Between the Lines:

How to Detect Bias and Propaganda in the News and Everyday Life

Eleanor MacLean

BLACK ROSE BOOKS   **Montreal**

Acknowledgements

Grateful acknowledgement is made to the following for permission to reprint parts of their work:

Canada-Wide Features Services Ltd., Ben Wicks cartoons.

Chicago Tribune-New York Times News Service, Animal Crackers cartoon, Author: Rog Bollen.

Development Education Centre (DEC) and Development and Peace, *Aid: the New Trojan Horse.*

Development Education Centre (DEC), *Underdevelopment in Canada: Notes towards an analytical framework.*

Development Education Centre (DEC), "Xingu" and "James Bay" by David Campbell, in *Through Arawak Eyes: songs and poetry of David Campbell.*

"The Corporation Haters", Herman Nickel and FORTUNE magazine ᶜ 1980 Time Inc. All rights reserved.

"The bottle baby scandal: milking the Third World for all it's worth" in *Mother Jones* magazine, December 1977, ᶜ Barbara Garson, author of MacBird and ALL THE LIVELONG DAY: The Meaning and Demeaning of Routine Work, Penguin (1977).

"The More or Less Scientific Method" from HOW TO WRITE, SPEAK AND THINK MORE EFFECTIVELY by Rudolf Flesch. Copyright 1941 by Rudolf Flesch. Reprinted by permission of Harper & Row, Publishers, Inc.

A passage from The Girl at Goldenhawk, reprinted by permission of the publisher, Harlequin Enterprises Ltd., from "The Girl at Goldenhawk" ᶜ 1974 by Violet Winspear.

On My Way to Work (Cuando Voy Al Trabajo) from the film "Companero". Words and Music by Victor Jara, TRO— ᶜ Copyright 1976 Mighty Oak Music Ltd. London, England, TRO-Essex Music International, Inc., New York. Used by permission.

"His Master's Voice" cartoon by May Ann Kainola.

King Features Syndicate, Inc., for Archie, Bringing Up Father, Hagar the Horrible and Blondie cartoons.

James MacLean and the Canadian Broadcasting Corporation (Radio) for an excerpt from a review of Athod Fugard's 'Sizwe Bansi is Dead".

Born Loser, Funny Business, Side Glances cartoons reprinted by permission ᶜ 1978 NEA, Inc.

Drawing by Modell; ᶜ 1978 The New Yorker Magazine, Inc.

Drawing by Mulligan; ᶜ 1978 The New Yorker Magazine, Inc.

LEN NORRIS and the VANCOUVER SUN, for Norris television cartoon.

The Estate of the late George Orwell, for excerpts from "Politics and the English Language", from *Shooting an elephant and other essays.*

Penguin Books Ltd., for an extract from the *Foreward* by C. A. Mace to J. A. C. Brown: TECHNIQUES OF PERSUASION (Pelican Books, 1963) Copyright ᶜ 1971 by Robert Cirino. Reprinted by permission of Random House, Inc.

THE AMAZING SPIDERMAN reprinted courtesy of The Register and Tribune Syndicate, Inc.

Warner Bros. Inc., for Bugs Bunny cartoons.

Weekend Magazine, for Christopher Munnion's "Last of the Few", 2 Dec 78 and Jim Christy's "The bloody road to Zimbabwe" 2 Dec 78.

"The long shadow of censorship", ᶜ John Wicklein, from "Electronic Nightmare," by John Wicklein, published by The Viking Press, New York, 1981.

Eric Wood and *Atlantic Issues* for the DREE Merry-Go-Round cartoon.

Care has been taken to trace ownership of the material used in the book. The publishers will welcome information that will enable us to rectify any errors or omissions.

Black Rose Books
3981 Boulevard St-Laurent
Montréal, H2W 1Y5, Québec

Reprinted 1988
Typesetting: McCurdy Printing & Typesetting Limited, Halifax, Nova Scotia.
Layout: Valerie Mansour. *Cover design:* Eleanor MacLean, Eric Wood.

Canadian Cataloguing in Publication Data

MacLean, Eleanor
    Between the lines : how to detect bias and propaganda
    in the news and everyday life

Bibliography: p.
Includes index.
Paperback ISBN 0-919619-12-6
Hardcover ISBN 0-919619-14-2
1. Mass media — Psychological aspects. 2. Journalism — Objectivity.
I. DEVERIC. II. Title.

P91.M23   302.2'4   C81-090103-X

Contents

Preface

The material in this book is introductory in nature, and is designed for adults. It has been assembled in such a way as to allow maximum flexibility, so it may be used in a variety of courses that deal with modern social issues. In its draft form it has been used in continuing education, high school and university courses, and has been found useful in Social Studies, History, English and Economics courses in particular. The fact that it has been found useful with this range of readerships has been convincing proof that distinctions between highschool, university and general readerships are artificial for introductory material. Moreover, what is taught in any school ought to be of interest outside the classrom as well . . . For these reasons, and because of the importance of the issues discussed, it is hoped that this book will receive a wider audience, both within formal education systems and in the community at large.

How to use the book

Each each chapter contains a number of suggestions for discussions, activities and further research. These suggestions, and the text itself, are meant to be catalysts. You will not find a full-fledged course, complete with step-by-step lesson plans, on the mass media or development. The book's main purpose is to initiate a *process of questioning and investigation.*The readings and suggested activities should supplement and complement rather than necessarily replace existing material or course outlines.

Each chapter is meant to stand on its own. It is not at all necessary to use them in their present sequence, nor is it necessary to use nearly as much information as is present in the book. You may even wish to use only part of one chapter.

The information, research and discussion suggestions cut across academic disciplines — as do, indeed, problems in the "real world" today. This book could play a small part in encouraging students to relate their educational training to their own lives, and in encouraging teachers of different subjects to work together. While recognising the possible problems inherent in such interdisciplinary work, I have also met many educators who, in the interests of the quality of education for their students, are making such extra efforts.

However this book is used, it will require the personal involvement, and work, of its users. The point is well made in the cartoon on the next page. There are no ready-made answers to pre-determined problems.

What is in this book

In this book, you will find some tools of analysis — sections on clear thinking, how the news is made, and how to detect bias. With some basic anayltical tools, one can learn how to read a newspaper, watch TV or "de-code" daily communication. In this way, readers can begin to examine, *for themselves,* the facts; to look beyond the stereotypes; to correct the many false impressions of others (and ourselves) that we get through the mass media.

An attempt has been made to present information in such a way as to favour egalitarian and non-intimidating relationships between

"Why doesn't the school board just buy some
LEARNING machines to go with the teaching
machines and then I could stay home?"

people. The student is as familiar with the content under study as is the
teacher. Such relationships promote participation and self-confidence
as well as *collective* confidence. There is no shibboleth and there is no
one proper approach — only a collective questioning process. With this
subject matter — the mass media — the economic and culturally
"disadvantaged" are on a more equal footing with the privileged.
Advertisements, cartoons and television are familiar to everyone.
Perhaps most important, this approach should allow people to identify
the pleasing or attractive elements that are part of certain
communications. However, users of the book should also be equipped to
distinguish between these good feelings, and specific commercial or
other messages communicated.

The book makes ample use of present sources of information
because a great wealth of information on many topics already exists.
However, it differs from others in that it proposes *an organised way of
approaching all this information.* Humour is also present in this book,
mostly in the form of cartoons. While the problems raised are very
sobering indeed, it would be distorting the reality not to include at least
a glimpse of the enjoyment of looking at the world from a critical
perspective. If one is critical of the way things are in today's world, it is
because one cares for it; wants to enjoy, with others, tomorrow's world.

Why such a book

In development education work over the years in schools and in the
community at large, I, like others, often have found that students,
teachers and the general public have almost no accurate information

on which to base their opinions on "Third World" or "development"-related issues. This is not because they are lazy or lack intelligence: I believe the problem lies in the limited number of information sources available to most people, and the poor quality of that information. Whatever the cause of the situation, educational efforts in such circumstances often had little context, as there was little background information (and often many misconceptions) about the issues being discussed.

Often after a TV broadcast about some aspect of the "Third World" (or other topic), the viewer can be left *more* confused than before about the fundamental issues involved. In the long term, this results in people becoming less and less prepared to examine any issues that appear distressing or confusing. Such issues do not disappear for our having ignored them, however, and often they are the very ones that have major implications for most people's daily lives, their happiness and indeed their survival.

The mass media — these most powerful sources of information — are generally not reliable or helpful for people trying to *understand* problems or issues facing underdeveloped and developed countries.

Those working in development agencies have deplored the mass media's neglect of the *basic questions of humankind's survival* — land use; food production; development of human and natural resouces; and many others. Such topics are thought not to "sell" very well. Only one of these kinds of issues is now given any attention by the mass media: energy — and this, only since the new-found power of the oil producers. Furthermore, even within this subject area, for example, there is still relatively little coverage of the many significant developments in alternative energy, some of which originate in the "Third World". Similar criticisms of media bias have been made by the labour movement, environmental, solidarity, women's groups and many others.

In recognising this inadequacy of our principal sources of information, however, I also had to recognise that first, there was no reason to believe that the mass media would change dramatically in their perspective and overall direction; and that second, they would continue to be the principal sources of information for the vast majority of Canadians, including ourselves. One should therefore take into account, in a formal way, the role of the mass media in forming the entire thought processes, the attitudes and the opinions of people today — the mass media's role in *educating* an entire population. An increasing number of people today are aware of this daunting if obvious problem: what seemed to be needed was to combine this realisation with a way to analyse the messages the media do relay.

No one book could disprove every false impression created by the mass media, and provide the appropriate "counter-information". However, a book might achieve the same objective by depending on the active participation of its readers. — Whence *Between the Lines*.

Aims and objectives

This book has two overall aims. First, by initiating a process of questioning and investigation, it should contribute to a better understanding of some of the major world problems which involve both Canadian and "Third World" societies. In particular, it should provide users with a method of analysis that will help them obtain sound information gleaned from a variety of sources. Second, the book attempts to show ways in which citizens can recognise and deal positively with major social problems; in particular it should contribute to the formation of independent thinking, which forms the basis needed for democratic institutions. Specific objectives for those using the book are:

> To identify principal ways of learning, and major sources of information (Chapter I).

> To distinguish between information (e.g., factual, theoretical, moral, aesthetic content), interpretation, and the overall message that is conveyed in any given communication, including the response the communication is intended to evoke (Chapters II, IV).

> To recognise this distinction between message, interpretation and information in daily communication (Chapter II).

> To gain a clearer picture of the ownership and control of the mass media, and how this affects the actual content of the mass media (Chapter III).

> To discover ways of finding and using alternative sources of information and analysis (All chapters).

> To encourage discussion, research and activities that will foster in the user the ability and desire to form independent judgments about current events through the steps outlined above (All chapters).

It should be emphasised that the alternative sources of information used, as well as the analysis of this book, ought to be subject to the same careful study as is being proposed for other sources of information. No one source of information is being promoted so much as a method for approaching all sources of information. Throughout the book, attempts have been made to clarify the writer's own perspective — as would only be fitting for a book of this nature! A mailing address has been included: your written comments and criticisms are welcomed.

E.M.

How did I form my opinion?

Acknowledgements

If I were to name all those who have assisted me in one way or another in the production of this book, I would need to publish a small telephone book: sincere thanks, first, to all the people whose names *do not* appear here — those working in office jobs, in public libraries, universities, corporate or government departments. While anonymous, their contributions have been nonetheless important, are remembered, and are well appreciated.

The worthwhile contribution of those who worked on a development education project some time ago must also be noted. *Between the Lines* was one of several resources prepared by individual members working on a joint CUSO-DEVERIC development education project. The idea of organising the material in this book form came to me in early 1977, in the course of project meetings with CUSO, DEVERIC and OXFAM staff and volunteers. Voluntary projects on tiny budgets can result in much information being assembled without there being further resources to complete or use it. This was the case for the work of some of those who contributed to the project but who have since moved away or have had to meet other commitments. Some of my ideas for *Between the Lines* were tried out first on the original working group. The following people, as members either of the project's working group or its Advisory Board, contributed to this overall project, of which my work was a part: Alex Bruce, Helen Buck, David Currie, Sharon Foley/Reilly, Howard Gardiner, Susan Johnson, Michael Lynk, Kate McLaren, Michael Menard, Jim Morrison, Peter Ross, Ron Stratford, Kass Sunderji, Nicola Swainson.

Kate McLaren and Jean Christie deserve very special thanks. Their efforts in support of the project and this book have been instrumental in the book's final appearance. As well, when David Currie was co-ordinator of the project, his encouraging me to pursue the ideas I had was essential to the circulation of the early drafts of this book.

Special thanks to all the teachers who helped the project: to the forty teachers surveyed who took the time to answer our questionnaires and telephone calls; to another selected twenty who stayed for hours in interviews with us; and particularly to the teachers who at various stages piloted some of our materials, including this book. They made very valuable criticisms and comments and suggestions. Carol Campbell's thoughtful criticisms and enthusiasm were particularly valued.

I am very grateful to all those other people who also took time to respond to this material in its draft form. I should like to mention in particular those who met with me on several occasions, either individually or as a group: Marc Allain, Nigel Allen, Phyllis Artiss, Deb Barndt, Alex Bruce, Joan Campbell, David Currie, Corrie Douma, GATT-Fly, Jim Guild, Susan Johnson, Claudette Legault, Rowly Lorimer, Gordon MacDermid, Harvey MacKinnon, Valerie Mansour, Dian Marino, Kate McLaren, Paul Robinson, Barbara Rumscheidt, and Ana Maria Quiroz. Each person read a draft of the book, and made many useful comments and suggestions. Our meetings together were not only enjoyable but showed the value of consultation. Many individuals gave helpful advice or suggestions, or responded to particular requests for information; for publishing suggestions and advice, the assistance given me by Ann Brimer, Howard Epstein, Angela Rebeiro, Michael Pitman and Paul Robinson was greatly appreciated. Robert Carty and Raymond O'Toole of LAWG gave indispensable advice.

I should particularly like to thank Glenda Redden, who always expressed interest and support when we contacted her, and communicated understanding rather than impatience at the long process of putting this material together.

This book could not have been produced without the co-operation and generosity of many individuals and institutions. For making facilities available for the use of project members, sincere thanks to the Atlantic Institute of Education, CUSO, Graphic Design Associates, the Halifax Teachers' Resources Centre, OXFAM; and Marc Allain, Claudette Legault and John Ure. The financial contributions towards the publication of this book by CUSO in the Atlantic Region and CUSO Development Education nationally, the Canadian Council for International Co-operation, the International Education Centre, OXFAM and the United Church of Canada also indicate the extraordinary co-operation and support we have enjoyed, and are deeply appreciated. The work of Jean Christie, Steve Seaborne, Anu Bose and Barbara McCann in arranging financing for the printing of the book is very much appreciated. I am grateful to the CUSO-DEVERIC Schools Project for a three-month contract to work on this material, and to OXFAM-CANADA's Education Programme, which allowed for an unpaid leave of absence for the same period, a subsequent month for editing and revisions, consultation time at the production stage and many, many hours for project meetings over the duration of the project.

A number of ideas contained in the book were developed during studies, while teaching, working with others in community activities, and just in discussions with friends. Thanks to professors, students and friends for these exchanges. I have noted others' suggestions or contributions wherever possible. The fine work of many writers, musicians, and artists who have dealt with some of the questions presented here from a multiplicity of angles has been a source of inspiration and delight, and has strengthened my resolve to complete a book that might point readers in the direction of a few of them.

The assistance I have received from all those named here in no way implicates them in what I have written, nor does it necessarily imply their agreement with views expressed in the book. Any errors or omissions are also my responsibility entirely.

For the production of this book, thanks go to many people: to Donna Treen for typing one of the earlier drafts under what is euphemistically called "less than ideal circumstances" in order to meet deadlines; to Nigel Allen and Bill Oliver for hours of photocopying; to Catherine Graham, Lana Joseph and Brian Murphy for proofreading; to Susan Johnson, Valerie Mansour and Heather Wood who consulted with Eric Wood and me on the design of the book.

Eric contributed an enormous amount of his time, energy and talent to virtually every aspect of production — from book design to suggesting improvements on the mock-ups of the pages and spending days on camera work.

A special place must be found for the special contribution of Valerie Mansour and the enormous volume of work handled by her in preparing the entire text for the printer, arranging for proofreading, and doing mock-ups of each of the pages for the printers. Her energy and good humour in working with Eric and me made the last, demanding stages of the book's production immeasurably easier. Eric and Valerie's talent, good cheer and generosity with their time were undeserved gifts for which I will always be very grateful.

Finally, I should like to thank especially members of my family, and the following people for their sustained interest, help and encouragement throughout this long process: Alex Bruce, Corrie Douma, Susan Johnson, Harvey MacKinnon and Barbara Rumscheidt.

I owe a special debt of thanks to all the friends who have remained such, despite my neglecting them while working on this.   E.M.

I. What gave you that idea?

Chapter I: What gave you that idea?

Introduction

Forming opinions

Thinking clearly

The mass media of communication

Further reading

Drawing by Mulligan; © 1978 The New Yorker Magazine, Inc.

"There is a perfect example of what is wrong with this country today."

"There is a perfect example of what is wrong with this country today."

Introduction

Who is biased and who is not? How can anyone know if what they hear or what they see on TV about a current event is true or not?

This book aims to explore these and other questions further. It will propose ways of interpreting the many "messages" we receive from each other when talking to one another, while watching television — while engaging in any form of communication. By developing methods of interpreting these many messages, you will be increasing your ability to *think clearly*. If people are to act independently and control their own lives, they must first be able to *understand* what is going on around them.

Developing methods of thinking clearly is perhaps increasingly necessary, given the importance and impact that various forms of communication have in people's lives. One scholar has noted that,

> . . . The unwillingness or the inability of people to think is a real danger to democracy. If a person does not know the difference between sound and unsound reasoning, he can't distinguish between the truth and false propaganda . . . [1]

Given the complex technology of communications and the increasing concentration of its ownership, the need for careful thinking and research is becoming more and more important, especially among young people. Acquiring these analytical skills should not be relegated to a particular course as a speciality, but should penetrate all the educational activities of students. The basic "survival skills" of responsible citizenship — the ability to make decisions based on sound thinking and accurate information —are going to become more and more important for young people in times to come. Here is the detached view of an expert in mind control:

> . . . although short-run propaganda may be directed at any age groups, that designed for complete and thorough indoctrination must be directed to children and youth since they are the most vulnerable to suggestion and persuasion techniques. Revolutionary political parties, religious bodies, and the manufacturers of cigarettes are all equally aware of this truth.[2]

We hope this unit will encourage you to reflect on the nature of communication in general; on the influence that the mass media have on us and on the way we view the world; on the particular interests represented by the mass media (Chapter III). We hope that at the same time our material will equip you with the necessary tools to analyse more closely all sources of information and ideas (Chapter II), including those presented in this book. Chapters V and VI open on to other dimensions of familiar problems and Chapter VI ends with suggestions for finding alternative sources of information. The urgent need for a careful and critical approach to communication, in order to have a truly free and democratic society, was eloquently discussed by George Orwell, and can be found at the end of Chapter II.

Forming opinions

Where do our ideas come from? How do we understand the world around us? On what basis do we form our ideas or opinions? In this chapter, we will begin to seek answers to these basic questions.

Why should we be concerned about *how* we learn things? The answer is that many of the things we experience or learn, whether in our daily lives or in the news, appear either extremely complex and confusing:
— "alcoholism"
— "child abuse"
— "vandalism".
Or else they seem completely unrelated to our own concerns:
— "the Middle East"
— "the Third World". . . . Yet we know that all these issues do relate to us in some way; but it is very difficult to figure out exactly *how* they do. We may have an opinion on any of these or other topics, or we may at least have very strong feelings about them. Often, however, we may have no idea why we think or feel the way we do. We need to know how we form our opinions before we can analyse them for their validity.

If you begin by examining your own opinions, and especially how you have come to hold them, you will have already gained some tools of analysis with which to study all sources of information. Eventually this method will allow you to understand better many issues and events, and you will therefore be better prepared to act on the basis of sound judgment.

Physical considerations
As human beings, we share a common trait with many other advanced forms of life in the

Signs: giving meaning to what we see

Here is a relatively uncommon sign. What does it mean? What issue would you guess it has been associated with?* What are some other signs more commonly recognised in everyday life?

*Free speech.

way we learn about our surroundings, about how to survive and prosper. Our nervous system resembles that of other primates: the five faculties of sight, hearing, smell, touch and taste inform us about our environment. The brain then puts all the information to our use, absorbing, retaining, recalling and co-ordinating millions of pieces of information every day.

The brain is continually ordering these sense perceptions it receives. Exactly how it decides on the basic patterns with which it organises data and, "understands" it as well, is still a matter of investigation. However, we do know that in making up patterns with which we "understand" things, many factors are involved, in a very complex process.

Everything that humans encounter provides *information* which the brain will select or discard as being useful or not useful: this occurs when we scan the newspapers, watch television, relax by just sitting in a chair — during all our waking hours.

In the same way, when we study our sources of information, we will find that the major part of the many messages we are given consists of the *presentation* of information, not the information itself. That is, facts, statistics and other data are presented in such a way that we will interpret them in certain limited ways.

Man and Beast

"The lower animals are generally *non rational*, but few of them are so positively *irrational* as man can be. It requires considerable sophistication to be irrational. No animal could develop the systematic delusions of the insane, nor are the 'lower' animals easy prey to advertisers or political propagandists . . .

. . . Man has the capacity to reason and to be influenced by reason in ways which a hungry tiger, for example, has not. It is an interesting and significant fact that political and religious propagandists, and advertisers, go so far as they do in thinking up (specious) argument addressed to the reason. These arguments are an unwitting testimonial to the rationality of man."

— C.A. Mace, in Foreword to *Techniques of persuasion* p.7

Capacity for Thinking
The evolution of the brain, from prehistoric reptile to modern humans, has been linked to skull size. As the brain grew, allowing for more intricate thought processes, certain skull bones (shaded) expanded to accommodate it. Today human cranial capacity averages about 80 cubic inches, roughly two thirds larger than a chimpanzee's. The human brain attained its present size in Neanderthal man 100,000 years ago.

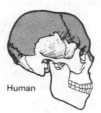

Human

Early chimpanzee

Primate

Early reptile

The brain's efficiency depends on the fact that it sifts and chooses all sense perceptions, and gives them an order and structure. When we focus on an object, of necessity we are not focussing on other objects. *Selectivity* is a basic and necessary fact of life for survival.

However, humans are said to differ from other primates and forms of life because, in addition to so many ounces of cells we call the brain, humans possess a *mind*. Not only do we store and use much more information than other known forms of life, but we "understand" it as well. This faculty is associated with human beings' ability to use creative language, as contrasted to simple codes or even highly developed ones such as those used by whales or porpoises. We possess not only this highly advanced sorting, storing and selection system, but also an ability to comprehend and transcend so many millions of bits of information: *we are able to make conscious judgments about the things we perceive around us*. Scientists, artists and philosophers have suggested that what makes human beings unique is our capacity to ask *why* (and to "understand" the answer).

Complementary to this ability to ask why is our ability to *choose* how we act. For exam-

Choice of patterns

Gestalt psychologists use such designs to demonstrate that the individual organises visual sensations into perceptions. The simple black and white pattern can be organised in two ways. The viewer does both, alternately perceiving a white vase against a black background or two silhouettes against a white background.

Learning

and

Thinking

In addition to certain reflexes and instincts, humans have learning and reasoning capacities. The ability to ask *Why* and understand the answer sets humans apart from other forms of life. Thinking is different than learning.

FACULTIES USED	SPECIES

Learning involves the use of one or more of the five faculties:
   touch
   smell
   taste
   hearing
   sight (e.g. colour differentiation.)
 	
A number of species can learn
   mimicry. Some can learn
   codes or isolated words;
   speech, in a rudimentary form, has
been learned by some primates in
laboratory tests.
	Many animals, including humans, make use of one or a combination of these faculties.
	
	Monkeys
	Whales, porpoises 

Thinking requires much more complex skills. The creative use of **language** is thought to be essential. **Argumentation:** **The irrational**	Human beings only 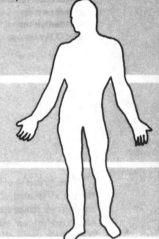
The rational	
The non-rational	

ple, we can choose to spend our evenings watching TV, reading a book, or working at a part-time job. On another level, history is filled with accounts of men and women who choose a certain form of action which would appear not to be in their own personal interests, but rather in the interests of an ideal or cause which they have chosen to make theirs. The lives of great composers, writers, religious thinkers and "heroes" often show the power of an idea, an ideal or inspiration to override an individual's concern with comfort, safety or personal goals.

If human beings' actions can be more than mere reflexes or instincts — indeed the result of conscious, intelligent choices — we are faced with the question: how do people make these choices, and on what do they base their decisions?

Our sources of information

When someone tells us something, or when we read a news story, how do we know that what we are being told is true or false?

To answer this, we first must review what possible sources of information are at our disposal. When people learn something or form an idea or opinion, on what have they based it? What are their sources of information? Generally, these sources fall into two main groups:

1. Direct experience. What we see, hear, smell, touch, taste ourselves. We know something has happened or the weather is such-and-such, for example, because we can see and experience these things for ourselves.

2. All other sources. From sources as diverse as radio signals from satellites or ancient

CONDITIONS UNDER WHICH LEARNING/THINKING TAKE PLACE

In a natural environment,	Under coercion,	Special interest groups
In a natural environment, animals sense "danger", a "mate", their "prey" etc. Basic, recognisable patterns can be formed and discerned.	**Under coercion,** a rat will learn to press a bar in order to eat or avoid electric shock. Physical techniques of persuasion, incl. drugs or torture, can "teach" subjects new behaviour or ideas.	**Special interest groups** can persuade or teach, by appealing to the senses. Commercial ads often heighten our awareness of our senses through e.g., the use of life-like photo images, or even "scratch and sniff" ads.
More complex patterns are developed.	"Brainwashing" can be a combination of physical and psychological assaults on the mind.	
The occult makes use of primitive forms of communication and irrational thought processes.	The occult can involve coercion, esp. of children. "Brainwashing"	Political: propaganda Religious: cults Commercial advertising
Most mental activity — daily discourse, scientific theory, philosophy, history mathematics — involves rational thought.	"Re-education" is a form of learning and thinking (e.g, prisoners are reasoned with, but are not free to leave until they change their views).	Political: election platforms Commercial: "learning systems", advocacy advertisements etc. Interest groups: positions in favour of or against something.
Intuition and "inspiration" are non-rational thought processes. — Poetry, artistic expression, and even some aspects of physics etc. are the product of non-rational thinking.	Psychosis and other disorders can be induced (the positive aspects of non-rational thinking and creativity cannot be induced).	Commercial: aesthetic appeal used often in advertisements (see J. Berger, *Ways of Seeing*)

Egyptian papyrus scrolls, we learn about things that we never experience directly ourselves. What we learn from these sources is based on *other* people's experiences, and *their* interpretation of them.

Clearly, our sources for most of what we know about the world fall into the second category. Every day, from radios, TV and conversations with other people, we accept as truth many hundreds of thousands of "messages" about the world around us.

What may not appear so obvious, though, is that we are constantly making judgments about the comparative value of those sources of information. Some people we believe more readily than others; some ideas we accept more easily than others; some we reject outright. This is why we now must examine more carefully how we make those judgments. What

method of analysis do we apply to all these sources?

Method of analysis

As we know from studying science in school, there are well-defined methods that are used to assess the relative value of any new piece of information. In most fields of human knowledge, these methods have been developed over centuries of work. In astronomy, physics, chemistry, mathematics, and science and technology in general, there are set methods and criteria with which we measure the validity of any finding. Similar critical methods exist in the humanities — in archaeology, history, linguistics, or literary criticism, for example. While some disciplines may have developed these critical apparatuses more fully than others, all have common features:

• certain working assumptions or hypotheses; as well as

• criteria for measuring the correctness of the hypotheses.

This method of analysis can be summarised as follows:

1. First, we state our working assumptions (hypotheses).
2. Next, we determine criteria with which we can test our hypotheses.
3. We test our hypotheses against our observations or through experiment.
4. We then take our findings, and assess them in relation to our original hypotheses.
5. Finally, we revise, reject or confirm our original working assumptions accordingly.

Thus, when engineers or architects set about designing a building or a bridge, they can reasonably accept certain working assumptions about physical laws of stress and gravity. Likewise in the humanities, translators accept certain working assumptions about linguistics and history, and are then able to decipher other languages. In this way, humans are able to build on each other's work.

The method of analysis we have just described has traditionally been associated with the world of science or higher learning. In this book, we are taking a step in applying a similar, sytematic analysis to the sources of information about world events — to approach all our sources of information — TV, films, newspapers — with an enquiring mind.

"Reading between the lines" is often thought of as an activity of rather sophisticated people — of those who perhaps have traveled widely or who might read two or more papers a day. In this book we will see how the person who comes across any piece of information — an ad, a news story, a cartoon —can "read between the lines".

To be able to deal intelligently and fruitfully with many problems today, people must develop their faculties of critical judgment. The methods for understanding events and trends around us must become more sophisticated and more carefully applied to daily life, so that we can determine when something is hearsay, innuendo, or when it is fact. We

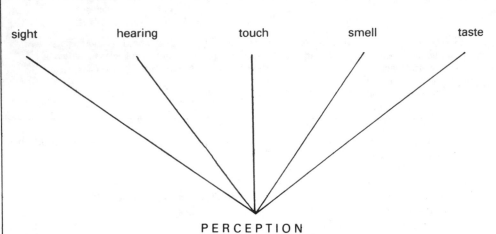

sight   hearing   touch   smell   taste

PERCEPTION
Most "intelligent" work is done with one or the other of the "noble" senses — sight and hearing (plus voice etc.).

Discussion

In class discussion, draw up a list of ways we communicate, and what combinations of senses are used — in TV, movies, theatre, silent movies, church, mime, etc.
What are the strong points of each of these forms of communication? Drawbacks?

should be able to tell when the facts we are presented with are relevant or when they are misleading, when we are faced with propaganda or when we have come across accurate information. In summary, we should be able to distinguish between error and truth.

Especially for current events, but also for daily life in general, we must make judgments about the comparative value of our sources of information, before we can feel confident that we understand a particular event.

Since our principal sources of information about the world today are the mass media of communication — TV, radio, newspapers, magazines etc. — they themselves require careful scrutiny. Are they reliable sources of information? Who has access to the mass media? Who owns and controls them? How does ownership of the media and access to it affect the kinds of programmes and ideas put forward by the media? The chapters which follow will discuss these questions.

Discussion/activities

1. Conduct a "brainstorming" session in your group.

A brainstorming session is one in which everyone says something — the first thing that comes to mind — when a word is mentioned. No one is allowed to criticise or ridicule another for what they say: the aim is to create a "storm" of ideas, words, pictures. Someone is designated to write them down on a blackboard. Later, they can be analysed.

2. Begin a log book for your group. Record the discussion so that you can compare ideas:
— at the end of sections in your course;
— at the end of the year.

3. Do you come across in your life any "modern world problems"? What "problem areas" do you encounter in everyday life:
— in the classroom?
— school?
— neighbourhood?
— family?
In smaller groups, individuals could choose a topic and write a two- to three-paragraph description of some "problem area". Then read it aloud to the group.

Was there enough information for everyone to understand properly what the problem was?

If so, what conclusions could people draw about the problem?

If there was not enough information, what questions did people ask?

4. Is *knowing* something the same as *understanding* it? (Examples: biology, a poem.)

Is *understanding* something the same as *accepting* it? What is the difference? Give some examples:
— in school life
— in family life
— in your community.

5. What is important to you? Can you determine your system of values? Do you believe in freedom of the press, or censorship?

Should everyone have the right to know what is going on in their own country and around the world? What countries are you aware of at present that do not ensure freedom of the press?

6. Included in this book is the United Nations Universal Declaration of Human Rights, which includes freedom of the press (Article 19). Do you agree or disagree with the rights as set out in this declaration? (Canada is one of the signatories of this declaration.)

7. With your group, draw up a list of ways humans communicate (speech, print, sign language such as semaphore etc.). What combinations of senses are used in TV, film, theatre, church worship, mime, etc.? For each form of communication, how much involvement, and what kind of involvement is needed by the people concerned?

8. Relate Article 29 of the Universal Declaration of Human Rights to the classroom community; school community; community at large.

Thinking Clearly

The following excerpt is from the book, *How to write, speak and think more effectively*. Its author, Rudolph Flesch, makes the point that:

> . . . science is forever self-correcting and changing; what is put forth as gospel truth cannot be science.

In other sections of this book, we shall examine this idea, as it relates to our understanding of the world, and our principal sources of information — the mass media.

THE MORE OR LESS SCIENTIFIC METHOD

Perhaps the most famous incident in the history of science occurred in the third century B.C. in Syracuse, Sicily. The mathematician Archimedes was taking a bath. His mind was busy with a scientific problem. King Hiero of Syracuse had ordered a golden crown and suspected the goldsmith of having cheated him by using some silver instead of the gold he'd been supplied with. The king had asked Archimedes to prove it.

Suddenly Archimedes noticed that his body caused some water to spill over. In a flash he realized the solution of the problem: he'd take the crown's weight in pure gold, dip it into water, and see whether the overflow was the same as that of the crown. Whereupon he jumped out of the tub, ran home naked as he was, and shouted to everyone he met: "Eureka! Eureka! . . . I've found it! I've found it!"

Perhaps the *least* famous incident in the history of science occurred in the twentieth century A.D. in the United States. The chemist J. E. Teeple was taking a bath. His mind was busy with a scientific problem. He stepped out of his bath, reached for a towel, dried himself, shaved, took another bath, stepped out of it, reached for a towel and discovered that the towel was wet. Thinking about his scientific problem, he had taken two baths. He had *not* found the solution to his problem.

The first of these incidents has been retold a million times; the second is trivial. Nevertheless, the second is the one that gives the truer picture of the scientific method.

In the first place, the story about Archimedes puts the spotlight on the happy discovery, giving the impression that this sort of thing is typical of a scientist's life. Actually, "Eureka!" moments are few and far between. Einstein once said: "I think and think, for months, for years, ninety-nine times the conclusion is false. The hundredth time I am right." And that's Einstein, the greatest scientific genius of our time. I leave it to you to estimate the percentage of correct solutions in an ordinary scientist's work. Most of their lives are spent like Mr. Teeple's half-hour in the bathroom, thinking and thinking and getting nowhere.

But there's a more important reason why Archimedes crying "Eureka!" isn't a good picture of a scientist. Today no scientist, dressed or undressed, would dream of telling people "I've found it!" as soon as he has hit upon a bright idea. Even less would he do the modern equivalent—announce his discovery immediately to the press. Just the contrary. He would take care not to breathe a word about it to anyone, but quietly go to his laboratory and run some tests—and more tests— and more tests.

A scientist today doesn't consider a bright idea as a revelation of the truth; he considers it as something to be disproved. Not just proved, mind you; it's his obligation as a scientist to think of all conceivable means and ways to *disprove* it. This habit is so ingrained in him that he doesn't even realize it any more; he automatically thinks of a theory as something to find flaws in. So he does experiments and hunts for every error he can possibly think of; and when he is through with his own experiments, he publishes his findings not in a newspaper but in a scientific journal, inviting other scientists to do some other experiments and prove him wrong.

And when the hunt for errors has subsided and a theory gets established and accepted—do scientists think they've got hold of a new truth? No. To them, all scientific findings are only *tentative* truth, "good until further notice," to be immediately discarded when someone comes along with another theory that explains a few more facts. Absolute truth doesn't even interest them; they get along very happily, thank you, with a set of working hypotheses that are good only at cer-

tain times and for cer:ain purposes. The most famous examp of this today is the theory of light. There is a wave theo that fits certain investigations, and a particle theory that f certain others. Years ago physicists stopped trying to find o which is true and which is false. The Danish Nobel prize wi ner, Niels Bohr, has called this the principle of compleme tarity, saying that after all "waves" and "particles" are on handy metaphors in dealing with certain facts; so why not u whichever is more practical at the moment? Never mind wh light is "really"; let's get on with the job of finding out wh it *does*. Or, as one physicist said, "Let's use the parti theory on Mondays, Wednesdays, and Fridays, and the wa theory on Tuesdays, Thursdays, and Saturdays."

For the layman, the most important thing about science this: that it isn't a search for truth but a search for err The scientist lives in a world where truth is unattainable, where it's always possible to find errors in the long-settled the obvious. You want to know whether some theory is rea scientific? Try this simple test: If the thing is shot throu with *perhapses* and *maybes* and hemming and hawing, probably science; if it's supposed to be *the* final answer, it not.

So-called "scientific" books that are supposed to cont final answers are never scientific. Science is forever s correcting and changing; what is put forth as gospel tr cannot be science.

But what does *science* mean? If someone asked you fo definition, you'd probably be on the spot. If pressed, y might come up with something like the definition in W ster's: "A branch of study . . . concerned with the observat and classification of facts, esp. with the establishment . of verifiable general laws . . ."

That's a pretty good description of what the word me to the average person. Does it mean the same thing scientists? It does not. In 1951 Dr. James B. Conant, w was trained as a chemist, published *his* definition of scien "An interconnected series of concepts and conceptual scher that have developed as a result of experimentation and servation and are fruitful of further experimentation observation." As you see, the two definitions are almost ex opposites. *You* think science deals with facts; a scien thinks it deals with concepts. *You* think science tries to est lish laws; a scientist thinks it aims at more and more exp ments.

And what is the scientific method? Your answer is apt be: "The classification of facts." Dr. Conant's answer is ag different. Look up *Scientific method* in the index of his bc *Science and Common Sense*, and you'll find this: "Scien method. *See* Alleged scientific method." In other words, Conant thinks there *isn't any* scientific method.

That surely is extreme. Even if there is no clearly defin scientific method, there's a way in which scientists w and it's certainly worth knowing about. Let's look at a c ful description by Dr. W. I. B. Beveridge, a British biolog

The following is a common sequence in an investi tion of a medical or biological problem:

(*a*) The relevant literature is critically reviewed.

(*b*) A thorough collection of field data or equiva observational enquiry is conducted, and is supplemer if necessary by laboratory examination of specimens.

(*c*) The information obtained is marshalled and c related and the problem is defined and broken down i specific questions.

(*d*) Intelligent guesses are made to answer the qu tions, as many hypotheses as possible being considere

(*e*) Experiments are devised to test first the likel hypotheses bearing on the most crucial questions.

" . . . clear thinking is rare. To approach it, we need above all that indispensable quality of the scientific spirit — humility. Like good scientists, we must be ready to sacrifice some of our personality and habits of thought as we face each new problem. For life's problems are always new, and defy all ready-made solutions."[3]

The key word here is *guesses* in (*d*). In the popular view the emphasis is on (*b*), the collection of data. But not among scientists. They like to distinguish between "accumulators" and "guessers," and they're pretty much agreed that it's the guessers that are important. In more fancy terms, you could say that the modern emphasis is on deduction rather than induction, or that the Aristotelian method is now more esteemed than the Baconian. What it comes down to is simply this: Our top scientists say we need more ideas rather than more facts: they want more Einsteins who just sit and think rather than Edisons who have a genius for tinkering in the laboratory. After all, Edison, as one of them has said, "was not a scientist and was not even interested in science."

Meanwhile, our research relies far more on accumulating than on guessing. General Electric, with its training courses in "Creative Engineering," is the exception; the American Cancer Society, which is openly resigned to "whittling away at this mass of mystery," is typical of the general rule.

Which is why Dr. Sinnott, when he was director of the Sheffield School of Science at Yale, said:

> It must be ruefully admitted that we have not produced our share of great new germinative ideas in recent years. In atomic research, for example, most of the fundamental theoretical progress was made either by European scientists or men who had received their training abroad. We are strong in application, in development and engineering, but much less so in the fundamental contributions of the theory on which all these are based. . . . We are in danger of being overwhelmed by a mass of undigested results.

And what is the method used by those hard-to-find "guessers"? If we try to analyze it, we come right back to Duncker's description of problem-solving, to his "solutions from below" and "solutions from above." Scientific problems are solved either by finding a seemingly irrelevant key factor or by applying a seemingly unsuitable thought pattern. Which means that scientific discoveries are made in one of two ways: by accident or by hunch.

Take any history of science, and you'll find that it is a history of accidents and hunches. Both types of discoveries are equally fascinating.

If you're interested in accidents, for instance, scientific history looks like this:

In 1786, Luigi Galvani noticed the accidental twitching of a frog's leg and discovered the principle of the electric battery.

In 1822, the Danish physicist Oersted, at the end of a lecture, happened to put a wire conducting an electric current near a magnet, which led to Faraday's invention of the electric dynamo.

In 1858, a seventeen-year-old boy named William Henry Perkin, trying to make artificial quinine, cooked up a black-looking mass, which led to his discovery of aniline dye.

In 1889, Professors von Mering and Minkowski operated on a dog. A laboratory assistant noticed that the dog's urine attracted swarms of flies. He called this to the attention of Minkowski, who found that the urine contained sugar. This was the first step in the control of diabetes.

In 1895, Roentgen noticed that cathode rays penetrated black paper and discovered X-rays.

In 1929, Sir Alexander Fleming noticed that a culture of bacteria had been accidentally contaminated by a mold. He said to himself: "My, that's a funny thing." He had discovered penicillin.

Of course, all these accidents would have been meaningless if they hadn't happened to Galvani, Perkin, Roentgen, and so on. As Pasteur has said, "Chance favors the prepared mind." What is necessary is an accidental event plus an observer with *serendipity*—"the gift of finding valuable or agreeable things not sought for." (Horace Walpole coined that beautiful word.)

On the other hand, if you're interested in hunches, scientific history looks like this, for example:

Harvey describes his discovery of the circulation of the blood:

> I frequently and seriously bethought me, and long revolved in my mind, what might be the quantity of blood which was transmitted, in how short a time its passage might be effected and the like. . . . I began to think whether there might not be a motion, as it were, in a circle.

James Watt invents the steam engine:

> On a fine Sabbath afternoon I took a walk. . . . I had entered the green and had passed the old washing house. I was thinking of the engine at the time. I had gone as far as the herd's house when the idea came into my mind that as steam was an elastic body it would rush into a vacuum, and if a connection were made between the cylinder and an exhausting vessel it would rush into it and might then be condensed without cooling the cylinder. . . . I had not walked further than the golf house when the whole thing was arranged in my mind.

Darwin writes about his theory of evolution:

> I can remember the very spot in the road, whilst in my carriage, when to my joy the solution occurred to me.

Kekule tells how he discovered the benzene ring on top of a London bus:

> I sank into a reverie. The atoms flitted about before my eyes. . . . I saw how two small ones often joined into a little pair; how a larger took hold of two smaller, and a still larger clasped three or even four of the small ones, and how all spun around in a whirling round-dance. . . . The cry of the conductor, "Clapham Road," woke me up.

Walter B. Cannon discovers the significance of bodily changes in fear and rage:

> These changes—the more rapid pulse, the deeper breathing, the increase of sugar in the blood, the secretion from the adrenal glands—were very diverse and seemed unrelated. Then, one wakeful night, after a considerable collection of these changes had been disclosed, the idea flashed through my mind that they could be nicely integrated if conceived as bodily preparations for supreme effort in flight or in fighting.

Does all this mean that some scientists are good at hunches and some others blessed with serendipity? Not at all. The accidental clue needs a receptive mind; the hunch has to grow from a study of facts. The good guesser works both ways, depending on what he has to go on. Here's one more example that shows a combination of both methods. It is typical of modern scientific research in many ways.

During World War II, a team of psychologists studied the propaganda effect of orientation films. Among other things, they tried to find out whether films changed the opinions and attitudes of soldiers who saw them, and whether and how these changes lasted. They had a hunch that the effect of the films would gradually wear off and that after some time, soldiers would forget the factual details and revert to their original opinion.

This idea may seem rather obvious to you. It seemed obvious to the psychologists too—but, being scientists, they decided to test it anyway. So they gave the soldiers a test after one week and another test after nine weeks.

As expected, the soldiers had forgotten most of the facts in the film during those eight weeks. But, "clearly contrary to the initial expectation," the general propaganda effect of the film—the opinion change—had considerably *increased* between the first and the second test. There was not the slightest doubt about it: the soldiers had forgotten the details of the film, but its message had sunk in deeper.

The research team cheerfully accepted this unexpected fact and immediately proceeded to account for it by a hypothesis. They found that it could be explained through a theory by the British psychologist, Bartlett, published in 1932. Bartlett had written that "after learning, that which is recalled tends to be modified with lapse of time in the direction of omission of all but general content and introduction of new material in line with the individual's attitudes." In other words, as time passes, we're apt to forget details but *reinforce* what we remember of the general idea.

Well, what have we here? Doubtless the research team made a valuable discovery. Yet the whole story is as unlike that of Archimedes in his bath as can be. For one thing, there is no single scientist, but a team of thirteen men and two women. Second, the discovery is exactly the opposite from what the scientists expected to find. Third, it is immediately connected up with an idea thought up by another scientist in another country, twenty years before.

And finally, there is no "Eureka!", no shouting from the housetops, no happy announcement to the world. Instead, after reporting their discovery and stating their hypothesis, the researchers add casually: "These highly speculative suggestions indicate some very interesting areas for future research." ■

Peretz/Kiev

Discussion

1. The article is entitled "The more or less scientific method." What did the author mean by this?

How could you apply the "scientific method" to daily activities? (Buying a car or clothes? talking about friends? reading a newspaper?)

2. The article gives some differing definitions of "science". In your science courses, what approach to scientific investigation do you take?

3. In the history of science, the condemning of Galileo is well known. History provides many examples of customs, practices or ideas that were widely accepted not all that long ago, but that no longer would be tolerated in present-day society.

For example, if you are female, do you think you should have the right to vote? The right to vote was only granted to women in Nova Scotia in 1918 (Apr. 26); in New Brunswick in 1919, PEI in 1922, Newfoundland in 1925 and Quebec in 1940!

The Election Act of the Dominion of Canada (1886) stated, "No woman, idiot, lunatic or criminal shall vote."

a. Can you think of any other examples of popular opinion changing over the years? (This could include burning at the stake of religious heretics; slavery; execution for stealing a loaf of bread; rock and roll music censored on TV; long hair causing family break-ups; women and smoking; men and housework.)

b. Are there any widely accepted ideas or customs that you think people might change their views on in the coming years? (Seat-belt legislation? capital punishment? right to unemployment insurance? welfare?) Would you agree or disagree with these changes?

c. How do you decide whether a change of public opinion is for the better or for the worse?

The mass media of communication

Our principal sources of information outside of family, friends and work are the mass media — TV, radio, movies, newspapers. Through them, we see the world.

If you are 15 years old or over, there is a remarkable storehouse of knowledge in your brain. You have *learned* literally millions of things. You may remember having learned facts or theorems for a recent test, but it is unlikely that you can recall having learned how to talk or tie your shoes — the acquiring of this knowledge is completely forgotten, though you still know how to do these things. While you are conscious of many things you have learned in the past, there is a whole world of knowledge that you have acquired *without consciously having done so*, and yet these things are indelibly printed in your mind.

You have learned many things — both true and false . . .

Things go better with

At   we do it all for

You have gained this knowledge through watching ads and listening to commercials. For three years of your life, your mind has been at work, watching ads.

The average person of 16 years has seen the equivalent of three years' worth of solid TV ad-watching, based on a normal work week.[4] In the typical American home, the male viewer, "between his second and 65th year, will watch TV for over 3,000 entire days — roughly nine full years of his life."[5]

The world of advertising is examined in more detail in Chapter II. Here we must remember, though, that *everything* we experience *informs* us about the world — from school textbooks, to commercials, to films like *Star Wars*, or whatever the most recent one is. It is impossible, then, to separate "culture", "sports", "entertainment" or "news" from "ideology": *we use all these things to construct a way of understanding the world — to construct a world-view.*

Because everything around us influences our thoughts, we must do two things when we are trying to find out *why* we think certain things or feel a certain way.

First, we must identify all the factors influencing our thoughts.

Second, having done this, we must analyse both their *form* (whether TV, a song, a picture etc.); and their *content* (what they say, what "message" they relay).

How are the ideas or values presented? What are they? What position are they asking us, implicitly or explicitly, to support or reject?

We will then have a better idea of what general messages we have been receiving, which are an important part of how we form opinions. As we will continue to discover, there are many factors influencing the way we see things — we are usually unaware of many of them.

Since television has already been singled out as a principal source of our information, ideas and opinions, we will start our study with it.

Activities

1. Define "ideology".

2. Try Step One on this page listing influences on the way you think.

3. "Average" people do not exist in reality, but the concept of the average person is a useful one for identifying general patterns.
a. How do you compare to the "average" Canadian? Spare time activities? Part-time job?
b. Determine the "average" in your group with respect to physical characteristics. Survey opinions on such things as recommended curfews. Show how the average of the group may not be the same as any individual response.

4. Conduct a poll on people's favourite TV programmes and characters. Ask them why they are their favourites. What personal characteristics make TV characters likable?
— warmth?
— humour?
— power?
— glamour?
— other . . .
Record your findings, and keep them for future reference in your group's course of studies.

ANIMAL CRACKERS

Television

It is difficult to underplay the importance of television — its impact on society, and its effect on our way of thinking, our way of *seeing the world*. Here we will not give detailed examination to other important mass media — radio, newspaper, magazines, telephones, cable TV, and other telecommunications media. While certain aspects of these media are touched upon in this book (especially Chapter II), the major work in these areas will have to be what you decide to pursue yourself.

Scope and impact

By the time average children enter kindergarten, they have already spent more hours in front of the TV learning about the world than the hours they would spend in a college classroom earning a B.A. degree.[6] One in five children spends more time watching TV than he would spend at a full-time job.[7] Television reaches almost all Canadian homes — 98% have at least one set, according to a recent study. In fact, more Canadian households in 1972 were without hot and cold water supplies, without baths or showers, without telephones or automobiles than were without televisions.[8]

The total amount of time we spend in front of the TV is staggering. Critics of this medium suggest 5 hours 15 minutes per day is the average viewing time; Canadian government publications put the figure even higher:

> Our ears and eyes are riveted to the tube more than 6 hours a day (the average viewing time in each home). And that is only a national average. Quebecers are even more avid viewers, averaging 6 hours 24 minutes a day.[9]

One Modern World Problems teacher in Nova Scotia estimated student viewing time in her school ranged from two to 50 hours a week . . . In Canada, about 40% of our leisure time is spent with television. TV ranks third (after sleep and work) as a consumer of time.[10]

Effects on lifestyle

Clearly, television plays a major part in modern life, and therefore should be examined carefully. It has appeared very recently on the scene, if we consider the length of time human beings have been communicating with each other. Television is just over one generation old. This is one of the reasons why the studies

". . . and how's life with YOU — what are YOU watching?"

measuring effects of TV are only now beginning to be widely circulated. Radio, an earlier form of mass communication, has been analysed. Its impact and its capacity to inform and persuade was made obvious in World War II. For example, a Danish Director of Radio noted rather startling correlations:

> When Denmark began 24-hour-a-day radio programming, the suicide rate dropped: 'In a modern society many people wait up at night, and radio has become a sort of companion to them. Many people have stopped worrying about the night, worrying that might lead them to think of suicide or even commit suicide.'[11]

If radio is seen as a constant companion, perhaps we should describe television as being both companion and mentor.

The following is intended to underscore the dramatic, far-reaching — and sometimes comical — effects of television on our lives and lifestyles.

- Medical doctors are encountering what they call "TV spine" and "TV eyes".

- " . . . it is clear that television has affected our lives in ways unrelated to its programme content. Brooklyn College sociologist Dr Clara T. Appell reports that of the families she has studied 60% have changed their sleep patterns because of television, 55% have changed their eating schedules, and 78% report they use television as an 'electronic babysitter'. Water system engineers must build city water supply systems to accommodate the drop in water occasioned by the toilet-flushing during television commercials."[12]

- "Rhoda marries Joe (*Rhoda*). Throughout the country people celebrate the event. Thousands of presents arrive at CBS headquarters on both coasts, at the local stations relaying the network feed, and at the offices of the MTM Company, the show's producers. The packages are addressed to Miss Rhoda Morganstern, the fictional lead."[13]

- Marcus Welby, M.D. received 250,000 letters from viewers seeking medical advice.[14]

- A parish priest in a city in the Atlantic provinces is asked to say mass for someone who is dying in a soap opera.[15]

For many, then, the distinction between reality and the world of television is clouded. It is, indeed, a "surrogate world". Even its unexpected effects are nevertheless dramatic:

A casual mention on television can affect viewers' attitudes and behaviour. After Rowan and Martin's *Laugh-In* used the expression, 'Look that up in your Funk and Wagnalls', the dictionary had to go into extra printings to satisfy a 20 percent rise in sales.[16]

In some places television has even come to be considered a *necessity of life*:

On July 28, 1976, N.Y. Governor Hugh Carey signs a bill exempting the television set from being appropriated to satisfy money judgements. The set now joins all other 'utensils necessary for the judgement debtor and family', immune from garnishment, along with wearing apparel, household furniture, tableware, cooking equipment.[17]

From your understanding of large cities and the lives of working people, why might television be considered a necessity of life?

Drawing by Modell; • 1978 The New Yorker Magazine, Inc.

"For best viewer supporting an actor or actress in a continuing drama or comedy series, the winner is —"

"Gerbner & Gross report a direct relationship between the amount of time spent watching television and a 'fortress mentality'. Heavy viewers of television are more likely to over-estimate the proportion of the general population involved in police work. They are more likely to over-estimate the danger of their own neighbourhood. They are more likely to have a sense of fear about daily life. They are more likely to over-estimate the probability of being involved in a violent crime . . . While many adults may be aware of the fictitiousness of television, it is hard for many people to distinguish between the real world in which they live and the television. . . . while people are aware that events portrayed on television are not 'really' happening, they believe that television accurately indicates that such things happen, how they happen, when they happen, where they happen, and to and by what sort of people they happen. Thus they develop mental sets modelled on the television portrayal of reality. They develop a cognitive map of reality patterned on the fictional world of television. As this conception of reality is shared by their peer or reference group, it has real consequences for their lives."

— Ontario Royal Commission vol. 6 (1976) p. 294.

Effects on our way of thinking

While these examples illustrate the impact of TV on how we spend our time or our money, perhaps just as important to consider is how TV, as a form of mass communication, affects our way of *thinking*.

Because TV appears to show us "real life", and can show us varieties of it from points of view and from places we could never experience ourselves, we can easily begin to believe that television describes the world — reality itself — more accurately, and with more credibility than other sources of information, other people or even we ourselves possibly could.

While on one level we know that of course TV is not always true to life, on another level, we unconsciously accept many of its messages as being inherently true, with relevance for our lives.

Without necessarily being aware of it, we accept as our reference points in the *real world* of daily experience the humour, drama, power and glamour of television.

It is 1980, on a golden summer evening on the Halifax Commons. A group of friends play softball. The bases are loaded, and a comedy of missed balls, slides into bases and players bumping into each other triggers full, and long laughter amongst the players and the half-dozen people in the bleachers who have come to watch. "That rates a beer commercial!" someone shouts . . .

"Cloning is irrelevant because it is already happening," according to former advertising executive and author Jerry Mander, who describes the effect of television on our very way of thinking: we have the same minds. All over the world, people have the same TV characters as companions, and they are learning the same things about the world from them. *The Waltons, Charlie's Angels* or *Hawaii Five-O* are part of TV's "universal curriculum".[18] According to Mander, TV does not allow people to use their powers of imagination — to dream. Radio listeners had to use their imaginations to create elaborate scenes, fabulous beauty, or terrifying monsters. But now it is as if television is saying to us, just as McDonald's ads do, "We Do It All For You".

Viewers become *passive recipients* of messages, not the *active participants* that they must be in order to understand poetry or other forms of communication.

Recently much has been said of how new TV technology will allow people to phone in responses to shows, thereby participating in TV. However, this is still fundamentally a response to stimuli. By its very nature the technology of mass communications does not admit of multi-directional emissions: people cannot broadcast to each other — they have to go through the TV or radio station, which has ultimate control. Mass media and TV, by their very nature, are one-way instruments of communication.

Television in particular shatters people's attention span and gives us a fragmented way of understanding things. Scores of issues may be touched upon in any newscast, but none may be dealt with in depth.

As a result, younger people today are said to lack a "linear sequential" understanding of things. That is, they do not follow an ordered, logical progression of ideas when they learn things. Rather, people "scan" information just as a television scans a screen with thousands of electronic impulses per second, picking up only a fragment of the image at any one time. Just as the brain forms a picture from the millions of dots that the electrons make on the TV screen, so our mind will "make sense" of all these impressions we receive. However, they will be just that — *impressions* — not the result of a rational, thinking process.

When we speak of TV's influence, then, we may be referring to any one of several factors:

● The effect of TV watching (leaving aside the programme content) on the way we spend our time, including what we *don't* do as well.

For example if we are watching TV, we don't have evening-long conversations with friends or spouses; we don't go for walks etc.

• The influence of TV programming on our attitudes, behaviour, and ways of thinking;

• The ways in which TV can be used to serve the interests of a particular group seeking "news coverage"; the ways in which TV can influence the actual outcome of the news (by swaying public opinion etc). Also the way in which TV people can decide what is "news". If an event is not covered, did it "happen" to any significant degree? This in turn actually affects the importance people attach to an issue, and how involved they become in it. The media, especially TV, can shape events depending on how it covers them.

• The use of television to serve economic interests; the role of "self-censorship" (a show must be "marketable" to some advertiser). Also, the staging of events which form public opinion is another way TV can be used to serve economic interests.

Children begin watching TV on a regular basis three or four years before entering Grade One, and most children watch television every day.[19]

Children between the ages of 2 and 5 watch an average of 22:57 hours of TV per week.

"The seven to 11-year old group watches 22:28 hours per week, and the teenage group watches 23:20 hours per week. With a possible maximum of 12 minutes of commercial time per hour, that's a lot of commercials."[20]

NEWS ITEM· OTTAWA PROBES TV RADIATION HAZARDS

(April 15, 1969)

"Your set is safe radiation-wise . . . have you checked the programs they've been exposed to?"

We have examined briefly some of the first two factors; in Chapters II and III the last two factors are examined.

Discussion/research

1. Do you agree with Jerry Mander's opinion of television (p. 18)? From this starting point describe the role you think TV plays in present-day society.

2. By the time children are about four years old, they have acquired the basic tools needed to communicate in every-day life.

a. With a tape recorder, tape several children's descriptions of their favourite TV episode (do not watch the show yourself).

b. From the cassette, reconstruct the plot.

Would your findings tend to confirm or contradict Mander's comments on TV's effect on our way of thinking?

3. What is the most-watched TV show in your group?

4. Are there any soap opera fans in your group? What gets people "hooked" on following the stories? Is *Another World* an accurate reflection of *your* world? Why or why not? Describe the world of your favourite soap opera.

5. In your discussion group, decide what the top five television shows are. Whatever they are — situation comedies, soap operas etc — describe the lives, occupations, houses, clothes, friends, situations and problems of the characters in these shows. Using specific references from these serials, describe the world, as it is depicted on the programmes which are most watched in your class.

6. Another World; The Waltons; Mork and Mindy; Dallas; Hawaii Five-O; Starsky and Hutch. By the time you read this, some of these TV shows may be well out of date. If so, what do people think of these shows? What has replaced them?

How do each of these shows differ from each other in the way the family, conflict, crime, social problems are dealt with? How "true to life" is each of the serials? How true are they to your life, in the Atlantic provinces?

7. Consider the quotation on page 17, in the light of your discussion about serials.

Can you think of any "real consequences" for people's lives, in your experience? If people's minds are continually slipping back and forth from the real world into the imaginary world of television serials to the point where some even confuse them, will certain character traits and ways of seeing the world rub off on the viewers? For example, is it possible that a young woman who has watched soap operas will be more likely to ask herself, "How much can I trust someone else?" . . . "Can a woman ever trust someone else?" . . . "Can a woman ever trust another woman when there's a man around?" . . .

8. What would happen if the characters of one show ended up in another serial? Create a skit, with "mistaken identity" as the axis of humour (e.g., *The Waltons* characters playing in *Another World*; Archie Bunker as host of *The Fifth Estate*; The Fonz as host of *Man Alive* . . .)

9. How would your week be different if you were denied TV? Try not to watch TV for a two-week period. Write a diary about what you do . . . your reactions to no TV.

10. How long are average commercials? Given the figures on television viewing by children, estimate how many commercials a six-year old might see in:
— a day?
— a week?
— a year?

Violence and television

The following article forms part of a report of the Ontario Royal Commission on Violence in the Communications Industry.

After reading the article, "Does violence shown on television distort viewers' beliefs about violence in the real world?", discuss it in small groups. What is meant by "social control"?

Do you agree with the author's viewpoint? Why or why not?

Does violence shown on television distort viewers' beliefs about violence in the real world?

Television Distorts Reality

The "uncertain mirror"[1] of television gives a weirdly distorted reflection of reality. Several[2] researchers have taken count of the kinds of characters that populate the world of entertainment television. Over three-quarters of that strange world is populated by young, North American, middle-class unmarried males. Children and old people account for only about ten per cent of the total population. When women are shown they usually occupy family roles, and in comparison to men, they are shown as being warmer and more sociable but less rational.[3]

The violence that is shown on television is also distorted. For example, in real life violence most often stems from close personal relationships.[4]. But on television violence is usually done by strangers.[5]. The crimes shown on television almost always involve violence, while in real life most crimes involve money or property and no violence at all.[6] About one-fifth of the characters in television drama are law officers and they act violently in about two-thirds of their appearances.[7] On the other hand, in real life police rarely, if ever, even draw their guns. Homicide is the most frequent television crime, but in real life homicide accounts for only a fraction of one per cent of actual crime.

But Who Believes It?

The world of television may show a grotesquely distorted version of the real world, but who really believes it?

Children do. Young children especially learn about the outside world primarily through televison – a fact that Canadian parents are quite well aware of.[8] In a survey study,[9] about half of the Grade One children interviewed said that the people on television were like everyday people. Some older children also believed that television characters and real people are alike most of the time. Even children in Grades Four and Five are often uncertain about the reality of what they see on entertainment television.[10] Almost half of the teenagers in a recent report indicated that crime programs "tell about life the way it really is."[11] Various studies have found that confusion between television fiction and reality is especially high among children who are more aggressive, and generally deviant,[12] and children from poor families or minority groups.[13]

Clearly a large proportion of children frequently confuse television and reality. How about adults? A single example is sufficient to demonstrate that many adults are capable of the same confusion. The popular televison program *Marcus Welby, M.D.* features Robert Young in the role of Dr. Welby. In the first five years of that program "Dr. Welby" has received over a quarter million letters from American and Canadian viewers, most of them asking for medical advice.[14]

And What Does It Matter?

Who cares if television distorts our perception of reality? Children may sometimes be amazed to find that Native People don't all live like "TV Indians." And, likewise, adults may be surprised to meet a real police

detective who turns out to be a very ordinary person. But there is little harm in this.

Some more sinister results of television distortion have recently been uncovered by George Gerbner, Dean of the Annerrberg School of Communication.[14] He and his co-workers have shown that heavy television users tend to develop a generally fearful and suspicious view of the world. Heavy television users are most likely to overestimate the proportion of people involved in law enforcement (reflecting television's version of reality). Similarly, heavy viewers tend to believe that most people cannot be trusted. The most striking evidence for the effects of television distortion comes from viewers who were asked to estimate their own chances of being involved in violence during any given week. Heavy television viewers were a good deal more likely to overestimate this possibility than were light viewers. Moreover, the exaggerated fear in heavy television users was held regardless of the age, sex, or education of the viewer.

Television, fear, and suspicion seem to go together. The obvious explanation for this is that the abundance of crime and violence shown on entertainment television causes people to be afraid. Of course this is not the only interpretation. It might be that especially apprehensive and mistrustful people spend more time in the relative safety of their homes, and thus watch more television than the average. This interpretation suggests that fear causes heavy television viewing. Perhaps the most plausible interpretation is that causation operates in both directions, creating a vicious circle.[15] Fear causes people to stay at home and watch television. Then the crime and violence shown on television increases their fear of the outside world. Television leads to fear, and fear leads to increased use of television – the classic self-perpetuating cycle of addiction. There is another disquieting interpretation as well.

Taking a wider view, Dr. Gerbner[14] sees the prevalence of television violence as a means of social control. The public fear and insecurity that are promoted by television violence produce an exaggerated concern for public order and an increasing dependence on the exercise of authoritarian power in our society.

Goranson, T. "TV violence effects: issues & evidence" Ont. Roy. Comm. On Viol. in Comm. Ind. Vol. 5: *Learning & media* p. 194

1 Canada, Parliament. Senate. Special Committee on Mass Media. *Report.* Vol. 1. *The uncertain mirror.* Ottawa, Queen's Printer, 1970) (Also known as the Davey Committee Report).

2 Gerbner, G. "Violence in television drama: Trends and symbolic functions." In G.A. Comstock and E.A. Rubinstein

(Eds.), *Television and Social behavior*, Vol. 1. *Media content and control.* Washington, D.C.: Government Printing Office, 1972. Pp. 28-187.

3 Tedesco, N.S. "Patterns of prime time." *Journal of Communication*, 1974, 24, 119-124.

4 Schloss, B., and Giesbrecht, N.A. *Murder in Canada.* Toronto: University of Toronto, 1972.

5 Gerbner, G. "Cultural indicators: The case of violence in television drama." *Annals of the American Academy of Political and Social Science*, 1970, 388, 69-81.

6 Silverman, R., and Teevan, J. *Crime in Canadian Society.* Toronto: Butterworth, 1975.

7 Liebert, R.M., Neale, J.M., and Davidson, E.S. *The early window: Effects of television on children and youth.* Elmsford, N.Y.: Pergamon Press, 1973.

8 Canada, Parliament. Senate. Special Committee on Mass Media. Report. Vol. 3. *Good, bad, or simply inevitable?* (Ottawa, Queen's Printer, 1970). (Also known as the Davey Committee Report).

9 Lyle, J., and Hoffman, H.R. "Children's use of television and other media." In E.A. Rubinstein, G.A. Comstock, and J.P. Murray (Eds.), *Television and social behavior.* Vol. 4. *Television in day-to-day life: Patterns of use.* Washington, D.C.: Government Printing Office, 1972. Pp. 129-256.

10 McLeod, J.M., Atkin, C.K., and Chaffee, S.H. "Adolescents, parents, and television use: Adolescent self-support measures from Maryland and Wisconsin samples." In G.A. Comstock and E.A. Rubinstein (Eds.), *Television and social behavior.* Vol. 3. *Television and adolescent aggressiveness.* Washington, D.C.: Government Printing Office, 1972. Pp. 173-238.

11 McLeod, J.M., Atkin, C.K., and Chaffee, S.H. "Adolescents, parents and televison use: Self-report and other-report measures from Wisconsin sample." In G.A. Comstock and E.A. Rubinstein (Eds.), *Television and social behavior.* Vol. 3. *Television and adolescent aggressiveness.* Washington, D.C.: Government Printing Office, 1972. Pp. 239-313.

12 McIntyre, J.J., and Teevan, J.J., Jr. "Television violence and deviant behavior." In G.A. Comstock and E.A. Rubinstein (Eds.). *Television and social behavior.* Vol. 3. *Television and adolescent aggressiveness.* Washington, D.C.: Government Printing Office, 1972. Pp. 383-435.

13 Greenberg, B.S., and Gordon, T.F. "Children's perceptions of television violence: A replication." In G.A. Comstock, and E.A. Rubinstein, and J.P. Murray (Eds). *Television and social behavior.* Vol. 5. *Television's effects. Further explorations.* Washington, D.C.: Government Printing Office, 1972. Pp. 211-230.

Greenberg, B.S., and Dervin, B. *Use of the mass media by the urban poor.* New York: Praeger, 1970.

14 Gerbner, G. and Gross, L. "Living with television: The violence profile." *Journal of Communication*, 1976, 26, 173-194.

15 Hadley, R. "The scary world of the TV addict." *Psychology Today*, 1976, 10, No. 3, p. 6. ∎

Discussion/research

1. Watching a lot of television creates a "bunker" or fortress mentality amongst TV's viewers, according to the experts testifying before Ontario's Royal Commission on Violence in the Communications Industry. The U.S. Senate (Dodd) investigation found that violence on TV was actively sought out by the networks.*

Why would the TV industry promote violence? Record your discussion; you may wish to return to this question at some point further along in the book.

2. Read and review the book *Four arguments for the elimination of television* by Jerry Mander (1978) N.Y. Morrow Quill Paperbacks. (This book was written by a former advertising executive of one of the United States' most prestigious advertising firms, and is recommended reading for this chapter.)

3. The name of the principal character in the popular TV series *All in the Family* is Archie *Bunker*. With reference to specific episodes, describe whether or not his surname is an appropriate one.

---

*"In spite of the industry's protestations that they do not use violence for its own sake, the Dodd investigation turned up some rather revealing memoranda to the contrary. An independent producer was asked to 'inject an adequate diet of violence into scripts' (overriding a sponsor's objections to excessive violence). Another network official wrote, 'I like the idea of sadism.' Still another was advised by memorandum: 'In accordance with your request, spectacular accidents and violence scenes of the 1930-1936 years have been requested from all known sources of stock footages. You will be advised as material arrives.' . . . No wonder the (Dodd) committee concluded that the networks 'clearly pursued a deliberate policy of emphasizing sex, violence and brutality on (their) dramatic shows.'." N. Johnson (1970) *How to talk back to your TV set* N.Y. Little and Brown, p. 40.

Further Reading

Let me speak!
Domitila Barios de Chungara (1978), trans. Victoria Ortiz. NY: Monthly Review Books

Four arguments for the elimination of television
Jerry Mander (1978) NY: Morrow Quill Paperbacks

Joyce Nelson (1977), short bibliography on television, available by writing to the Canadian Broadcasting Corporation, Ideas programme

New Internationalist
In particular, this magazine's October 1976 issue on global media. Monthly $15/year, 175 Carlton Street, Toronto, Ontario M5A 2K3

Television: the critical view
Horace Newcomb (1979) ed. and intro. NY: Oxford University Press

Ontario Royal Commission on violence in the communications industry report
(6 volumes, 1976)

Audio/visual

"Television: a Surrogate World"
Joyce Nelson, producer, four-part radio broadcast, CBC *Ideas* series

Fahrenheit 451
(16 mm colour film, 112 min.), director Francois Truffault, available from Universal Films, 77 Germain St., Saint John, N.B.

II. Getting the message

Chapter II: Getting the Message

BUMPER GRAIN HARVEST AROUND WORLD
RAISES FEAR OF A FOOD CRISIS

— Newspaper headline[1]

"It's not bombing — it's air support."

— Air Force Colonel[2]

"Well the system was designed as a fail-safe system, and
as such was not required to carry out the tests."

— Aircraft safety official

(Several defective DC-10 aircraft crashed, killing over 500 passengers.)[3]

Introduction

The above quotes are reminders of what can happen when people do not think clearly. They underscore how important it is that we understand the consequences of our words and the positions or policies we support.

However, most of the daily messages we receive are not as obviously contradictory, confusing or fallacious as the examples just given. Yet, if we were to examine more closely some of the daily messages we receive, how well would they actually rate?

The aim of this chapter is to explore ways of analysing clearly the many types of messages that we receive in daily communication. The tools of analysis presented here will help you to "read between the lines". Being able to read between the lines and use critical judgment in daily life will help you to base your opinions and actions on a solid foundation. This ability to analyse things clearly is often associated with a very small, sophisticated or academic minority. However, most people have this ability: they lack only the tools of analysis with which to work. In this chapter, we will introduce a good number of them.

Working assumptions

We should begin by recalling that humans never cease to receive messages, even if these messages are only ones from their environment (It's cold, it's hot; the bus is coming; I read the ads on the bus). We are continually *making sense* of our surroundings, accepting or rejecting the millions of messages that come our way. Most often this is an automatic, instantaneous and unconscious process.

In this chapter, we shall try to examine part of this process, as if it were in slow motion. In this way we can see how it works, how we come to hold certain views or opinions. In particular, we shall look at the various ways in which people can be convinced by an essentially unsound argument.

Second, we should remember that everything that surrounds us *informs* us about ourselves and our world — classified ads, mail-order catalogues, records, photographs, school books, personal conversations. All give us messages of some sort.

Thirdly, it should be noted as well that even as this book is being written, some of its examples and illustrations will become dated in some ways. It will be your responsibility to find examples for study and discussion in your own newspapers and daily life. This is why the entire book (and this section in particular) is to be considered an introduction: you yourself must continue the work.

The "raw data" to be analysed in this section include such things as editorials and daily conversations — subject matter that you are familiar with. What may be new are the methods of analysis we propose, and the examples and illustrations you yourself bring to this section.

Because you are familiar with the subject matter, you will be able to judge for yourself the meaning, use and value of the method of analysis we propose. You should remember that the critical approach we are proposing should be used to judge this book itself, as well as other sources of information!

Fourth, it is important to note that there is no such thing as an "objective" attitude, news report or scientific theory. In this book, you may sometimes find the word "facts" in quotation marks. This is because, in the very process of selecting something worth recording as a fact, a person is making a subjective choice. All scientists, historians or observers have to make subjective choices in their work: humans, by their very nature, are *subjects,* not objects. They must consider some things more significant than others.

However, some people are better than others at distinguishing their working assumptions, personal interests, methods of work and analysis. Also, some are better than others at ensuring that the statements they make are open to various forms of verification. Such care and discipline is often incorrectly called an "objective" attitude in a scientist, historian or journalist.

Finally, with some practice in recognising various techniques of persuasion, you are likely to be thinking more clearly yourself, and thus will be better equipped to make sound judgements in your own daily life.

Language

Language performs three functions. It communicates facts or theories. It expresses

Checklist for careful thinking

These general questions are useful to keep in mind when assessing the meaning and value of any argument, story, conversation or other communication you encounter.

What is the source?
Is the source of information friendly or unfriendly to the point of view expressed? Can I determine the viewpoint of the source itself?

What is the basic message?
What is the basic point being made? How does it relate to any wider issues connected to it?

What is presented in support of the point of view?
If a logical argument is being put forward, are the assumptions upon which it is based correct? Is the reasoning sound?

If the statement or argument can be proven with evidence, what evidence is brought forward? Is it relevant? Is it convincing?

Is anything omitted?

What types of examples are used to illustrate a point? Are they pertinent or misleading?

How is the message being conveyed?
Are the techniques used to persuade me fair ones?

Who stands to gain?
If the point of view presented is adopted, what individuals or what interests stand to gain?

our own emotions or stirs the emotions of others. And it can spur people to action. When you tell your friends that you have gone hiking in the country, you are communicating a fact. When you tell your friend how warm it was, how you could swim in the lake at the end of the trail and what a wonderful afternoon you had in the warm and quiet pine forest, you are communicating facts, but you are also expressing your feelings and perhaps stirring theirs. When you try to get your friends to come with you, you are trying to get them to act.

Within two or three sentences your language may play all three roles. In this section, we are primarily interested in language as it affects the way we *think*.

Humans of course communicate to each other through language. However, language can be *any* organised system used by humans to communicate amongst themselves. We have all heard of "computer language": this is just one more way of communicating, as is English, French, Micmac, Cree or any other language. All these languages have structures and assign meanings to them. These meanings are known to users of the language. Because humans can *understand* each other, they are able to work and create things with each other, and build on each other's work.

We will be examining many techniques of persuasion. *We are all persuaded to one viewpoint or another. The important question is: was this persuasion based on clear thinking, or on unsound or unfair techniques of persuasion?*

Let us start by looking at some cases of decision-making that may be quite familiar.

Exercise: clear thinking

Explain clearly how you thought about a question before reaching a decision. Here are some ideas of things you may have thought about; you likely will have many more to suggest.

Shall I take an after-school job?
Shall I work during my summer vacation?
What subjects shall I choose in school?
Shall I plan to go to university? trade school? get a job right away?
Shall I copy someone else's written assignment (or give them mine to copy over)?
Shall I take up smoking cigarettes (or quit smoking)?

Determining the Overall Message

In determining the *overall message* in any given communication, we must divide the message we are presented with into two categories — the message's form, and its content.

Message = content + form

A message is composed of two things:

1. **Content:** This is *what* is presented — the information, "facts" or theories put forward in support of an idea. The content of a message can include logical, moral, or aesthetic arguments — it also includes personal feelings.

The actual content of a message usually is only a small part of the overall message we receive. Most of our messages are in some way "packaging".

2. **Form:** This is *how* something is presented, — how we convey what we want to express. We shape our information, ideas or feelings: we give them a *form*.

When we have communicated ideas to someone else, we have given them a *message*, which has a meaning: if we have been successful in conveying our messages, the other person will understand our words, gestures the same way we meant them.

It is not necessarily bad that most of our messages are made up of form (interpretation) rather than content (facts, etc.), because we know that the brain's intelligence and efficiency is based on selectivity.

However, to know whether the selection and presentation of information is sound, we must also be sure to start by *ranking carefully* our sources of information. We have to determine the credibility of our sources. Then we have to see whether their position is valid, before accepting it.

Credibility

We will have a better idea of how credible our sources of information are once we know the answer to these four questions:

1. **Who is the source?** Who is giving me the message? Is it an individual, a government official, an ad company, a scientist?

2. **What knowledge do they have?** What knowledge or experience do they have in the area on which they are speaking?

3. **What techniques of persuasion are they using?** What techniques are they using to per-

suade me? Are they appealing to any particular emotion or bias?

4. What is their motive? Why might they want to persuade me to their point of view? What is their own particular stake in the issue being discussed?

By taking these questions into account, we can decide how much time we should give to examining a certain point of view. Then, we must look at the actual content of these sources of information. We may seek out other sources as well, to test the validity of the position. We may also be able to test the position against our own experience. We should then take a fifth step.

5. Is this a conventional or unconventional position? Is the view expressed generally in line with accepted ideas on the subject? If so, are the general premises valid? If the position is an unconventional one, how is it different from the conventional view? Does this differing view have some merit?

After establishing these points we will be able to decide whether we need to consider any further someone's position. If it does merit further consideration, we will then have to take a sixth step, and decide on the validity of the position that is put forward.

'However, the Chilean man-in-the-street appears to have few complaints.'

LNS

Validity

We have to determine the validity of a position: whether it is true or false.

6. Is the statement true or false? Is the reasoning and argumentation sound or unsound? Have I isolated any factors in the position that are unsound or untrue? Are these factors central or peripheral to the main position? Is there a coherence to the overall position?

Finally, after determining the credibility of the source and the validity of the statement, we must then decide whether the statement has validity for us: is it in harmony or conflict with all the other ideas and values we hold? We must accept or reject the position.

Acceptability

7. Will I accept or reject this statement? On the basis of the above criteria, and my personal and community values and interests, do I accept or reject this position? If I accept or reject the position, are there any consequences I can foresee, for myself or others?

While all these steps may seem complicated, we follow them every day of our lives, to some extent. For example, if you hear rumours about a friend of yours, if you have good judgment, you generally will examine the credibility of the source before spending too much time needlessly worrying (Is the source of the rumours someone who is jealous of my friend? a rival or personal enemy?).

Discussion

Imagine some daily scenarios in which the seven steps outlined here might be used.

Bias and propaganda techniques:
How is a position being built?

We can examine a statement that is made in a newspaper, an ad or a film in the same way that we might examine a house or an apartment block we were considering moving into. How sound is the structure? How well has a particular position been built?

What are your first impressions? Do you like the picture, statement or idea you are presented with? After answering this question either way, you must examine more closely *why* you hold this view.

Is the argument or proposition built on a sound foundation? Even if the foundations are good, are you sure that the argument constructed on top of them is as sound? Can you recognise any signs of short-cuts that those who know the tricks of the trades of persuasion can get away with? Can you see past any cheap gagetry that might make you *think* that the argument was of the highest calibre and the construction was of the finest, whereas in reality it is covering up cheap and shoddy work?

In the following sub-sections, we will look at bias and propaganda techniques, with these ideas in mind.

Shaky foundations: Starting off wrong

There are several general ways in which unsound arguments may be built. The very basis on which they rest may be unsound.

A compelling argument . . .

"Shut up," He Explained:

My 14-year old daughter, Kim, wanted to wear a black arm-band to school to demonstrate against the war. I told her I had no objections if she really understood the facts. So I took a lot of time to tell her how we got involved in Vietnam, and the situation there and so on. She said, "I understand what you're saying, but I don't agree." So I explained the whole situation again, about the 1954 accord, and the 1962 accord, and she said, "All right, but why not just get all of them out of there?" So I said, "Kim, I have given you the arguments for not just getting out, and you just haven't given me a logical argument against it. So there will be no black arm-band and no participation in a demonstration!"

Oct. 6, 1969

U.S. Vice-President Spiro T. Agnew

Bold assertions. People sometimes give no reason at all for the views they hold; or they accept without question what political or religious leaders say. When asked why he will not do something, a child may retort with the unanswerable "—Because!". When people make bold assertions, they praise or condemn public figures, friends or enemies without sufficient evidence to do so.

"Our community had a visit of what is unquestionably the finest hockey club in Canada." Words like *unquestionably, indisputably* should be looked at very closely, as should such expressions as *But the truth is* (has it been proven?) or *The fact is*. "The Prime Minister was speaking for all Canadians when he said . . .". Can such statements be proven? If not, they should be modified accordingly: "Our community had a visit of the widely acclaimed X hockey club, which has won sixteen games in a row." "But the truth is" should often be replaced with "however".

Untrustworthy authorities. We can be reasoning improperly if we do not carefully distinguish between various authorities. People are authorities in certain fields, but not in all fields. Famous Canadian recording artists and sports stars have sold consumer products or the services of banks by appearing in commercials and advertisements. While famous or accomplished singers may be authorities on singing, this does not make them an authority on unrelated topics like consumer items. Their authority in these fields will depend on studies. Thus, the worth of their opinion should be ranked along with that of any individual with equal intelligence and knowledge of the subject.

Moreover, if a celebrity is receiving large sums of money or other rewards to endorse a product or policy, their claims must be examined all the more closely.

Reasoning with the wrong facts. Another factor contributing to faulty reasoning is reasoning with entirely the wrong facts. Sometimes, even in reasonable discussions, irrelevant or misleading points are introduced in support of an argument (see *Ignoring the question* as well). For example, after the nuclear reactor accident at Three Mile Island in the United States, a nuclear physicist had his picture taken for newspaper wire services with his infant, the cooling towers forming a backdrop. This supposedly "proved" how safe they were . . .[4]

When examples or statistics are given, we must ask:

a. Are these appropriate references for the topic at hand?

and

b. Is there any important information or consideration missing? Leaving out the most important information or the major opposing argument is a common device.

Are "two sides" of an issue really presented? Or are they presented in such a way as to favour one over the other? Is the opposing side *really* presented, or is it presented as a "straw man" that can easily be knocked down? Often with controversial issues two contrasting views are presented:

> But sometimes this seemingly fair technique is a front, behind which the agents can completely shut out sides of the controversy they don't approve of. They present only those sides that they find acceptable or responsible — or those so bizarre as to be ridiculous. The public is thus deprived of any opportunity to consider all sides.[5]

Rationalisation. Sometimes we make up reasons for doing something that we wanted to do all along, but are unwilling to admit it. If we would rather go skating than help clean up the yard, we say "I need the exercise and relaxation. Skating will give me the strength I need for my biology exam."

Downright lying. From fabricated stories of atrocities during the Crusades (which triggered real atrocities) to the Nazi propagandist Goebbles' directive that "If you are going to lie, tell a big lie," this technique is used with rather alarming success.

Faulty premise for an argument. Analyse the following: "Immigrants are taking away jobs from Canadians. They shouldn't be allowed in the country." Is the premise a correct one?

Exercise

Of the following, which would you describe as an example of logical reasoning? Which would strike you as a rationalisation? Add an example of rationalisation that you have made yourself.

1. Instead of finishing my history homework, I'll go downtown for a while and just let my

"Don't worry about it. One day you're feeling down and you dish out 20 years to some poor devil. The next day you feel great and everybody gets a suspended sentence. It all evens out in the end."

mind work on it, and then maybe tomorrow morning before school I will have figured out how to answer that question. They say that if you give your mind a break the answers come easier.

2. I'm not going to try out for the team. The coach has probably already picked the team so I wouldn't have a fair chance anyway.

3. Instead of taking out the garbage myself, I'll get my younger brother to do it. Young children need to become responsible and grow up sometime.

4. At the other regional highschool, the students organised themselves and got the buses to come later, so that everyone could stay for the after-school clubs and sports. Because I'd like to be able to play with my other friends who have to leave after school and I know others do too, I'm going to ask around amongst the students to see if we can do the same thing here.

Review: shaky foundations

Here is a review of faulty reasoning techniques that have been studied so far:

Bold assertions

Untrustworthy authorities

Reasoning with the wrong facts

Rationalisation

Downright lying

Faulty premise for an argument

Faulty construction: illogical or unsound ways of arguing

Some arguments and positions have basic weaknesses in their construction. We should be able to identify them clearly. Here are some of them.

Hasty generalisation. Generalisations, based on much learning and research, are what allow great civilisations to flourish: people are able to build upon each other's work. If we make a generalisation on a representative sampling, we are likely to make a sound generalisation.

However, generalisations based on a few unrepresentative samplings are likely to be faulty. If someone says, "Both Bill and Terry Walsh were on the first string basketball team; therefore both their younger brothers will probably also be stars," this person has jumped to a conclusion. The generalisation is based on only two examples. Besides, human beings are too complex to be reduced to many generalisations: they often differ as much within a family as not.

By hasty generalisations, then, we mean arguing that what is true for one or more particular cases is true for *all* cases without exception.

Mistaking the cause. When two things happen at the same time, we sometimes say one caused the other. While this is correct in some cases, in others it is not. For example, if a skin outbreak disappears after a young person

has used a certain product advertised to eliminate skin blemishes, is it *necessarily* the product that has cleared up the skin? What about the special attention s/he may be paying to other important factors (diet, exercise, sleep, frequent changes of bedlinen, etc.)? Each of these things may be major or minor causes for the effect which has been produced.

Cause-effect relationships do explain many things, but it can be dangerous to ascribe a cause to an effect without serious and careful examination.

False analogy. An analogy is the relationship between two things which are similar in many, though not in all respects. In logic, one assumes that if two things are similar in one or more respects, they will be similar in other respects. Arguing by analogy can sometimes quickly clarify a question or heighten our awareness of an issue, but false analogies can be hard to pinpoint and often difficult to refute.

Because analogies often catch the imagination, they can be very persuasive devices. If, however, an analogy is not useful in furthering a discussion, you need not refute every point using the terms of the analogy — it may be that the analogy was a false one to begin with.

Ignoring the question. Ignoring the question is avoiding or missing the real matter to be discussed. If the question is: Resolved, that the students should receive credit for participation in the camera club; and the debater spends all his/her time proving that extra-curricular activity is valuable to students and improves their ability to get along with each other, this person is ignoring the question, since many extra-curricular activities can be valuable to students — basketball, organising a dance, part-time jobs, etc.

The historian Macaulay criticises this fallacy of arguing beside the point when he says, "The advocates of Charles I, like the advocates of other malefactors against whom overwhelming evidence is produced, generally decline all controversy about the facts, and content themselves with calling testimony to character. He had so many private virtues! . . . A good father! A good husband! Ample apologies indeed for fifteen years of persecution, tyranny, and falsehood!"

Another common way of ignoring the question is cracking jokes instead of dealing with the argument seriously. This can often distract the listener, or make the other person look stupid or pedantic for sticking to the point. Someone might think discussing power rates is *"boring"*, but if they are the issue at hand, it is ignoring the question to make such a comment.

The *"straw man"* argument is a form of ignoring the question. The person wanting to convince another of the validity of his/her case sets up a "straw man", which then can be easily knocked down. This knocking down of spurious argument can pass for serious argumentation about the real issue.

Appealing to tradition or prejudice are other ways of ignoring the question.

Begging the question. When people beg the question, they are assuming the truth or falsity of what they are trying to prove. When a person argues that someone is not a great blues singer because there are no great blues singers alive today, s/he is assuming the truth or validity of a larger statement which includes the one he started to prove, and hence is begging the question. When an editorialist says, "The disgraceful and pointless practice of strikes must be put to an end," s/he is assuming that strikes are disgraceful and pointless, instead of trying to prove them to be so, and therefore is begging the question. One way of begging the question is so common as to go almost unnoticed. For example, "Rightly or wrongly, the company has threatened to pull out of the area if it doesn't get the concessions from the government. Therefore we should pressure our Member of Parliament to see that the company gets them."

The way it works, in grammatical terms, is to place the major assumption in a minor part of the sentence: the question being begged (namely, *whether the company will pull out)* is a dependent clause and the principal clause, the main focus (that is, *we should pressure government to give the company what it wants)* remains uncontroversial.

Attacking the person, not the argument. "Don't tell me you've been listening to that malcontent Matthews! He's a born trouble-maker — that's all." Or, "When you're a little older, you'll get a little less idealistic and a

Changing usages and meanings

Over the years, words take on new connotations and meanings, or shed them, as the language continues to evolve. Such words as *Communist, Capitalist, Fascist* at one time referred to specific and clearly defined groups of people, as did *Christian* centuries ago. However, words can in effect change in meaning over time, either taking on pejorative or favourable connotations or losing their original, specific meaning. What once was an everyday word may later carry a "loaded meaning".

An interesting example of this change in a word's connotation appears in an entry in Nova Scotia's Registry of Deeds. A man, who today would probably describe himself as a "businessman", in 1917 put, as his profession, "Capitalist".

little more realistic." Called *ad hominem* arguments, these statements attack the person rather than the arguments s/he presents. They are not reasoning statements.

The unscrupulous might use the personal shortcomings of an author, scientist or political opponent to discredit a position or research that was entirely unrelated to that shortcoming. (E.g., "Because Hemmingway was a heavy drinker none of his writings could be worth much.")

Pointing to an enemy. A successful technique often used by skilled politicians is to deflect criticism from themselves by pinpointing an enemy. In this way they can claim to be *for* something and *against* something else (the enemy). In the extreme, the rise of Fascism and Nazism in the 1920s and 30s was in large part due to the manipulative skills of its leaders, who blamed the real hardships of people on unreal, or fabricated "enemies" — Jews, gypsies or other political parties.

Misusing statistics. Disraeli once said, "There are lies, there are damned lies, and there are statistics."[6] People often use statistics to "prove" statements that the figures do not prove at all: this may be a case of carelessness, simple inaccuracy, or yet again downright dishonesty. Though they can be very useful, statistics must be used carefully and in moderation. Even the most painstakingly done statistical surveys must be examined closely, because it is not always possible to describe reality accurately by reducing it to numerical data. A survey or opinion poll should never be the sole basis on which you make a decision.

Meshing fact with opinion. Sometimes fact is presented with the same emphasis as opinion, so that the opinion takes on some of the credibility of the fact. This is closely related to Begging the Question and other categories, but deserves special attention.

What is fact and what is opinion in the following sentence?

"Southern Africa is being overrun by Communists."

What does the verb connote? What do the nouns denote?

Review: faulty construction

Here is a review of further techniques of faulty reasoning that have been studied so far.

Hasty generalisation

Mistaking the cause

False analogy

Ignoring the question

Begging the question

Attacking the person, not the argument

Pointing to an enemy

Misusing statistics

Meshing fact with opinion

Exercise: recognising shaky foundations or faulty construction of an argument

In most of the following, the reasoning is faulty. In each case of unsound or unconvincing reasoning, name the fallacy or defect and show clearly that the argument is not convincing.

1. Potatoes don't grow well in Yarmouth. I planted some in my garden and they didn't grow.

2. Hemmingway, the great American novelist, was a heavy drinker. Therefore heavy drinking is not a serious hindrance to accomplishment or success.

3. Finishing highschool doesn't matter. Look at all the people who are millionaires without finishing school.

4. My eyes are sore. I must be studying too much.

5. The shares of Zed Company are on the way up, and should double in value before the end of the month. Gordon Ellison, who can sell me some and has already made a fortune on the stock exchange, told me so.

6. People who don't listen to opera are ignorant and boorish, because if they did have any culture, they'd be listening to it every Saturday and they'd realise what they're missing.

7. I'm not a racist, but I'll never rent a room to one of those foreign students again. I did once, and she left without paying the phone bill.

8. Brent Burton should never speak at a rally. Last week when he tried to speak after those people were hurt in the fight, his voice was shaking and his hands were trembling.

9. Because I passed the Christmas exam in French, I should do okay at Easter.

10. Jack Benson, who only talks to the best looking girls in the school, asked me to meet him after school; therefore I must be one of the best looking girls in the school.

11. Elio Bartoli, an Italian immigrant businessman, was recently sent to jail for tax evasion. Italians shouldn't be allowed to get start-up grants for small business because they just abuse them anyway.

12. Everyone knows that walking alone at night is very dangerous. Therefore if a woman is out late at night by herself she's just asking for trouble.

13. Millions of dollars' worth of merchandise is shoplifted every year. What difference will it make if I just take one thing every once in a while? One pair of jeans here or there won't make a difference either way.

14. Our family has always voted conservative. Therefore I will vote conservative.

15. Sarah only takes twenty minutes to get all her math homework done. That's all the time it takes me too. Maybe I'll get an A in it as well.

16. I've had trouble starting my car lately. Apparently this can be caused by a run-down battery. I'll get a new one tomorrow.

17. Roy's suggestions for the basketball tournament are impractical. He's so obnoxious anyway.

18. I've enjoyed every album that has been put out by that group so far. Here's their new release. I'll probably like it too.

19. Since the average person in our city only uses the bus 1.3 times a week, we are announcing the following reductions in service...

20. The media, rightly or wrongly, tend to cover only sensational events, so we'll have to think of a "gimmick" if we want coverage.

21. Many scientists feel nuclear power plants are safe, so I shouldn't worry.

Discussion/research

1. How could the guidelines set out in this unit be of use to you in your own personal life, for determining what is the true interpretation of an event
— with friends?
— with teachers, parents?
— where you work?

2. Have you noticed others making generalisations based on faulty reasoning or unsubstantiated rumours? What are some examples?

a. Prepare a short presentation on these events in history:
— Persecution of Jews
— McCarthy period in U.S.

b. Prepare a presentation on media coverage of Quebec.

c. Examine the literature put out by the Ku Klux Klan.

*"Meaningless statistics were up one-point-five per cent
this month over last month."*

Tricks of the trade: intentional distortions

In addition to watching out for unsound reasoning, we must try to ensure that we are not being tricked into taking a position, through intentional distortion. Some people have considerable skill in masking the tenuous nature of their arguments.

Twisting and distortion. The distortion: John Kulik said being a father was a heart-breaking experience and nobody in their right mind would ever choose to become one.

What he actually said: "I'm lucky to have two great kids that I love more than I can say. But for all the men who have been laid off at the plant, being a father without a job, without any way of putting groceries on the table, is a heart-breaking experience, and I'm worried about the next generation, because nobody in their right mind would ever choose to become a father without knowing how to care for his kids."

The first sentence completely twists this fictional character's point of view. The interpretation given to his words has completely altered the original meaning: the full quotation shows the original meaning. It is often difficult to see through this kind of distortion.

Selective omission. Sometimes a half-truth or incomplete truth can do more damage than an all-out falsehood. A political candidate may try to gain votes by saying that his rival once voted against what had become a popular measure. He will not mention that the particular bill voted on had had unacceptable clauses in it, and that once they had been removed the candidate had supported the bill. By omitting such important information, the dishonest person can create a completely false impression. Such omissions are also hard to spot, unless we take the time to find out what the other side says.

Selecting, out of a mass of complex facts, a few to serve one's own purpose while intentionally ignoring other significant data is a common persuasive device.

Incomplete quotation. Seeing something in quotes doesn't necessarily ensure the truth of the quotation. This applies to radio and television interviews as well. What a person says can be edited in such a way that it is still a quotation, but no longer represents fairly their real meaning.

"I don't really want to run for student council if it's going to get mean or become a popularity contest," said Janet. Paul quoted Janet as saying "I don't really want to run for student council." By only quoting part of what she said, Paul gave a completely false picture of Janet's position.

Exercise: studying incomplete quotations

The following sentences have brackets surrounding parts of the sentence. Discuss how the meaning of the sentence changes, depending on whether you quote part of it or the whole sentence.

1. (It's annoying to listen to him speak) when the sound system is so bad you can hardly make out what he's saying.

2. I've never found that (Ian is unreliable).

3. (Jacqueline would never go out with anybody) until she'd finished the assignments she'd agreed to do.

4. (When it comes to conversations, Cheryl doesn't have much to say), but what she does say is very important.

5. (Nuclear power is as safe, or safer, than a number of other forms of energy supply, according to all the foremost nuclear physicists) who attended the conference.

Recently a reader wrote into *Maclean's* magazine, complaining that the ironic intent of his letter to the editor had been lost when the magazine published it without the final sentence. How did the deletion of the final sentence alter the meaning of the letter? (We have reprinted the entire letter below.)

> Regarding a number of complaints claiming that the preponderence of flesh in *Macleans* is inappropriate in a news publication I must take exception to this selfish criticism. Don't let *Macleans* be spoiled for the rest of us. If they want news, let them read a news magazine.[7]

Quoting out of context. Several women were joking in the lunch room about whether it was their wardrobes or their qualifications that ensured job security, when Jennifer mentioned that her legs ached when she wore a certain type of shoe. "I guess you're not qualified enough to keep the job," was the reply by someone, and everyone chuckled. Later it was rumoured that it was an open secret that Jennifer wasn't really fit for the job. What had been said in good fun had been taken out of context, and used maliciously.

When people are quoted out of context, their words may be reported, but the overall message has been distorted.

Exercise

1. Show how, in the following fictitious review of a real article, a passage has been taken out of context:

> The author praises *Readers Digest,* saying 'Each issue contains fascinating tidbits, interesting episodes, informative articles and beautiful advertisements. It is a pleasant experience for the reader . . .'. (Page 232 'The biggest myth of all', *Don't blame*

the people, reproduced on page 66 of this book.)

2. Show how the quotation used in this <u>fictitious</u> review has distorted the real intention of the author. The book in question is the book you are reading now; the page number is that listed in this book:

> The book is a compendium of propaganda and persuasion techniques. The author of *Between the Lines* even suggests that those using the book should try using as many dishonest persuasive techniques as possible (p.49, question 4a).

Innuendo and baseless speculation

Innuendo is a remark with an underlying criticism or accusation. Individuals, groups or causes can be discredited in almost unnoticeable ways by the manner in which they are described, which subtly questions their credibility.

"Members of this group have been in and out of jail over the past 10 years." Were there any charges laid? Was anyone found guilty of a crime? What was the offence?

"It's been proven that this group is associated with alcoholics" (with wife-beaters, with ex-convicts, with separatists, etc.). What is the *nature* of the association? By simply linking a person or a group with an "undesirable" element, that person or group can be discredited. Also, by "clustering" different groups and saying another one has been "connected" with them, all are considered as undesirable as any one of the group.

During the 1950s McCarthy era in the United States, this charge was made by a lawyer, Richard Milhouse Nixon, who was beginning to make a name for himself:

> Ninety-six per cent of the 6,926 Communists, fellow travellers, sex perverts, people with criminal records, dope addicts, drunks and other social security risks removed under the Eisenhower security program were hired by the Truman administration.[8]

Beware also of coverage that has speculation at the core of the story or assertion:

> *Government sources denied that there is a mass exodus from Quebec.* (We think: if the government has to deny it, perhaps there is evidence that in fact there *is* a mass exodus . . ?).

It is also possible to attribute a motive or attitude to someone else through innuendo, and yet not be charged with slander or libel:

> The case before you, ladies and gentlemen, is that John Hill wants compensation for the oil slick's damage to his fishing gear. Now maybe he wants to fish again, or maybe he'd like to live off UIC, or even retire to Florida with the settlement money — I don't know; but you must decide if he is entitled to it.

Discussion/research

1. What are some examples of how the Parti Quebecois has been described by its detractors? How have some of the critics of the Canadian Union of Postal Workers (CUPW) described this union?
2. Describe the criticisms levelled at any group or individual involved in public controversy.
3. The truth of a negative proposition is impossible to verify. What implications can you see this having?

Cheap gadgetry: more persuasive devices

We have called the final area to watch out for in analysing the messages we receive "Cheap gadgetry". To use again the analogy of the building, these techniques would be like the velvet-cut wallpaper hiding a hole in the wall or the dinette chandelier that makes you forget to check how good and how adequate the wiring is in the house. Certain emotional or other appeals *in themselves* may be harmless enough; but they can be devastatingly powerful when directed at someone who has not been alerted to their persuasive power.

Such techniques encourage people to think uncritically, to accept ideas, political positions and values without thinking about them for themselves. They can subtly undermine independent thinking.

Testimonial. Though Mike Macho, movie star, endorses a certain political candidate, what qualifications give him expertise in the political sphere? Just because someone famous or well-respected says something does not make everything they say true. Has the person based his/her position on reliable information? Are they being paid to say what they're saying?

A combination of the Testimonial and Bandwagon appeals is the *my-kind-of-product* appeal. It may sound more personal, but the statements have no more meaning for their personal stamp: "George Brown is my kind of candidate"; "That's my [name of car]!" It is nevertheless an effective device: we see a nice person with an enviable lifestyle in warm and friendly settings endorsing something. All this invites us to be a part of that life, by buying the product or supporting whatever they support. We may be so swayed by our identification with this person that we forget to examine the product itself.

Political positions or products that are endorsed by someone you admire are not necessarily better than others.

Band wagon appeal. You may hear that "everybody" is behind a certain candidate, subscribing to the *Express* or ordering a particular drink at the night spots. But if you think your candidate, your paper or your orange juice is better, don't change your mind just to hop on the bandwagon.

Plain folks. "Hello, friends, I'm glad we can have this heart-to-heart talk this evening. You 'n I know how hard it is these days for everybody, and I'd just like to take only two minutes of your precious time, neighbours, to tell you how you can change your whole life."

The Plain Folks approach uses the appearances of simplicity and honesty, without any particular connection to reality.

Snob appeal. This is just the opposite approach to the Plain Folks tactic. "A new and exclusive menu of Baron Hamilton's has been especially created only for the most sophisticated of gourmets." Words like *exclusive* and *sophisticated* can convince us that certain things are preferable, without any direct relation to their merits.

Glittering generalities. In some situations, abstract words like "happiness" or "brotherhood" can lead us to forget to ask what exactly they are referring to. We can thus accept the whole statement that surrounds the glittering generality, with all its vague implications.

While all of us might quickly agree on what a *laundromat* is, we might have a harder time agreeing on what *co-operation, justice, democracy, law and order* or *peace* are. This is because they, like happiness, refer to a general state of things, not things themselves.

Getting people to accept glittering generalities without examining the basis on which they are made, is one of the more common, and most lethal, of propaganda devices.

Before endorsing a *far-reaching reform* or buying an *ideal home product*, lay bare and examine the reasons given for such a claim. Then decide.

Here are some other glittering generalities; which others could you add to the list?

the man in the street	terrorists
a man of the people	freedom fighters
our proud history	dissidents
our glorious fatherland	subversives
this country of ours	traitors
God is on our side	dupes
the good of all	armchair radicals
pigs	reactionaries
bleeding hearts	do-gooders

hijackers
sob sister

Exercise/discussion

1. Define the following:
democracy
national unity
national security.

2. In 1980 Canada's Solicitor General Robert Kaplan defined *subversion* as an attempt to bring about change in society "by unlawful means — improper means".[9] Discuss. (E.g, what might be considered "improper" but not be illegal? Who decides what is "improper"? *media* Who decides what is "illegal"?) *courts*

Name-calling. By simply having called someone a "pillar of the community" or a "troublemaker", "self-righteous" or "patriotic", you have not proven your statements. Labels such as "malcontent", "paranoid",

"This 'pig' business upsets me. Why can't they simply call people horses' asses, as we did?"

"neurotic", "naive" mean nothing until convincing evidence is produced to substantiate such claims.

If you hear name-calling, stop and put the name calling to this test:

1. What does the name mean?

2. Is the speaker trying to appeal to my emotions or to my reasoning abilities?

3. Did they prove that the label is applicable to the person?

Another technique related to name-calling is using in a derogatory way such qualifiers as "so-called", "self-styled", "calling itself".

Examine the following (fictitious) news story:

> The ragged clutch of neurotic women calling themselves "Concerned Mothers" continued to whine about day-care and wave their makeshift signs outside the legislature till past midnight, when more than one person wondered if they even cared where their own children were.

Some questions to ask:

The ragged clutch	What specifically does the adjective refer to? What does the noun connote?
of neurotic women	What justifies the use of the adjective?
continued to whine	What justifies the use of the verb?
makeshift signs	What does adj. imply?
more than one	How many more? Who were they? How does the author know?
wondered if	Is such speculation warranted? Is there any basis for it?

Exercise: studying name-calling

1. What are some examples of name-calling (include words describing women, men, ethnic minorities)?

2. What would be a "neutral" or less emotionally-charged word for these names (e.g., chicks/women; dude/man; scab/strikebreaker; . . .)?

Using stereotypes. Closely related to name-calling is the use of stereotypes to build one's argument. A person or group of people can be categorised in a way that covers all aspects of their lives and personalities: men have mechanical, intellectual, managerial abilities, women have cooking, social and child-rearing abilities, etc. While some element of reality may be present in a stereotype, stereotypes in themselves do not reflect reality.

Transfer. The politician who is out kissing babies on the election trail may be the first to cut back on hospitals or schools once s/he is in office. Or, someone may have no demonstrable regard for the well-being of the citizens of their country, but by surrounding their campaign literature with maple leafs, they could trick the gullible into thinking that they will "serve the country" better than another. By *associating* themselves with symbols (a flag, a baby) or institutions we revere (photographing themselves outside a church or parliament buildings), they can stir our feelings and deceive us in such a way that we accept a programme apparently endorsed by institutions or agencies we respect.

Scientific slant or appeal to authority. In our society science is highly respected. But pseudo- (or false) scientific claims abound, especially in advertising. "Wash daily with Formula D, and see the germ count go down .." By transferring our faith in science or a particular authority to the faith in what is being promoted, the unscrupulous can succeed in convincing us that their product or policy is better than others, without actually proving *how* it is superior to others.

Here are some of these appeals; what are some others?

"35% more absorbent . . ." — More absorbent than what?

"pH factors" — What about them?

"U.S. Dept. of___approved" — What does the approval mean? Can the product be sold if it hasn't been approved?

Repetition. If a statement is repeated often enough, in time it can come to be accepted by its audience. Constant repetition can range from advertisements ("Players Please") to political slogans ("Ein Volk, ein Reich, ein Fuhrer"). What are some present-day words, ads or slogans that are often repeated?

Co-optation. A remarkably powerful characteristic of the advertising industries and other campaigns is their ability to co-opt or use to their own purposes the very ideas or themes that their opponents and critics put forward. For example, "Roll back prices" was a political slogan before a large food chain in Canada used it in its promotional material. Ads actually "serve the people", according to an ad executive, echoing the slogan made famous by the Chinese communist leader, Mao Tse-tung.[10]

Abuse of language

Abusing language could be considered a persuasive devise in its own right, inasmuch as it can lull us into accepting ideas without really understanding them very clearly.

While some of the other techniques we have discussed have been abuses of ideas or values, the abuse of language as a whole is an abuse of our thought processes — the very way we express ourselves and the way we think.

If someone's speech is careless, hackneyed or unintelligible what reason have we to believe that their *thinking* is any more careful, more original or more intelligible?

Carelessness. If you say you saw a group of *young juveniles* what does the *young* add? Why say they were running at seven *a.m. in the morning* when one or the other expression will do? Instead of saying they are *one of the*

DECISION-MAKING POSITION WITH A VEGETABLE MARKETING UNIT

most unique teams you know of, why not decide whether or not they're unique (and prove it) or use another more fitting adjective? Having *the same thing in common,* and *overexaggerate* are other examples; what are some that you have come across? Redundancy is one form of carelessness; if you are speaking carefully, each of your words will have a function and meaning.

Careless use of language can result in ridiculous statements. On a national Canadian radio show, it was stated that "Home insulation sales have literally taken off this year".[11] Insulation sales can no more *literally* "take off" than the Nova Scotia talk-show host can say with a straight face, "I completely agree with you, up to a point."[12]

These are nuisances; however other forms of carelessness in speech have more serious implications. For example, the word *insurgent* is often used incorrectly in Third World news reporting. On 17 July 1980, there was a violent military coup in Bolivia. It took place during the period when the elected government was trying to establish its administration, and 19 days before the elected president was to take office. Yet according to the CBC news, *"insurgent* miners"[13] in one part of the country finally surrendered to the junta on July 25. The dictionary meaning of insurgent is:

> *insurgent adj., rebelling against a lawful government or civil authority.*

Who were, in fact, the insurgents?

Hackneyed (or fashionable) phrases. "On stream", "downtime", "go situation" . . . the list of hackneyed expressions could be almost endless. Many of them may have a tenuous connection with some branch of technology or science, but of their original meaning only the technical ring remains. It can continue to impress, however, and can distract the listener from what might otherwise be a completely dull or unimaginative idea. "Conditions will remain strong wind-wise"[14] is a rather roundabout way of saying winds will remain strong. While we still get the general message, the pseudo-technical formula gets in the way of expressing a simple, yet useful piece of information.

Certain word groupings can become inseparable, and language by formula takes over: a truce is almost invariably an *uneasy truce;* certain countries invariably qualified with *war-torn; ailing* goes with Premier, *on-going* with evaluation, *free-swinging* with debate.

Like careless speech, hackneyed speech in itself may have no malicious intent, but it does

Now, Mr. Edwards, I know that you believe you understand what you think I have said, but I'm not sure you realize that what you hear is not what I mean.

reflect on the poor *quality of the thoughts* being expressed. A Canadian example of language by formula, with some serious implications, is the familiar expression, the "Balkanisation of Canada", used by Canada's Prime Minister among others.[15] In using such a formula, the speaker assumes a) that there is agreement on the historical facts; and b) that there is agreement on the interpretation of these events (e.g., determining cause-effect relationships, or determining that the results were injurious to the states concerned). Such sweeping assumptions are unfounded; such a formula confuses rather than clarifies an issue. In this way, fuzzy language reflects either fuzzy thinking or a deliberate attempt to obscure the real issues.[16]

Exercise: fashionable and hackneyed phrases

1. Some common expressions of the 1970s are listed below. How many of them can you decipher? Put them in your own words:

on stream   downtime
go situation   go the _____ route
down the road   at this point in time
turn the corner   get a handle on (something)
turn around   thing)

2. What are some fashionable or hackneyed expressions that you hear today in everyday speech?

3. According to a national CBC television announcer, Quebeckers *"spoke with one voice"*[17] in voting No in the May 1980 Quebec referendum. The actual results of the referendum were 59% No to 41% Yes.

a. Discuss the announcer's interpretation of the vote.

or

b. Prepare a research paper on media coverage of this referendum (including paid commercials).

"Newsspeak". By newsspeak, we mean language that distorts, confuses or hides reality. Words may bear no relation to their original meaning. During the Vietnam war, soldiers created a verb, *to off*, meaning to kill; *air support* meant bombing and strafing. The Johnson and Nixon administrations in the United States became infamous for creating their own vocabulary — the word "newsspeak" refers both to George Orwell's *Nineteen Eighty-four* "newsspeak" and government official's unscrupulous "management" (or manipulation) of the news. Here are a few examples:

misspoke: lied. Used often by President Nixon's Press Secretary Ronald Ziegler.

stonewall: whatever happens, admit nothing.

operative statement: ("This is the operative statement. The others are inoperative.") Don't pay any attention to what we said before. (Note that it is not a question at any point of telling the truth or not.)

accelerated pacification: Pentagon terminology for the bombing of Cambodia.

neutralized: killed.

condolence award: money paid to the family of a South Vietnamese civilian killed by mistake.[18]

When asked about the hotly denied rumour (later proven to be true) that the U.S. had invaded Laos, the President's Press Secretary commented, "The President is aware of what is going on. That's not to say there is something going on." Newsspeak expressions fill the air with words so that clarity of meaning — and responsibility — is lost. They also give their speakers a few more seconds to figure out what they are going to say next. Those appearing before hearings into the Watergate scandal commonly used such expressions as: "at that point in time", "being in a position to (do or say something)"; "evaluate and make a judgment in terms of a response".

Like Careless or Hackneyed Language, Newsspeak is an abuse of language. However, the scope and nature of the abuse has far more sinister implications than the others, because such an abuse is intentional.

In order not to fall into unthinking acceptance of ideas, you should make sure you really understand them first.

"When *I* use a word," Humpty Dumpty said, in a rather scornful tone, "it means just what I choose it to mean. Neither more nor less."

"The question is," said Alice "whether you *can* make words mean so many different things."

"The question is," said Humpty Dumpty, "who is to be master. That is all."

Lewis Carroll, *Through the looking glass*

A good way of testing this is to see if you can put someone else's ideas in your own words. Thus you can become a translator without knowing a single foreign word. You are translating from English to English: you do this whenever you detach ideas from one set of words and attach them to another — as you do, for example, when you write a letter or give a speech. Detaching your ideas from your words in this way lets you find out whether you *have* any ideas — or just words.[19]

About four thousand years ago in China, it was said that,

> The beginning of a wise policy is to call things by their right name.

The wisdom of that saying could hardly be more relevant today.

© 1975 by Warner Bros Inc

Exercise: abuse of language

1. "Translate" the following sentences by putting them into your own words.

    a. Concerning the economy, "it's pretty bad both in short-run and long-run terms".

    b. "Under the white paper, offshore banks would have been able to own 10 per cent of their Canadian subsidiaries and corner 15 per cent of the Canadian financial market."

    c. "I am not advancing that my thought processes are absolutely devoid of obscurity." — Solicitor General Jean-Jacques Blais, on contradictory statements made by RCMP officials and federal cabinet members.[20]

2. Collect examples of bureaucratic or other confusing language and prepare a "simultaneous translation" for a class skit.

3. Conduct a survey in your school or local shopping mall, using a tape recorder. Ask people to define words used in everyday speech — for example, what is a "billion"? What does "radioactive" mean . . .?

4. Read James H. Boren's *When in doubt, mumble: a bureaucrat's handbook* (1972 NY: Van Nostrand Reinhold).

    a. Prepare a review of the book;

    or

    b. Prepare a skit on the basis of some of the ideas in this book.

5. Within the Soviet Union, people who speak out against the government are called *subversives*. The same people are called *Soviet dissidents* by people in the West.

Discuss the use of these terms, and the points of view they represent. Are there any parallels in our own country?

6. General Augusto Pinochet, leader of Chile's military dictatorship, has described his form of government as "authoritarian democracy". Discuss.

Review: tricks of the trade

Here is a review of the further persuasive devices studied so far.

Twisting and distortion

Selective omission

Incomplete quotation

Quoting out of context

Innuendo and baseless speculation

Cheap gadgetry:

    testimonial

    bandwagon appeal

    plain folks

    snob appeal

    glittering generalities

    name calling

    using stereotypes

    transfer

    scientific slant

    repetition

    co-optation

Abuse of language:

    carelessness

    hackneyed (or fashionable) phrases

    newsspeak

Exercise: studying persuasive devices

Each of the following sentences contains one or more persuasive devices. Which ones are used? In some cases two or more are used.

1. Give her the watch all women want; individually crafted with exquisitely hand-tooled gold and silver . . . in exclusive stores only.

2. Marginol, that new spread that costs less and goes further, is becoming a favourite among many millions of Canadians with less to spend and more to feed. Marginol contains none of those harmful animal fats that can cause problems, because it's 100% pure marginol! Join the millions of happy Canadians who are finding that marginol tastes almost as good as the other spreads — and costs less! Marginol!

3. Only the woman who has been sky-diving in the Andes or the man who would take home slips of plants for his observatory from the great restaurants of the world would appreciate a Marauder. If you have to ask what it is or how much it costs, it's not for you.

4. The advertisement shows a man in a white coat with a stethoscope around his neck, talking to an anxious-looking woman. The advertisement reads: "Everywhere doctors are telling their patients there's no magic cure for anxiety and sleeplessness, but they know Sleeponit will help. Sleeponit helps. Ask your doctor about it."

5. That self-styled union leader thinks she can tear down our time-honoured institutions by trying to run for city councillor. How does she think she is going to manage the affairs of the city when, by the accounts of a few men I know, she can't even manage her own affairs?

6. The discriminating art collector and investor will be interested to know that Chelsea Galleries has recently acquired, by private London auction, several fine examples of the unique, early Obbledobber school of painting (black and blue period). Viewings are by invitation only. Please make all enquiries at The City Club or The Whispers Country Club.

7. Friends, this is the moment you and I — that we've all been waiting for. Our good ol' friend Hank Tatum has just got here in his honest-to-goodness beat-up ol' '72 Plymouth to tell us how he'll help us all out if we put him in on election day. We all know Hank and how honest and clean-livin' he is. Why I remember back in '64 he returned a wallet a little ol' lady had lost. Hank's an honest and clean-livin' fella, just the kinda person we need. He's my candidate, and I hope he's yours too.

8. Criterion demands perfect performance, excellence and precision in every one of its cars, from hand-crafted interior to electronically tested axles. That's why those who insist on quality and detail will settle for nothing less.

9. Give yourself a Perfect-O power saw, the quality saw. You deserve the very best.

10. Hospitals across the country are using Natty Nappies. Natty Nappies keep baby dry and happy — help prevent that sore diaper rash caused by wetness. The reason why so many are using Natty Nappies is that they're scientifically proven to absorb more moisture! Here's Cheryl Macho, pretty wife of actor Mike Macho: "I'm the wife of a famous movie star, but I'm also a Mom who loves her kids. That's why I start them off with only the best —Natty Nappies."

11. If you believe in the freedom of this great country of ours; if you believe in the freedom of our business and our free-enterprise system; if you believe in bringing back the old virtues — maybe my opponent would call them "stuffy" — you will join the millions of patriotic Canadians and vote for X on your ballot!

12. I got rid of that nagging cough, and you can too, with Poppindrops. Try Poppindrops, and the new menthol-flavoured Poppinmentholdrops. You'll like them!

13. Friends, we all made a mistake in not planning our energy future before now, but you 'n I know that our company has been serving this great land of ours for many years now, and that together — we at Oh-Oh Oil and all of Canada — together we're just gonna have to find a way out of this energy crunch. So I know I can count on you to pull together with our engineers 'n technicians who are workin' around the clock to find new sources of energy. So turn them lights off an' pay yer bills on time. Everybody's gotta do their part, cause that's how we're gonna beat it. I know I can count on you.

transfer, distortion, innuendo

14. The picture is a political candidate looking out of the page, in the background a vandalised home. The text reads, "Some of the candidates in my riding probably don't care that this house has been ruined by vandals. Well I do care. Vote for the (only) party that cares. Vote X on election day."

distortion, selective omission

15. If the Government gives in to the demands of the investigators, the security of the nation itself may be at stake.

hackneyed phrase

16. Human nature being what it is, you shouldn't feel angry if she'd been lying to you all this time.

hackneyed phrase

17. My country right or wrong.

name calling

18. Back-to-work legislation could never affect me because my union isn't a troublemaker like theirs is.

name calling

19. That biologist's report needn't be taken very seriously — he's working for that radical ecology group, and probably couldn't get a professional job anyway.

hackneyed phrases

20. The investigation showed there was corruption in high levels of government. Ho hum. So what else is new?

plain folks, abuse of language, hackneyed phrase

21. Now the environmental group, in all its self-righteousness, can holler about pollution and disease, but the fact is, we need the jobs.

"De-coding" some messages

In the preceding exercises, a number of persuasive devices were examined. But most of the examples were fictional. Now, we must attempt to recognise faulty reasoning, bias and other persuasive techniques in real, day-to-day communication.

Interpersonal communication. What you hear around yourself — at school, at your job, with friends, at home — is the subject matter.

1. For a period of one week, try to pay particular attention to what you hear people saying to you and to others. When you can, note

down exactly what is said, or something that will remind you of the conversation.

2. Write down what persuasive techniques or other reasoning processes which seemed a) sound to you; and b) unsound. Refer to specifics (Hasty Generalisation, Bandwagon appeal, etc.).

3. Outline the reasons for your classification.

4. Discuss your results in small groups and make a group report to the class.

5. If your class has decided to have a reporter and log book, don't forget to enter the results.

6. Look through the preceding pages (bias and propaganda techniques), and select two or three techniques. See if you're able to get away with using them in discussions with friends, families etc. Report on your success/-failure to do so, and discuss.

The rest of the discussion on this critically important area is up to you, the reader. We will go into further detail with some of the other messages that must be "de-coded". However, we have included one exercise that contains a few examples of faulty reasoning or persuasive techniques.

Exercise

Examine the following quotations, which are from real life, making full use of your faculties of critical analysis. Under what category — Shaky Foundations, Faulty Construction, Tricks of the Trade etc. — would you place them? Explain. (Refer to the specific devices such as Mistaking the Cause, Hasty Generalisations etc.)

Example:
Here is one definition of "National Security":

> Freedom of the President to pursue his planned course was the ultimate national security objective.[21]

It was given by Egil Krogh, White House aide, who was convicted of illegal activities during the Watergate scandal. "I see now," he said when being sentenced by the judge, "that the key is the effect that the term national security had on my judgment. The very words served to block critical analysis."

Shaky Foundation

1. (CP) — 'A nuclear power plant meltdown is so improbable that the Atomic Energy Control Board feels there is little use in studying the consequences of such an accident', board president Jon Jennekens said Friday.

'No one knows what would happen so you assume that meltdown and melt through wouldn't happen', he told an Ontario legislature committee investigating nuclear generating plants in the province.[22]

name calling

2. Commenting on consumer activist Ralph Nader, whose research uncovered design faults causing fatal car crashes, industrialist Henry Ford said,

> Frankly, I don't think Ralph Nader knows very much about automobiles. He can read statistics and he can write books . . . but I don't think he knows anything about engineering safety into automobiles.[23]

Shaky Foundation

3. With regard to the effects of spruce budworm spraying on children, Canada's Deputy Minister of the Environment J. B. Seaborn is quoted as follows:

> Everybody's genuinely worried about the effects on the kids, but in our view the case is far from proven.[24]

name calling / *pointing to an enemy*

4. In the United States, following countrywide opposition to the government's foreign policy in Southeast Asia, and the shooting deaths of a number of students on two campuses, U.S. Vice-President Spiro Agnew had this to say of the increasing unity and numbers of students and faculty members who were opposed to the invasion of Cambodia:

> Those who would tear our country apart or try to bring down its government are enemies, whether here or abroad, whether destroying libraries and classrooms on a college campus or firing at American troops from a rice paddy in Southeast Asia . . . They are a small, hard core of hell raisers who want to overturn the system for the sake of chaos alone . . . They are encouraged by an equally small number of faculty members who apparently cannot compete legitimately within the system or do not choose to do so.
>
> It is my honest opinion that this hard core of faculty and students should be identified and dismissed from the otherwise healthy body of the college community lest they, like a cancer, destroy it.[25]

5. The same Vice-President also described opposition to the present administration in this way:

meshing fact w/opinion

> When I talk about troublemakers, I'm talking about muggers and criminals in the streets, assassins of political leaders, draft evaders and flag burners, campus militants, hecklers and demonstrators against candidates for public office and looters and burners of cities.[26]

attacking person / *false analogy*

6. . . . you are a communist and as such deserve to be treated in the same manner as I would be treated if I endeavoured to carry on in Russia as you are doing in Nova Scotia.

— From a June 1940 letter by the Minister of Labour to Charles Murray, a Nova Scotian who with others was organising a fishermen's union in the Lockeport area. The letter was telling him to stop his union work.

glittering generalities / *fuzzy language*

7. To develop the new culture based on progress and science which upholds the lofty ideas of genuine independence, democracy and progress against imperialism, fascism and reaction.

— From a Canadian political party's platform in the May 1979 elections. This was one of the "social and cultural tasks" to be undertaken by the party.

faulty premise

8. 'The RCMP must have felt it necessary, otherwise they wouldn't have made the request,' Beatty said. RCMP witnesses gave similar replies last month when their files showed that they passed along data along to other police forces across the country, often without recorded reasons.[27]

— Robert L. Beatty, a retired government employee explaining illegal access to Social Insurance files by the RCMP, other police forces and many other government agencies.

bold assertion / *pointing to an enemy*

9. I believe many Americans resent the smugness demonstrated among some elements in the press to the effect that 'it is our job to get to the bottom of everything, no matter who it hurts' . . .[28]

— Former Governor of Texas and Secretary to the U.S. Treasury, John Connolly, concerning press coverage of government scandals.

10. I'm a Protestant, a Republican and a free-enterpriser, which means I am biased in favour of God, Eisenhower, and the stockholders of Time Inc.[29]

false analogy

— Henry Luce, who was President of Time Inc.

11. Supt. Cobb said it is the RCMP security service's 'duty to protect democratic institutions,' such as the PQ, and to this end he felt justified in using 'disinformation' and 'disruptive tactics' to prevent infiltration of the separatist political party.[30]

rationalize

— RCMP superintendent explaining the RCMP's fabricated FLQ communique calling for violent revolution.

Advertising

In this section, we will look at how advertising works. Whether we are aware of it or not, advertising has a major influence on our thoughts and our "world-view" — the way we understand the world around us.

Advertising makes use of some of the techniques of persuasion we have just studied. Advertising influences people's ideas about what they want, about what they need; it affects how people view themselves in relation to others.

Why do ads work so effectively? How do they work? The *Reviews* for detecting faulty reasoning and propaganda techniques, as well as the *Checklist* for careful thinking are very useful for understanding how ads work.

Ads are carefully made by very creative people. Those who invent promotions for cars, cigarettes or perfumes know human beings well — their feelings of insecurity, their hopes

What we want is something new. If it does anything, so much the better.

and ambitions. Ad people also consult market surveys and psychological research, putting this information and their creativity to their advantage. Ad people *know* how we feel; they know themselves. They know that we all have some anxiety . . .

For the young or unattached:
Am I really attractive? Will he/she like me? Do I look all right? Do I have bad breath or body odour? Do I fit in with the others?

For parents:
Am I a good mother/father? Am I a good provider? Do I love my children? Do I care enough to send the very best? As an ad executive put it,

> A housewife is buying satisfaction. She wants her clothes to be clean — but she also wants to feel good about their being clean.[31]

The people who create the ads also know we all have some fantasy, some dream. We would like to be like some of the attractive people in the ads we see; we would like to share in their lives.

Here is the profile of Charlie, a person created by an advertising department. Her name was given to what would become the world's best-selling perfume:

> Charlie seemed to capture modern woman's purposeful new self-image. 'Charlie strides without being strident,' explains Paul Woolard, president of Revlon's U.S. Cosmetics and Fragrance Division. 'She's twenty-seven, single, has a job, and supports the women's movement, though she's no bra-burning libber. Most of all, she's happy as hell in an era of dissatisfaction.'[32]

"Of course no one NEEDS it, Willoughby! That's where you people in advertising come in."

"I used to enjoy TV in the old days, when commercials had more involved plots."

Ads catch your attention. They stimulate the imagination. Their power is the *power of suggestion*. They sometimes make you imagine yourself in a wonderful world, full of the products (and promises) they promote.

At other times ads do not stimulate the imagination at all. They are repeated so many times that they enter the consciousness by wearing down its resistance to them. A senior advertising executive complained in a rather humorous way in a trade journal:

> The most familiar [ad idea] is known to the client as the 'slice of life.' To the agency it's the 'Hey Marge' and to the outright cynic it's the 'two ------s in a kitchen' format. You know it well — too well. A neighbour walks into a kitchen, without knocking, at the instant a highly specific problem rears its ugly head. The child, perhaps, has just anointed his jeans with a mix of ketchup and gravy. The neighbour (------ number two) just happens to be toting a shopping bag containing the product which will solve the problem.[14]

Discussion

1. What are the good feelings we associate with Coca Cola? Sprite? McDonald's? How do they relate to the product? Describe what is happening in one of the ads. What do you learn about the product? Analyse in depth one recent McDonald's ad, and present your findings to your group, with some discussion questions.

2. What are the attractive characteristics of cigarette ads? What are the elements in the ads that we like? (e.g., good looks, glamour, status, etc.) How do they relate to the product?

3. In your opinion, what is the emotion or attribute that advertisers emphasize most frequently? Can you make such a broad generalisation? Or does it depend on the product? Why (or why not)?

4. Create ads for something you are in favour of.

    a. Try using as many dishonest techniques as possible.

    b. Try using as many persuasive techniques as possible, but that are all honest, truthful and in keeping with your code of behaviour and lifestyle.

Discuss the results with your group.

Ads can be low-key or high-powered, depending on the image they are intended to project. Many of the appeals used by advertisers are directed at basic human feelings of goodness; or fear, sexuality, power, etc.:

It's new
    different
    free
    a time-saver
    a money-saver, economical
    healthy
    luxurious ("you *deserve* the best")
    scientifically improved
    lemon-scented . . .

A TV program is what they give us for watching commercials.

YOU GET WHAT YOU PAY FOR . . .
YOU PAY FOR WHAT YOU GET . . . .

. . . It is often felt that because corporations 'subsidize' the media through advertising that the audience gets its entertainment free. This could explain the high levels of tolerance in terms of advertising saturation people endure. But nothing could be further from the actual situation. As Judy La Marsh has pointed out: *'The public does not seem to appreciate that it also pays for the cost of private TV . . . by its purchase of the advertiser's product or services*'* . . . To think that the cost of advertising is borne by corporations is sheer lunacy. Each dollar is transferred to the consumer who is at one and the same time the audience. If they ever came to realise how much they are really paying to listen to the radio, watch television or read a newspaper or magazine, they may demand quality but as it is the cost remains hidden behind a charade of the corporation paying the piper; the corporation calls the tune but the consumer pays.

— Wallace Clement (1975) *The Canadian corporate élite*
*Emphasis ours.

Trends in public opinion and "fashionable" issues find their way into advertising. For example in the:

1960s, "Revolutionary" products were promoted for the "now" generation . . . Then in the

1970s, Women's issues marketed many products (e.g., the ad for underarm deodorant: "BAN: A WOMAN'S ART OF SELF-DEFENCE"). As well:

Ecology, conservation . . . (e.g. "We're producing more steel but polluting less" — Dofasco)

Consumers' interests . . .

Health and fitness[34]

Canada and national pride . . .

1980s? What might be some trends in the 1980s?

Through a process of co-optation, one takes over the language and symbols of one's critics and uses them to one's own advantage. The serious issues of, say, women's rights or ecology are thus trivialised and neutralised. Ads that are "critical" of the mass media business could even be used to sell an idea or product . . .

Activities

1. Collect ads and bring them in for discussion. What techniques are used in each one? Use the list of devices (bandwagon, scientific slant, etc.) studied for analysing them.

2. Form small working groups, and begin to collect magazine ads on the following:
— cigarettes
— alcohol
— beauty products
— (other).
Be sure to note down what magazines they came from. What techniques were used
— for each magazine?
— each product?

3. Study ads *by magazine*. Determine the readership of each magazine. How are the ads related to the stories or "copy" in the magazine? Assemble ads from one magazine without indicating the title of the magazine, and present them to another working group. See if, by looking at the ads, people can guess what the magazine was about and who the readership was (i.e., *Maclean's, Good Housekeeping* etc.).

4. Switch advertising "copy" (text or script) of two products. For example, use *Chanel No. 5* ad approach to advertise a $1.44 sale at the K-Mart . . .

5. "It's the real thing"
a. Design a poster or an ad "proving" this statement.
or
b. Design a poster, with this slogan, using irony.

6. Establish a log of television time in prime time, and around news time. Write down the "plots" of ads as well as the items carried in the news. Write down the outlines of TV stories.

How would you describe an evening of programmes? What thoughts, emotions, go with what programmes or ads?

7. In the earliest days of television, these were the sponsors of the original "Mickey Mouse" show:
Carnation Milk, B & B Enterprises, Brystol Meyers, Campbell Soup Co., Coca-Cola, General Mills, S. C. Johnson (Gold Seal Wax), Lettuce Inc., Mars, Mattell, Miles Laboratories, Nunn, M & M, Morton Salt, SOS (scouring pads), Vicks Chemicals, Welch's Grape Juice.

   a. Compile a list of sponsors for two or three different TV programmes that are popular today.

   b. Present the list(s) to your group, and see if others can guess what show is being broadcast by what commercials are shown.

   c. Was your group able to come close to guessing the kind of programme that was on? Why/why not?

   d. The Bureau of Broadcast Measurement (BBM) conducts surveys to determine the popularity of the shows we watch on TV. Their findings are used to determine the cost of advertising time during certain programmes. In this way, television *audiences* are also considered advertising *markets* (potential purchasers). Discuss the implications of this.

8. In 1978 a series of TV promotional spots were made by General Foods for the Canadian National Institute for the Blind (CNIB). The 60- and 30- second spots suggested that employers should think about hiring the blind because blind people are good employees. Some TV stations passed them as Public Service Announcements (at no charge) and others re-

> "People always tend to make friends with other people who have similar beliefs, attitudes, social status, education etc. Very rarely will anyone be close friends with someone who is extremely different . . . Advertisers realise this and build their persuasive appeal around people who are most like the people in their target audience."
>
> E. Tate, 'Viewer perceptions of selected programmes,' Ontario Royal Commission on Violence in the Communications Industry Vol. 6, p. 296.

fused to run them for free because they were "too much of a plug for General Foods."[35]

Discuss. (E.g., What is the difference between an ad and a Public Service Announcement? Who should decide, and on what basis should they decide?)

A key element in persuasion is establishing a common bond between the persuader and the person being persuaded. Establishing this bond is of course the way all people communicate. However, it can be used to take advantage of people's good will, their fears or aspirations. Some people are persuaded by a down-home approach, others by a scientific slant, others by identifying themselves with glamourous figures. In a paper titled "The American value system: premises for persuasion," E. D. Steele and C. Redding set out 25 "shared cultural values" that underlie most American thinking, and therefore are key characteristics to use in order to persuade. They include:

> puritan morality (sub-themes honesty, simplicity, co-operation, orderliness, personal responsibility, humility, and self-discipline), achievement and success, effort

As marketing requested it

As sales ordered it

As manufacturing built it

As supply delivered it

and optimism, sociality and considerateness, external conformity, generosity and patriotism.[36]

Looking at this list, it is easy to see how clearly, such characteristics appear in some ads (McDonald's) and in appeals of political parties.

However, there are other ads (notably alcohol, cigarettes and cosmetics) that would not necessarily fit into this framework of values. Perhaps this is because the former (food, political representation) are considered necessities of some sort and therefore require "serious" consideration while the latter (alcohol or perfume) fit into a "luxury" category, and therefore are set loose from practical or more "serious" considerations. Luxuries — and nonessentials — can be chosen on our whim: our fantasies, then, must be appealed to for these items.

Many critics of advertising claim that ads create false needs amongst those who see them. We do not entirely agree with this view. We suggest, rather, that ads play upon some of our *real needs* — the need to feel attractive, to feel accepted, to be secure — or happy, interesting, or daring ... The needs themselves are not false — only advertising's suggestion that they can be met by purchasing things.

Discussion/Research

1. Discuss the "shared cultural values" premise for persuasion. Do you think there is merit in the suggestion that advertising for luxuries and non-essentials appeals to other aspects of our personality (e.g., fantasies) than our reasoning abilities?

2. The paper quoted on page 54 was on the American value system. Would you see any differences between the American value system and the Canadian one? Although many ads originate in the United States, some are made in Canada, and others are altered slightly for Canadian (and regional) audiences.

If you have friends in the U.S., arrange for them to exchange issues of the same magazines that you are collecting in Canada (e.g. *Time*). What ads are different? In what ways? Can you propose any possible explanations for the differences?

3. The Coca Cola bottle is a symbol of freedom and peace."[37]

Why would an expert in public relations think this? How has this beverage acquired this quality of symbol?

4. Advertisements take into account the results of years of psychological testing. Psychologists can predict that certain cigarette brands will appeal to certain personalities. Some tests are said to be deadly accurate. A U.S. researcher, Donald Armstrong, administered Rorschach psychological tests to subjects who had a strong loyalty to some specific brand of cigarette. Though this was all he knew about his subjects, he reported that

> ... just looking at [the test results] you knew immediately the brand the poor devil *had* to smoke. We were right 80 times in a row.[38]

a. Gather together a large number of ads for cigarettes, from a variety of magazines (young people's magazines, housewives' magazines, sports, business magazines etc.)

b. Do a "profile" of the person smoking the different cigarettes. What sort of worlds does each of the characters live in?

5. I need a cigarette ... I need a drink. Does the person "really need" a cigarette, or is it the relaxation, status or image that the cigarette is supposed to provide? Describe the various factors in a situation which lead people to say they need a drink or cigarette (at a dance;

As plant installed it

As advertising sold it

What the customer wanted

'We'll be back in a minute with Harlan Harris' Sports Extra, Jules Bernmeier and the weather. Jimmy Cunningham's Entertainment Plus, Judith Enright's Fashion Notes, Grady O'Tool's Celebrity Interview, Maria Dellago's Budget Center, Murray Vaughn's Mr. Fix-It Shop, and me, Biff Brogan, with a note on the news.

assignments that are due; too much work; family arguments . . .). How else might one deal with these situations?

6. Cigarettes: are they stimulants or depressants? Alcohol: a stimulant or depressant? Coffee . . . Valium . . . Prepare a research paper on one form of addict or drug dependency, examining causes, and contributing factors (including the role of stress, peer pressure, advertising etc.).

7. 'People told us we were nuts to sell cookies, too. But if you merchandise properly you can make anything go.'[39]

This is the comment of Wat-a-Tan, a company with plans to put tanning salons in shopping malls and office buildings across Canada. The owner is also head of a giant cookie business: if he can sell cookies, he reasons, he will be able to sell suntans, if they are "packaged" properly.

The head of the skin cancer group of the B.C. Cancer Control Agency (where the shops started) is Dr. David McLean. He says the ultraviolet bulbs used for these sessions emit wavelengths of light of the sort that have been shown to produce cancer. The Executive Director of the National Cancer Institute, Dr. Bob Macbeth, concurred: ultra-violet radiation is a known carcinogen.

a. Do you agree with the owner who says that people should be allowed to "merchandise" *anything?*
If you are in favour of some advertising regulations, what would be the basis of them? What would be the basic principles underlying them? Draw up a summary of them.
If you think the "free market" should decide what is sold and what is not sold, what, then, is the role of advertising?

b. *If people are stupid enough to go for products that are harmful to them, they deserve what they get!*
Do you agree with this position, or disagree? Do a research paper on smoking. Sources you may wish to consult include: *Don't blame the people* (listed at the end of the chapter); *Mother Jones* magazine feature issue: "Smoking: the truth no one else will print."

News and current events

These are the well-known questions that every good news report is supposed to answer:

Who?	When?
What?	Where?
How?	Why?

A person can be said to have really understood a news item if it has given this information. But do regular news reports actually answer these questions adequately — especially the question *Why?*

Why are the streets of a Middle-Eastern capital filled with angry crowds for months, or years? Why is there a military coup in a Latin American country? Why have people numbering in the thousands got themselves arrested for sitting in a government office or nuclear site?

We have examined how persuasive techniques can be used in our day-to-day communication with others, and we have examined how they are used in advertising. Now we must turn our attention to "de-coding" the news.

In the preceding activities in this chapter you can find some methods of analysing every-day messages. Throughout these activities you are encouraged to develop a healthy scepticism of all sources of information and analysis (including this book). This is because *all* sources of information have some inadequacy. However, this fact cannot be used as an excuse by people who want to side with whatever source they prefer listening to, on the grounds that all have some drawbacks. If one is seeking more than "ammunition" for an entrenched position, one must be prepared to examine seriously information and ideas that may challenge or contradict one's own.

In attempting to get accurate information about any current event, you will have to adopt an alert and thinking attitude while watching the news or reading a paper. You cannot remain passive: you must become ac-

In the eye of the beholder . . .

On October 14, 1976, the first General Strike in Canada was called since the historic 1919 Winnipeg General Strike. The National Day of Protest was declared over the question of government-imposed wage controls.

The following juxtaposition illustrates how sharply interpretations can diverge on exactly the same event. The headlines are from the commercial press; the quotations were made by labour officials in their own press.

STRIKE MODERATE SUCCESS, BUT DIVISIONS THROW DOUBT ON REPEAT.
— *Globe and Mail*

"It was terrific"
— Len Stevens, director, district 3, Steelworkers

THOUSANDS WALK OUT . . . BUT LIFE GOES ON.
— *Toronto Star*

"Canada's labour movement took a giant step forward on October 14th"
— Louis Laberge, President, Quebec Federation of Labour

PROTEST DAY GETS COOL RECEPTION
— *Edmonton Journal*

"I was enormously proud."
— Lyn Williams, Director, District 6 Steelworkers.

DAY'S SUCCESS VARIES WIDELY
— *Ottawa Citizen*

"You are making history."
— Joe Morris, President, Canadian Labour Congress

FEWER PARTICIPATE THAN PREDICTED
— *Halifax Chronicle-Herald*

"There can be no turning back to nice safe business as usual unionism."
— David Archer, former president, Ontario Federation of Labour

THE DAY OF PROTEST PROVES NOTHING
— *Montreal Star*

". . . the beginning of labour's offensive."
— C. S. Jackson, President, United Electrical Workers

Based on: Canadian News Synthesis Project, *Making History: labour and the press after the Day of Protest*, Toronto 1977.

tively engaged in a questioning process. *What is being left out of this story? What is being emphasized?* — These and many other questions should spring to mind when the news comes on.

Any number of the techniques of persuasion previously discussed may be present in your local newspaper or radio broadcast. Those who are "making the news" — and the writers or even editors — may be using such persuasive techniques consciously or unconsciously.

In addition, there are cases of intentional, hidden bias. In the early days of radio, a CBS newscaster was given these suggestions on how to hide an editorial:

> Use such phrases as 'it is said', 'there are those who believe', 'the opinion is held in well-informed quarters', 'some experts have come to the conclusion'. Why keep on saying 'I think' and 'I believe' when you can put over the same idea much more persuasively by quoting someone else?[40]

However, bias is not confined to political speeches or newsreporting. It can be present in any human communication. While we may think of the scientific community as being rather far removed from the question and outside the realm of bias, this could not be further from the truth. Indeed, though there are many examples of outrageous bias in newsreporting, perhaps the *effects* of this biased reporting may not be as dramatically evident as have been the effects of biased thinking in the scientific community. A recent case in point is the effects of bias amongst scientists in Canada over mercury poisoning, which decimated the Ontario Indian communities of Grassy Narrows and White Dog:

> The extraordinary coincidence apparent to one studying these events was that every scientific researcher and physician outside the governments' services who looked at the problem reacted with alarm and demands for urgent action, while virtually every scientist, researcher and physician on the staffs of government departments, and ministries, or contracted to do studies for them, was exuding comfort and complacence. Difficult to avoid recalling George Orwell's response to co-optation: 'A bought mind is a spoiled mind.'[11]

A medical doctor in the Three Mile Island nuclear accident area put it very simply:

> If you don't want to find something, then you don't look for it.[12]

Research

1. Research the spruce budworm spraying controversy. Make sure you represent accurately the opposing positions, and conclude by taking your own position on the validity of one or the other positions.

2. Prepare a research paper on any current controversy, in which appeals are made to scientific theory and data to justify positions.

3. Do you watch the news (read the newspaper)? Why?

4. Conduct a survey of your group or community:

   a. How many people watch the news? How many read a newspaper? Find out what newspapers are read by what general age group. Do people read any other print materials?

   b. What are the principal reasons given for watching (or not watching) the news, reading the paper etc.?

   c. Was there any correlation between age and the kind of printed material that people read?

   d. Do people think they are affected by world events? In what way? Ask for examples.

5. Will you ever be in the news? Why or why not?

Bias and quality of news reporting

When a story does not distinguish clearly between its author's interpretations and the facts being reported, it is a biased or slanted report. Let us examine the hypothetical example given under the Name-calling heading earlier in this chapter (page 40).

> The ragged clutch of neurotic women calling themselves 'Concerned Mothers' continued to whine about daycare and wave their makeshift signs outside the legislature till past midnight, when more than one person wondered if they even cared where their own children were.

The (fictional) author is editorialising while giving the report. The result is a lack of relevant information. For example, was a bill on daycare being debated in the House that night? What was the group actually saying about daycare?

Newswriters may be unconscious of their own biases: praise or slurs may slip almost unnoticed into their reports of issues or people they personally like or dislike.

How can we recognise bias in the daily newspapers or news broadcasts? Hidden and unconscious bias can come in the form of any of the techniques of persuasion already studied so far. If you use the methods of analysis described earlier in this chapter, you will be able to detect some of the signs of bias.

Here is the first paragraph of a feature article on the Spring 1980 Quebec referendum campaign:

Passage A

Bold assertion attacking the person

In times of tedious calm, Rene Levesque is as irascible and aimless as a cranky old pump sucking at an empty well. When the pressure returns, his cantankerous clatter settles into the determined purr of a smooth-running piston. Wednesday, sweat running in rivulets from his temples to his neck, the 57-year-old firebrand stood before a spell-bound crowd in the Chaudière River Valley town of Ste-Marie and proved he is at the peak of his power to *emotional words* bait, bully and beseech Quebeckers into national independece. Grandiloquently, under a Ben Hur backdrop of a boldly lettered OUI soaring skyward, the Quebec premier proclaimed: 'A 'yes' will mean the end of a long beginning — and the beginning of the affirmation of our maturity as a people.'

Maclean's 28 Apr 80

How would you describe this passage, in relation to bias? Refer to any specific persuasive devices you can identify.

Here is one possible re-write of the passage:

Passage B (fictional)

Quebec Premier Rene Levesque spoke before a very attentive crowd in the town of Ste-Marie in the Chaudière River Valley. 'A 'yes', said the 57-year-old leader, 'will mean the end of a long beginning — and the beginning of the affirmation of our maturity as a people.' Sweat poured from his temples as he spoke.

What does Passage A tell you that Passage B does not? Why does the last sentence of Passage B sound so incongruous? Here are the facts in the paragraph that can be empirically verified (ie, they can be proven or disproven):

	True	or	False
On Wednesday,...........	yes		
Rene Levesque	yes		
spoke before a crowd.......	yes		
in the town of Ste-Marie,..............	yes		
in the Chaudière River Valley...................	yes		
The crowd was "spell-bound" (very attentive)	(?)		
Sweat ran down his temples..................	yes		
He is 57 years old..........	yes		
He was speaking in front of a giant OUI sign.........	yes		
He is the premier of Quebec	yes		
He said, "A 'yes' will mean the end of a long beginning . . ."	yes		

Here are other statements from the paragraph:

	True	or	False
During tedious calm Rene Levesque is irascible and aimless	?		?
His delivery can range from cantankerous clatter to a determined purr	?		?
Levesque is a firebrand	?		?
He is at the peak of his power....................	?		?
His power is to bait, bully and beseech Quebeckers..............	?		?

This second group of statements are much of what *gives meaning* to the facts. Passage B above did no more than state a series of facts that could be proven to be true or false; it did not give meaning to them. It has not described the atmosphere of the meeting. Therefore reporting the fact that the speaker was sweating strikes the reader as slightly peculiar, rather than being an integral part of the overall scene being described.

Here is another possible re-write:

Passage C (fictional)

Wednesday's rally will never be forgotten by the people in the town of Ste-Marie, in the Chaudière River Valley of Quebec. Rene Levesque, Premier of Quebec, stood before his spell-bound audience, describing the future of Quebec and the hopes of all Quebecois. Behind him, the bold OUI lettering soared skyward, as if to symbolise the dynamism of the crowd that night, and the growing popularity of the Yes movement. It has already gathered momentum in this first week of the referendum campaign, and is 'taking off' all over Quebec. Levesque made his way through the singing, chanting, applauding crowd, which pressed in upon him as he had passed across the front of the auditorium and up onto the podium. But in the heated, packed auditorium, once the 57-year-old leader began, you could have heard a pin drop. 'A 'yes,' said Levesque, sweat running in rivulets from his temples to his neck, 'will mean the end of a long beginning — and the beginning of the affirmation of our maturity as a people.'

While the viewpoint of Passage A might be described as one of grudging recognition of a charismatic leader, the viewpoint of Passage C is one of obvious adulation. Passages A and C have both given contexts for the quotation and facts contained in the stories.

FORMULA FOR PROPAGANDA

This formula for making headlines comes from a description of actual techniques used widely in Latin America by various sources of propaganda:

HEADLINE = SUBJECT + VERB + OBJECT

Scapegoat term	Groundless accusation in future	Glittering generality
SUBJECT	VERB	OBJECT
Terrorists	plan to attack	political system
Extremists	(or)	public education system
Guerrillas	threaten	Armed Forces
Socialists		Freedom
Secret communists	plan to infiltrate	Supermarket
	plan to *"descabezar"*	*El Mercurio*
	(Sp., physically behead)	(newspaper)
		Middle Class
		National Security

(Based on: Fred Landis, "The CIA makes headlines," Liberation, Mar/Apr 75)

Activity

1. Try making your own propaganda headlines.

Example: P.Q. referendum threatens democracy.

2. Propaganda flourishes in times of crisis (or "perceived" crises). Analyse headlines during the October 1970 period.

Checklist for monitoring the media

These questions help determine the quality of media coverage of news or current events. The same questions are easily adapted for radio and TV coverage.

Importance

What importance was given to the item?

Prominence: — On what page did the article appear (or Radio/TV at what point in the newscast did the item appear?)

Space: — How many column centimetres did the article measure? What size type was used?

On a given issue, how many items appeared on it?

Were any news stories neglected?

In your judgement, was the importance given to the main items justified, in relation to other news items?

Use of photographs

Are photographs or other illustrations used? How are they used? Do they give a favourable or unfavourable treatment of their subject?

How often are photographs used on a given issue? How big are they? What aspect of a person or story do they highlight?

What is the source?

Is it possible to identify clearly the people who are the sources of stories (their name, occupation, where they live . . . e.g., "Janet Smith, city reporter for the *Times*")?

If the story is from a wire service, is this noted anywhere? (E.g., "Business News Service".)?

Can I clearly identify who is being quoted in the story (their name, occupation, relation to the story being covered . . . e.g., "Daniel Landry, a farmer in the area and spokesman for the group")?

Angle of the story

What aspect of the story was played up?

How are humourous comments used? What do they imply? Admiration? Ridicule?

Are dramatic or tragic human interest stories used to symbolize a larger social condition? If so, how? How much information is provided on the larger social condition?

Information

What information is provided? Do I have any unanswered questions? (Are they significant?)

What is the percentage of straight factual reports given in the news item? What is the percentage of opinion, voiced either by the reporter or someone quoted?

Point of view or bias of the reporter

Were there any veiled character slurs in the reporting or personal attacks? Any noticeably reverential treatment of a particular issue or person?

U.S. GOVERNMENT
ECONOMIC FORECAST

SUNNY, MILD

Editing

The extension of the incomplete or inaccurate quotation is the editing of an entire news story or feature in such a way as to distort the real situation being reported on. The only sure way such distortions can be detected is to be present at the event being described or to know someone who was there. One example from the Maritimes will illustrate how it works. A newspaper story:

> NO VIABLE ENERGY ALTERNATIVE TO NUCLEAR POWER, CHURCHMEN TOLD — SACKVILLE (Special) — Two professors from the University of New Brunswick in Saint John told United Churchmen here Saturday there is no viable alternative to nuclear energy if Canadians wish to maintain their present life-style.[43]
>
> *Chronicle-Herald*

The rest of the article expanded on these points. In reality, however, there were *three* speakers at the conference. The third speaker, also a professor, had made theological reflections and a critique of nuclear energy, including a critique of the two other speakers' arguments (all three had each other's main points in advance). This was indeed a "Special" news report from the conference, as the paper indicates . . .

While the above example appears to be an intentional distortion in editing, with television drastic editing of hours of tapes down to a minute or two for TV becomes mandatory because of high costs and the risk of losing viewer interest in watching TV at all. This imposes serious limitations on what *kind of reality* the mass media can in fact report on. Only the dramatic, the sensational, will "rate". TV's limitations in this area were described thus:

> Presenting events exactly as they occur does not fit with the requisites of television news . . . Given the requirement that a network news story have definite order, time and logic, it would be insufficient in most cases to record from beginnning to end the natural sequence of events with all the digressions, confusions and inconsistencies that more often than not constitute reality . . . Cameramen seek out the most action-packed moments; and editors further concentrate the action.[44]

The author describes what he considered to be distorted TV coverage of a five-hour student demonstration:

> . . . when the happening was reduced to a two-minute news story for the NBC Evening News, the editors routinely retained the violent scenes, building up to them with quick cuts of speeches and crowd scenes . . . The process of distilling action from preponderantly inactive scenes was not perceived as any sort of distortion by

any of the editors interviewed. On the contrary, most of them considered it to be the accepted function of editing; as one chief editor observed, it was 'what we are really paid for.'[15]

The action shown in a newscast, the way the principal actors are pictured, the commentary, the very choice of subject matter — all these editorial decisions influence the way the viewer or reader perceives the event being described:

> By featuring a dramatic and symbolic story or a momentous event in a person's life, the media can move its audience to empathy, indignation, tears, joy or action. We should thus pay attention to the type of dramatic stories the media feature as contrasted to those it neglects.[16]

PRESS BIAS . . .

(Headlines of Paris newspapers reporting the journey of Napoleon across France, on his return from Elba March 9-22, 1815)

March 9

THE ANTHROPOPAGUS HAS QUITTED HIS DEN

March 10

THE CORSICAN OGRE HAS LANDED AT CAPE JUAN

March 11

THE TIGER HAS ARRIVED AT CAP

March 12

THE MONSTER SLEPT AT GRENOBLE

March 13

THE TYRANT HAS PASSED THROUGH LYONS

March 14

THE USURPER IS DIRECTING HIS STEPS TOWARDS DIJON

March 18

BONAPARTE IS ONLY SIXTY LEAGUES FROM THE CAPITAL
He has been fortunate enough to escape his pursuers

March 19

BONAPARTE IS ADVANCING WITH RAPID STEPS, BUT HE WILL NEVER ENTER PARIS

March 20

NAPOLEON WILL, TOMORROW, BE UNDER OUR RAMPARTS

March 21

THE EMPEROR IS AT FONTAINBLEAU

March 22

HIS IMPERIAL AND ROYAL MAJESTY
arrived yesterday evening at the Tuileries amid the joyful acclamations of his devoted and faithful subjects

Activities

1. Who? What? How? When? Where? Why? Sometimes reports do really answer all these questions; often they don't. Find examples of good and bad reporting, and discuss them in your group. Refer to the Checklists and Reviews (pages 28, 33, 35, 44).

2. Cut out and bring in three editorials which you think are good ones, and after pasting them in your book, write under each what you think its merits are.

3. Write an editorial on some topic in this week's news. Have half your group write a "good" editorial (well researched, clearly argued), and the other half write the World's Worst Editorial (unsound or illogical arguments, name-calling etc). Which kind of editorial was easier to do?

4. "Translate" an article of interest from a daily paper. (see p. 44, Abuse of language, in this chapter)

5. Choose a news item from your paper. In list form, note the facts, statistics, and events reported.

Was the coverage noticeably favourable or unfavourable to the issue in question? Rewrite the story, using the same facts, but giving a different interpretation — strongly favourable or unfavourable — to them.

6. Compare two opposing articles on the same topic, political figure or current event. Did both give facts to support their cases? Did the facts presented differ? How? How much use did each article make of emotional words (e.g., epithets, abstract nouns like "democracy", "Canadian unity" etc.)

7. Choose a speech given by a Canadian public figure, and re-write or "translate" part of it. In the introduction, place the excerpt and the speech in context, including a description of the event or problem in question. The conclusion to your paper should include your comments and opinions about the same question.

8. Here is an example from the past of the use of bias in reporting:

> Fast-talking Nikita Krushchev carried his good-will sales campaign to San Francisco yesterday, still acting more like a

peace-loving peasant than the most dangerous man in history.[47]

a. Who was Nikita Krushchev? How is he viewed in the West today, in relation to the history of his country and its relations with countries like the U.S.?

b. What personal attributes or habits are associated with some Canadian politicians or public figures? Can you give any examples of when they have been used to cast an unfavourable light on their abilities in their work? A favourable light?

9. Analyse one night's television newscasts, using the techniques of analysis described in this section. How many stories were covered? Take one story and determine what was learned from the item.

10. A good test of the quality of newsreporting can be personal experience. Have you ever been involved in an activity or event that was covered by the media? Was the coverage and edition true to the spirit of the event?

11. The company *offered* a 5% cost of living adjustment; the union *demanded* 20%.

Examine the language of labour reporting, looking for hidden bias.

12. Try this experiment with the Evening News on TV with a friend. Have one person just listen to the sound and not watch the screen and the other person watch the set as usual. Discuss the news after its over. What were the major impressions of each of you? What do you gain by watching the TV image? What might you lose? *objectivity*

13. Compare two papers that were published on the same day in your own area and from somewhere else. Were the headline stories the same? Measure each story, and list all of them in order of importance (column centimeters). Compare this list to the other paper's list.
Were there any noticeable differences?

14. Compare two papers (or newsmagazines) which you know have divergent editorial positions, listing headlines, column centimeters etc. *story titles or direction*

15. Examine the rubrics of *Maclean's* or another popular magazine, over the period of a couple of years.

Getting the message: working hypotheses

Working hypothesis

1. Origin. Knowing who emits any given piece of information is essential in determining the credibility of the source.

> **Examples:**
> — If a company sells liver tonic, can its own laboratory tests be acceptable as the only necessary, impartial judge of the effectiveness of the tonic? (Or studies by mining companies on industry-related diseases)? *No*
> — If a government department was the regulatory agency covering safety standards for nuclear power plants, would it be a credible body to investigate an accident in a plant? (or police for an enquiry into illegal activities by the police)? *No*
> — If a special interest group promotes a certain point of view, can it be accepted (or rejected) on the basis that it identifies itself as an interest group? (Anti- or "pro-development" groups; Taskforce for Churches and Corporate Responsibility vs. Cdn. Association of Church and Businessmen)? *No*

2. Sponsor. Similarly, knowing who pays for promoting a certain policy or point of view is important.

3. Beneficiary. Who will benefit? Conversely, *who stands to lose* if a project goes ahead? (E.g., see the Nestlé's Bottle Baby debate)

4. Techniques. Analysing techniques used to put across a message will help uncover the nature of message itself.

5. Content. Studying the selection of facts and authorities on which arguments are based is essential. Argumentation and logic as well.

6. Conclusion: the message. From the above steps, it will be possible to suggest an interpretation of the *overall* message presented — what the receiver is intended to think or conclude.

Thus:

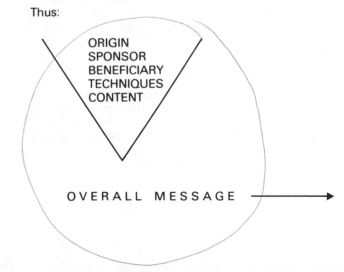

ORIGIN
SPONSOR
BENEFICIARY
TECHNIQUES
CONTENT

OVERALL MESSAGE

Questions to ask

— Can I determine who is presenting a particular stand?
— What might be the motives of those involved?
— How credible are these sources of information?

— Where must I look for an alternative view?

— How have they tried to persuade me?
— How is subject presented?
— What are they appealing to? Emotions or reason?
— Is the same point restated several times?
— Can the claims be substantiated?
— What facts are selected? omitted?
— Are the facts correct or incorrect?
— Is the conclusion a logical progression from the argument?
— Are the arguments presented logical?

— What is the final message?
— What action or position does the message lead us towards? As a result, will I be more likely to:
buy something?
vote for someone?
associate a particular product with a concept or feeling?

Is it true or false?

Two different views from Canadian papers

During the May 1979 federal elections, several of Canada's major churches produced an election kit, *Will the Candidate Please Explain?*, designed to highlight certain issues that might be brought to the attention of political candidates. The responses to the kit from within the press varied greatly . . .

FROM CHURCHMEN, A CURIOUS DOCUMENT AND GAME PLAN FOR INFLUENCING CANDIDATES

(Financial Post 19 May 79. Abridged.)

In the current federal election, who is in favour of:

● 'More effective redistribution of income' through increases in income taxes and a guaranteed annual wage . . . .

● Economic sanctions against South Africa, South Korea, Chile and Argentina . . . .

● Making immigration into Canada easier for 'those who struggle against right-wing dictatorships in Latin America,' specifically by disregarding information from 'security forces in repressive and torturing dictatorships.' . . . .

● 'Political institutions which allow for self-determination' for the aborigines of the North — which, clearly, would weaken Canadian sovereignty in an era of vital strategic and economic importance.

THE ANSWER:

(A) The Communist Party of Canada (Marxist-Leninist), or

(B) The Flat Earth Society, or

(C) The Anglican, Roman Catholic and United Churches of Canada?
PROBABLY all of the above. The churches make their position clear in *Will the Candidate Please Explain?*, a broadsheet issued for the election . . . . It contains statements and sample questions on various suitable progressive causes, prepared by a variety of inter-church 'task forces,' plus odd interlopers such as the radical Latin American Working Group, whose allegiance is somewhat more terrestrial.

Ambush
In their covering letter, the officials urge Canadians to distribute the broadsheet, and to lure candidates to meetings where they can be ambushed with the questions . . . .
. . . For the policies the churches favour will not in reality bring about the ends they claim to desire. The 'chief obstacle to peoples feeding themselves' is **not** 'the worldwide industrialisation of agriculture.' In fact, it's the only hope . . .
Focus left
. . . The broadsheet's secular emphasis didn't bother [the United Church spokesman] him, he said, since the key issue is 'the human personality.'

As for its being left-wing, he said, it was just that the church was 'standing still at a time when society is moving so far to the right.'

When persecution of Christians was at its height in Uganda, Anglicans in the West asked their Ugandan brethren what they needed. The answer was: an urgent shipment of clerical collars. The Westerners were amazed. Didn't the Ugandans want food? Medicine? The latest booklets on corporate responsibility? No, said the Ugandans in the simple faith of early Christianity, they had to have clerical collars. When the people were being herded together for execution, it was essential that they should be able to identify their priests.

It will be easy, when this happens here, for Canadians to turn to the local clergy. They will be the ones wearing 'Save the Rosenbergs' buttons, or, for the more contemporary, 'Stop the War.'

But who will want to?

CHURCHES RAISE SOME REAL ISSUES

(Toronto Star 21 Apr 79)

With the election campaign limping along in a fog of personality-bashing, it's refreshing to find one public group determined to get some thoughts about real issues out of the politicians.

The "ecumenical election kit" put out by the Roman Catholic, Anglican and United churches lists moral and social concerns and urges members to ask questions about them at election meetings.

The paper properly avoids attacking or endorsing any party in the campaign. It simply outlines the issues which, in the view of the churches, should be discussed.

In Canada's internal affairs, there are questions of a guaranteed annual wage to reduce poverty and of a national food policy to counter Canada's increasing dependence on imported food. Internationally, the paper questions Canadian investment in foreign enterprises which compete with domestic industry and Canada's relationships with repressive regimes in South Africa, Chile and Argentina. It asks why military spending is going on while social programs are being cut back.

Not everyone would agree with the churches' priorities or with the policies they seem to be urging. Nevertheless, they are right to insist that their views be considered and their questions answered.

Most Canadians are far too content to let the politicians themselves define the issues and debate them on their own terms.

Discussion — propaganda

There are no rules in such a game. Hitherto acceptable norms of human conduct do not apply. If the U.S. is to survive, long-standing American concepts of 'fair play' must be reconsidered. We must learn to subvert, sabotage and destroy our enemies by more clever, more sophisticated and more effective methods than those used against us. It may become necessary that the American people be acquainted with, understand and support this fundamentally repugnant philosophy.[48]

This quotation is from a report by the American Hoover Commission (1954), which is cited in John Stockwell's book *In search of enemies*. Stockwell, a former CIA agent, describes what he now believes is massive and wanton carnage that has no value to American foreign policy.

1. What is your initial reaction in reading this passage?

2. Now, look at it more closely. What is the underlying reasoning of this position? *LICENSE TO SUPPRESS*

   a. *"If the U.S. is to survive . . ."*. What kind of survival is implicated in the rest of the passage? What kind of a society is envisaged? If "fair play" is expendable, what will be the characteristics of the society envisaged? *POLICE STATE*

   b. *"It may become necessary . . ."*. Who would make these decisions? What conditions would lead them to make them? From this passage, who is assumed to be in control? *GOVT*

   What are the implications of this passage? *FRIGHTENING*

The Reader's Digest: The Biggest Myth of All

The following article is from the book, *Don't blame the people*, 1971, NY: Random House, by Robert Cirino. The book shows how the news media use bias, distortion and censorship to manipulate public opinion.

> There is one copy of the Digest which not only will never be thrown away but is actually framed. It belongs to an oil geologist, working in a part of the Venezuelan jungle inhabited by Motilone Indians. As he and his party were returning to camp, they were attacked, and an arrow struck him from behind. Since the Motilones used poison arrows, he was sure he was going to die. In camp he found that he was unscratched. The arrow had been embedded in a copy of The Reader's Digest which he had put in his hip pocket.
>
> *Reader's Digest*, February 1969

The *Reader's Digest* was the first mass-circulation magazine to use the word "syphilis." This was a courageous act for a mass-circulation magazine because up to 1936 the word had been taboo. The *Reader's Digest* was one of the few out of thousands of mass media agents to crusade from the very beginning against the hazards of smoking. The *Digest* was alone in the middle 1960's in crusading against the vast sums of money being spent to send a man to the moon. And what the *Reader's Digest* does is important as probably no other single publication so effectively shapes the attitudes of its readers—who number an estimated 80 million world wide. For millions who pay little attention to regular news media, the *Digest* serves as a capsule guide to what's going on in the world. Every doctor's office, supermarket check stand and drug store prominently features the *Digest* with its quickly and easily read articles. The *Digest* is important for another reason—it stands alone without competition; no other magazine of this type has even one percent of its 28 million paid monthly circulation. If the *Digest* has a one-sided bias in its selection of articles from 500 different magazines, then its 80 million readers in effect are being propagandized. On the other hand, if the *Digest* is earnestly trying its best to select and present a cross section of viewpoints as expressed in the nation's magazines, it is indeed offering its readers a valuable service.

The *Digest* claims that this is what it is doing—acting as a representative digest of the tens of thousands of articles published monthly in the nation's many magazines. On close examination this claim turns out to be grossly misleading. George Bennett, a statistician, classified all *Digest* articles and found there are three kinds. One is a genuine reprint of an article first appearing in some other magazine. Another type used is the plant—an article written by or for the *Digest*, but planted in another magazine first so that when it later appears in the *Digest,* it looks like a genuine reprint. These articles are often given free to smaller magazines such as the *American Legion Magazine,* the *Kiwanis* or others like them. This is a method of extending *Digest* influence even beyond its own readers to include the readership of about sixty other magazines which accept plants. The third type of article is a *Reader's Digest* original—one that is written solely for or by the *Digest* and printed nowhere else. Bennett found that from 1939 to 1945 genuine reprints accounted for only 42 percent of *Digest* articles while *Digest* originals or plants accounted for 58 percent.[1] Since 1945 the *Digest* has become more and more fond of its own articles, and as a result about 70 percent of the articles in the 1960's were *Digest* originals or plants, and only 30 percent were genuine reprints.[2]

Another *Digest* claim is that through its selection of articles it presents both sides on controversial issues. This claim turns out to be even more false than the claim of being primarily a digest. From 1950 through 1969, the *Digest* presented 84 articles dealing with Vietnam. Of these, 81 supported the U.S. policy in Vietnam while three were neutral. During this time there was not one single article criticizing the U.S. Policy, although many congressmen, senators and retired generals had written many dissenting articles which appeared in various magazines. Typical of the tone of most *Digest* articles was one in February 1956 on:

THE BIGGEST LITTLE MAN IN ASIA

who, according to O. K. Armstrong, a favorite *Digest* writer, was President Diem, South Vietnam's notorious dictator who was eventually overthrown by his own people. The subtitle for the article said:

HE SHOWS THE WAY TO PEOPLE WHO ARE DETERMINED TO BE FREE

The article, which had Diem fighting colonial exploitation and "Red" agression, ended by stating: "In the midst of the dark storms that threaten Asia, President Diem stands like a beacon of light, showing the way to a free people."[3] The *Digest* ended its 81 article crusade for the war in December 1969 by featuring its own editorial backing the establishment's policy plus an article by the press corps' most enthusiastic supporter of the Pentagon, Joseph Alsop. In his article titled

THE VIETCONG IS LOSING ITS GRIP,

Alsop asked the American people for more patience. *Reader's Digest's* own editors wrote 18 of the 84 articles on Vietnam. Of the *Digest's* stable of favorite writers on the topic, Alsop was featured three times, Hanson Baldwin six times and Richard Nixon three times, beginning with his 1964 article:

NEEDED IN VIETNAM: THE WILL TO WIN

Another characteristic of the *Digest*—important in our understanding of its effect on its worldwide readership—requires the following background information, upon which I base my opinion concerning the role of private U.S. corporations in the Latin American economy. Each year U.S. corporations take out from Latin America much more in profits than they invest. In 1968 more than a billion dollars, five times the amount invested, was repatriated to the United States. In addition, the rich raw materials of the region are exploited to give Americans, not Latins, a higher standard of living. Furthermore, large U.S. corporations through their political power have been the authors of a U.S. foreign policy that sanctions using foreign aid money (and the Marines, if necessary) to guarantee the survival of dictatorial governments who are sympathetic to U.S. corporate interests. Critics of U.S. corporate activity and foreign policy use these facts to argue that the people of Latin America suffer from being exploited by U.S. corporate investments and corporate influenced political power. Even the very conservative leaders of the Latin nations are now complaining that Latin America gives to the United States more than it receives.[4]

In 1969, President Nixon, a long time supporter of corporate economic and political policies in Latin America, admitted to Chile's

Foreign Minister, Gabriel Valdes, that U.S. private investment in Latin America was a matter of business, not aid.[5] The exploitative character of U.S. corporate activities in Latin America is the reason that even loyal supporters in Peru, Chile and Bolivia, as well as the establishment's enemy in Cuba, have nationalized large oil and mineral holdings of U.S. corporations.

As we shall see, the *Reader's Digest* apparently wants to keep its readers from being exposed to critical viewpoints based on these facts. From 1950 through July 1969, the *Digest* selected 99 articles favorable to U.S. foreign policy and corporate activity in Latin America compared to only 2 unfavorable and 10 neutral articles.[6] One of the more memorable ones, in a historic sense, was the December 1950 article titled:

DO YOU KNOW WHAT'S HAPPENING SOUTH OF THE BORDER?

The subtitle carried the answer:

A DECADE OF PHENOMENAL PROGRESS . . . PROMISES BETTER DAYS AHEAD

The author was Michael Scully, a *Digest* favorite, whose 14 articles constituted almost a third of the 43 articles on Latin America selected by the *Digest* in the Fifties. Most of the articles favorable to the U.S. presence in Latin America dwelt on the great benefits that Latin Americans received as a result of U.S. corporate investments, missionary activity or foreign policy. The two articles unfavorable to U.S. activity were both critical of U.S. foreign policy, not U.S. corporations. This left U.S. corporations with an unblemished twenty-year record of humanitarian portrayal by the *Digest* during a time when many journals and small magazines had numerous articles criticizing U.S. corporate activities in Latin America.

From 1950 through 1959 the *Digest* sided with investor-owned electric power companies against the customer-owned power companies. It published 9 articles dealing with the issue; all 9 either praised the private power companies or attacked the customer-owned companies and government policies which made them possible. William Hard, one of the *Digest's* own editors, wrote 6 of the 9 articles on the subject. In the very same issues there were full page advertisements from the investor-owned companies (which cost $55,000 per page).All tolled, the *Digest* receives about a quarter of a million advertising dollars annually from the private power companies.[7] It's not necessary to subject *Digest* articles to any rigorous analysis to decide where their bias is on this issue. Albert L. Cole, while General Manager of the *Reader's Digest*, told the Edison Electric Institute in 1961: "We are on your side. We have shown this repeatedly by articles published in *Reader's Digest* over a period of many years."[8]

From 1945 through 1959 the *Digest* presented 9 articles criticizing the concept of socialized medicine while shutting out completely the other side of the debate. Reo Christenson, writing in the *Colombia Journalism Review*, noted that the *Digest* attacked Medicare three times, at the same time shutting out those supporting Medicare.[9] The *Digest* presents so one-sided a view of government activity in helping the unfortunate that Christenson was able to state in 1965:"In none of these categories was I able to find a single article since 1945 presenting welfare state activities or concepts in a generally favorable light."

The *Digest* has always looked favorably toward "hard working men"—that is, as long as they don't join a union. Christenson found that from 1952 to 1965 the *Digest* had 49 articles critical of the labor movement, 5 neutral and 8 favorable. An earlier study by John Bainbridge found 13 articles unfavorable to organized labor, many written by *Digest* editor Willim Hard, compared to only 3 favorable.[10]

Christenson also found 5 articles favorable to the House Un-American Activities Committee and other Congressional committees investigating radical organizations, but none pointing out the abuses and violations of rights by these committees. Not all Congressional investigations were supported by the *Digest*. They printed a March 1963 article saying there were too many government investigations, claiming they "harassed industry" and were costly to the public.

The *Digest's* attitude as revealed by its treatment of controversial issues also expresses itself as conservative and ultra-conservative in the political arena, even though the *Digest* claims to be non-partisan. Christenson found that during President Truman's last four years there were 14 articles favorable to his administration compared to 44 which were critical. Bainbridge found earlier that articles critical of Franklin D. Roosevelt and his administration outnumbered those favorable by a 3 to 1 ratio.

While the *Digest* kept its readers aware of the hazards of smoking and had the courage to deal with syphilis before anyone else, it published only one article on hunger in America from 1945 through 1969, and this was not until November 1968.

The *Digest* has consistently through the years warned of the threat that labor unions pose to democratic processes. However, from 1960 through 1969 not one article appeared pointing out the danger posed to democratic processes by the military-industrial complex even though President Eisenhower had made it the subject of his farewell address to the nation in 1960. During this ten years there was not one single article drawing attention to military waste or the excessive stockpiling of nuclear arms.

From 1940 through 1959, there were many articles about automobile accidents and safety, but not one of them mentioned car design as a factor in causing accidents or making accidents less serious for the victims. In the 1960's there was mention of the need for seat belts, but no mention was made of auto manufacturers' lack of enthusiasm in designing safe cars. Typical of the *Digest* attitude toward the controversy was a September 1965 article titled:

HOW GOOD ARE AMERICAN CARS?

The subtitle read
: THEY'RE AMONG THE BEST BUYS

IN THE WORLD TODAY

An April 1964 article asked
: WHAT ARE THE REAL CAUSES

OF AUTO CRASHES?

The answers were mechanical failure due to lack of maintenance, inadequate driving skills and poor highway environment. Mechanical failure due to poor automotive engineering or construction was not mentioned. The article did mention that at least half of those killed could have been saved if they had used seat belts, but there was no mention or complaint about the fact that the automobile manufacturers were not including seat belts as mandatory equipment in all·new cars and had opposed legislation that would require them to do so. It wasn't until August 1966, more than two years after the *Digest* reprint, that Congress finally passed a law requiring seat belts as mandatory equipment in all automobiles.

A February 1964 article ended with the conclusion: "Today's cars are the safest we have ever had." That may have been true, but it wasn't saying much because the 1964 cars were still without the many life-saving safety features that critics had been suggesting for more than 25 years. As one engineer prominent in automobile crash research said in early 1965, "One has only to examine the current model automobiles to find many flagrant examples of complete disregard for the most rudimentary principles of safety design."[11]

The *Digest* didn't flinch when it came to exposing prison conditions from 1945 to 1959. However, the way in which the articles were written would tend to convince the reader that though the situation was deplorable, good men were in charge and something significant was being done to improve the prison system and its approach to rehabilitation—a very misleading idea since treatment of prisoners in United States prisons was and still is deplorable. There were 9 articles focusing on courageous prison reformers who had worked miracles. There were only two articles which exposed conditions and at the same time revealed that nothing much was being done. In my view, based on my research for this book, this is a standard technique used by the mass media when handling a controversial topic. The situation is painted in the blackest of terms with no holds barred, and then the article concludes by giving the impression that good intentioned men are in charge and progress is being made—so there's no sense in getting aroused or pushing for radical change.

The *Digest's* dedication to the establishment is also revealed in the way they treat establishment leaders and their corporations. Warren Boroson found that the March 1965 reprint of an *Esquire* magazine article on American gasolines omitted the sections exposing deceptive advertising gimmicks.[12] *Digest* protection of big business was also shown in its coverage of the issue of pollution. Back in 1962 the mass media were still able to keep pollution from being a big issue. It was even fashionable to question whether people like Rachel Carson, author of *Silent Spring,* were loyal Americans or were doing the country any good by exposing major polluters and embarrassing the pesticide industry. Boroson notes that the *Digest* selected an article from *Time* dealing with the charges in Carson's book. The reprint was featured in December 1963 with the title:

ARE WE POISONING OURSELVES WITH PESTICIDES?

The subtitle established the tone of the article by stating:

**HERE ARE THE REASONS WHY MANY
SCIENTISTS DISAGREE WITH THE AUTHOR**

The article concluded by claiming that, "many scientists . . . fear that her emotional outburst in *Silent Spring* may do more harm than good."

Advertisers spend $60 million each year to advertise in the *Digest*. This must affect the *Digest's* selection and editing of articles. The titles of many *Digest* articles appear to read like advertisements for establishment concerns. A few of these are: FROM HENRY TO EDSEL TO HENRY, HOWARD JOHNSON—HOST OF THE HIGHWAYS, UNITED FRUIT'S INTERNATIONAL PARTNERS, BANKS THAT BUILD NEW BUSINESSES, STEEL—OLD GIANT WITH NEW

TRICKS, HEAVENLY WAY TO RUN A RAILROAD, and HOME
SWEET ELECTRIC HOME.

The *Digest* permits advertisers to use the exact same layout, print,
and style as regular *Digest* articles. This makes it hard to tell the
difference between an advertisement and a real article (and reading
the ads often won't help because the message of ads and articles is
often the same). To discourage deceptive advertising, the Federal
Trade Commission requires magazines to place the word "advertisement" on ad copy that could be confused with editorial matter so that
the reader may have a way of telling the difference between the two.
In November 1967, the *Digest* published a $240,000 advertisement
from the Pharmaceutical Manufacturers Association. It was an eight-
page section composed of four different article-like editorials glorify-
ing the drug firms and attacking the practice of buying drugs—at a
considerable savings—under their generic names. The first page had in
small type the words "special advertising section." There were then
seven pages and three more advertisement articles with no identification as advertisements. On the last page was the notice: "First in a
series published as a public service by the Pharmaceutical Manufacturers Association." Wisconsin's Senator Gaylord Nelson, a critic of
practices that sustain the high cost of drugs, described this and other
advertising practices of the *Digest* as "calculated deception."[13]

One of the *Digest's* most arrogant acts in defense of its advertisers
and the advertising ethic was its censorship, through its own publishing company, Funk and Wagnalls, of Samm Baker's book, *The Per-
missible Lie: The Inside Truth About Advertising*. Robert Shayon notes
that after this setback, Baker bought the rights from the *Digest*-owned
Funk and Wagnalls Publishers and sold them to World Publishing
Company, a Times-Mirror subsidiary who promised full-page ads
which were to state: THE BOOK THAT *READER'S DIGEST* SUP-
PRESSED. World later decided this would be in "bad taste" and left
it out of their ads. Baker also claims that World failed to spend the
full agreed-upon advertising budget to promote his book. The *Digest*
found other companions in its effort to shackle the book. While Baker
received many TV and radio interviews in Europe, "Today," "To-
night" and the "Merv Griffin" show turned down repeated requests
for the author to discuss his book on their shows. Baker, a retired
advertising man with thirty years experience on Madison Avenue and
eighteen books to his credit, commented that he ". . . hadn't realized
the prevalence and overriding power of censorship by conglomerate
communications interests"

The *Digest*, in an obvious effort to avoid the need to censor any
future books, promised to exercise control over all future Funk and
Wagnalls manuscripts.[14]

An extra bonus for the establishment leaders occurs when the *Digest*
decides to honor them as highly respectable individuals. Bainbridge
found an average of 2 articles a year on Henry Ford. One pictured the
industrialist in most saintly terms by asking in a title: "ARE GAN-
DHI AND FORD ON THE SAME ROAD?" In the 1960's the *Digest*
still sees the leaders as great benefactors: "JOHN D. ROCKEFELLER
JR.'S GREATEST GIFT" was featured in September 1960. To round
out the decade ten years later in December 1969 was an article titled:
"WHY I BELIEVE IN PHILANTHROPY," written by John D. Rockefeller III. (Those reading the *Digest* might find it rather difficult to
reconcile these portraits with the hatred that millions of Latin Americans feel toward Nelson Rockefeller and what he represents.)

Since 1961, the *Digest* has had a "Press-Section." It's the first feature readers come across as they turn the pages. This section includes various editorials from newspapers representing the entire spectrum of the mass media press. The balanced selection of newspapers serves as a cover for the selection of editorials with a bias favoring *Digest* interests and values. It is an easy task to find among any newspaper's editorials one or two that express the viewpoint of the *Digest*.

The *Digest* has condensed many great books over the years, but it is careful not to reprint any books that attack its own special interests or ultraconservative values. Some of the books the *Digest* runs have been denounced by responsible reviews. The *Nation* magazine pointed out that the *New York Times* denounced the right-wing book,*The Road Ahead*. The*Times* saw the book as significant because it was one of: ". . . the latest and most extreme manifestations of endemic hysteria presently affecting a considerable segment of our society."[15] Apparently the *Digest* editors did not mind the possibility that this right wing hysteria might spread; when they introduced the book they printed only that part of the *Times* review that said it was one of the two "most important books about the contemporary American scene that we will have this year." The readers were left unaware that the *Times* thought it important only because they considered it a noteworthy example of hysteria.

The *Digest* apparently isn't satisfied with propagandizing its readers by selecting articles to favor its own views by 80 to 1, 20 to 1, 5 to 1, or 3 to 1 margins. Many of the articles it writes or selects contain flagrant errors. The Area Development Administration found twenty different instances where "IS THIS THE WAY TO FIGHT THE WAR AGAINST POVERTY?"was misleading or factually inaccurate. The article was written by a member of the *Digest* staff. Boroson also notes that another staff writer, James Daniel, wrote an article about unemployment that caused the director of the Bureau of Labor Statistics to reply: "I cannot recall having read a short article in which so many inaccurate statements were presented in support of such unwarranted conclusion."[16]

The *Digest* does not have to write all their misleading or factually inaccurate articles, for there are plenty to choose from—some of them by Congressmen. Representative Frank T. Bow's "THE GREAT MANPOWER GRAB" claimed that the U.S. Employment Service was undermining the people's right to choose the kind of work they want. After analyzing this article Reo Christenson stated:

> The author is able to provide no evidence whatever that the U.S.E.S. or anyone else had such a goal in mind, except that the service is helping many high school students about careers. . . . The *Digest* did not inform its readers that Representative Bow has close relations with private employment agencies, which have a special interest in restricting the U.S.E.S.[17]

Inaccurate articles plus the *Digest's* ultraconservative bias and Republican partisanship have not passed unnoticed by politicians:

> The *Digest* has been lambasted by President Truman for printing 'a pack of lies,' by Sen. Mike Mansfield for being 'irresponsible,' by Sen. Joseph Guffey for being 'a tool and toy of a power-crazed publisher,' by Rep. Elmer J. Holland for its 'hit-and-run-journalism,' and by Rep. Emanuel Celler for refusing to print 'the views of the underdog, or that of minority groups.'[18]

Digest readers are unaware of widespread criticism of the *Digest* because its editors use one of the oldest propaganda techniques in the trade to convince its readers it is responsible, fair and infallible. The *Digest* steadfastly refuses to print any rebuttals or make retractions or corrections no matter how biased the article or glaring the inaccuracies. This technique has been so successful that even the *Digest's* most learned readers have been fooled. Teachers order 500,000 copies a month for use in American classrooms. If teachers used the magazine to help students learn techniques of implanting hidden bias the practice could be justified. But the *Digest* is seldom used for that purpose. It is used by teachers who don't warn students that the *Digest* is a masterpiece of deceit.

The American Education Fellowship Conference for Parents and Teachers made an attempt in 1947 to alert teachers about *Digest* deceit. They adopted a resolution calling the attention of teachers to the fact that ". . . the *Reader's Digest* carries the implication that it is unbiased and comprehensive in its selection when it is in fact otherwise." Teachers would have been lucky indeed if they found out about this warning. The *New York Times* placed this announcement in one small paragraph near the bottom of an article on Page 64 whose headline,

WIDER RECOGNITION OF SCHOOLS URGED,

carried no hint of the *Digest* condemnation buried below.[19]

Despite false *Digest* claims, the critics must admit the *Digest* is a vital magazine. Each issue contains fascinating tidbits, interesting episodes, informative articles and beautiful advertisements. It is a pleasant experience for the reader; nothing difficult is required of him. He does not have to edit, arrange, select, balance or deliberate on what is happening in the United States and the world—it is all done for him through the painless vehicle of entertaining selections. But the reader and society pay a price for being entertained and informed by the *Digest*. They receive and assimilate, unaware, a bias which gives them a view of the world that is so distorted it limits the alternatives they must consider in meeting their challenges. There is no opposite bias in mass media to compete, expose or balance *Digest* bias. No regulations exist requiring the *Digest* to give equal treatment to competing ideas, perspectives and selections. The result is that over fifteen million *Digest* buyers in the United States are excluded—to the extent they depend on or believe the *Digest*—from taking part in deciding what is true from among competing interpretations and information. The *Digest* bias has decided what is true for them.

1. John Bainbridge, *New Yorker,* December 1, 1945, p. 40.
2. *Time,* February 2, 1967, p. 47, and Reo M. Christenson, "Report on the Reader's Digest," *Columbia Journalism Review,* Winter 1965, pp. 31-36.
3. P. 144.
4. *New York Times,* June 12, 1969, p. 1.
5. Ibid.
6. Favorable articles include those depicting U.S. missionaries and large Latin American corporations.
7. Quoted in Metcalf, *Overcharge,* p. 148.
8. Edison Electric Institute Bulletin, June 1961, pp. 184, 246-8, as quoted in Metcalf, *Overcharge,* p. 149.
9. Christenson, *Columbia Journalism Review,* Winter 1965, p. 33.
10. Bainbridge, *New Yorker,* December 1, 1945, p. 44.
11. *New York Times,* January 27, 1965, p. 1.
12. Warren Boroson, "The Pleasantville Monster," *Fact,* March-April 1966, p. 7.
13. *Columbia Journalism Review,* Winter 1967-68, p. 24.
14. Robert Shayon, *Saturday Review,* November 1969, pp. 48-49, and *Columbia Journalism Review,* Summer 1968, p. 3.
15. February 18, 1950, p. 157; *Reader's Digest,* February 1950, p. 1.
16. Boroson, *Fact,* March-April 1966, p. 26.
17. *Reader's Digest,* October, 1964; Christenson, *Columbia Journalism Review,* Winter 1965, pp. 31-32.
18. Boroson, *Fact,* March-April 1966, p. 3.
19. *Newsweek,* December 4, 1944, p. 84.
20. November 24, 1944.
21. Seldes, *Never Tire of Protesting,* pp. 82-92.
22. March 16, 1947. ∎

Mass Culture

Television, advertising and the news media have now been studied as important sources of information. They are also major vehicles of mass culture.

Mass culture informs us in a general way about ourselves and our world. Mass culture forms the environment for our ideas and our thinking — and that of people all around the world. Our ideas "germinate" in this culture (in this sense the bibliogical meaning of the word culture applies, too). People in the Annapolis Valley, in downtown Toronto or in the slums of Sao Paulo, Brazil, all see the familiar red and white logo with its message: *Coke adds life.* In the 1970s the most-recognized figure on this planet was reported to have been the boxer Muhammed Ali.

People are not accustomed to examining in a systematic or formal way the pictures, sounds, and objects that surround them in everyday life. This book challenges you to do so, as all these things are immensely important in creating a person's world-view. Examining mass culture has been put at the end of this section, because perhaps its messages are the most difficult to decipher.

Mass culture is culture for thousands, millions — masses of people. For our purposes, we will use the ordinary dictionary meaning of culture:

> culture n. the training and development of the mind/ the refinement of taste and manners acquired by such training/ the social and religious structures and intellectual and artistic manifestations etc. that characterise a society.

While some of the "refinements" of the second definition — oil paintings, opera and ballet — are part of culture (and we usually think only of them as culture), they are not part of *mass* culture. With few exceptions, they are restricted to a small segment of the population. By contrast, advertising, TV and other media are designed for millions of people.

The characters found in mass culture are part of our lives. Sometimes they are irritating intruders; sometimes likable individuals — welcome and anticipated guests. Ronald McDonald, The Walton Family, Donald Duck, the Man from Glad, Josephine the Plumber, Mary Tyler Moore, Archie Bunker . . . each character is known by us and becomes part of our lives for half an hour, or thirty seconds.

Advertising and television are two principal forms of mass culture. However radio, the record and movie industries are other forms of mass culture, as are magazines, spectator sports, horoscopes, popular magazines, cartoons and comic books. All of these forms of mass culture are important to examine because all of them give us *messages*.

Some of these messages have made a deep imprint on our consciousness, on our understanding of ourselves and the world.

In some cases, the messages of mass culture may be very simple. For example, top-selling records on the radio often have straightforward messages (song title: I Want to Dance; message: I want to dance). Other messages and songs however are not so simple at all. In this book, we will not examine such forms of mass culture as movies, rock songs or sports any further: these will be areas of study for you, the reader. Anyone who does pursue research in this area is likely to find very interesting, challenging, and perhaps surprising

information. In the following pages we will examine an area which may seem at the outset an equally surprising area of study for a book with a serious purpose: cartoons and comics. They are forms of mass culture.

Discussion/research — mass culture

1. We have included sports in our list of vehicles of mass culture. Does this surprise you? Do you agree with this inclusion? We think the definition of mass culture includes such activities (particularly spectator sports). Justify with examples your agreement or disagreement with this position.

2. Prepare a research paper on the Politics of Sport, referring especially to the Olympic Games.

3. Do a research project on whatever rock group is at present considered the most popular, controversial or successful. See what you can find out about the group's history, how they got together, who backed them financially; how their promotion has been done. Choose one or two representative songs and analyse them (theme, language . . .) What messages do they contain?

4. Review the book. *Rip off the big game: the exploitation of sports by the power élite,* by Paul Hoch (1972), NY: Anchor Books.

5. The founder of a French publication modeled on the American *People* magazine said,

> We cannot, as in America, have show business personalities on our cover all the time. Too many Frenchmen will keep their distance if they think we only deal with shows. *Saga* will have politicians, writers, lawyers on its covers, that is, a full range of members of the community.[49]

a. The French publication is supposed to be more representative of society, showing its *"full range"*. On the basis of what its publisher has said, would you agree that it in fact represents the full range of people in society? Why or why not?

b. What possible reasons might be given for the lack of coverage of, say, industrial workers, fishermen or housewives in such magazines? Would you agree or disagree with these reasons? Why or why not?

With a newspaper like this . . .

Control of the mass media, whether it is in American-dominated Latin America or Soviet Russia, produces its own humour among people who are affected by it. Because we live in Canada and North America, most of the material presented in this unit is about our media system. But, to encourage you to look beyond our book, we will make space to include something else. Here are some jokes people tell in the Soviet Union:

A foreign journalist was interviewing a worker in Gdansk.
'Do you find your job rewarding?'
'In every respect.'
'And what's your apartment like?'
'Modern, spacious and cheap.'
'How do you spend your leisure?'
'I go to the opera and the theatre. I attend evening classes to broaden my education. I play football at week-ends.'
'Do you possess a radio?'
'Of course I do. How else would I know how to answer your questions?'

* * *

The Party Secretary was reporting to a meeting on his recent visit to his native village of Ivanovo, several hundred miles away in the remote steppe-land.

'I could hardly believe my eyes, comrades,' he said. 'The poverty-stricken village of my youth has now developed into a bustling industrial township. When I was a lad, before the revolution, the Ivanovo peasants lived to a man in reed-huts. Now they live in modern housing estates grouped around a magnificent Palace of Culture and a brand-new sports centre.'

Everyone was deeply impressed. When question time came round, only one old man raised his hand to speak.

'Comrade speaker, I was in Ivanovo only last week, and I didn't see any modern housing estates or Palaces of Culture. All I saw were a few reed-huts and a broken-down old barn.'

'Comrade!' said the speaker severely, 'you should travel less and read *Pravda* more often.'

* * *

Two Russians were sitting in a factory canteen, each rolling himself a cigarette.
'What is your opinion of *Pravda*, comrade?' asked one of them.
'An admirable paper. After all, didn't Lenin himself found it?'
'And *Izvestia*?'
'Not bad. I find I get quite a lot out of it.'
'What about *Trud*?'
'To tell you the truth, I've never smoked it.'

Excerpts from Benton, Greg and Loomes, Graham, *The big red joke book* London: Pluto Press (1976).

The wonderful world of comics

Studying critically and systematically *all* sources of information is important if you want to understand how people form opinions. Humans *give meaning* to their experiences. Thus, we must examine all aspects of our experience, including comics. For these reasons comics and other forms of mass culture should be subject to the same critical analysis as would be applied in areas that have traditionally enjoyed more serious study — such as political studies, literary criticism, science or other disciplines.

We find justification for studying comics from educational authorities themselves. The creator of the World of Disney, American Cartoonist Walt Disney was described by the Superintendent of Public Instruction of the US's largest educational system as "The greatest educator of this century — greater than John Dewey or James Conant or all the rest of us put together."[50] There are Disney strips in five thousand newspapers, translated into more than 30 languages, spread over a hundred countries.

. . . I glance at the comics, perhaps only for a few seconds. But like any repetition, these images and impressions settle in my subconscious, like silt in a river. Just as surely as deltas are formed by a long and continual sedimentation process, so my thoughts and attitudes are formed by my environment, including the apparently "meaningless" messages of cartoons.

What messages do cartoons and comics give us?

Like TV or newspapers, comics do communicate messages, but like the other media, they are a vehicle of communication. One cartoon can differ from another in content and message as much as one TV show can differ from another, or one book from another. We propose the following general categories for analysing cartoons.

Critical cartoons

In this book, we have used cartoons to illustrate some points. All of them attempt to make some form of humourous commentary on the subject matter being discussed.

Critical cartoons challenge our general outlook on things. They may range from the mildly humourous or whimsical to the savagely satirical. Although the cartoons have been drawn from a variety of sources, the cartoonists have found something laughable in certain situations, and have made social commentaries on them. These commentaries might be summed up by saying,

> There is something inherently illogical, unfair, or absurd in the present state of affairs in our society.

Here is a Critical cartoon with nuclear safety as its subject matter:

Focusing on the absurd statement of "how time flies" makes a point about the dangers of the situation in a way that technical papers, sophisticated arguments or carefully done research cannot.

'Retiring, eh? Gosh, how time flies. I can hardly believe you've accumulated 40 equivalent years of radiation already.'

Similarly, a commentary on make-work projects:

Or a commentary on women and work:

Or on aid programmes to other countries:

"Because you've done it successfully your way for generations, it doesn't mean it works."

In one way or another, these cartoons are social commentaries that are critical of the way things are. To a greater or lesser extent, they challenge us to look afresh at our ideas about ourselves or the world around us.

Reinforcing cartoons

However, there are other cartoons that reinforce our accepted ideas about the world, rather than propose new, critical ideas. The social commentary of these types of cartoons could be summarised by saying,

> *Human beings and society are as you see them in the cartoon; right now things couldn't be much different, and shouldn't be, really.*

In general, when we look at a Reinforcing cartoon, we may identify in some way with a character because we can picture ourselves in that situation. Or we may identify a cartoon as being funny (and "true" in some sense) because it fits in with how we already view others. However, are our accepted ideas *always* correct ones? To make its humourous point, the Reinforcing cartoon often relies on stereotypes. Women may be stereotyped:

"I think she's coming out of the anesthesia...she's
asking for her charge cards!"

Or, when a woman is found in an unconventional occupation, for example, it is reassuring to know that she really hasn't changed at all . . .

"So there we have it — five in favor and one who wants 'to sleep on it.' "

Cartoonists may put a woman in an absurd context, which makes her social concerns look equally absurd. In this cartoon her concerns are presented as a ridiculous obstacle to what she was really made for doing (and what she really wants to do):

"I'm **attracted** to you, too. But first, where do **you** stand on nuclear energy?"

In Blondie and Dagwood, we find not only the stereotype of a woman . . .

. . . But we also find the continuation of the parents' stereotypes in their offspring.
Like father, like son:

Dagwood's son will, like his father, be seen rushing somewhere — already late for his destination. None of the members of the Bumstead family are ever really in control of their lives: like her neighbour, Blondie chronically overspends, and something always puts Dagwood behind schedule for the day.

At home, he is asleep on the couch or in the bathtub. At work, he is seen, by himself, at his desk. What Dagwood actually does all day in his work is apparently not worth noting. He will continue to incur (for unknown reasons) the wrath of Mr. Dithers:

Bolting out of the house to work, dodging the fury of his boss, desperately trying to catch up with his wife's overspending, the likable Dagwood is set upon from all sides. As if he didn't have enough trouble on his own, Dagwood comes across "real-life" hardships. The stereotype of the harried, American male who is taken advantage of at every turn, encounters the stereotype of the poor . . .

From a reading of Blondie and Dagwood, one might infer that the poor were poor because they wanted to be; and that essentially they were content with their lot in life, as Dagwood presumably is with his:

The humour in the unexpected is well done. We laugh at such a turn in a comic . . . but is it possible that just part of our smile might come from a subconscious relief . . . that there is a funny ending, that everyone is in their proper place, where they are destined to be?

Characters from Reinforcing cartoons often allow the reader to feel superior to them. A more recent cartoon makes the position of Dagwood (and other characters) all the more explicit: by name, the Born Loser:

We may smile at Thornapple's foibles, or those of the most famous loser of them all, Donald Duck. But perhaps there is an instant of vague uneasiness, a slight apprehension that possibly we, ourselves might in some way resemble them, or share in some of the same conditions . . .

Donald, Walt Disney's world-famous character, is the frustrated worker, humiliated by his boss (yet vitally dependent on him); the unemployed slouch, always trying to find an easy way out,

He is today's Everyman, always in turmoil, constantly searching. A study on this cartoon character described him thus:

> Donald Duck represented a new kind of comedy, suited to a new age: a symbol not of courage and wit, as Mickey had been to the '30s, but an example of heroic failure, the guy whose constant efforts toward gold and glory are doomed to eternal defeat.[51]

Research has shown that intelligence is not an important factor in determining a person's susceptibility to techniques of persuasion. What is important, it seems, is how adequate a person feels. Robert Cirino notes that,

> . . . Perhaps it is not entirely an accident that the poor, the labourer and the ordinary middle class workers are pictured in the media in such a way as to make them feel inadequate . . . This partly explains the biggest miracle accomplished by media owners — the turning of the labourer and the middle class against the hungry, the poor, black and brown.[52]

Fantasy cartoons

Finally, there is a third type of cartoon which differs from the Critical or Reinforcing cartoon. While the Critical cartoon may use imaginative and improbable incidents to challenge our ideas, or the Reinforcing cartoon may use them to make its point, this third type of cartoon uses fantasy as its central device.

The Fantasy cartoon does not appeal to the sense of humour or critical faculties so much as it appeals simply to the imagination. There are romance fantasies — Dr Morgan, Mary Worth; there are power fantasies — Spiderman, Mandrake the Magician; there are war, violence, pornographic and other fantasy comics.

If the Critical cartoon asks the reader, *"Is this the way you want things to be?"* and the Reinforcing cartoon says, *"This is the way things are, so look on the bright side,"* the Fantasy cartoon says to the reader,

> *You can see the way things are (unhappy, miserable, dangerous, unjust), but imagine if you had the lover you dream of; if you had unlimited powers . . . how things would be different . . .*

The Critical, the Reinforcing and the Fantasy cartoon — all three are social commentaries of one kind or another. All three have readers who have casual, momentary encounters with their messages. These readers are living, breathing people who are forming attitudes and opinions from their environment, which includes cartoon messages. They are working people, they are the jobless, the old, the young . . . they are union members; they are strike-breakers . . .

Cartoons are one small aspect of mass culture. In some ways, their simplicity makes their messages easier to "de-code" than the more complex messages of, say, film or a TV show. None of these messages are neutral.

Research/discussion

1. Describe several cartoon characters. What are their likable attributes? Weaknesses? What place in society does each of the cartoon characters occupy?

2. Referring to Robert Cirino's observations on page 82, comment on the cartoons that appear on the following pages, or that appear in your daily newspaper. What occupation in society does each of the characters have? What role do they play? Do you agree with the author? Substantiate your position with specific references to characters, situations, dialogue, etc.

3. Although he is from Britain, the cartoon character Andy Capp is recognised easily by many Canadian readers. The Halifax *Chronicle-Herald* carries his cartoon regularly. Save his cartoons over a period of several weeks (or obtain one of his comic books.)

Imagine that you are a social worker. List the problems you would find in the Capp household.

4. Prepare a presentation for your group on fantasy comics, literature and films that deal with inter-galactic travel and warfare. For a humourous interlude in your presentation, you may wish to show a short spoof of the plot of a well-known movie. The film, *Hardware Wars* (colour, 10 min. approx, 16 mm), can be obtained by writing to International Tele-Film, 47 Densley Avenue, Toronto, Ontario.

5. Examine the following comic strips. Try to identify the humourous elements of some of them. What place in society does each of the characters occupy? Is what each character is saying in keeping with his/her role in society? Why or why not?

6. Imagine yourself as an archaeologist. Imagine that you know nothing of North American society and that all that remains of North American civilisation are the few artifacts that had been uncovered and that are now under your study. They are comic books.

From these few remains, you must try to piece together a picture of North American society — its social realities (crime rate, family situation) and its value system (friendship patterns, etc.).

a. Describe the world of Peter Parker, the adolescent who can transform himself into Spiderman. What kind of a society do you find?

b. Since of course you are not an archaeologist and North American society has not vanished, you can compare these elements of our mass culture with *real* social indicators. How close does the world of Peter Parker resemble the real world?

7. Use the same analytical process for another form of mass culture (movies, sports, records, paperback novels).

"Fifty per cent sex and fifty per cent violence. That's the balance we've been looking for!"

8. Research into American television viewers from 1969 to 1977 found that people who watched a great deal of TV were in large numbers at the lower end of the social stratum, had lower educational qualifications, less hopes for "bettering themselves" and far higher worries about crime and law and order. A study of programme content found that 64% of the major characters and 30% of all characters in the crime programmes were either perpetrators or victims of violence. "There is a marked difference between this fiction and the fact that from 1970 US statistics, there was only 0.32% of violent crimes per 100 of the population."[53]

    a. Discuss the role of mass culture in influencing society's attitudes and opinions.
    b. Prepare a research paper on crime comic books and war comic books. Try to determine the readership, and analyse the content of one or two representative comics. Would your findings tend to confirm or call into question the television study?

9. Read and prepare a book review of Dorfman and Mattelart's *How to read Donald Duck,* a book that in 1973 was burned by Chile's military dictatorship and permanently banned from a number of Latin American countries. This book appears in the recommended reading suggested at the end of this chapter.

10. Constant and subtle use of bias over hundreds of years has created racism, chauvinism, respect for the rich, contempt for the common labourer and the poor, and respect for religious leaders no matter how short-sighted or inhumane their use of political power is.[54]

Essay

Using examples from the mass media, apply the techniques covered in this section to prove or disprove this statement. Be sure to give sufficient examples and adequate documentation.

or

With the same quotation in mind, discuss the notion of *heroism,* as it is depicted in mass culture. (You may wish to examine, by contrast, the dangers involved in the daily work of fishermen, miners or industrial workers.)

"The cartoons below are examples of Co-optation." Discuss this statement.

Impact of propaganda and advertising

We now must examine the effects on society of propaganda and advertising. It is possible that you have never personally experienced any dramatic instances of propaganda or unclear thinking. However, if you begin systematically to "read between the lines" in daily life, it is likely that before long you will notice how common unfair persuasive techniques are, as are fundamental flaws in the logic of certain positions. A startling example of this occurred when supposedly intelligent officials could put signs in the LaHague nuclear reprocessing plant in Europe advising workers that,

IF THERE IS A CRITICAL REACTION YOUR BEST PROTECTION IS TO FLEE.[55]

One tends not to question authority, especially when it claims to be acting for one's "own good".

The absurdity of suggesting this action as the "best" option for protecting oneself, under such circumstances, is staggering in its implications.

Does advertising actually do any harm or any good?

In Canada well over $2 billion is spent each year on advertising (all media).[56] In the United States, approximately the same amount is spent on TV advertising alone, on the assertion that it is the most effective advertising medium. Even in 1975 the price for a one-minute ad on *The Waltons* was $122,000. An ad that lasts 30 seconds can cost $250,000 to broadcast.[57] It has been estimated that a person is bombarded by about 1,500 advertising messages a day.[58] An unusual example illustrating the power of ads to influence people's consumption patterns was found during the U.S. ghetto riots in the late 1960s: the most looted products were also the most advertised.[59] As one advertising critic noted,

You don't spend millions in this business *not* to affect people![60]

Supporters of advertising say that the purpose of ads is to inform consumers about products. However, a more critical view would be that the aim of commercial advertising is to encourage people to consume — whether or not they need to or can afford to.

Yet it can be difficult to measure the specific impact of advertising or propaganda messages in Canada. The mass media have reached most cities and communities through TV and advertising. Because almost all Canadians are reached by them, there are few "control groups" who are not receiving the same messages whose behaviour, values, or buying patterns can be compared to our own.[61] While we have seen some serious evidence that people are in fact deeply influenced by what they hear and see through mass media, some people may still question that this influence can have any dramatic or harmful effects.

For this reason we include the following series of articles. The first describes the effect of advertising of one consumer product in the "Third World" — infant formula. Similar effects of advertising have been documented in isolated communities in Canada, especially in the North.

The subsequent articles highlight the infant formula debate.

(*Mother Jones* is a high-circulation "alternative press" magazine noted for its investigative journalism.)

This article first appeared in the December 1977 issue of *Mother Jones* magazine.

THE BOTTLE BABY SCANDAL

MILKING THE THIRD WORLD
FOR ALL IT'S WORTH

By Barbara Garson

Photography by Ira Sandler

"In 1970, I visited a small town called Aliagua, in a very rural area of Luzon. . . . During my visit, an old friend of my family, who knew that I was a doctor, approached me and asked me to visit his newborn child, who was very ill. The baby was less than ten days old. He was burning with fever, dehydrated and suffering from severe diarrhea. I asked the mother how she had been feeding the baby and she replied that she was using Enfamil. She told me that this had been given to her on discharge from the hospital in Cabanatuan where she had delivered the child. The milk was given to her by a nurse who told her that her milk was 'inappropriate' for the baby."

So writes Dr. Jesus T. De La Paz, who practices obstetrics and gynecology in the Philippines. According to Dr. La Paz, 80 per cent of the sick infants in the pediatric ward at his country's San Pedro Hospital are bottle fed. Why?

Throughout the Third World, from Haiti to Venezuela to Nigeria to the Philippines, new mothers are leaving maternity wards with tins of powdered milk—free samples—supplied by American, Swiss and Japanese companies. In an attempt to do what's modern, what's best for their babies, they abandon breast feeding. And then, like the family in Aliagua, they try to reconstitute a powdered formula where they have no clean water, no suitable pot for sterilizing, insufficient fuel to boil their one bottle and nipple several times a day, and no refrigerator for the milk.

Above all, they do not have money to keep on buying enough formula. A laborer in Uganda would have to spend 33 per cent of the average daily wage to feed an infant on powdered milk. In Pakistan the figure is 40 per cent. In Haiti a secretary, a relatively well-paid worker, spends 25 per cent of her salary for substitute infant food. And so what happens is that poor mothers start to "stretch" the formula. In 1969 the National Food and Nutrition Survey of Barbados asked mothers of bottle-fed infants two to three months old how long a can of milk lasted. The can contains a four-day supply. But 82 per cent of the mothers said they made it last anywhere from five days to three weeks.

Some mothers who have run out of formula have been found mixing cornstarch with water to give the baby something that looked like milk. Others use cocoa, tea, or simply sugar water to stop the crying, at least temporarily. The British charity organization War on Want found a Nigerian mother feeding her baby water alone. She had seen the bottle and nipple pictured on a billboard and thought the manufactured items themselves provided the nourishment.

Unsterilized and diluted bottle formula exacerbates the two most common causes of infant sickness and de around the world: malnutrition diarrhea. Actually, the two are "sy gistic," as the doctors say: each ma the other worse. Underweight bal are prone to the infections that cr diarrhea. And the baby with const diarrhea receives less nutrition fr what food it does get.

Since the late '60s, health official poor countries have been seeing th symptoms combined in a syndrc sometimes called Bottle Illness. In so hospitals in Africa these severely hydrated babies are kept aside in b labeled "Lactogen Syndrome" (Lac gen is the Nestlé Company's powde formula). Dr. D. B. Jelliffe, a dis guished British pediatric nutritio who now heads the UCLA School Public Health's Division of Populati Family and International Health, labeled the syndrome "commercioge malnutrition."

Whatever you call it, the syndrc involves no new diseases. The diarr results from the Third World's pre lent bacterial and amoebic infectic which can be contracted from drink unboiled water. The malnutrition ta the form of marasmus (shown by sunken eyes, prominent ribs, thin li arms and legs we've seen in the Ban, desh posters) and kwashiorkor (p face and feet, anemia and apathy).

What *is* new about "Bottle Illness the early onset of these poverty dise: in children. Ordinarily mother's m *even of an underfed woman*, will pro adequate nourishment for at least early months. For a year to 18 mon more it can sometimes provide a g protein supplement. Of course it is g for the mothers to eat well, but, un

mother is virtually starving, the baby
ts nourished.

Furthermore, mother's milk provides
imunities against various diseases—
mething all the more important in
untries with few public-health meas-
es. No matter what water the mother
inks, the baby receives breast milk
latively free of the local infections.
hen poor people breast feed, malnu-
ition doesn't usually appear until well
to the second year of life. Recently
e Inter-American Investigation of
ortality in Childhood, conducted by
e Pan American Health Organization,
oranch of the World Health Organiza-
in, checked into the causes of some
,000 deaths in 15 areas of the world,
ostly in Latin America. The research-
s found that because of the decline of
east feeding, childhood deaths from
alnutrition now peak in the third and
urth months of life.

Of course death is only the extreme
sult. Milk companies would find little
ofit in distributing those free samples
every infant was going to die in two or
ree months. But one of the horrible
pects of this new form of malnutrition
that protein deficiency in the early
onths seems more likely to lead to per-
anent brain damage. We won't know
e full effects of malnutrition that be-
as at birth until 15 or 20 years from
w, for it had been relatively rare in
e world until widespread bottle feed-
y came along.

For ghoulish family planners, let me
ip to point out that bottle-baby deaths
e not an effective population control.
ither, they tend to _increase_ popula-
n. Study after study has shown that,
gardless of the availability of birth
ntrol, people do not start having
aller families until they feel secure
at their children will live to adult-
od. When children die, people go on
iving big families in the hope that at
st one or two children will survive.
irthermore, the decline of breast feed-
g may increase population, because
re is some truth to the old wives' tale
t you don't get pregnant while you're
irsing. It's not foolproof birth control,
: lactating mothers do have children
ced farther apart than bottle-feeding
others.

"FOODS YOU CAN TRUST"

The bottle baby problem really be-
i in the late 1960s. By then it had be-
ne clear the U.S. birthrate was head-
for an all-time low. Figures from

Europe told the same story. Baby-
oriented businesses throughout the developed world knew that they had to
think of a strategy to cope with the
baby bust.

Some companies diversified, but the
big push went into finding new markets
in the Third World. Ross Laboratories,
for example, is the subsidiary of Abbott
Labs, which manufactures Similac and
Isomil. In 1969 the overseas portion of
Ross' pediatric sales was 14.3 per cent;
by 1973 it had risen to 22.2 per cent,
amounting to $31.3 million. Following
the same strategy, Bristol-Myers (En-

LACTOGEN

LACTOGEN
NESTLÉ

; THE VERY BEST MILK FOR YOUR BA

famil and Olac), American Home Products' Wyeth division (SMA, S-26, Nur-
soy) and, biggest of all, the Swiss corporation Nestlé (Lactogen) expanded
like mad. Throughout Asia, Africa and
Latin America, the airwaves and the
billboards began filling with slogans like
"Right from the Start—the Foods You
Can Trust."

Soon nutritionists began to object.
After a series of meetings organized
through the U.N., the companies agreed
to modify their approach. Now their
signs said things like: "The Next Best
Thing to Mother's Milk." Their pamphlets spoke vaguely about the times
when breast feeding is "inappropriate"
or "unsuccessful." More important, in
the last few years the milk companies
have almost entirely dropped billboards

and radio spots. They concentrate now
on the most effective and direct approach to the new mother. The majority
of the companies give out free samples,
pamphlets, posters and contributions of
equipment directly to hospitals; they
give services to and sponsor conferences
for the doctors and nurses. Thus, the
woman from Aliagua was given Enfamil
by the nurse when she left the hospital.
In some countries (Guatemala, for instance) "milk banks" connected with
the hospitals sell a supply of formula
to new mothers at cut rates, so it takes
them a couple of weeks before they have
to buy it on the open market and realize
how expensive it really is.

But Nestlé, Bristol-Myers and some
of the others don't stop with the hospitals. Bristol-Myers, for instance, has
hired former consumer activist Bess
Myerson as a consultant; her name and
photo adorn a new publicity brochure.
More important, some milk companies
now hire their own special "milk
nurses." Dressed in nurse-like uniforms,
they travel around in countries such as
Jamaica or Malaysia visiting new mothers, providing gifts and advice, weighing
the babies—and leaving infant formula
samples. These "mothercraft personnel" or "milk nurses," incidentally, may
or may not be medically trained. Indeed,
the use of fully trained nurses as sales-
women is probably the more harmful
practice, since it depletes a developing
nation's small supply of medical personnel.

Dr. Roy E. Brown is a nutritionist
and pediatrician, now at Mount Sinai
medical school, who has practiced
abroad for 11 years, including time in
the Bangladesh refugee camps. (There,
incidentally, he used a simple and successful technique to promote "relacta-
tion" among mothers who had previously ceased breast feeding.) He told
me about a pediatric nurse he knew in
Ethiopia in 1963:

"She was a beautiful woman who
was not only an Ethiopian nurse but a
nurse tutor. She had been to Sweden,
where she got advanced training to
teach other nurses. She was married
and had one child of her own. She left
the hospital when a milk company offered her three times what she was getting paid as a nurse.

"I saw her again in 1974. She had two
children and was still employed by the
milk company. I had become increasingly disturbed by what I had seen of
bottle feeding around the world, and I

Milk company advertisements.

tried to talk to her about it. She said she understood my point of view, but she wanted to make a good living. Her defense was that she did not advise people to stop breast feeding; she simply gave them information if they 'couldn't breast feed.' Besides, people were giving up breast feeding anyway, so at least she would supply them with a wholesome product and instructions."

MAKE YOUR BABY WHITE

Mary Lee, a housewife in Malaysia, wrote this letter: "On 23rd August, 1976, I had an interview with a Bristol-Myers mothercraft nurse by the name

of Mrs. Ho, who came to my house at my request. Mrs. Ho was wearing a white nurse's uniform and informed me she is a State Registered Nurse who trained here in University Hospital, Kuala Lumpur. On arrival Mrs. Ho presented me with a free sample tin of Enfamil powder infant formula without my asking for it. I told her I was thinking of weaning my baby from the breast, to which she said that Enfamil 'is just like breast milk.' She even pointed out on the sample tin the content 'choline,' which she assured me would make my baby's complexion beautiful and fair. In this community mothers feel it is very important to have fair skin. . . ."

Mary Lee happens to be a doctor's wife. She was not particularly impressed

by the white uniform, nor was she intimidated when the nurse worriedly weighed her baby. And she doesn't seem interested in making her baby more white with Enfamil. But what about a poor and unsophisticated woman?

Or what about a not-so-poor and -unsophisticated woman? During World War II, my mother, otherwise honest and patriotic, bought black market lamb chops. This was because her pediatrician prescribed an exact diet for each baby he treated. Four ounces of lamb chop, two ounces of cereal, three ounces of mashed banana. And this I was fed (and re-fed) despite the fact that I threw up three times a day for three years.

Before I was ready for the scraped lamb chops and mashed banana, I was bottle fed with a formula that entailed much measuring, sterilizing and breaking of bottles. Worst of all, the doctor set me on a four-hour feeding schedule. My parents later told me how I cried stubbornly, sometimes for two and a half hours straight, while they sat in agony waiting for the scientifically determined moment when they could give me the bottle that would bring immediate silent satisfaction.

How could they do it? Why didn't they just pick me up and feed me the way their mothers had done? Well, my father's mother was dead and, besides she had lost children while feeding the old way. And my mother's mother was an immigrant who spread newspaper on the floor after she washed it and kept live fish in the bathtub to make gefilte fish at Passover. I was going to get the best scientific chance in life.

And here's an even more sophisticated woman. When I was to deliver, I chose a hospital that allowed Lamaze and featured rooming-in. They brought me the baby after isolating her for hours, and I nursed contentedly for a couple of days. Then the nurse said "The baby is not gaining any weight. Not an ounce after any feeding."

"But she's sucking," I insisted, "and she's not crying. Let me keep trying."

Then the doctor came in: "Not a single ounce."

I agreed reluctantly to let them start her on formula while I gave it a few more tries. But I knew the bottle would curtail the baby's sucking, and there wouldn't be too much hope after that.

While I was giving it that one more try, a woman who was cleaning the floor

NESTLÉ MEN WATCH A BABY DIE

In an interview broadcast on West German radio stations in 1975, Dr Elizabeth Hillman, a pediatrician on the staff of the Kenyatta National Hospital in Nairobi, described the following incident:

"A short while ago . . . the Nestlé representatives came to visit us at the hospital to ask if we had any opinion about the War on Want publication that had been translated in Switzerland and retitled, 'Nestlé Kills Babies.' They really wanted us to say that Nestlé did not kill babies. We discussed this at length with them, and were not able to say, of course, that Nestlé either does kill or does not kill, statistically speaking. But, to illustrate the point, I mentioned to these two gentlemen that there was a child over in our emergency ward . . . who was very near death, because the mother was bottle feeding with the Nestlé's product [Lactogen, a milk preparation], and I asked whether they would like to see the baby.

"I took the two representatives over into our emergency ward, and, as we walked in the door, the baby collapsed and died. I had to leave these two non-medical gentlemen for a moment . . . and help with the resuscitation procedure. It was unsuccessful. And, after the baby was pronounced dead, we all watched the mother turn away from the dead baby and put the can of Nestlé's milk in her bag before she left the ward. . . . It was a vivid demonstration of what bottle feeding can do—because this mother was perfectly capable of breast feeding. The two men walked out of that room, very pale, shaken and quiet, and there was no need to say anything more . . . ."

ith no white uniform, said to me: "That baby's not gettin' a thing."

"What do you mean?"

"Look," she said, pinching me oughly. "It's all clogged up." She howed me how to put a hot washcloth n my breast and squeeze hard. After n hour of hard work, milk started to ow. Apparently the 24-hour delay fter the baby was born had caused the ilk to "back up." I should have nursed ght away or started squeezing the ilk out by hand. If it weren't for the eaning lady, I, like the woman in iagua, would certainly have found at under modern conditions I was one f the many who "couldn't nurse."

The same thing happens in the Third World. There, too, people are being cut ff from their past, moving away from heir families. The Green Revolution *Mother Jones*, August 1977) sends for- er subsistence farmers off the land nd into the *favelas*, barrios, and shanty owns in the city. There, with modern edical help, many will find breast feed- g "unsuccessful" or "inappropriate." ome can't nurse because they work or ope to work. Most, however, will hoose more freely not to nurse. What ould they do if the baby cried on the us? Some don't want to be bothered. ut most want to do what's best for eir babies. They want to give their hildren the start that will help them ut of the *favela* and into the modern orld. Like buying an encyclopedia.

In the scantiest slum store they will nd the powdered milk prominently splayed. (A chart in the February 977 issue of the Brazilian trade journal *Modern Supermarket* shows that baby ormulas have a profit margin of 72 per nt. This is three or four times higher an the profit margin for most other ems.) On the labels of these products e pictures of plump, smiling children. nd so, healthy mothers are feeding eir babies watered-down imported ilk in contaminated bottles in the hope e all share—to do the best by one's ildren.

THE NUNS GO TO COURT

The bottle baby problem has not ne unnoticed. Activists have been hting Nestlé in Europe for some time, d in the U.S. the Interfaith Center on orporate Responsibility (ICCR)— nnected with The National Council of hurches—has been publicizing the is- e widely, especially to church groups. erefore, when the Sisters of the Pre-

cious Blood, a Catholic teaching order based in Ohio, realized several years ago that they owned stock in Bristol-Myers, they quickly made the connection.

The Sisters tried first to speak to corporate executives about the problem. They found Bristol-Myers more difficult to deal with than the other milk companies, who were, if nothing else, at least willing to talk politely. Eventually, unable to get satisfaction, the sisters submitted a stockholders' resolution asking for information about Bristol-Myers' sales policy abroad. In a proxy statement urging defeat of that resolution, the company said, among other things: "Infant formula products are neither intended, nor promoted, for private purchase where chronic poverty or ignorance could lead to product misuse or harmful effects."

> "The small grave is decorated with a crushed milk can and a little baby bottle. Mothers put Lactogen cans and feeding bottles on their babies' graves, for they believe to the end that powdered milk and feeding bottles were the most valuable possessions their babies once had."

Now it can in some cases be a violation of Securities and Exchange Commission (SEC) regulations to make misstatements in proxy material. After further frustrating dealings with Bristol-Myers, the Sisters of the Precious Blood eventually filed a lawsuit against the company on these grounds. The strategy of the suit was to expose the lie. The Sisters attempted to show, first, that the company *did* promote its Enfamil formula to chronically poor people and, second, that the people who bought it were too poor or ignorant to use it safely.

As all TV viewers know, court testimony must always be based on firsthand knowledge. You can't submit sta-

tistical reports or get up and say "as everybody knows . . ." So, the Sisters and ICCR painstakingly collected testimony from 15 countries. There are affidavits that read something like: "I, Dr. So-and-So, living in the town of Such-and-Such, Venezuela, or Indonesia, or Guatemala, went to the following grocery stores in poor neighborhoods where I personally saw cans of Enfamil on sale." One exhibit was an Enfamil ad on the back page of the Barbados phone book, as personally observed by the witness, of course.

There are personal interviews, like these taken by Dr. Arthur L. Warner in Guatemala, where one in four slum mothers he talked to was bottle feeding:

"**Family B.** A young mother of two living in a shanty hillside settlement of Guatemala City decided to wean her baby at ten days, because a friend told her the milk was no good and too weak. She purchased Enfamil on the suggestion of a doctor in the public health 'well-baby' clinic. Her husband earns $3 a day (of which she spends about 75¢ for the infant's milk). They 've without safe water and beside an open sewer. Their shack has many openings for flies. They have no refrigeration. She is illiterate. She must haul water . . . from a community spigot.

"**Family C.** A mother of three, living in a shanty development in Guatemala City, decided to wean her baby at two months because the child wasn't gaining fast enough and was sickly. A clinic nurse had suggested her milk had gone bad. [Local] water, generally considered contaminated since the earthquake . . . Fuel costs are high. . . . Boiling water costs the family up to $5 a month."

A doctor in Jamaica reviews the cases of 37 patients referred to the Tropical Metabolism Research Unit for severe malnutrition. "Twenty-five received infant formula. Five died."

And so the Sisters of the Precious Blood compiled thousands of pages. In one way their brief is an impressive document, and in another it is almost pathetic—this patient piecing together of minute firsthand accounts to show the worldwide workings of imperialism. To show what everyone knows.

In May of this year the case was dismissed, though the Sisters are appealing. The decision, by Federal Judge Milton Pollack, though a little difficult to read, appears to say:

The shareholders' resolution was only a request and wouldn't be binding on the board of directors even if it had passed. Therefore, it just doesn't matter. The court doesn't have to consider whether the proxy material contained a misstatement or whether the affidavits submitted by the Sisters are true, because no irreparable harm was done to any shareholder.

There is no law preventing corporations from doing irreparable harm to Third World babies.

BOTTLE ON THE GRAVE

Leah Margulies, small, lively and radical, heads the project on bottle feeding for the Interfaith Center on Corporate Responsibility. "I was hired with the general assignment to develop the relationship between multinational corporations and world hunger—agribusiness, cash cropping, you know. But it is very difficult to make it graphic that the world is starving, not because of drought, or floods, but because of economic dependency."

"So you decided to use the baby bottle case as an example?" I suggested.

"I didn't really decide. It grew up around us," Margulies said. "I did extensive research on multinationals in the early '70s. I was anxious to show the effects of the *normal* operations of capitalism, not the big scandals or fuck-ups. So I read *Fortune, Harvard Business Review, Forbes,* annual reports, speeches by corporate executives.

"And I developed my thoughts about economic dependency. The corporations operate in the Third World in a way that creates overall economic dependency as horrifying, impoverishing and unnatural as the dependency of a healthy mother on expensive powdered milk. The import of unnecessary powdered milk—forget Coca-Cola—now takes about one *billion* dollars a year from the Third World.

"But I tell you the truth, even after documenting the entire lawsuit—the facts, the figures, the affidavits—sometimes I still don't believe myself. I don't believe the world could be starving, that babies could be sick and dying just for a little profit.

"Like you remember the story about the graves in Zambia?"

I remembered it well. The film *Bottle Babies,* used widely by the church groups, ends with a shot of a child's grave near Lusaka, Zambia. The small grave is decorated with a crushed milk can and a little baby bottle. The narrator says, "Mothers put empty Nes-

A Nestlé salesperson shows his wares to East African mothers.

tlé's Lactogen cans and feeding bottles on their dead babies' graves, for they believe to the end that powdered milk and feeding bottles were the most valuable possessions their babies once had."

"Well, last week," Margulies continued, "I happened to see the film *Last Grave at Dimbaza.* The film is about apartheid, not about bottle feeding. No mention was made of that. But it shows the poverty and the horrible infant mortality. The film ends with a shot of those infant graves. My heart jumped. There —you could make it out if you knew what it was—there was that little can of powdered milk.

"But still, when you immerse yourself back in our U.S. reality once again, you don't believe it. For instance, the president of American Home Products is a kindly, charming man. I go in there with a room full of church people. We are all middle class. And this lovely gentleman says, 'Do you believe we would deliberately harm babies?' "

I questioned Margulies about the stockholders' approach. Did it make sense to ask corporations on their own to stop selling? Or to limit their market to the tiny number of Third World mothers (certainly under five per cent) who really can't nurse? She felt that the educational effect on the participating religious groups made it worthwhile. Also, the publicity can't hurt. And pressure here creates the climate for real

regulation in the Third World. So fa though, the countries attempting to reg ulate milk companies are few. I Guinea-Bissau baby formula is avai able only by prescription. Papua Ne Guinea is cracking down on advertis ments. In Jamaica, mothercraft perso nel are forbidden to enter the hospital though it seems that some still do. An in any case, they are active in all th slums. Malaysia and Guyana, amon other countries, have launched nation, breast-feeding campaigns. But of cours their resources are limited compare to milk company advertising budgets.

"I HAVE AN APPOINTMENT"

Like Margulies, I, too, found myse suffering bouts of doubt. Infants cr ing from hunger when there is all th milk they need? Maybe this is just radical "cause." Something blown u out of proportion.

I must check it out, I felt, someplac more neutral and scientific. . . .

At the U.N. I spoke first to Dr. Jacc Schatan of the Protein Advisory Grou He is a mild, thin man, very reasonab sounding, but sad. He is Chilean.

"What is the scope of this bottl feeding problem? Is it really so dange ous?"

"Everywhere there is a marked tren of decline of breast feeding." Dr. Sch tan speaks in U.N. Reportese, thoug his gestures show concern. "It is a tren

ccompanying urbanization. I could not
ell you the exact percentages for each
ountry, but we can easily estimate the
ost to the developing nations in the
illions."

"Billions?" I asked. (He has an accent,
nd he mumbles.) "Billions with a *B*?"

"With a B."

"Do you think there could be legis-
ation restricting the companies?"

"The Protein Advisory Group pro-
ides information from scientists to the
J.N. system, not to countries. However,
would say you need legislation not in
elation to sale, but legislation facilitat-
ng breast feeding for urban women. If
  mother works eight hours, there
hould be a time and place to nurse at
ork. This is not done except in a few
f the ... uh ..." (The pause is cautious,
ainful; finally, he gives up and uses the
ord.) ". . . socialist countries. And of
ourse education. There must be an
ducational campaign."

Next I went to UNICEF, where I
poke to L. J. Tepley, senior nutritionist.

"How did the question of bottle feed-
ng first come to your attention?" I
sked.

"And just how could I be concerned
vith children's nutrition without its
oming to my attention?" (Tepley, a
tocky American, is as bluff and direct
s Schatan is cautious.)

"Is it really as dangerous as some
hink?" I asked.

"Does any of those papers . . ." (He
ointed to a bundle of charts, reports
nd articles I had been collecting all
veek and was now spilling on his office
oor. They were from the Columbia
Medical School, Mount Sinai Hospital,
he U.N., the Consumer's Union, the
Brookings Institute, the ICCR, the milk
ompanies themselves.) "Does *any* of
nem say bottle milk is *good* for poor
eople? Here." (He handed me an
normous envelope for all my papers.)
"We know the effects. They are awful.
No one doubts it."

"Then why is it spreading?" I asked.

"The causes are two. Ignorance and
money. Not necessarily in that order."

"What can be done?" I asked. "Can
he milk companies be regulated?"

"I have to go," said Mr. Tepley. (I
ad dropped in on him unannounced
round lunch time.) "I have an appoint-
ent."

AND IN NEW YORK ...

A couple of years ago, the chief of the
New York City Health and Hospitals
Corporation announced proudly a
money-saving contract with Ross Laboratories, the Abbott subsidiary that
makes infant formula. Till then the city
hospitals had been spending some
$300,000 a year on Similac. But Ross
was going to slash next year's price to
less than $100,000, and in the third year
of the contract the hospitals would be
getting all the Similac they could use for
free.

I decided to take a look around Lin-
coln Hospital in the Bronx. When I got
to the maternity ward, it was feeding
time. The sign in front of the swinging
doors said, "No entry. Mothers with
babies." While I waited, an orderly
wheeled in a cart loaded with cases of
Similac. Here they use the more expensive pre-mixed formula in individual
disposable nursing bottles.

After a while I went down to the pre-
natal clinic. I asked the pregnant women,
all black or Puerto Rican, whether they
were going to breast feed or bottle feed.
The answers were unanimous.

"What if I'm on the bus when the baby
gets hungry?"

"If you're in the house with just your
husband, okay. But if there are friends
or family, then you have to go into the
other room."

"I eat a lot of junk. The baby would
drain me."

"My milk wasn't good enough for my
first one."

"What if you're out in the street? You
can't just whip it out!"

In English, Spanish and sign language, the response was clear. Total
repugnance at the idea of breast feeding.

I asked whether the nurses or doctors
had said anything about breast feeding.

"They said Similac was just as good."

"They said you have to eat a certain
diet, and I couldn't eat all those special
vegetables."

"They give you pamphlets that say
you should choose yourself."

The pamphlets handed out at the pre-
natal clinic are published by Carnation.
The more detailed one, "You and Your
Contented Baby," does indeed admit
that "the breast-fed baby seems to have
fewer digestive upsets than the bottle-
fed baby." However, the seven-step instructions for breast feeding include language like "compress the nipple and the
brown tissue horizontally," along with
medical illustrations of areola and si-
nuses and indecipherable diagrams labeled "correct and incorrect positions
for baby's jaw." This makes it all seem
much more complicated than simply
heating up a formula. Not to mention
the fact that the picture of Carnation
milk is in color and labeled "For over
35 years, millions of babies have thrived
on Carnation Evaporated Milk formulas." A second, simpler pamphlet says
nothing at all about the advantages of
breast feeding.

Pamphlets notwithstanding, it is the
official policy of the pre-natal clinic that
breast feeding is best. The intake nurse
told me that she is supposed to mention
it to each mother. "But I know that
they are going to say 'Echh, I can't do
that.' And then there is a language barrier. I can give directions in Spanish,
but I cannot talk about personal things.
I do mention it, though, when I think
they may be interested. And if one
woman a week says 'Yes, I'd like to try,'
then I feel very rewarded."

Back up in the maternity ward, the
babies had been put away. After an initial period of isolation, they are brought
to the mothers every four hours, along
with the bottles of Similac.

I stood with a group of new mothers
in front of the nursery window talking
about breast feeding, while we watched
the nurse inside feed a newborn from a
Similac bottle.

I asked the women if they knew what
the formula would cost.

A couple said, "I have no idea." Some
gave me a figure: "$5.50 a case," "$1.50
for the quart can of concentrate." One
lady said, "I don't know what it will cost
me because I don't know if they're giving mine Similac or Carnation." Apparently she was under the impression
that she would have to continue to use
whatever the hospital started the baby
with.

But the majority of mothers said, "I
won't have to pay for it because I'm on
this program." The program was WIC
(Women Infant Care), a federal program
offering health care to mothers and well
infants. One of the inducements to remain with the program is a monthly

supply of baby products, including bottle formula.

"WILL YOU MAKE A PROFIT?"

"I called Bristol-Myers," I said to
Leah Margulies.

"Yeah?"

"And they put me on to Ed Simon in
the P.R. office."

"Oh, yeah?"

"I asked him if any of your charges had affected their sales promotions abroad."

"What'd he say?"

"First, he said I was obviously prejudiced because the question implied that the charges were true. Second, he said, 'While not acknowledging any of the claims, it is safe to say we've made every attempt to strengthen our control over the sale of infant formula.'

"And then he started to read me all the clauses from their guidelines:

'Detailed information on infant formula . . . will be directed only to physicians and medical personnel. . . .

'Mothercraft nurses will perform in a manner comparable to government-sponsored public-health nurses, with their primary concern the assistance of mothers in the proper care and feeding of their infants, whether breast or formula fed. . . .'

"I was busy scribbling, trying to get it all down as fast as I could. Finally, I said, 'With all those restrictions, do you sell more or less Enfamil?' "

"What did he say?"

"He said they couldn't discuss information regarding the sale of specific products."

"One of the Sisters of Mercy made the same point during our meeting with Abbott in Chicago," said Margulies. "They were being very agreeable about modifying their sales techniques. 'Use of mass media will be dropped . . . no radio, billboards . . .'

"Well, as we were about to leave, one of the Sisters said, 'Tell me, if you stop selling to people who are too poor to use the product safely, will you still make a profit?'

"There was absolute silence. It must have been a full minute.

"Finally one of the corporate executives picked it up and said:

" 'That is the crux of the problem.' ▪

Discussion

1. According to the author why are new mothers not breast-feeding their babies?

2. How do the companies get women to bottle-feed their babies?

3. Why do the milk companies try to market their products in the "Third World" when it is clear these people cannot afford the products?

4. "Bottle Babies" is an example of the devastating effects ads can have. In defending the role of advertising, ad agencies say that they are informing people about the product — not that they are trying to get people to buy something regardless of the consequences. What do you think?

5. What would you say the needs were of people in the "Third World"? Are they being met? Why or why not? (If you have kept a log book, remember to record the ideas of the group.)

Statement from the President of Nestlé (Canada) Ltd.

Since the *Mother Jones* article on Bottle Babies was written, a great deal more has happened in connection with the infant formula debate. Among other things, an international meeting sponsored by the World Health Organisation (WHO) and UNICEF deplored the use of advertising in promoting infant formula, and made a series of recommendations. Also, an international boycott of Nestle's products has had increasing success. There has been a corresponding increase in the public relations activities of Nestle's. As the "information war" escalates, so do the techniques of persuasion.

Reprinted here is a statement by Nestle's in which its President declares that "In the spirit of the WHO/UNICEF meeting, Nestle intends to move forward in every possible way to continue to play a constructive role in the battle against infant malnutrition world-wide." . . .

From: Nestle (Canada) Ltd.   October 1979
         1185 Eglington Avenue East
         Don Mills, Ontario
         M3C 3C7

Ref: Raymond Peterson (416) 429-4411

STATEMENT FROM M.E. HANSEN, PRESIDENT

NESTLE (CANADA) LTD.

"I am pleased to announce that the parent Nestle company in

Switzerland has endorsed the statement issued October 12th by the World

Health Organization and UNICEF on the marketing and distribution of

infant food products.

The statement was issued by WHO/UNICEF following a four day meeting

in Geneva in which 150 representatives from industry, governments, the

medical profession, and consumer groups participated. A major element of

the statement was a recommended ban of all sales promotion and promotional

advertising to the public of breastmilk substitute and supplement products.

Nestle terminated consumer advertising and direct consumer promotion of

such products in July, 1978.

The WHO/UNICEF statement further announced the organization of a

process by which WHO/UNICEF will develop an international code of marketing which will also serve as a model for governments to adopt. Nestle has already encouraged and co-operated in the formation of codes of conduct in several countries and will continue to do so.

In announcing Nestle's support of the WHO/UNICEF statement, I would like to point out that Nestle participated in the Geneva meeting together with other members of the International Council of Infant Food Industries (ICIFI), whose members account for 85 per cent of the sales of baby foods in the Third World. ICIFI's president, Ian Barter, described the Geneva meeting as 'a constructive and important landmark in the battle against malnutrition'. He also pledged the industry's determination to cooperate with WHO in establishing the more detailed international code of conduct.

The Nestle parent company in Switzerland was proud to have participated in the Geneva meeting, which brought together all interested parties in a constructive spirit to reach agreement on ways to improve the health and nutrition of infants and children throughout the world.

Our company associates itself completely with the position taken by ICIFI on behalf of all members and supports wholeheartedly the final statement issued by WHO/UNICEF. Current Nestele policies are totally consistent with these recommendations. Where there may be a need for further clarification, the company intends to adopt the most stringent measures to avoid any practice that could be interpreted as inconsistent.

The Geneva meeting and the agreement reached as a result of it are seen as the most important and most positive developments to date on the complex issue of infant nutrition. In the spirit of the WHO/UNICEF meeting, Nestle intends to move forward in every possible way to continue to play a constructive role in the battle against infant malnutrition world-wide." ■

Here is the response to the preceding Nestle's statement, made by the Interfaith Centre on Corporate Responsibility (ICCR). It contrasts Nestle's interpretation of those recommendations with the recommendations themselves . . . .

INTERFAITH CENTER ON CORPORATE RESPONSIBILITY

A Sponsored Related Movement of the National Council of Churches
475 Riverside Drive   •   Room 566   •   New York, NY 10027 (212) 870-2293

WHY THE NESTLE BOYCOTT MUST CONTINUE

The Nestle Company is mounting a massive public relations campaign aimed at stopping the increasingly successful Nestle boycott. They are attempting to convert into a public relations victory the actual setback they suffered at the recent WHO/UNICEF meeting on Infant and Young Child Feeding in Geneva. Nestle contends that their marketing practices are in agreement with the recommendations issued by the WHO/UNICEF meeting, thus making the boycott unnecessary. The truth is, however, their marketing practices remain inconsistent with the letter and spirit of the WHO/UNICEF recommendations. The boycott must not only continue, but it must intensify in order to preserve the important gains made at the meeting. Only sustained pressure can prevent Nestle and the other infant formula companies from making " interpretations of convenience" that distort the spirit of the meeting, ie. the overwhelming consensus among non-industry participants on the need for strict controls on industry activities.

The WHO/UNICEF recommendations clearly call for far-reaching restrictions of marketing and promotion of infant formula. WHO Director General, Dr. Halfdan Mahler said that the industry was "morally obliged" to change these practices and added, "There is no way industry can get away with what they've been doing in the past and say they have our blessing." Yet Nestle Managing Director, Arthur Furer disagreed that changes were required in a newspaper interview. "We do not feel restricted in any way in our commercial activities by the WHO recommendations. On the contrary, the gradual changes Nestle has introduced in the past five years are completely in line with the recommendations."(Interview with Arthur Furer, <u>Tages Anzeiger</u>, an important Swiss-German newspaper, October 19, 1979.)

Nestles is using their distorted interpretations of the recommendations to justify precisely the activities that the meeting sought to ban. The following comparisons of the WHO/UNICEF Recommendations with the Nestle interpretation reveal Nestles' strategy to disguise promotion as education or charity.

On Advertising

WHO Recommendation: "There should be <u>no</u> sales promotion, including promotional advertising to the public of products to be used as breastmilk substitutes or bottlefed supplements and feeding bottles." (emphasis added).

Nestle Interpretation: "Advertising of an educational nature, which is regarded as beneficial by the state, is allowed. This would include educational and informative posters." (Furer, <u>Ibid</u>.)

On Free Samples

WHO Recommendation: "Advertising or promotional distribution of free samples of breastmilk substitutes through health service channels <u>should not be allowed.</u> Artificial feeding <u>should not</u> be openly demonstrated in health facilities." (emphasis added)

Nestle Interpretation: "Furthermore, we would agree to a more selective delivery of samples to the clinics and hope that WHO and UNICEF would instigate precise sets of rules about this within the relevant international code. Indeed it must not be overlooked that the samples are in many cases a help to clinics in developing countries who do not have extra funds at their disposal." (Furer, <u>Ibid</u>)

On Company Personnel

WHO Recommendation: "<u>No</u> personnel paid by companies producing or selling breast-milk substitutes should be allowed to work in the health care system, even if they are assigned more general responsibilities that do not directly include the promotion of formulas, in order to avoid the risk of <u>conflict of interest.</u>" (emphasis added)

Nestle Interpretation: "Each individual state must decide if it wants to call on people who are employed by the baby food industry and at the same time have a diploma in child care, to help impart information which will benefit mothers... It is simply unjust to condemn being involved in this instructive action...because the state doesn't have at its disposal the necessary personnel and they have

previously been pleased to have been able to draw on the producers of baby foods to work with them." (Furer, <u>Ibid</u>.)

Nestle's interpretations do not accurately reflect the position of
WHO/UNICEF which made their official position clear in their Background Paper
released before the meeting. The Background Paper was prepared by independent
scientists on the basis of recent research and extensive field experience. Ther
recommendations reflect an objective assessment of what is needed to protect babies.
The meeting's recommendations, on the other hand, represent the result of a
tough negotiation-bargaining process where industry stymied the desire of most
of the meeting's participants to enact more forceful steps. In other words, the
final recommendations, rather than representing a consensus of the meeting, actually
represent the most that concerned national governments, UN agencies, experts, and
the nongovernmental organizations could successfully advocate over the vigorous
opposition of the industry.

If the Background Paper's explicit recommendations had been adopted and
enforced, the industry would have been compelled to make major changes in its
practices. So industry lobbied intensely against them before and during the
meeting. Ian Barter, President of ICIFI (the industry trade association of which
Nestle is a member) a ttacked the Background Paper in the press as "unscientific
and unworthy of that name." ICIFI placed a full page ad in the <u>International Herald
Tribune</u> on the first day of the meeting to advertise its "public relations concept"
of "shared responsibility" — which means that industry wants as much right to
determine infant feeding practices as governments and health workers. ICIFI
hired its own scientists to prepare an industry critique of the Background Paper,
attacking WHO/UNICEF's conclusions.

During the meeting, industry refused to follow the official agenda and
repeatedly sought to substitute their own versions. At one point they tried to
"blackmail" the meeting by threatening to walk out. Industry set up a lavish
"hospitality suite" and wined and dined delegates.

   The area of medical promotion provides an example of how industry distorted
what WHO/UNICEF wanted to accomplish. The WHO/UNICEF Background Paper confined
the industry information to ethical and factual information only for "consideration
of product composition." The final recommendations lack this specificity --
the result of industry lobbying against such precision. Now Nestle's Managing
Director Arthur Furer claims that "Manufacturers must retain the right to inform
doctors and paramedical personnel about the preparation and use of such products."
This difference is substantial. "Product composition" restricts information to
that which helps health workers choose the right formula for a particular patient,
while Furer's definition justifies the extensive medical promotion that Nestle has
been doing for decades.

The Chairperson of the meeting, Dr. Fred Sai (Ghana), made it clear that
"what took place was a <u>first step</u> for WHO/UNICEF to go ahead with a machinery
for working out, based on these considerations, an appropriate code (of·conduct for
the baby foods industry) and machinery of enforcement." (emphasis added). The
real work of the coming months will be to translate these general principles into
concrete codes and models of national legislation.

Continued pressure on the industry is absolutely crucial in this phase of code
making. WHO/UNICEF need our help to strengthen their hand in dealing with the
industry so that the WHO/UNICEF official position -- so strongly expressed in the
Background Paper — will prevail.

Nestle counter-strategy is to remain as vague as possible for as long as
possible. For example, after protesting self-righteously that they will
always sit down with their critics, Nestle just turned down (October 19, 1979)
a formal request by INFACT and 40 national organizations endorsing the boycott
to identify the differences that remain between them. Nestle refused to meet with th
boycotters because they know that they would have to explain precisely what changes
they will be making. This would thwart their public relations strategy of pretendin
follow the WHO/UNICEF recommendations, while making "interpretations of convenience."

Nestle, in fact, has not met any of the boycott's four specific demands.
While they have suspended mass media advertising, other forms of direct consumer
promotion continue, as do free samples, "milk nurses", and intense medical promotion. Experience demonstrates that Nestle has not followed even its own weak
self-regulatory codes.

Only sustained pressure can prevent backsliding, which will result in weak
codes and more sick babies. We have come so far and accomplished so much; to
stop the boycott at this critical moment would jeopardize the progress we have
made to date. As WHO Deputy Director General Dr. T.A. Lambo asked on the opening
session of the meeting: "Are we really ready to give up something to help satisfy
the unmet needs of hundreds of millions of infants, young children, mothers, and
families in the world?" Responsible boycotting is needed to finally eliminate
irresponsible promotion. ■

Discussion/research

1. What is Nestle's public position on infant
formula feeding?

2. What is the Interfaith Centre's position?

3. What does the ICCR mean by "interpretations of convenience"?

4. Prepare a research paper on the Bottle
Babies issue.

Finally, we include for your examination an article which appeared in *Fortune* magazine. Amongst both the promoters and critics of infant formula feeding, there are many who would agree that the Bottle Baby issue is only a symptom of a larger problem . . . This article describes the major critics of corporations' policies as being "The Corporation Haters".

(*Fortune* carries articles on many aspects of the business world, and is noted for its coverage of "Fortune's 500" most powerful businesses. This article appeared in the 16 June 1980 issue of *Fortune*.)

The Corporation Haters

by HERMAN NICKEL

The fizzling of Ralph Nader's "Big Business Day" gives corporate America little cause for self-congratulation. Americans may be getting a bit bored with the Savonarola of the consumer society, but most of them don't think much of corporations either. As late as 1968, when a Yankelovich survey asked whether business strikes a fair balance between profits and the public interest, 70% answered yes. By last year, the yes vote was down to a mere 19%.

How much of this decline can be credited to Nader and other anti-corporate crusaders is impossible to measure, but they have certainly done their best. According to the strident placards they have raised in the public arena, American business is morally bankrupt. The indictment reads this way:

U.S. corporations thrive on racist suppression in South Africa and profit from starvation wages in the Caribbean and parts of Asia. Hand in glove with corrupt and repressive governments in Central America, giants of U.S. agribusiness like Castle & Cooke and United Brands try to perpetuate the pattern of dependent plantation economies, blocking the emergence of self-reliant, truly independent nations. At home and abroad, huge conglomerates variously rape and poison Mother Earth, whether through strip-mining, herbicides, or pollution. Once their old mills and factories start losing money, runaway employers leave behind dying communities, like so much industrial waste. Life itself is threatened by the reckless construction and operation of nuclear power plants. Even innocent children are not safe from the greedy corporate reach. Seductive TV commercials lure them to nutritionally worthless junk foods. Worse yet, by pushing infant formula on Third World mothers who can neither afford it in sufficient amounts nor prepare it properly, the companies are responsible for the disastrous consequences of a significant falloff in breast-feeding. "Ten million Third World babies are starving because of the heartless, money-hungry activities of powerful multinational companies," a fund-raising letter of the Infant Formula Action Coalition (INFACT) charged last year.

The common theme is plain enough for even the slowest learner: in the capitalist economic system, profits and social responsibility simply do not mix.

If all this sounds like a replay of the New Left of the protesting Sixties, in many ways it is. The spirit lives on in segments of the environmental and antinuclear movements, in Barry Commoner's Citizens party, in the pages of *Mother Jones*, the counterculture's bright newsmagazine, and in the work of such radical think tanks as the Washington-based Institute for Policy Studies.

The movement gets religion

Surprisingly, however, the real clearinghouse of the anti-corporate campaign today is at 475 Riverside Drive in Manhattan, where on ground donated by the Rockefellers sits the gray office block that houses the National Council of Churches and its ecumenical affiliate, the Interfaith

102

Center on Corporate Responsibility (see box, page 128). On first impression, the gap between the moderate-conservative mood of mainstream churchgoers and the militant zeal of the church functionaries on Riverside Drive is astonishing. But the confluence of radical Christian and radical Marxist thinking has been under way for some time without arousing much opposition from individual congregations. On the Protestant side, this new orientation began with a generalized sympathy toward the economic plight of the Third World and took a specifically anti-business direction in the World Council of Churches' five-year-old campaign against the supposed depredations of the multinationals. On the Catholic side, the activating influence has been the "liberation theology" emanating from radical priests in Latin America. The WCC Program on Transnationals proclaims that to achieve the new Just, Participatory, and Sustainable Society, dubbed JPSS, "the basic organizing principle is struggle." The invitation to a "Christian-Marxist Dialogue" sponsored by the Maryknoll Mission Institute last summer explained that "the inherent evils of gross capitalism and the inadequacies of our democratic system at this time have brought the social teachings of the Church in direct relation to the dynamics of Marxian thought."

Theologian Michael Novak, who has been developing a spiritual rationale for capitalism (see page 132), says that the fact that the National Council of Churches gave its amen to the World Council program signals a reversion of American Protestant thinking from the pragmatic liberalism of Reinhold Niebuhr to a Christian social utopianism. Because Niebuhr understood the fundamental difference between "moral man and immoral society," he had no illusions about socialist panaceas. This, as John C. Raines observed in *Christianity and Crisis*, made Niebuhr a prime target for the New Left, which saw his theology as a "buttress to the liberal establishment."

The Pope takes a stand

Today the most powerful warnings against seeking salvation through radical social and economic change are coming from Pope John Paul II, and they are drawing similar fire. "This idea of Christ as a political figure, a revolutionary, as the subversive man from Nazareth, does not tally with the Church's catechesis," he told the General Assembly of Latin American Bishops in Puebla, Mexico, last year.

The new ideological compatibility between church activists and the New Left has led quite naturally to cooperation on a practical level as well. For student radicals of the 1960's, one way to turn the "struggle" into a steady job is to join the issues staff of organizations like the Interfaith Center on Corporate Responsibility, where they have come to occupy some key positions and coordinate and orchestrate those shareholders' resolutions that almost every chief executive of a large American corporation is familiar with by now. To generalize, the resolutions seem designed less to uplift the world's less fortunate people than to indict the business establishment.

Much of the data on which the church activists rely are supplied by radical research organizations. For South African issues, the Institute for Policy Studies and the American Committee on Africa provide properly revolutionary analyses. Another important research resource is the unabashedly pro-Castro North American Congress on Latin America in New York. One NACLA report on Guatemala, under the headline "A Vanishing Breed," featured the photographs of prominent Guatemalans. Ominously pointing at them from the lower left corner of the page is a revolver. But the publication of this thinly veiled hit list has not kept NACLA from receiving church funds for its studies. "Two and two makes four, no matter who says it," shrugs the Reverend Howard Schomer, world-issues secretary of the United Church Board for World Ministries. For the radicals, the alliance with church groups has many other tangible advantages. It provides a way of conducting political programs behind the shield of tax exemption, and access to a large organizational network. The church activists can gather information from missionaries throughout the world and disseminate propaganda to the memberships of participating churches. Above all, the religious connection provides respectability and legitimacy. What better way to challenge the existing system than to brand it as an offense to the will of God?

In order to attract broad support, the church activists have chosen to present business-related issues as morally clear-cut and simple—when in fact they are usually complex, morally ambiguous, and involve difficult policy trade-offs. How moral, for example, is the pursuit of a boycott strategy that might help bring about an apocalyptic racial war of liberation in South Africa? A good many black South Africans, who would not be privileged to follow this exciting but bloody drama from comfortable observation posts in the U.S., say that it is neither moral nor wise. Even though the people working on Castle & Cooke's banana plantations in Central America earn far less than the U.S. minimum wage, would they be better off if the company decided to move elsewhere? Is opposition to nuclear power in the U.S. really the only possible moral position when the alternative is more death and disease from the mining and burning of fossil fuels and greater energy problems for the Third World?   *SOLAR?*

But propagandists know that complexity and ambiguity actually feed the demand for simple answers, whether the issue is strip-mining, South Africa, or nuclear power. The infant-formula issue provides perhaps the best example of all as to how this process works.

Why mothers stop nursing

No one questions that marketing of infant formula in the Third World can pose serious problems. Everyone, including the infant-formula industry, agrees that breast-feeding provides the best and cheapest nutrition for babies. Because mothers who are lactating are less likely to conceive, breast-feeding also helps to space out births. Therefore, marketing practices should not induce mothers who otherwise would be willing and able to breast-feed to switch to the bottle.

But feeding patterns are intertwined with social change. This was the experience in the West, where the industrial revolution went step by step with declines in breast-feeding, long before commercial infant formula became available. In the least developed parts of the Third World, breast-feeding still prevails. But an overworked and poorly fed mother who is rearing many children in an urban slum without the help and support of the traditional extended family is often unable to continue producing enough milk to nourish her baby. At that point the question is not whether supplementary foods are needed, but which supplementary foods to use. The superiority of infant formula over all infant foods other than breast milk is beyond dispute. Some substitutes, such as skim milk, lack sufficient fat and can cause dangerous dehydration.

In the terrible distortions of the anti-corporate propaganda, however, the big food and pharmaceutical companies are deliberately "hooking" Third World mothers on formula by giving free samples to doctors and hospitals. The mothers stop lactating but cannot long afford a product that costs 50 cents for a day's ration. The charge that companies are destroying the precious bond between the breast-feeding mother and her baby makes for powerful propaganda. As Mark Ritchie, all-round San Francisco activist, has put it, "It links the capitalist system —and the way it organizes our lives—to people's very personal experience."

Every protest movement needs its special villain, and in Nestlé S.A.—which has about a third of the Third World market for infant formula—the activists found an unlikely but richly rewarding target. Proud of its 100 years in the service of wholesome nutrition, the prim Swiss food giant (1979 sales: $12 billion) was simply not accustomed to having its rectitude challenged. When Senator Edward Kennedy's subcommittee on health scheduled hearings on the issue in 1978, Nestlé's world headquarters in Vevey saw them as an improper attempt to hold foreign companies to account for their activities outside the U.S. Though its American managers in White Plains, New York, were well briefed on the subject, Nestlé sent an executive from Brazil, Oswaldo Ballarin, who opened with the charge that the whole issue was really "an indirect attack on the free world's economic system." Kennedy weighed in with heavy sarcasm, and the hapless Ballarin was all but laughed out of the room.

Even with such unwitting assistance from Nestlé, the movement has had to overcome a glaring weakness in its case: the virtual absence of reliable data to uphold the basic premise that promoting infant formula by giving away free samples is a significant factor behind declines in breast-feeding. The use of infant formula apparently increased sharply in the Soviet Union, where there is no promotion, but breast-feeding has staged a strong resurgence in the U.S., where baby formula is heavily promoted. Nor is there any clear correlation between the feeding patterns of Third World countries and infant mortality and morbidity. Infant death rates are generally highest in backward rural areas, where the benefits of science—including infant formula—haven't yet penetrated. Breast-feeding has dropped dramatically in Singapore—and infant mortality has declined to a rate lower than in the U.S.

It may well be that some Third World doctors are handing out samples too freely. But even if they and their patients were grossly irresponsible—and this is not a charge that the church activists care to make in plain language—the death toll could be no more than a minuscule fraction of the ten million commonly alleged.

Only about six million Third World babies drink infant formula, and the benefits easily outweigh the risks.

Bill Moyers was shocked

But when it comes to propaganda, fact matters less than emotion. Here the movement can rely on three powerful films. "Bottle Babies," produced by West German filmmaker Peter Krieg in Kenya in 1975, was later condemned as "emotional, biased, and exaggerated" by Dr. Nimros O. Bwibo, a Nairobi pediatrician who appeared in it. But it is highly effective as an organizing tool. "Into the Mouths of Babes," a CBS Reports production with Bill Moyers, is of the same genre and last year won an award from the American

Film Festival. Finally, there is "Guess Who Is Coming to Breakfast," produced by the Packard Manse Media Project on grants from the National Council of Churches and others. What these films have in common is plenty of heartrending footage of malnourished babies and distraught mothers, who testify that they had become dependent on a product they couldn't afford.

The mind-set created in this way is implacably confrontational. As Professor Luther Gerlach, a University of Minnesota anthropologist who has been studying the movement, points out, this serves a vital "energizing" function. Companies that reciprocate the hostility may unwittingly strengthen their opponents.

A Guide to the Anti-Corporate Network

Though the anti-corporate movement lacks centralized organization, it functions effectively as a loose coalition. At the local level, activists for one cause often help out campaigners for another. A principal coordinator is the New York-based Interfaith Center on Corporate Responsibility, an ecumenical affiliate of the National Council of Churches in which 17 Protestant denominations and 170 Catholic orders and dioceses participate.

A companion organization is Clergy and Laity Concerned, which began as an antiwar group but dedicated itself to "join those who are angry and hate the corporate power which the U.S. presently represents." The National Council of Churches also helps to fund the Washington Office on Africa and the Washington Office on Latin America, which lobby for tighter controls over the activities of American multinationals.

The pro-Castro North American Congress on Latin America in New York also has churchly ties. Created after the U.S. intervention in the Dominican Republic, it found its first home at Interchurch Center in 1966; it has played a leading role in the campaign against Castle & Cooke, and one of its staffers went on to found a separate source of anti-corporate intelligence, the "Corporate Data Exchange."

The Washington-based Institute for Policy Studies is to the anti-corpo-rate movement what the Rand Corp. is to the government. Its co-founder and senior fellow, Richard Barnet, is not only a revisionist analyst of the Cold War, but also author of *Global Reach*, a highly critical text on multinationals. The anti-corporate network even has an advertising agency, the Public Media Center in San Francisco, which produces polished copy for the various causes.

In adapting the system's own tools to their ends, the activists have discovered the interlocking directorate. Timothy Smith, the 37-year-old director of the Interfaith Center, recently served on Nader's Big Business Day advisory board. Many of the groups are backing the Infant Formula Action Coalition in their boycott of Nestlé.

Money for these activities has come from a variety of family foundations, notably the Samuel Rubin Foundation. Its benefactor was chairman of Faberge, and his daughter, Cora Weiss, was a prominent crusader against the Vietnam war. More important is the contribution that has come from millions of unsuspecting churchgoers, and indeed from every American taxpayer. Practically all the movement's organizations are tax-exempt, either as church groups or because the Internal Revenue Service has accepted their assurances that they are primarily "educational" organizations.

LaDonna Harris, a Comanche activist and Barry Commoner's running mate on the Citizens party ticket, delivered the opening pep talk to about 100 delegates attending the annual conference of the Infant Formula Action Coalition in Washington last March. One of the conference themes was that the promotion of infant formula should be banned not only in the Third World but among America's poor, including reservation Indians.

Abbott Labs turns the other cheek

One company that didn't fall into this trap is the Ross Laboratories division of Abbott Labs, which fights with Bristol-Myers, Wyeth, and several other companies for the non-Nestlé portion of the Third World market for baby formula. Working with Sister Marilyn Uline of the Adrian Dominicans, who represented the Illinois Committee for Responsible Investment, Ross's President (now chairman) David Cox introduced a number of new precautions against marketing abuses, including new labels, new mailings to physicians, and new warnings to retailers.

Sister Uline began the dialogue with a conviction, which she still holds, that a willingness to move toward confrontation is necessary to make corporations listen. But as the dialogue continued, she was "a little amazed," as she puts it, that others in the movement seemed more interested in "baiting" the Ross people than listening to what they had to say. She was particularly taken aback by an encounter with Leah Margulies, the brash and aggressive director of the infant-formula campaign at the Interfaith Center for Corporate Responsibility.

An English major out of Boston University, Margulies had done some reading on multinationals while working at the Economic Growth Center in New Haven and playing flute and bass guitar for the New Haven Women's Liberation Rock Band. The reading "blew my mind," Margulies says, and in 1974, though an atheist herself, she landed a job with the Interfaith Center to work on multinational issues.

The way Sister Uline remembers it, Margulies had this to say during a conversation about businessmen: "But Mar-is that she was "co-opted" by the infant-formula industry.

A revealing absurdity

Even rougher treatment was meted out to Dr. Dana Raphael, a longtime associate of Margaret Mead. As director of the Human Lactation Center in Westport, Connecticut, Raphael was one of the first to detect the dangers in the falloff in breast-feeding in the Third World and to question whether the infant-formula makers were behaving responsibly. But according to Raphael, when she suggested that the companies could help solve the problem by devising cheap but nutritious local weaning foods, Tim Smith, the Canadian-born director of the Interfaith Center, sneered at her: "I always knew you were in their pockets."

[margin handwriting: ? NOT CONSISTENT]

The movement's stated goal is the total "demarketing" of infant formula. In testimony before Congressman Jonathan Bingham's subcommittee on foreign trade last year, Edward Baer, an ICCR staffer, explained what demarketing is supposed to mean by citing socialist Algeria. There the importing and distribution of infant formula is in the hands of a state monopoly, and all brand competition has been eliminated. What Baer failed to add is that imports of infant formula have risen from 2.5 million half-pound cans in 1976 to 12 million in 1979, and are expected to reach 16 million in 1980. Baer's reply is that the steep rise in infant-formula use in Algeria does not bother him, since it is taking place under government aegis. This reduces the controversy to the absurd but revealing proposition that capitalist infant formula kills babies, but socialist infant formula does not.

[margin handwriting: ? GOVT. SUPERVISED?]

[margin handwriting: HALF TRUTHS]

Once the case has been stated so baldly, there is a temptation to dismiss it out of hand. The economic effect of the anti-formula crusade so far has not been painful. For two years now, the activists have been boycotting all Nestlé products, but the company finds the effects so negligible that it has kept making new American acquisitions (Beech-Nut baby foods), even though the products are promptly added to the boycott list.

But the movement cannot be shrugged off that lightly. One of the most interesting dimensions of the infant-formula campaign is the extent to which it has gained support among what Irving Kristol and others have called the "new class" of influential functionaries among congressional staffs, research organizations, and the bureaucracies of the federal government and the United Nations.

A Theology for Capitalism

One theologian who does not accept the contemptuous view of capitalism held by the Christian activists is 46-year-old Michael Novak, a Catholic. Formerly the Ledden-Watson Distinguished Professor of Religion at Syracuse University, Novak has spent the last two years at the American Enterprise Institute developing a Christian case for the market system. He notes that "the strength of the business community in concentrating on the practical order carries with it profound weakness in the fields of theory and ideology." Still he finds it remarkable that a system responsible for an "unprecedented explosion of human inventiveness and enterprise" should be disparaged as "vaguely immoral." The system not only conferred wealth on the people of the U.S., but vastly expanded markets for the goods of the Third World.

In his spiritual rationale for the market system, Novak, who used to be attracted to democratic socialism, stresses the relation between capitalism and democracy. "Capitalism may flourish without democracy," he argues, "but democracy without capitalism is very hard to achieve." He says that the theology of the Christian activists reminds him of Dostoevsky's prediction in *The Brothers Karamazov* that when the Antichrist comes he will proclaim that spiritual questions must wait until material problems are solved. According to Dostoevsky, the devil's message will be: "Feed men and then ask of them virtue."

---

ilyn, they're all bastards. If they weren't they'd be living like we're living and doing what we're doing." Sister Uline suggested that her order withhold a shareholders' resolution because of the progress she was making in her talks with Ross. But without Uline's knowledge, another religious order entered the resolution instead, with Margulies's blessing. Sister Uline subsequently resigned from the campaign and is now awaiting reassignment by her order. The word being spread by some militants in the movement

One man who could testify to this is Dr. Mamduh Gabr, who as Egyptian Health Minister in 1978 vainly pleaded with the U.S. Agency for International Development for $5 million worth of infant formula for the babies of Egyptian mothers who could not breast-feed. He was turned down for fear that this could "subject the entire U.S. AID assistance program to undeserved debate and criticism."

AID stacks the deck

More recently, the AID Office of Nutrition awarded a $1.2-million research project on the determinants of infant-feeding patterns to a team led by Dr. Michael Latham of Cornell University, one of the earliest and most vociferous proponents of the Nestlé boycott, who helped get the National Council of Churches aboard by asserting that his examination of the scientific evidence left "no room" for doubt that Nestlé was guilty of for-profit infanticide. The award was all the more peculiar because Latham was the highest bidder. His study will cost almost twice

---

As the church sees it, socialist formula is good for babies.

---

the sum originally budgeted—and his proposal was adjudged inferior to competing ones in the first round of judging by a technical panel. Clearly self-conscious that the objectivity of their conclusions would immediately come under attack, Latham and his associates offered to delegate "perhaps the most sensitive part of the study," the marketing component, to an independent market-research firm. But assisting with the integration of these data into the overall findings will be none other than James Post, associate professor of management at Boston University, who led an INFACT workshop on the "demarketing" of infant formula in Washington, D.C., earlier this year.

Meanwhile, the main battleground has shifted to the U.N. Nestlé supported this change of venue, and it is possible, though not likely, that the U.N. will be able to come up with marketing guidelines better than those already being followed by the leading companies. The first hearings

(INNUENDO)

in Geneva last October were not especially promising. After listening to a bitter exchange of charges and countercharges, an African delegate rose to offer an old saying that "when two elephants fight, it is the grass that suffers."

What can corporations learn from this bizarre campaign, which is still far from over? At first glance, cooperation and compromise do not seem to be a promising course. Ross Laboratories tried that, and has been targeted as villain No. 1 in a new campaign against the selling of infant formula to America's poor. But this new campaign is transparently silly. Baby formula could account for only about 10% of a poor family's food-stamp budget. Would the church care to take on that other mainstay of the welfare mother, Pampers?

— YES!

The benefits of compromise

By its willingness to listen and make changes, Ross did manage to appeal to the many sincere people in the movement who are more interested in constructive results than endless battle. When the zealots move on to hotter causes, this quiet minority, including such experts as Dr. Raphael, may become the new majority.

A straw was blowing in the wind at the recent General Conference of the United Methodist Church in Indianapolis. By 510 votes to 398, the plenary session overruled a proposal by its "Church and Society" committee that it endorse the Nestlé boycott. The church voted instead to seek a "constructive dialogue" with the infant-formula companies. In proposing this approach, theologian Paul Minus specifically cited the Ross experience.

Having been through this fiery furnace, Ross and the other companies that make infant formula have learned a lot about handling sensitive issues. Ross has appointed a nine-person task force to study Third World concerns. It reports directly to the chairman, David Cox, who says that he has been devoting most of his time to such problems.

"Of course," Cox says, "in that time I might have been thinking of new products and better productivity." But he accepts the need to deal with these questions in a serious way. He offers the opinion that the activists may be doing corporations a good turn by prodding them to prove they can meet social challenges. Thus the Marxists marching under the banner of Christ may help the private-enterprise system to adapt and survive —even though that may be the last thing they want to see happen. ∎

← SNOW JOB

Epilogue . . .

In January 1981, the *Washington Post* published leaked memos from Nestle's which showed that the company had co-opted some of the World Health Organisation's highest officials and secretly financed anti-boycott propaganda which was disseminated as "impartial" journalism. The article "The Corporation Haters" figured among the materials produced for the pro-Nestle campaign. Herman Nickel, the Washington editor of *Fortune* magazine, received $5,000 from a conservative Washington foundation to write the article. The foundation also reprinted the article for wide distribution. The memos showed the company's plans to make a pro-Nestle film through the foundation and to fly Mr. Nickel to Switzerland to "encourage" the author's impartial journalistic efforts.

Discussion/research — bottle babies

1. What are the main points of the article, *The Corporation Haters*?

2. Discuss the title of the article.

3. "He said that they said that . . ." How does the author describe the position of critics?

4. The author concludes the article by suggesting that critics might even "help the private-enterprise system to adapt and survive — even though that may be the last thing they want to see happen."
Refer back to the *Mother Jones* article and the circular from the Interfaith Centre on Corporate Responsibility: what is the *first* thing that they want to see happen? What are the obstacles to this change of policy?

5. You have an example of how the Interfaith Centre replied to Nestle's statement (p. 95). You now also have a more general position put forward by supporters of present corporate policy (p. 99).
If you were on the side of those who criticise company policies, how would you analyse this article and respond to it?

6. Complaining about the similarity of ads and the frustration that a creative person in an ad agency can feel, an ad executive maintained that,

> Despite what the marketing people say, the problem most often begins with the similarity of products.[62]

a. Do you agree with the ad-man's explanation of why certain ads appear to be all the same (e.g. laundry detergent)?

b. If the products, for example in the soap industry, are so similar and there are only three major companies in control of all the different major brands, what conclusions could be drawn about the role of advertising in this case?

ROLE OF ADVERTISING

Publicity [advertising] has another important social function. The fact that this function has not been planned as a purpose by those who make and use publicity in no way lessens its significance. Publicity turns consumption into a substitute for democracy. The choice of what one eats (or wears or drives) takes the place of significant political choice. Publicity helps to mask and compensate for all that is undemocratic within society. And it also masks what is happening in the rest of the world.

Publicity adds up to a kind of philosophical system. It explains everything in its own terms. It interprets the world.[63]

— J. Berger, *Ways of Seeing*

---

7. Comment on John Berger's interpretation of ads (above), agreeing or disagreeing with it. Support your position with examples and quotations from present-day advertising.

8. Here are two different points of view:

• "Freedom of speech is not for sale at $50 a minute."[64]

(1939: Leonard Brockington to a Canadian Parliamentary Committee)

• "What is advertising?

Essentially it's free speech that somebody pays for. It's a force that supports free choice in the market place of ideas . . ."[65]

a. Try to list reasons to support each point of view.

b. Describe what you think would be the interests or motives of people holding either point of view.

c. Define the term "freedom of speech". In your opinion, is it possible for advertising to promote freedom of speech? Why or why not?

9. The CBS bills itself as "the world's largest advertising medium".[66] CBS is also one of the largest of the "information industries", broadcasting international news coverage the world over. What conflicts of interest could arise between the advertising and the news departments of the same network?

10. Contact the editor of the paper that is most widely read in your community (even if it is a supermarket giveaway). Interview him/her about the paper's advertising and editorial policies. Will they accept ads from anyone and everyone? Will they accept articles written by anyone and everyone?

11. Comment on the two following quotations as they relate to the structure of our economy and society.

I believe advertising today occupies a crucial role in providing the driving power for our expanding economy because it is the dynamic ingredient in the movement of goods and services. Without advertising, mass production and mass distribution could not have been achieved. Without mass consumption we cannot build an economy of the proportions necessary to support our national objectives in either military defense or human defense.[67]
— Career pamphlet

The industrial system is profoundly dependent upon tv and could not exist in its present form without it . . . Radio and TV are the prime instruments for the management of consumer demand.[68]
— Economist.

12. A man's relationships (whether they are with people, ideas or possessions) are healthy to the extent to which they are based on reality and not on pretence. But the subtlety and pervasiveness of advertising have created a social climate in which it is almost impossible to have a real relationship with anything, and most of all with one's possessions. It is astonishingly difficult today to know whether one really needs a particular article or has been made to feel one needs it. Advertising is essentially based on fraudulence. It promises that we may escape from our tensions, our loneliness, our lack of inner peace — by buying things."[69]

a. With this quotation as your starting point, arrange a class discussion on what people feel their *needs* and their *wants* are, and how advertising affects (or does not affect) their views. Arguments both for and against the author's position should be supported with concrete examples from daily life.

b. List the last 10 things you bought. Write down why you bought them. Were they necessities, or "non-essentials", or luxuries? Describe your reasons for buying them.

c. In a writing assignment, construct an "interior monologue" (what someone thinks privately to themselves) of someone you know (yourself?). The person is walking through a shopping mall.

Politics and the English language

We conclude this chapter with an excerpt from an essay by the English author, George Orwell. It was written in 1946; its wisdom and relevance — and the urgent need to heed its warnings — are all the greater today.

Politics and the English Language

MOST PEOPLE WHO BOTHER WITH THE MATTER AT ALL WOULD admit that the English language is in a bad way, but it is generally assumed that we cannot by conscious action do anything about it. Our civilization is decadent and our language—so the argument runs—must inevitably share in the general collapse. It follows that any struggle against the abuse of language is a sentimental archaism, like preferring candles to electric light or hansom cabs to aeroplanes. Underneath this lies the half-conscious belief that language is a natural growth and not an instrument which we shape for our own purposes.

Now, it is clear that the decline of a language must ultimately have political and economic causes: it is not due simply to the bad influence of this or that individual writer. But an effect can become a cause, reinforcing the original cause and producing the same effect in an intensified form, and so on indefinitely. A man may take to drink because he feels himself to be a failure, and then fail all the more completely because he drinks. It is rather the same thing that is happening to the English language. It becomes ugly and inaccurate because our thoughts are foolish, but the slovenliness of our language makes it easier for us to have foolish thoughts. The point is that the process is reversible. Modern English, especially written English, is full of bad habits which spread by imitation and which can be avoided if one is willing to take the necessary trouble. . .

As I have tried to show, modern writing at its worst does not consist in picking out words for the sake of their meaning and inventing images in order to make the meaning clearer. It consists in gumming together long strips of words which have already been set in order by someone else, and making the results presentable by sheer humbug. The attraction of this way of writing is that it is easy. It is easier—even quicker, once you have the habit—to say *In my opinion it is not an unjustifiable assumption that* than to say *I think.* If you use ready-made phrases, you not only don't have to hunt about for words; you also don't have to bother with the rhythms of your sentences, since these phrases are generally so arranged as to be more or less euphonious. When you are composing in a hurry—when you are dictating to a stenographer, for instance, or making a public speech—it is natural to fall into a pretentious, Latinized style. Tags like *a consideration which we should do well to bear in mind* or *a conclusion to which all of us would readily assent* will save many a sentence from coming down with a bump.

A scrupulous writer, in every sentence that he writes, will ask himself at least four questions, thus: What am I trying to say? What words will express it? What image or idiom will make it clearer? Is this image fresh enough to have an effect? And he will probably ask himself two more: Could I put it more shortly? Have I said anything that is avoidably ugly? But you are not obliged to go to all this trouble. You can shirk it by simply throwing your mind open and letting the ready-made phrases come crowding in. They will construct your sentences for you—even think your thoughts for you, to a certain extent—and at need they will perform the important service of partially concealing your meaning even from yourself. It is at this point that the special connection between politics and the debasement of language becomes clear.

In our time it is broadly true that political writing is bad writing. Where it is not true, it will generally be found that the writer is some kind of rebel, expressing his private opinions and not a "party line." Orthodoxy, of whatever color, seems to demand a lifeless, imitative style. The political dialects to be found in pamphlets, leading articles, manifestos, White Papers and the speeches of under-secretaries do, of course, vary from party to party, but they are all alike in that one almost never finds in them a fresh, vivid, home-made turn of speech.

In our time, political speech and writing are largely the defence of the indefensible. Things like the continuance of British rule in India, the Russian purges and deportations, the dropping of the atom bombs on Japan, can indeed be defended, but only by arguments which are too brutal for most people to face, and which do not square with the professed aims of political parties. Thus political language has to consist largely of euphemism, question-begging and sheer cloudy vagueness. Defenceless villages are bombarded from the air, the inhabitants driven out into the countryside, the cattle machine-gunned, the huts set on fire with incendiary bullets: this is called *pacification*. Millions of peasants are robbed of their farms and sent trudging along the roads with no more than they can carry: this is called *transfer of population* or *rectification of frontiers*. People are imprisoned for years without trial, or shot in the back of the neck or sent to die of scurvy in Arctic lumber camps: this is called *elimination of unreliable elements*. Such phraseology is needed if one wants to name things without calling up mental pictures of them. Consider for instance some comfortable English professor defending Russian totalitarianism. He cannot say outright, "I believe in killing off your opponents when you can get good results by doing so." Probably, therefore, he will say something like this:

"While freely conceding that the Soviet régime exhibits certain features which the humanitarian may be inclined to deplore, we must, I think, agree that a certain curtailment of the right to political opposition is an unavoidable concomitant of transitional periods, and that the rigors which the Russian people have been called upon to undergo have been amply justified in the sphere of concrete achievement."

The inflated style is itself a kind of euphemism. A mass of Latin words falls upon the facts like soft snow, blurring the outlines and covering up all the details. The great enemy of clear language is insincerity. When there is a gap between one's real and one's declared aims, one turns as it were instinctively to long words and exhausted idioms, like a cuttlefish squirting out ink. In our age there is no such thing as "keeping out of politics." All issues are political issues, and politics itself is a mass of lies, evasions, folly, hatred and schizophrenia. When the general atmosphere is bad, language must suffer. I should expect to find—this is a guess which I have not sufficient knowledge to verify—that the German, Russian and Italian languages have all deteriorated in the last ten or fifteen years, as a result of dictatorship.

But if thought corrupts language, language can also corrupt thought. A bad usage can spread by tradition and imitation, even among people who should and do know better. The debased language that I have been discussing is in some ways very convenient. Phrases like *a not unjustifiable assumption, leaves much to be desired, would serve no good purpose, a consideration which we should do well to bear in mind*, are a continuous temptation, a packet of aspirins always at one's elbow. Look back through this essay, and for certain you will find that I have again and again committed the very faults I am protesting against. By this morning's post I have received a pamphlet dealing with conditions in Germany. The author tells me that he "felt impelled" to write it. I open it at random, and here is almost the first sentence that I see: "[The Allies] have an opportunity not only of achieving a radical transformation of Germany's social and political structure in such a way as to avoid a nationalistic reaction in Germany itself, but at the same time of laying the foundations of a co-operative and unified Europe." You see, he "feels impelled" to write—feels, presumably, that he has something new to say— and yet his words, like cavalry horses answering the bugle, group themselves automatically into the familiar dreary pattern. This invasion of one's mind by ready-made phrases (*lay the foundations, achieve a radical transformation*) can only be prevented if one is constantly on guard against them, and every such phrase anaesthetizes a portion of one's brain.

I said earlier that the decadence of our language is probably curable. Those who deny this would argue, if they produced an argument at all, that language merely reflects existing social conditions, and that we cannot influence its development by any direct tinkering with words and constructions. So far as the general tone or spirit of a language goes, this may be true, but it is not true in detail. Silly words and expressions have often disappeared, not through any evolutionary process but owing to the conscious action of a minority. Two recent examples were *explore every avenue* and *leave no stone unturned,* which were killed by the jeers of a few journalists. There is a long list of flyblown metaphors which could similarly be got rid of if enough people would interest themselves in the job.

I have not here been considering the literary use of language, but merely language as an instrument for expressing and not for concealing or preventing thought. Stuart Chase and others have come near to claiming that all abstract words are meaningless, and have used this as a pretext for advocating a kind of political quietism. Since you don't know what Fascism is, how can you struggle against Fascism? One need not swallow such absurdities as this, but one ought to recognize that the present political chaos is connected with the decay of language, and that one can probably bring about some improvement by starting at the verbal end. If you simplify your English, you are freed from the worst follies of orthodoxy. You cannot speak any of the necessary dialects, and when you make a stupid remark its stupidity will be obvious, even to yourself. Political language—and with variations this is true of all political parties, from Conservatives to Anarchists—is designed to make lies sound truthful and murder respectable, and to give an appearance of solidity to pure wind. One cannot change this all in a moment, but one can at least change one's own habits, and from time to time one can even, if one jeers loudly enough, send some worn-out and useless phrase—some *jackboot, Achilles' heel, hotbed, melting pot, acid test, veritable inferno* or other lump of verbal refuse—into the dustbin where it belongs. ■

Discussion

George Orwell's *Nineteen Eighty-Four* appeared in 1949. His original title for the novel was *Nineteen Forty-Eight,* but publishers overruled his choice, and it appeared as we know it now. We are now living in the "far-off" point in the future that the changed title suggested.

What elements of the novel are applicable today? At the time the book appeared, what point that Orwell was trying to make would have been lost with the changing of the title?

Further Reading

A.I. in quotes
Amnesty International (1976) London: Amnesty International

Ways of seeing
John Berger (1973) Harmondsworth: Penguin

The Washington connection and Third World Fascism
Noam Chomsky and E. S. Herman (1979) Montreal: Black Rose Books

Don't blame the people:
How the news media use bias, distortion and censorship to manipulate public opinion, Robert Cirino (1971) NY: Vintage Books

How to read Donald Duck
Ariel Dorfman and Armand Mattelart (1975) NY: International General

How to write, speak and think more effectively
Rudolph Flesch (1960) NY: Signet

How to lie with statistics
Darrel Huff (1954) NY: WW Norton & Co.

Crime of the 20th century
Mother Jones magazine (1979), special November issue on the impact
of dumping of unsafe products in the Third World. 625 Third Street,
San Francisco CA 94107 USA.

Tomorrow's epidemic? Tobacco and the Third World
Mike Muller (1978) London: War on Want

**Ontario Royal Commission on violence in the communications in-
dustry report**
(1976)

Audio/visual

Ways of seeing
On the imaginary world created by advertising, and on the real world
of work, with a focus on women. (colour film, 16 mm, 25 min., available through DEVERIC, Halifax, DEC, Toronto, or other centres across
Canada.

Bottle babies
on the effects of infant formula promotion in the Third World (16 mm
colour film available from CUSO Development Education.)

The formula factor
on the effects of infant formula promotion, focusing on the Caribbean
and native peoples in Canada, hosted by Roy Bonisteel. (Colour film,
16 mm, available through the National Film Board.)

I. F. Stone
a film about this remarkable journalist, (black and white 16 mm film,
40 minutes approx., available from the Canadian Filmmakers Distribution Centre, 144 Front Street, Toronto, Ontario.)

III. This message was brought to you by...

Chapter III: This message is brought to you by . . .

Introduction

How do we know about things going on in other parts of the world or even in our own country? Most of us find out by watching TV, listening to the radio or buying a newspaper. How does that news get made? Who decides what is news?

If the old saying is true, "He who pays the piper calls the tune," we will have to find out who owns and controls the mass media in ✳ order to know what interests they might represent, and therefore what point of view they are likely to reflect.

The information presented in this chapter is intended first to give some information about Canadian and world media ownership; and second to stimulate thought and discussion. Those who might disagree with any position put forward in these pages are encouraged to prepare counter-arguments.

Imagine you and your friends wanted to start up your own radio station.

What kind of music would you play? What kind of programmes would the radio station have? . . . What recording artists would get the most air time? What kind of mix of programmes would you have? . . . Would you try for no ads, or for better ads, . . . ? How would you decide?

Would you like your radio station to have sports news? What contacts or equipment would you need to get such coverage? How would you go about getting local news coverage? National coverage? International news? How would you try to establish and build up your listening audience?

What other practical things would you need to start up the radio station? — transmitter, studio, turntable . . . ?

Imagine the *minimum* you would need.

Discussion/Activities

1. Keep good notes of your discussion. Go through the same process for television; and for a newspaper.

2. Invite a local station manager in to explain what is involved in running a radio station. How many of the necessary factors had you thought of? Did you miss any?

3. "He who pays the piper calls the tune." What does this expression mean? Can you describe any *personal* experience that would confirm this maxim (for example, use of the family car.)?

1. Where the news comes from

How does the Six O'Clock News get together? Who makes up the news, and how does it come to us? Here is a brief description of the news-making process.

Networks

For TV, there are networks of newsreporting. The CBC and CTV are national networks across Canada (the CBC also has a radio network). Global Television in Ontario and TVA (Télédiffuseurs Associé) in Quebec have networks for their provinces. CBS, NBC and ABC are the networks in the United States, and the BBC is Britain's network.

Camera crews, reporters and researchers in various places cover an event and transmit the story to their broadcasting station and, depending on whether the producers think the story is worth relaying to other regions as well, it is sent to other broadcasting stations.

The news "item" can be relayed by microwave or by satellite to other parts of the country or world. For international coverage on TV, the three largest have by far the most impact: Viznews (British); UPIIN (British-American, owned 50-50 by UPI and ITN) and CBS Newsfilm (American). Most "Third World" countries depend entirely on these services for TV coverage.

Wire services

Radio, TV and newspapers also use wire services. Major ones in Canada are CP (Canadian Press), AP (Associated Press, an American cooperative), UPI (United Press International, a commercial American concern), Reuters (British) and AFP (Agence France-Presse, French). These are virtually instant forms of communication as well, which use teletype and other telecommunications equipment. News stories from all over the world come in "on the wire" and are reprinted or broadcast on air within minutes of delivery.

CP, the source of much of our information about Canada — and other Canadians' source of much of their information about us in the Atlantic — is a co-operative which is owned by member newspapers. The cost is shared on the basis of its 115 member papers' circulation. The service operates non-profit. CP has a similar broadcast service for radio and television, Broadcast News (BN).

Each local CP office makes up the news for the wire service by reading the local papers and sending stories out on the wire service. Through the same process, papers across Canada receive news about each other's regions. Although CP reporters do cover some stories themselves, most of the news comes from their monitoring the local press. CP will do stories on request as well — for example the *Vancouver Sun* might ask for a particular story on forestry in the Maritimes.

Of the 114 Canadian daily newspapers in 1971, 104 belonged to CP. According to a 1970 Special Senate Committee on Mass Media*, "More than 70 papers rely on CP for *all* the news they publish beyond what is written locally by their own staffs." *(I: 230)*

This means that when people in the Maritimes read wire stories about Quebec or Alberta, the stories are generally from the point of view of the local papers. They are not necessarily independent reports. That is, it is likely the wire service stories will have taken the local papers' basic points of reference, interviewing perhaps the same people, considering the same events as being newsworthy.

Nationally CP employs about 180 editors and reporters. CP has staff members at the U.N., New York, Washington, London and Paris, and a stringer in India. It occasionally sends teams of reporters overseas to cover major events like the Olympics. One CP reporter

---

*Referred to as the Senate Committee, abbreviated to *Sen.* for references.

in Ottawa concentrates on international affairs.[1] It also has agreements with Reuters, AP and AFP which allow it to process international news from these services, and release the Canadianized version as a CP story. Here is a description of how this has been done:

> The Canadianization process is a rather fascinating one. The following examples of Canadianization were observed during a 24-hour watch of CP copy in CP's New York bureau during the summer of 1969.
>
> • the word 'President' was changed to 'president'; . . .
>
> • the name of a community, 'Centerville' was altered to 'Centrevile';
>
> • the term 'the nation's' was altered to 'in the U.S.';
>
> • the reference to 'The Duke of Edinburgh, the Queen's husband', was changed to 'Prince Philip'; . . .
>
> • a reference to 'enemy' in a story from Viet Nam was altered to read 'North Vietnamese-Viet Cong'.
>
> As all the above examples illustrate, the process of Canadianization does not alter the basic story content, only adjusts minor points that might irritate Canadian readers[2].

After CP comes Canada's second-largest wire service, UPC, United Press Canada (the former UPI, United Press International in Canada. A commercial service, UPC is 80% owned by the Toronto Sun and 20% owned by UPI[3]. After a year as a Canadianized operation it was reported still to have "a general manager who's British, a heart deep in Texas and an American editor-in-chief."[4] The heart deep in Texas refers to where UPC's information is stored on computer. But things *will* improve for the Canadian service, the American editor said, for Canada "is an important state to us"[5]. . .

Other services

There are also a number of other news services in Canada. The Southam News Service gives coverage for papers in its chain, as does Thomson. The Dow Jones wire carries business news into newspaper offices, and there are services that provide the media with ready-made articles produced by the Public Relations departments of business and industry, such as the Business PR Newswire, a subsidiary of Western Union.[6]

There are many more services that offer news and feature material by either mail or teletype: the syndicates of the *Toronto Star,* the London *Observer.* the *Manchester Guardian,* the *Times* (England); the *New York Times;* Publishers Hall; Miller Services; National Geographic News Service; Religious News Service; Gallup Poll, and many more.

Newspapers do have out-of-country correspondents. There was a total of 19 of them around the entire world for *all* newspapers in Canada in 1974[7] . . . According to Charles Lynch of Southam News Service there are fewer Canadian correspondents abroad than at any other time in the past 30 years.[8] A recent survey found that only a few of the larger newspapers had their own foreign correspondents, and few of these were based in Third World countries. For example, the London correspondent for the Toronto Star covered Europe and the Middle East. Southam News Services' writer who covers Asia is based in Ottawa. A correspondent based in Paris covers the Middle East. Thomson newspapers rely heavily on Thomson News Services, which have a foreign affairs columnist and a business columnist based in Toronto.[9]

Broadcast News is the CP news service for radio. Three other main radio services exist. News radio is connected to the American CBS network, Contemporary News is connected to UPI, and Standard Broadcast news is connected to NBC.

Discussion

1. What are some of the major issues discussed in your newspaper? Measure coverage in terms of column inches/centimeters (do not forget to include advertising).

2. How would you rate the media in your area:
— for coverage of local issues?
— national issues?
— international issues?

3. Have you come across any cases where coverage of an event or issue has been biased or misleading? Can you picture a situation in which this might happen?

4. A chain is only as strong as its weakest link.

In relation to *quality,* how strong is the "chain" of newsreporting in our country in terms of accurate, independent news? How strong is the chain world-wide?

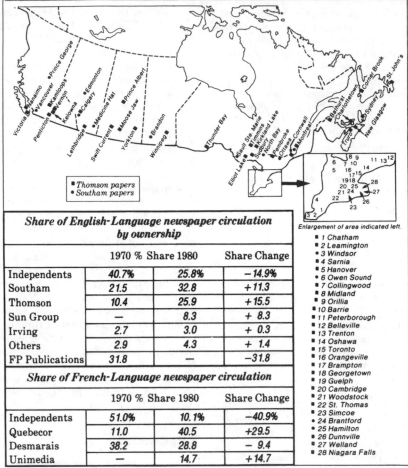

Share of English-Language newspaper circulation by ownership			
	1970 % Share 1980		Share Change
Independents	40.7%	25.8%	− 14.9%
Southam	21.5	32.8	+11.3
Thomson	10.4	25.9	+15.5
Sun Group	—	8.3	+ 8.3
Irving	2.7	3.0	+ 0.3
Others	2.9	4.3	+ 1.4
FP Publications	31.8	—	−31.8
Share of French-Language newspaper circulation			
	1970 % Share 1980		Share Change
Independents	51.0%	10.1%	−40.9%
Quebecor	11.0	40.5	+29.5
Desmarais	38.2	28.8	− 9.4
Unimedia	—	14.7	+ 14.7

Enlargement of area indicated left.

- 1 Chatham
- 2 Leamington
- 3 Windsor
- 4 Sarnia
- 5 Hanover
- 6 Owen Sound
- 7 Collingwood
- 8 Midland
- 9 Orillia
- 10 Barrie
- 11 Peterborough
- 12 Belleville
- 13 Trenton
- 14 Oshawa
- 15 Toronto
- 16 Orangeville
- 17 Brampton
- 18 Georgetown
- 19 Guelph
- 20 Cambridge
- 21 Woodstock
- 22 St. Thomas
- 23 Simcoe
- 24 Brantford
- 25 Hamilton
- 26 Dunnville
- 27 Welland
- 28 Niagara Falls

Sources: Thomson Annual Report 1980 and *Maclean's* magazine.

2. Ownership and control

We know that most of the news we receive comes from the mass media and now have a general picture of how the news is made. The next question is: who controls these outlets for the news?

Newspapers

The national newspaper chain that is found throughout the Atlantic provinces is the Thomson chain. One of the two largest chains in the country, Thomson's papers are spread right across Canada. Controlling newspapers in Canada with a total circulation of approximately 2.4 million, the Thomson chain is found in the cities and outlying areas of Canada. Its principal owner, Mr. K. R. Thomson, is also joint chairman of the International Thomson Organisation, whose interests include the *Times* and *Sunday Times* of London, England, numerous holdings in South Africa, and over 119 newspapers in North America (44 in Canada).

The second-largest newspaper chain — Southam — owns fewer dailies (14), but also has a giant total circulation (approx. 1,260,000). What Southam lacks in wide geographical influence it makes up for in huge circulations in large urban areas. (Southam also controls the largest book retailer in Canada, Coles, with 167 outlets across the country.)

These two newspaper chains alone control 58% of newspaper circulation in Canada.

In Nova Scotia, apart from the Thomson chain, the two daily newspapers of any significant circulation are both owned by one family.

In New Brunswick, the Irving family has 100% ownership of four of the five English-speaking dailies, and has controlling interest in the fifth. It has been suggested that significant influence is exercised over the sixth daily as well, the French l'*Evangéline,* through extensive advertising *(Sen. II: 62).*

In PEI, the one daily that is not a Thomson paper is owned by the Sterling Newspaper chain. The chain's president, Conrad Black, is president of the Journal's publishing company, and one of the richest and most powerful financiers in Canada. Among Mr. Black's holdings one finds such huge complexes as Dominion Stores, Hollinger Mines, and Noranda Mines.

In Newfoundland, two of the three dailies are owned by the Thomson chain, the third being owned by the Herder family, who in 1979 sold the first two to Thomson.

Overall, the concentration of newspaper ownership is three times as high in Canada as it is in the United States.[10] Daily newspapers appear in about 90 Canadian cities, but at last count, just four Canadian cities — Toronto, Edmonton, Calgary and St. John's — had competing English language dailies under separate ownership.[11]

Television

The ownership of television in this region is linked to larger TV broadcasters in other parts of Canada.

In Nova Scotia, there is one private broadcasting network for the province, the Atlantic Television System (ATV). It is 50% owned by the president of Toronto's giant CHUM broadcasting group. Among CHUM's subsidiaries one finds Telephone Stores Ltd, National Security Systems, Accu-Tab Computer Services Ltd, and the Ottawa Football Club. Another 30% of ATV is controlled by the Nathenson family.

In New Brunswick, the Irving family controls all private television stations.

In Newfoundland, Geoffrey Sterling owns all private television stations throughout the province.

There are no commercial TV broadcasters in PEI. We should note that US stations have greatly increased their broadcasting to Canada — and most dramatically to the Maritimes.[12]

Concentration of ownership

Further information on the rest of the media in the Atlantic region can be found in the Appendix. It is fair to say that concentration of ownership in other print and electronic media is also very high; in general the situation here is similar to that found elsewhere in Canada. The overall trend is towards "a decline in

'How little we really own, Tom, when you consider all there is to own.'

competition and growth of monopoly and oligarchy."[13]

The structure of the media has changed, but the mythology surrounding it has not. The 1970 Special Senate Committee on Mass Media noted that

> . . . conventional wisdom still cherishes the image of the 'independent' owner-editor, a tough but kindly old curmudgeon who somehow represented the collective conscience of his community. If this image ever had validity, it hasn't now . . . *(Sen.I:5)*

In 1970, the largest newspaper chains (Thomson, Southam and FP Publications) controlled 45% of daily circulation. FP has since been bought out by Thomson, and many other mergers have taken place. At the time the Senate Committee *(I:19)* found that of the 116 dailies in Canada, 66% were group-owned; of the 97 private TV stations, 48% were group-owned, and of the 272 radio stations, 47% were group-owned. For the publishing and printing industry, just four companies control 42% of the total value of that business. With the next four largest (eight in total) they control 66% of the business. [14]

Here is what a researcher for the Senate Committee said six years after its study:

> We warned that concentration of media ownership was increasing and would constitute a threat to freedom of expression. When we wrote that, 66% of the nation's media outlets were owned by chains or groups; today the figure is 90%.[15]

Illusions and realities

Canadians generally like to think of themselves as being part of a classless or at least a middle-class society. A 1980 poll showed that the majority considered ourselves "Middle-Class" — a full 25% more than actually fitted the income definition used, which itself was a very modest one.*

The illusion seems more comfortable to live with than the reality: we would *rather not* think of ourselves as "not in charge" of our lives, our entertainment, news, our very ideas. Understandably, we tend to want to identify ourselves with those who are in fact making the decisions about our entertainment, news and culture. Yet network executives can earn in the range of 1 million dollars a year in salaries alone[16] — hardly what most Canadians earn.

It is important to note this general misconception, because many of us mistakenly interpret relative comfort or personal wealth for membership in the class of people who actually own and control most of the wealth in this country — the people who make the major decisions about investments; about the future directions Canada's industry, trade and resources will take. The vast majority of Canadians do not belong to this small group of people who control Canada's business and financial institutions, and media outlets. A Royal Commission on Corporate Concentration found that just *under 6%* of all corporations in Canada accounted for over 90% of all the assets of the country, and 86% of sales. A mere 29 corporate giants, *0.02%* of Canadian businesses, hold 35% of all the assets in the country.[17] When one is reminded that corporate executives often hold directorships in several

*The definition includes people whose household incomes range between $13,000 and $28,000 per year — in the range of at least *one tenth* the income of a corporation executive. (*Maclean's* 10 March 80, p.48.)

corporations, the scope and depth of concentration of control is astounding.

A Statistics Canada report issued in late 1979 showed that a handful of Canada's major business families controlled seven out of the ten largest groups of corporations.[18]

In reality, then, a small group of people actually control the major media of newspapers, TV and radio. Each of these media invest in one another; this further concentrates ownership in the media:

> . . . concentration of ownership in the media [is] not confined just to concentration within the major media (newspapers, television and radio) but across the media as well . . . [The] largest publishing interests also held numerous broadcasting outlets. For example, Southam Press has 26 broadcasting outlets, Thomson 10, Sifton and Maclean-Hunter nine each. There was also concentration within the broadcasting companies without publication interests; for example, Moffat Broadcasting has 10 outlets . . .[19]

In the television industry, there are only eight independents without network affiliation.[20]

The chains or groups of companies are in turn owned by a still smaller group of people who have investments in many areas. This small group of immensely wealthy and powerful people has been called "The Canadian Corporate Elite". The author of a book by the same name states:

> Actually, the overlap [of the media élite] with the economic élite is extensive, almost one-half the members are exactly the same people. Moreover, those not overlapped resemble very closely the economic élite. The

conclusion must be that together the economic and media élite are simply two sides to the same upper class; between them they hold two of the key sources of power — economic and ideological — in Canadian society and form the corporate élite.[21]

Listing the hundreds of companies that major media owners in Canada are directors of would fill up page after page of this book.

Rather than do this, we suggest you examine the work of Wallace Clement and others who have done extensive research in this area. He found that

Not only do the media élite coincide as overlapping social circles and have common class backgrounds with the economic élite, they are in very large part identical people.[22]

Champions of Freedom of the Press . . .

THE DOORS OF INJUSTICE

SENECA FALLS, New York — In 1976, an ex-policeman disappeared while fishing on Seneca Lake in Upstate New York. Two men were arrested and accused of his murder, even though the body was never found.

Carol Ritter, court reporter for Gannett Rochester Newspapers, went to cover the pretrial hearing for the accused.

When she arrived at the courtroom, Ritter and other reporters were barred from the hearing on the pretext that the accused would not be able to get a fair trial if the pretrial hearing was covered by the press.

The Gannett Rochester Newspapers strongly disagreed and challenged the judge's right to close the doors of justice to the people, including the press. They took that challenge to the Supreme Court of the United States.

Gannett believes no judge should have the right to shut the people and their free press out of such pretrial hearings, where an overwhelming majority of criminal prosecutions are resolved.

Can you imagine up to 90 percent of all court cases being settled in secret? Gannett could not. But on July 2, 1979, the Supreme Court ruled it could happen.

Gannett protests vigorously this abridgment of the First Amendment. Not only has the Court limited journalists' access to gathering and reporting the news for the public, but it has also

trampled on the people's freedom to know, the cornerstone of our rights as a free people in a free society.

The freedoms of the First Amendment must be cherished, not shackled.

At Gannett, we have a commitment to freedom in every business we're in, whether it's newspaper, TV, radio, outdoor advertising or public opinion research.

And so from Burlington to Boise, from Fort Myers to Fort Wayne, every Gannett newspaper, every TV and radio station is free to express its own opinions, free to serve the best interests of its own community in its own way.

Gannett
A world of different voices where freedom speaks.

Giant media complexes, like any of the large companies, engage in Public Relations campaigns, especially when they feel it is necessary to maintain their image.

This American ad is a very clear example. It advocates Freedom of Speech, as guaranteed by the U.S. Constitution: by advocating something many people agree with already, the newspaper chain successfully *associates itself* with values and principles that people believe in. — The catch is that many people are *also* critical of the dozens of media take-overs that have followed one upon another over the past decade. They are concerned, precisely, with Freedom of the Press under such conditions.

This ad appeared in September 1979, just after it was reported that the huge Gannett chain gained control of two more big newspapers, seven TV stations and 13 radio stations.

. . . and Market Surveys

In another publication, however, this is what its President, Al Newharth says:

"Basically we respond to our reader studies. Whatever diet the readers want, we custom tailor the paper for that diet. . . That's no great practice of journalism, but it's what the readers want."

Ad: *Atlas World Press Review* Sept 79, Newharth interview *Working Papers for a New Society*, Jul 79

The following, from the social pages of the *Globe and Mail,* illustrates in a rather unusual way the overlap of powerful people in the worlds of finance, business, government and communications. As the columnist notes, the groom has controlling interests in Dominion Stores, Domtar Inc., Hollinger Mines, and Standard Broadcasting. The footnotes were added with the research of Wallace Clement, [23] author of the *Canadian Corporate Elite;* the original article appeared on 17 November 1978.

Blacks invited 'people we're fond of' to party

Mr. and Mrs. Conrad Moffat Black were married in July in Grace Church on-the-Hill; she is the former Shirley Hishon Walters of Montreal.

Their first large party was held recently at the York Club and the bride looked lovely in a simple plum-shade silk blouse and silk paisley-patterned skirt, mid-calf length with a side slit to the knee.

Among the first to arrive were Lieutenant-Governor Pauline McGibbon, who was on her way to speak at a dinner in Barrie. Others who left early were the Roland Micheners[1] and the Sydney Hermants[2] — they went on to cocktails with Mr. and Mrs. C. Malim Harding[3] in their Rosedale home. The Blacks and the Hardings had each invited the other to the coinciding parties.

As explained by Shirley Black, "We asked the people we're really fond of." And so one saw Rev. John E. Erb, who officiated at their wedding, with Mrs. Erb. And some of the Old Guard like Mr. and Mrs. J. Harold Crang,[4] Joseph Sedgwick, the Terence Sheards, Maj. Conn Smythe,[5] Mr. and Mrs. Charles B. Stewart,[6] Mr. and Mrs. Douglas H. Ward and the E.P. Taylors.[7]

Mr. Taylor told me he's lost 60 pounds, and had to cart all his suits to London to be taken in.

"You look wonderful," I told him. "How did you lose?"

His answer, "I didn't do anything. I think it's age. I'm outliving everyone."

Col. and Mrs. Kenneth L. Campbell came with their houseguests Mr. and Mrs. J. Barry O'Brien of Ottawa; Mrs. Charles L. Gundy[8] was escorted by photographer Ken Bell, and with their wives were Mr. Justice Charles Dubin, Donald C. Early, Deputy

Crown Prosecuting Attorney Stephen C. Leggett, John C. Lockwood[8a] and Charles Rathgeb.[9] Also there were Mr. and Mrs. John H. Taylor[9a] with their son-in-law and daughter Mr. and Mrs. John Craig Eaton.

The Blacks used to live back-to-back to the Eatons — also present were Mrs. John David Eaton, Mr. and Mrs. George R. Eaton and Mrs. Thor Eaton. Other long-time friends were Fruma Bell, Mr. and Mrs. Robert Dale-Harris of Uxbridge, Mr. and Mrs. Leighton McCarthy,[10] David F. Jewell and Mrs. Jewell, Mr. and Mrs. Morton Simcoe and Mr. and Mrs. Thomas McMahon, who've recently moved from Montreal to Toronto.

Conrad Black is the author of Duplessis,[11] which came out one year ago. His publisher, John G. McClelland, was at the reception and others in the publishing world who attended were Douglas G. Bassett,[12] St. Clair Balfour,[13] Floyd S. Chalmers,[14] J. Douglas Creighton, George N.M. Currie, Michael C. de Pencier,[15] Gordon N. Fisher[16] and Michael C. Sifton.[17]

Other authors there were Peter Charles Newman, Richard Rohmer and Madeline Kronby.

Members of the media there included John W.H. Bassett,[18] Anthony F. Griffiths,[19] Betty Kennedy[20] and her husband G. Allan Burton,[21] Adrienne Clarkson, Philippe de Gaspe Beaubien,[22] Barbara Frum and her husband Dr. Murray Frum, Fraser Kelly,[23] Frederick Langen with his fiancee, Helen Meyer, Edward S. Rogers,[24] and Morton Shulman[25] with Mrs. Rogers and Mrs. Shulman.

Relations present included Mr. and Mrs. Bruce E. Brymer, Mr. and Mrs. Robert Gillan and their daughter

Janice, the Gordon P. Oslers[26] wit their daughter and her husband M and Mrs. Robert Beverly (Biff) Ma thews,[27] Mrs. Conrad S. Riley,[28] Nar cy Riley, and Mrs. W. Culver Rile and her daughter Mrs. Robert a Langley.

From the political arena were th following with their wives — Edw A. Goodman,[29] Senator John M Godfrey, Jerahmiel S. Grafstein, Donald S. Macdonald, Rob Parke recently elected Conservative MP f Eglinton, John P. Robarts,[32] Dav Smith,[33] John Napier Turner,[34] ar two Liberal candidates for the ne federal election, Roy MacLaren ar James S. Peterson.

Also there was Michael Arth Meighen, the former national pre dent of the Progressive Conservati Party of Canada. He's now a cons tant to TV Guide magazine. He w with his wife, the former Ke Dillon. They were married in t spring and are living in Roseda She's the daughter of Richard Dillon, Ontario's deputy provinc secretary for resources developme and Mrs. Dillon. Kelly is head of t personnel department at Gene Foods.

Conrad Black and his brother Montegu Black 3rd, with associat recently took over Argus Corp. L This includes control of Domin Stores, Domtar Inc., Hollin Mines, Massey-Ferguson and St dard Broadcasting.

Business friends with their wi were Thomas Bolton,[35] Albert L. F ley,[36] Anthony S. Fell,[37] Henry Jackman[38] and his son H.N.R. Ja man[39] Igor Kaplan, Douglas W. N loney,[40] Donald A. McIntosh,[41] V tor A. Rice, Albert A Thornbroug and William O. Twaits.[43] Bank here included R. Donald Fullerton,[44] Russell E. Harrison,[45] Hartland Molson MacDougald,[46] Richard M. Thomson[47] and J. Page R. Wadsworth.[48]

And after the hullabaloo in the financial world about the dispute relating to the valuation of the Ravelston Corp. shares between the Meighen group and the Blacks, all has been settled.

Who's who: footnotes

Former governor-general. 2. President, Imperial Optical. 3. Harding Carpets. Crang and Ostiguy stockbrokers. 5. The Leafs. 6. President, Simpson's. 7. E. P. Taylor founder, Argus Corp. 8. Chairman, Wood Gundy investment brokers. 8a. Chairman, Lever Brothers. 9. President, Comstock International. 9a. Chairman, Bramalea Consolidated Developers. 10. Canada Life Assurance. 11. See review, *ThisMag*, July '77. 12. Inland Publishing, Toronto Argos. 13. Southam Press. 14. Maclean-Hunter. 15. Key Publishers, *Toronto Life*. 16. President, Southam Press. 17. President, Armadale Communications. 18. Baton Communications. 19. Canadian Cable Systems. 20. CFRB. 21. Chairman, Simpson's 22. President, Telemedia Communications. 23. CTV. 24. President, Rogers Communications. 25. Author, *How to make a million and profit from inflation.* 26. Vice-chairman, British Steel Corp. 27. McCarthy and McCarthy. 28. President, Dominion Tanners. 29. Goodman and Goodman, Conservative fundraiser. 30. Liberal fundraiser. 31. Former federal finance minister number one. 32. Former Ontario premier. 33. Recent Toronto mayoral loser. 34. Former federal finance minister number two. 35. President, Dominion Stores. 36. President, Hollinger Mines. 37. President, Dominion Securities. 38. President, Dominion and Anglo Investments. 39. Chairman, Empire Life. 40. Senior general manager, IAC Ltd. 41. Fraser & Beatty. 42. President, Massey-Ferguson. 43. Imperial Oil. 44. Chief general manager, Canadian Imperial Bank of Commerce (CIBC). 45. President, CIBC. 46. Clement doesn't know this one but is very intrigued by the name. 47. President, TD bank. 48. Chairman, CIBC.

ZENA CHERRY

Blacks invited 'people we're fond of' to party

"Now you see our desperate application for a price increase from our point of view, Mr. Pepin."

3. How do present trends affect the media's message?

You may well wonder what difference it could make if only a few people control the mass media of communication. What real effects can this have on news coverage or analysis? How do these trends affect the actual content of the media's message?

There are at least six ways in which the present trends in ownership and structure of the mass media can affect the kind of news or programmes we receive.

(i) Obvious conflict of interest or censorship

The first way that the media can be influenced by present trends is the most obvious: through conflict of interest or censorship. Because of the other holdings that a media owner might have, news affecting these other holdings might not appear in the media outlets s/he owns. Here is an example from our region.

On January 6, 1971, a fire and explosion ripped apart the crew's quarters aboard the oil tanker *MV Irvingstream* in the Saint John, N.B. harbour. Five men were killed. The Irv-ing newspaper, the *Telegraph Journal* said editorially that the cause of the *Irvingstream* disaster was that the federal government did not provide sufficient fire boats (even though its own news story reported that the fire chief had ruled out fireboats as a significant factor). An inquest into the accident was held, and the company was accused of negligence. There was no editorial mention of this in the paper. *"As far as the casual reader knew, five men had died because Ottawa didn't provide fire boats."*[24]

In a presentation to the Senate Committee on the Mass Media, writer and journalist Silver Donald Cameron cited a case where the Fredericton *Gleaner* did not print an investigation of welfare abuses, because the results of the investigation did not jibe with the paper's policy.[25] Other cases of accidents and pollution caused by Irving interests have not been covered by Irving's media[26] . . .

From the national media, a rather telling example of manipulation can be found in the Toronto *Globe and Mail*'s selective editing of an important book review. The book in question was *The Canadian corporate élite*. The section of the review dealing with ownership of the media was taken out! (See appendix.)

"Freedom of the press belongs to those who own one."

A famous example of interference in the entertainment sphere was the cancellation of a prime-time U.S. comedy and satire programme of the 1960s, *The Smothers Brothers*. The show's hosts took an anti-war stand, and often lampooned the statements of government officials. Despite extremely high ratings and widespread public objections to its being cancelled, the show was summarily taken off the air. The official reason given was minor contract violations and declining popularity. In private, however, a CBS official gave a different reason: "One of them had been sticking his finger in the network's eye and something had to be done."[27]

More recently in the United States, the noted scholars Noam Chomsky and Edward Herman experienced first-hand what they described as "an authentic instance of private censorship of ideas". Their book, which finally appeared in 1979, had had 20,000 copies printed in 1973, but at the last minute publishers recalled the book, even though a full-page ad for it had been placed in the New York Review of Books. Printed flyers that listed the monograph as one of the publisher's titles were destroyed, and officers of the company

were told that distribution of the recalled book would result in their immediate dismissal. The publisher, Warner Books, had decided that the meticulously documented publication, *The Washington Connection and Third World Fascism* was "unpatriotic". The authors noted with irony that the same publishers had pleaded "freedom of the press" in justifying the promotion of former President Nixon's memoires of illegalities and corruption. The authors comment:

The uniqueness of the episode lies only in the manner of suppression. Usually private intervention in the book market is anticipatory, with regrets that the manuscript is unacceptable, perhaps 'unmarketable'.[28]

In Canada, Ian Adam's best-selling novel, *S Portrait of a Spy*, was only re-released in 1981, after a three-year period when the book was kept off the market. Though the book was fiction, the threat of a libel suit *had had the effect* of censorship, the publishers withdrawing it themselves.

(ii) Vulnerability to influence from advertisers

Another way the content of the media can be influenced or distorted is through the influence of advertisers. The Senate Committee report tells of a "classic case of advertising nervousness" occurring when the CBC rescheduled a particular episode of its series *Quentin Durgens MP*, to avoid its coinciding with the introduction of a new line of automobiles. That particular episode was about auto safety. General Motors was the sponsor of the programme . . . *(Sen.II:149)*. In Nova Scotia, the radio station CJLS in Yarmouth was also shown to have altered news broadcasts so as not to offend advertisers. *(Sen.I:92)*.

Advertising finances most of the media: 73% of the newspaper and periodical industries' revenue comes from ads; 93% of the gross income of the broadcasting industry. This advertising does not come from widely based sources in society, but instead from a narrow corporate élite: as a whole, the mass media derive 70% of their advertising revenue from just 100 major companies, half of which are U.S. controlled *(Sen.I:243;246; II:120)*.

Do advertisers deliberately control and manipulate the mass media? Author Wallace Clement points out that it is not even necessary to argue that the advertiser directly determines the content of the media:

> It is enough to know that the media owners are very aware of the limits of tolerance and they need to remain within these limits.[29]

Journalists point out that any Canadian newspaper's clippings file on Eaton's will show how carefully the media treat large advertisers. Stories are always very carefully written, and usually highlight some charitable or community-oriented aspect of the giant business. However, in addition to the favourable coverage of the company, there are also obvious gaps in coverage:

> Just as revealing (but more difficult to trace) are the stories that do not get printed, for instance of a brutal middle-management cleanout in Eaton's store in Winnipeg or of a mass firing of maintenance in Toronto in the mid-1960s.[30]

In its own promotional material, *Maclean's* magazine shows the close connection between the way news and advertising are handled:

> A good magazine works because the readers count on two kinds of information: editorial and advertising. They enjoy, trust and respond to both.
> *Both together.*
> . . . The magazine that promotes the interlock between editorial and advertising is the magazine that flourishes.[31]

NB

The 1970 Senate Committee concluded that the economics of advertising ultimately determined all other decisions basic to the operation of a newspaper or broadcasting station *(Sen.II:19).*

The 1980 purchase of the FP Publications chain by the Thomson newspaper chain received wide criticism because of the influence Thomson's other holdings could have on its own papers. Thomson's holdings include oil and gas companies and hundreds of others, including the Hudson's Bay Co., which controls Simpsons and Zellers and part of Simpsons-Sears — all major advertisers. When Thomson was poised, ready to take over The Bay, in 1979, *Toronto Star* financial columnist John McArthur commented,

> . . . it is particularly, and obviously, potentially dangerous for newspapers, radio and TV stations to be connected by ownership to the very industries they depend upon for ad revenue and on which they are expected to report impartially and fully.[32]

(iii) Quality of programming

A third way in which present trends in media ownership can affect the media's product is in quality of programming.

As papers, TV and radio stations fall into the control of fewer and fewer groups, there is a decline in the competition and pride in quality that sometimes characterised independent media outlets. For a variety of reasons — which include lack of competition and a man-

agement made up of professional businessmen rather than professional journalists — the quality of programming slips from mediocre to worse. Describing the level of journalism in the dozens of radio stations that are part of large media groups, a journalist noted,

> In many small stations, there are what is called the rip and read announcers: they simply rip the pre-written newscast off the wire and read it.[33]

The Halifax papers the *Chronicle-Herald* and *Mail-Star* were seen by the 1970 Senate Committee to be "uncomfortably close to being typical of too many Canadian dailies". The editorial failure of such publications does not stem primarily from "news suppression", according to the committee:

> It stems, rather from what Dr [Donald] Cameron calls 'enforced laziness' — the imposition by newspaper ownerships of an atmosphere in which editorial initiatives are unwelcome. People who want to practice vigorous, independent journalism do not thrive in such an atmosphere. *(Sen.I:90)*

.ie typical Canadian newspaper has become

> ... the kind that prints news releases in-tact, that seldom extends its journalistic enterprise beyond coverage of the local trout festival, that hasn't annoyed anyone important in years. Their city rooms are refuges for the frustrated and disillusioned, and their editorial pages a daily testimony to the notion that Chamber-of-Commerce boosterism is an adequate substitute for community service. It is our sad impression that a great many, if not most Canadian newspapers fall into this classification. Interestingly enough, among them are some of the most profitable newspapers in the country. A number of these newspapers are owned by K. C. Irving. *(Sen.I)*[34]

When there is a tacit understanding in a newsroom that certain stories are best left alone to avoid trouble, the result is the kind of coverage just described — on trout festivals.

Supporters of media take-overs have claimed that if a newspaper is part of a large chain, its quality will actually improve because the chains have more resources at their disposal. However, a 1978 study in the U.S. found results to the contrary. It compared 28 chain-operated papers with the same number of independently-owned papers. The papers were comparable in size (circulation) and time of day at which they appeared. Papers *without* chain affiliation had 16% more national news, 35% more international news, and 25% more local and regional news. The unaffiliated papers also featured more staff-written stories (rather than syndicated news).[35] Other studies have also shown that chains tend to raise both the newsstand price and the advertising rates of papers that they take over, but they do not make efforts to improve content.[36]

While no study (such as those just mentioned) is definitive, we have not found any serious evidence to support a different interpretation: media takeovers do not improve the quality of news, nor do large chains compete more fiercely in a way that produces a better product. Indeed what we were able to find in Canada confirmed the results of the American studies.

A case in point is the relationship between what were, until early 1980, two of Canada's rival newspaper chains — Southam and FP Publications. While they appeared to be adversaries, apparently competing with each other, they got along remarkably well in Vancouver, BC. There, they put out the two dailies together: the *Sun*, owned by FP and the *Pro-*

"Since the activities of this company are a matter of public record, the purpose of this meeting is to devise means of covering our tracks in the future!"

vince, owned by Southam. Both papers were published by Pacific Press, whose ownership was shared on a 50-50 basis by Southam and FP, and were produced out of the same building *(Sen.II:62)*.

FP has now been consumed by a still larger giant, Thomson.

Southstar is another example — a company jointly owned by the Southam chain and the *Toronto Star*. It publishes *Today*, formerly called *Canadian Weekend*, in turn a merger of the old *Weekend* and *Canadian* magazines. The new hybrid of course cut in half the number of articles needed for every issue — and hence the number of writers, editors, artists and others needed. While operating costs would be lowered and advertising revenue concentrated still further, the reading public in effect was receiving less and less.

On August 27, 1980, the Southam chain closed down its paper, the *Tribune* in Winnipeg, leaving an unrivalled Thomson daily there, while on the same day the Thomson chain closed down its paper, the *Journal* in Ottawa, leaving the Southam chain unrivalled there. There were charges that these closings constituted restrictive trade practices, and a Royal Commission of Inquiry was established to investigate.

The reason given by Canada's famous Lord Thomson of Fleet for media take-overs is

clear: "I buy newspapers to make money to buy more newspapers to make more money."[37]

In a recent study, the declining quality of journalism in Canada was documented by the University of Quebec at Montreal. Fewer and fewer journalists are investigating stories on their own. Researchers found out that for the period under study, 67% of TV news coverage was exclusively the thought and opinion of government officials.[38]

(iv) Distortions caused by limited access to media

The fact that very few people have access to the media can affect the actual messages they relay as well. The very images the media relay (e.g., wives of Texas oil millionaires, spies, police, etc.) bear no relation to the lives and work of the vast majority of people in this country or around the world. The result is a distortion of reality.

For examples, of the 6,900 radio stations in the United States in 1971, blacks owned only eleven, though they formed 10% of the American population. Of the 848 TV stations, blacks owned none.[39] The thousands of blacks who keep America's industries working, those who teach in its cities, work in its mines or harvest its crops, do not appear in American television images.

Similarly, Canadians as an entire people are almost invisible in their own mass media programming. Few prime-time TV shows are Canadian or have Canadian content, apart from hockey. Testifying before Canada's Senate Committee, one advertising executive criticised the way editorial decisions are made in the mass media:

Fond recollections of advice to be ruthless

Before he sold the prestigious *Times* of London to an Australian scandal-sheet millionaire, Ken Thomson insisted he would close down the paper rather than sell it at a lower price. Reminiscing on earlier days, Canada's media millionaire said he was sure that his father would have wanted him to do this. Sharing a family story with reporters, he remembered the old days, when his father had sold his very first radio station. Didn't it make him sad?, he had asked his father.

> He says, 'Son, there's a time to buy and a time to sell.' And he says, 'Don't ever let sentiment get in the way.'

(22 Oct 80 CBC-TV news)

All the news that fits . . .

In the midst of a union organising drive in the 1930s, the *Halifax Herald* abruptly withdrew its labour reporters, and a news blackout on the drive ensued. One of the organisers, Charles Murray, asked the *Herald's* publisher why the paper had done this. Didn't he think the paper had a responsibility at least to report the facts? His reply:

> "We've no obligation to build your union for you."

The measure of editorial acceptability becomes 'How does it fit?' or 'Will it interest the affluent?' As a consequence, the mass media increasingly reflect the attitudes and deal with the concerns of the affluent. We don't have mass media, we have class media — media for the upper and middle classes.

The poor, the young, the old, the Indian, the Eskimo, the blacks, are virtually ignored. It is as if they don't exist. More important, these minority groups are denied expression in the mass media because they cannot command attention as the affluent can.[40]

Distortions can also be caused by limited public access to the information that mass media do possess. When an experienced journalist wrote the Southam newspaper chain to protest against a travel article that appeared to him to be a thinly disguised public relations article for a large private Canadian airline, this was the reply he got from the paper's publisher:

The investment is paying off: for us and for our advertisers.

When you advertise in Maclean's, you're investing in an environment where nothing is passive, where the relationship between writer and reader hinges on issues of importance, on a sense of urgency, a promise of *the news that matters*.

Above: Maclean's bid to advertisers in the Financial Post, 2 December 78. Note hundred-dollar bills coming out of the magazine.

I think perhaps you have become so accustomed to investigative reporting that you have fallen into the trap of assuming that you have some right to detailed knowledge and information in any area that crosses your mind. Such is really not the case . . .[11]

He had asked whether the writer was from the marketing department or a bona fide journalist. Although the journalist's concerns proved to have been well founded, the paper was under no obligation to report to its readers the nature of the distortion — promotional material passing for news.

(v) Unconscious bias

However, perhaps the most unsettling trend today is the subtlest and most difficult to recognize.

Far-reaching and profound in its influence, it may be the least tangible. This is the often unconscious distortion of events and issues that results when the interests of a newspaper, TV station or other media outlet coincide with the way a journalist already views the world.

A study done for the Royal Commission on Corporate Concentration, titled *The newspaper and freedom of information*, recognises how ownership can affect the content of newspapers. Media owners could

easily influence the general orientation of a newspaper and thereby can influence news content in many ways. Thus, through selection of managers at the supervisory level, the choice of editorial writers and journalists, monetary and intangible rewards, biased guidelines and direct intervention owners can considerably influence the handling of the news.[12]

When the *general orientation* of news reporters, commentators, researchers, editors and producers reflects that of the owners, it then is a matter of chance if journalists uncover a "real story" — not a matter of profession. If all of them have similar starting points and outlooks on the world, the news and the images they make for the mass media become "homogenised".

(vi) Technology

"— But ownership of the media by a few people is necessary and inevitable! In an age when technology is increasing in sophistication (and hence cost) almost by the month, and especially in a country as big as Canada, who else but the very rich could afford to own a newspaper or a TV station?"

Some variation of this position can be heard quite often.

Technology itself, the argument goes, requires increasing interdependency, and thus increasing control. The small number of media owners is necessary — in fact inevitable, according to this argument.

Technological change is already a major global issue today, and will indeed present increasingly acute problems as time passes. Unemployment, trade barriers, and many other trends cannot be fully understood without considering its impact. However, we must first remember that technology does not develop magically on its own, and then confront humans with a *fait accompli*. Humans create technology for specific reasons, with research and development financing of some kind. Technology may well surprise a society that is not prepared for it. However, this happens because the people who are responsible have not informed society of these developments or their implications (for example, the connection between automation and unemployment, or nuclear technology and its risks).

Furthermore, refining and improving high technology (as is done in the media industries) is a deliberate choice that is being made over refining and improving other, medium or low technologies. Which technology — high, medium or low — is the *appropriate* technology? Who has the power to decide? Author Robert Cirino suggests that the myth that only the other side uses propaganda does not deal with the decided bias that is introduced into the media by technical or financial requirements of high technology. He maintains that "all the people in the world are in a state of being propagandised by the very technical and financial nature of modern communications."[13]

Just as the tail does not wag the dog, technology does not determine the media's future: *those who control the media determine its technology*. For this reason we must ask some basic questions.

• Who makes the decisions to develop these increasingly sophisticated (and interdependent) technologies? How has the development of these new technologies been paid for?

• For what reasons have these new technologies been developed? In what institutions was the original research done, and for what reasons?

Attempting to provide all the specific answers to such questions is not the aim of this book. However such crucial questions must never-

theless be asked when examining ownership and control of the media. High, medium or low technology in itself is neither good nor bad: the *use it is put to* determines this.

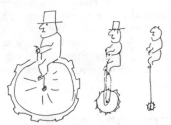

Finally, the question of increasing sophistication of mass media technology must be clearly separated from that of programme quality. Instant communication does not guarantee that the *quality* of news is improved. For example, the quality of newsreporting in a paper is not necessarily any better because computerized telecommunications equipment allow stories to be written, edited, typeset for printing and relayed to other computer terminals all in one, nearly instantaneous operation. Such technology accelerates information exchange, but can in no way guarantee that the information itself is of any worth.

Discussion
Is there any difference between controlling the communications industry and controlling other sectors of the economy?

Conclusions
These, then, are some of the ways in which present trends in the media can alter the kinds of news we receive — or the very way we see the world.

The concentration of ownership and control in the mass media is dramatic. As wll, any significant access* to the media by the majority of Canadians is extremely limited. Indeed the mass media, by their very nature, are one-way media: they are not designed for receiving or exchanging mass messages — only giving them.[14]

We have also seen how prevalent the use of unsound or unfair techniques of persuasion

---

*(ie, prime-time TV or radio, major film or record industries or large-circulation print media; decision-making and direction of programming, etc.)

can be (Chapter II). With the mass media of communication, however, bias is broadcast instantly and in all directions. There is little chance of anyone replying or correcting any distortions they create. When one considers all these factors in combination, the question of media ownership becomes all the more relevant. We have given some indication of the fundamental difference this concentration of power and control can make.

Whether or not it matters to you depends on whether you are interested in really knowing what is going on around you, and around the world.

Discussion/research

1. The owners of large corporations and owners of large media complexes have been described as being in a *symbiotic* relation to one another. What does "symbiosis" mean in this context? *Revenues needed by M/M*

2. It is the business of newspapers to make money.
— Lord Roy Thomson[45]

a. Who was Lord Thomson of Fleet? (One suggested reference: *Maclean's* 30 Apr 79.)

b. Prepare arguments for or against his statement (Ref. Wallace Clement, "Dominant media complexes," *Canadian corporate élite*, p. 306-323).

3. Management's obligation is to protect the interests of those stockholders.
— Chairman of the Board, CBS[46]

Discuss.

4. All forms of communication (including this book) represent certain interests. The point of course is to determine what interests are represented in any communication, and to decide where one's own interests lie, compare these to one's code of ethics (and then, presumably, act accordingly).
Can you determine where your interests lie?

5. Given present trends in the mass media, can the rights set out in the Universal Declaration of Human Rights (Art.19) be guaranteed? What rights do you feel you should have? Should everyone have the same rights?

6. Commenting on the general reading public's fascination with science in the past three or four years, an official of Time-Life publications said his company was in a position to "market" science. Magazines with science cover stories were the "best selling", and therefore they would be marketing a number of new publications to satisfy this market.[47]

a. What are the merits and drawbacks to this form of "marketing" of scientific ideas?

b. If you were the general editor of a science series, what major themes or issues would you want to cover in the series? On what basis would you make your editorial decisions?

c. Prepare a research paper on the present series that popularise science. What major areas are covered? What ones are not covered?

7. Freedom of the press is guaranteed only to those who own one.
— A. J. Liebling
Discuss.

4. Where does government fit in?

We hope something has been conspicuous by its absence in our discussions so far.

That is any mention of the government — whether in the form of the CBC or any regulatory body — in the control of information in society.

A government may decide to regulate all information flow in one way or another in its country; it may create its own information sources. In Canada, we find some variations of both these activities.

"I see creeping socialism, chiselers on relief and the erosion of fiscal integrity in government!"

The CBC

With the establishment in 1936 by the Canadian Government of the Canadian Broadcasting Corporation (CBC), a public system of broadcasting was created. This includes CBC Radio, CBC English TV, and the radio and TV services of Radio-Canada. Similar institutions exist in Britain (the BBC, British Broadcasting Corporation) and in France (the ORTF, Office de Radio-Télédiffusion Française). No body of similar scope exists in the United States, the largest broadcaster in the world (although there does exist a small Public Broadcasting System).

The CBC is a Crown Corporation, and as such provides a public service to the whole of Canada. It is available to 96% of the Canadian population. The whole of Canada of course includes the "non-profitable" parts of Canada like the North, and relatively non-profitable parts like the rural areas of the Maritimes, Newfoundland, Labrador, the prairies etc. CBC television is available to 97% of the Atlantic population and an average of 94% of Canada's total population. As an autonomous, non-commercial network, the CBC receives an annual grant from Parliament, is responsible to it, and communicates with it through the Secretary of State.

The CBC's autonomy has been seriously jeopardised by direct U.S. programming in our country.* Only passing reference can be made here to the profound effect US prgraming has had on our society, our culture, and in the final analysis our selves. In short, the CBC attempts to provide Canadian programming — news, entertainment, in-depth studies —

with Canadian content and done by Canadians, in both official languages. As it does this, it competes with U.S. programming (through commercial TV networks and cable TV in Canada). Yet it must also compete with the border US stations that beam programmes directly into Canada without even the minimum legal Canadian content requirements that commercial stations must fulfil. In the case of American beaming of programmes, the profits of the commercial US stations (which come from advertisers, who pay well for this access to our livingrooms) do not go to Canada, and are therefore not re-invested in programmes done by Canadians. American border stations cream off an estimated $20 million a year of Canadian advertising money as well.[18]

Despite these obstacles, the quality of CBC programming is still superior to that of its commercial counterparts. In doing research for this book, we found that commercial TV and radio produced little of note in regular news or current affairs programmes. Perhaps it is not coincidental that the most reliable programmes that do exist, dealing with thought-provoking and carefully researched issues, have been produced by the CBC, which has some measure of independence from advertisers and ratings.

While recognising this strength, however, we must not leave the impression that the CBC is a homogenous structure consistently reflecting the best of investigative journalism, ideas and the arts. The quality of programming varies greatly within CBC radio and television, and within individual programmes.

CBC Radio's best-known current affairs show is a case in point. Though *Sunday Morning* has produced excellent documentaries on other topics, its coverage of Iran, for example, could hardly be called courageous. At key

*In a 10-year study period (1967-77), the Maritime provinces showed the most dramatic increase in receiving US broadcasts: from none in PEI or Nova Scotia to 31% and 64% of the population respectively. In New Brunswick 56% of the population could receive at least one US station. CRTC (79) Special Report on Broadcasting in Canada, Vol. 1, p.31.

points in Iran's recent history, the programme ignored or downplayed the immense suffering of ordinary people in Iran, and instead portrayed the country's dictator, the Shah, as a stern but gentlemanly father figure whose well-meaning reforms had somehow just not worked out. When U.N. Secretary-General Kurt Waldheim visited the country, *Sunday Morning* reported that he was shown a child whose arms had been "allegedly cut off"[49] in front of his father. Though other sources such as Amnesty International had long described the U.S.-backed regime as having a record of torture that was "beyond belief", *Sunday Morning* chose to ignore mentioning this when the Shah died. Instead it spoke of the coming to an end of a "2,000-year reign", repeating the absurd historical fiction created by the Shah's family itself. His last 18 months, after being overthrown and driven out of Iran by a massive uprising throughout the country, were "a lonely existence", according to the sympathetic report. There was no mention of the imprisonment, torture and deaths of thousands of peasants, children, professionals, trade unionists and others throughout the country during his dictatorship.[50]

The award-winning filmmaker, Peter Watkins describes the unwillingness of CBC television to support initiatives that might turn out to be controversial. After having invited him to make a film for television, CBC-TV changed its mind. Watkins recalls,

> I proposed to show what could happen if the newly constructed reactor in the Philippines (partly fuelled by Canadian uranium) went into melt-down. The CBC abruptly withdrew its offer of work, and the letter confirming their rejection of the Philippines film was typed two days before the Harrisburg accident in the United States.[51]

National Film Board

In 1939 the National Film Board of Canada was established, taking over the old Motion Picture Bureau. A Crown Corporation, the Film Board has a mandate to produce and distribute Canadian films. While it also has produced some excellent films, on a number of occasions the NFB has not funded films in order to avoid controversy. On other occasions, it has supported films which are thinly veiled public relations films for business or industry (e.g., a film on the Ford motor company, which was then shown around the world).

The NFB's film library is open to the public, free of charge.

Regulatory bodies

Government regulatory bodies oversee the operations of business or utilities that are deemed to be public concerns. The only part of the mass media with a regulatory body is the broadcasting industry. Certain sections of the Criminal Code of Canada deal with obscene or hate literature, but there is no body that deals with the ownership, control or Canadian content in newspaper, book publishing or printing. The Combines Investigation Branch or the Restrictive Trade Practices Commission of the federal government could have influence over certain aspects of the ownership of the print industry, but neither has exercised it.

A Press Ownership Review Board was one of the recommendations strongly argued for by the 1970 Senate Committee on the Mass Media: it has not been acted on. An entire study, *The newspaper firm and freedom of information* by the Royal Commission on Corporate Concentration, and others by the Secretary of State on the publishing industry in Canada have been produced as well. No action has resulted.

The film and record industries have no regulatory body, although films are subject to local boards of censors who rule on matters of obscenity and violence but have nothing to do with such questions as ownership, control or Canadian content.[52]

For radio and television broadcasting and cable systems in Canada, there is the federal CRTC (the Canadian Radio-television and Telecommunications Commission). Established by the Broadcasting Act of 1968, the CRTC licenses all private and public broadcasting. The Ministry of Communications holds the responsibility for the CRTC. Broadcasters must meet Canadian content and other requirements to qualify for a licence. The CRTC issues licences to broadcasters, much in the same way that businesses get liquor licences or motorists driver's licences. Similarly, if it is proven that the licence holder has been in violation of any of the rules and regulations, the licence can be revoked. Public hearings are conducted at the time of licence renewals; any member of the public can make an intervention at these hearings. All licence holders or applicants must list full information about ownership and control of their company.

While it has a wide mandate, the CRTC has been criticised for not being able to deal effectively with such fundamental questions as American programmes and concentration of ownerships of the electronic media. At all times 80% of Canadian TVs are on American programmes — more than when the CRTC was established twelve years ago.[53] If the CRTC is the "industry's watchdog", then it seems to have caught itself in a fine tangle of restricted areas of investigation and other competing government departments for jurisdiction ... to the point where the watchdog can do little if anything.

Discussion/research

1. Does your family or anyone you know listen to the CBC? What role does the CBC play in your community? What role do you think the CBC plays in Canada today?

2. There has been increasing discussion of a "user pay" approach to services in this country. Some provinces, for example, are introducing "user pay" fees at hospitals. Arrange a debate where the "user pay" position is discussed, including the "user pay" concept for the media. (For example, who would pay for the news and feature stories?).

3. Given the international situation (trends towards concentration of media ownership), what should the CRTC do in Canada?

4. Do a research essay on the CBC.

5. Considering the general state of the media in Canada, the CBC is like a temporary patch on a blow-out.

In a well-documented essay which takes into account the question of ownership raised in this section of the book, discuss this point of view. (The image suggests that there is something wrong with the present state of affairs. In your presentation, be sure to clarify whether you agree or disagree with this viewpoint.)

Other government intervention

After examining the other aspects of government relations to the mass media, we cannot ignore, at the level of media content, some more direct interventions by governments.

An almost invisible form of government influence on the mass media is the promotion of an administration's policies and programmes through government public relations departments. According to one Canadian study, 67% of TV news coverage was exclusively the thought and opinion of government officials.[54] While this fact might be attributed in large part to the laziness of the press, other examples of government influence cannot be so explained.

In a quickly-forgotten but nevertheless highly significant brief to the Canadian Radio-television and Telecommunications Commission (CRTC), former CBC *National* news announcer Peter Kent detailed four incidents in which he said intervention by the Prime Minister's Office resulted in either special or broadened coverage of the Prime Minister. The most recent example had been Prime Minister Trudeau's "hours-before-showtime" demand for live coverage of his widely criticised August 1978 economic programme.[55]

The Canadian Government is also the country's biggest advertiser, and at times its advertising has had obvious political dimensions. During the 1980 Quebec referendum, the Federal Government flooded the mass media with overt or thinly disguised "pro-Canada" messages. In the days preceding the referendum, government health ads urged Quebec drinkers to say, "Non, merci." Ads reminded Quebec tourists that the Rocky Mountains provided "so much to stay for." In a *Saturday Night* article, Morris Wolfe reported that during one hour of a widely viewed tennis championship on CFTM, a private French-language station in Montreal, federal ads appeared nine times:

... at 2:04, the Department of Energy, Mines and Resources; at 2:08, Customs; at 2:15, an ad urging people to buy Canadian; at 2:17, the Department of Regional Economic Expansion; at 2:37, Health and Welfare; at 2:41, Energy, Mines and Resources (again); at 2:51, Public Works; at 2:53 Energy Mines and Resources (yet a third time); at 2:58, a tourism ad.[56]

Though the Quebec government tried to stop the Federal campaign, a superior court judge in Montreal ruled in favour of Ottawa.

Regarding outright censorship, as we know, in totalitarian states such as the USSR or Argentina, the state controls the press through direct suppression. However, even in our own country government censorship exists, though this fact is not widely known. Over and above the examples cited earlier of film censors and police interception of obscene and hate literature, there are about 35,000 books, films, videotapes and other materials forbidden entry into Canada under Canadian customs laws.[57] Until a *Maclean's* magazine story on censorship was written, this list included William Faulkner's *Sanctuary* and James Joyce's *Ulysses*! There are still no clear guidelines, and even Members of Parliament cannot find out exactly how much is being censored or even what materials have been refused entry to the country.

Even with this brief glance at how government relates to the mass media, it would be difficult to miss seeing three distinct trends. First, government-financed bodies such as the CBC and NFB do create some kind of alternative to the private media, but other government departments with specific mandates to oversee the mass media have taken little if any effective action to prevent or control corporate take-overs in newspapers, broadcasting and other private media. At the same time, other government departments are themselves using the mass media to further the interests of the administration in power. And finally, still other government departments exercise censorship powers that are generally unknown to the Canadian public or its elected representatives.

5. The global village

We have had a glimpse at the media in our region and in Canada. How do we fit into the international picture? How do the mass media work world-wide?

Let us start by recalling what is perhaps obvious: that the United States is by far the largest source of mass media in the world. Former U.S. Presidential Adviser Zbigniew Brzezinski has noted that 65% of all world communications are emitted from the United States alone.[58]

On a clear, dark night its satellites are visible — blinking across the sky, beaming the news, weather conditions, hockey games or Muhammed Ali to the world. The night news comes into homes nestling down to sleep in the Canadian winter. The news features a swimming meet that is taking place that instant in the blistering sun of Australia: we in Canada may know who the winner is before the contestants do.

The awesome power of mass media to influence how we view the world and ourselves is as important as the business aspect of the global media. Here we will outline briefly some aspects of international media ownership.

Concentration of media ownership is taking place across the globe much in the same way as it is in Canada. Here are a few indications of global trends:

• The American oil company Atlantic Richfield owns the prestigious English weekly, the London *Observer*.

• America's oldest continuously publishing paper, the *New York Post* has been bought out by an Australian press conglomerate.[59]

• The Canadian Thomson newspaper chain is listed among the top 100 foreign-owned companies in the United States.[60] In addition to the more than 119 papers owned in North America, Thomson has large holdings around the world.

The International Thomson Organisation has interests in book publishing companies, some broadcasting interests, a travel business (including an airline), North Sea oil companies. ITO has purchased an American textbook publisher, a microfilming company and 21 gas-producing wells in Mississippi.[61]

• The giant FIAT car-manufacturing company, owned by the Agnelli family, has amongst its holdings textbook and encyclopedia publishers, and Bantam Books (including the rights to over 1,500 titles of which one, *The Exorcist*, has sold over 20 million copies). With the Rothschild family (Fundy Tidal power, Churchill Falls), the Agnellis share a British subsidiary of children's books. FIAT has 20% ownership of the successful French "Livre de Paris" of Hachette publishers, and has the

TOP 50

How does your daily reading rate in global terms? Here, in order of circulation, are 50 of the world's biggest publications. M = Monthly, F = Fortnightly, W = Weekly, D = Daily.

	Publication	Base	Frequency	Circulation (millions)
1	Readers Digest	USA	M	29.0
2	Pravda	USSR	D	9.0
3	Isvestia	USSR	D	8.4
4	Komsomolskaya Pravda	USSR	D	7.7
5	National Geographic	USA	M	7.6
6	Penthouse	UK	M	6.7
7	Asahi Shimbun	Japan	D	6.5
8	Playboy	USA	M	5.8
9	Good Housekeeping	USA	M	5.7
10	Time	USA	W	5.3
11	News of the World	UK	W	5.2
12	Sunday People	UK	W	4.1
13	Sunday Mirror	UK	W	4.1
14	Hore Zu	W. Germ.	W	4.0
15	Daily Mirror	UK	D	3.9
16	Bild Zeitung	W. Germ.	D	3.6
17	Sunday Express	UK	W	3.5
18	The Sun	UK	D	3.5
19	Peoples Daily	China	D	3.4
20	Radio Times	UK	W	3.4
21	Newsweek	USA	W	3.3
22	TV Times	UK	W	3.2
23	NY Sunday News	USA	W	3.0
24	Mainichi Shimbun	Japan	D	3.0
25	Daily Express	UK	D	2.7
26	Fernsehe woche	W. Germ.	W	2.4
27	Bild am Sonntag	W. Germ.	W	2.3
28	Burda Moden	W. Germ.	M	2.2
29	NY Daily News	USA	D	2.1
30	Modes et Travaux	France	M	1.8
31	Bonne Soiree	France	M	1.7
32	Daily Mail	UK	D	1.7
33	Funk Uhr	W. Germ.	W	1.7
34	Womans Weekly	UK	W	1.7
35	Glamour	USA	M	1.6
36	Nihon Kaizai Shimbun	Japan	D	1.5
37	Sunday NY Times	USA	W	1.5
38	Stern	W. Germ.	M	1.5
39	Brigitte	W. Germ.	F	1.4
40	Bunte	W. Germ.	W	1.4
41	Europa	Belgium	M	1.4
42	Sunday Times	UK	W	1.4
43	Wall Street Journal	USA	D	1.4
44	Daily Telegraph	UK	D	1.3
45	Al Ahram	Egypt	D	1.2
46	Chicago Tribune	USA	D	1.2
47	Los Angeles Times	USA	D	1.2
48	Selecciones de Readers Digest	USA	M	1.2
49	Bild und Funk	W. Germ.	W	1.0
50	Quick	W. Germ.	M	1.0

Notes:
1. For comparison, the biggest publications in *Canada*, *Australia* and *New Zealand* are: *Toronto Star* (0.8m) *Sun News Pictorial* (0.6m) and *N.Z. Herald* (0.2m) respectively. *(New Internationalist 0.017m)*.
2. Sources: *BRAD, Advertisers Annual, Publishers, UNESCO.*
3. As figures for certain publications were not available this list may not be exhaustive.

— from *New Internationalist*, Oct 76

German subsidiary of the American Praeger publishers.[62]

• The New Brunswick-based Irving media empire is connected, through its oil and other holdings, with Standard Oil of California. Since 1973, Standard Oil has owned 49% of Irving Oil, although this was only publicly disclosed in December 1979. Standard Oil oversees as well a huge agribusiness in California.[63]

• Four of the largest record companies in the world — CBS, MCA, RCA and Warner — are affiliated with giant corporate complexes that are also involved in films and book publishing.[64]

• The Nova Scotia pulp and paper mills Bowaters-Mersey are part of a giant world-wide conglomerate owned by the British-based forest products company. Bowaters-Mersey owns 51% of the Washington *Post*. Bowaters' largest customer (80% of production) happens to be the Washington *Post*.[65]

Networks

The top TV networks in the world are closely integrated with hundreds of related and non-related companies.

NBC is a subsidiary of RCA, as are Hertz, the Commercial Credit Company, Random House publishing, and Defence Electronics Products, to name some.

CBS is part of a group of companies reported to include the publishers Holt Rinehart and Winston, Columbia Records, Creative Play-things and the New York Yankees baseball team.

ABC network is part of PBC-Paramount, which in turn is linked to Gulf & Western. The Gulf & Western empire includes among other things, sugar and breakfast cereal companies, plantations in the Dominican Republic, Paramount Pictures, the TV series *Happy Days* and the New York Rangers. ABC has extensive media holdings in Latin America and other parts of the '"Third World".[66]

PTL In terms of U.S. size, after the NBC and CBS networks and before ABC comes the fundamentalist PTL (meaning "Praise The Lord", or "People That Love") network. With earth satellite stations across the globe, PTL beams live broadcasts 24 hours a day around the world, and has a staff of over 500, claiming a viewing audience of nearly 20% of the entire U.S. viewing public. Another fundamentalist network, CBN (Christian Broadcasting Net-

work) also has installed world-wide satellite communications and employs a staff of 700.

Both PTL and CBN are expanding to include sports coverage, situation comedies, variety and soap operas, with a fundamentalist message. As CBN's advertising consultant Bob Bloom notes, "we are trying to sell a product and that product is Jesus Christ."[67] At the time of writing, these two networks appeared to be the most far-reaching and significant new developments in media network ownership.

South Africa's attempts to purchase the Washington *Star*, and a 50% interest in UPI television before the information scandal broke in 1980, demonstrate the mass media's

vulnerability to be purchased by any interests that bid on them.

Wire services

As for wire services around the world, the Big Five news agencies control global news and information flows. These five are AFP (Agence Fance Press), AP (Associated Press, United States), UPI (United Press International, United States), Reuters (English) and TASS (Telegraph Agency of the Soviet Union).

AP feds 17 million words a day to 10,000 subscribers with journalists in 110 countries with an estimated daily audience of 1 billion.

UPI transmits 14 million words a day to 7,000 subscribers in 90 countries.

Reuters distributes one and a half million words a day in six languages to subscribers in 155 countries. It has 529 permanent correspondents.

AFP journalists in 110 countries put out three million words a day to 12,000 subscribers . . .

TASS is the official news agency for the Soviet Union. Its news is disseminated in Soviet-bloc countries.

None of these major agencies is from the "Third World". All the "Third World" countries, then, must rely almost entirely on outside sources for news about each other. They are furthermore dependent on outside sources for such things as specialised radio and TV technology, and newsprint. Add the dependency of "Third World" media on First World technology and resources to its dependency on international wire services, and we can get some idea of the extremely limited view of the "Third World" that can be presented in the mass media.[68] There are also fewer and fewer full-time correspondents abroad. The Overseas Press Club of America's survey showed the following downward trend in numbers of foreign journalists:

1969	929
1972	797
1975	429

The decline has been more rapid since the survey was completed.[69]

The mass media view of the "Third World" is inadequate. Crises and disasters are highlighted, giving little or no context for stories. Also there are very few English-speaking journalists who can speak any of the hundreds of languages of the peoples who live in the countries they are trying to report on.

A study by the Ottawa-based International Development Research Centre (IDRC) found

---

Sometimes the most ordinary things can prove to reveal startling realities when examined more closely.

One such example is a reference, made in passing on a current affairs radio programme. It was simply mentioned that 700 "top opinion-makers" had been invited to the White House for an explanation of a U.S. government policy. *(CBC Sunday Morning 24 June 79)*

What is striking is not necessarily the fact that journalists and media people can allow themselves to be the objects of such obvious forms of flattery and influence-peddling (700 people clearly cannot ask a press secretary for amplification of a particular point, or conduct an interview). More striking, rather, is that it *is* in fact possible to identify 700 people, bring them into a building together and then expect them to leave and "make" the opinions of the 220,000,000 other people in the United States, and by extension many millions more in Canada and around the world.

that where there was coverage on the "Third World" in the Canadian press, almost absent from it was any mention of such key issues as population, energy, food and positive development efforts. Instead political upheavals, business affairs, international crimes and personalities received coverage.[70]

Why it is that news networks focus on these kinds of issues is a complex question that needs much fuller treatment than can be given here. However, the question of increasing concentration and control of news media and communications generally cannot be ignored.

Sensational . . .

The profits in the communications industries are phenomenal. These figures are from the *Financial Post's 125*. The article told the reader to "Write 1978 down in the record books" as a very good year for profits . . .

Profit Margins

Communications:	4th quarter profit margin
Baton Broadcasting	11.6%
Maclean-Hunter	6.8%
Selkirk Holdings	16.3%
Southam Inc.	8.7%
Thomson Newspapers	22.4%
Torstar	5.2%
Western Broadcasting	21.0%

The average rate of profits for the communications industry was 11.6%, a full five percentage points higher than the average overall profit for all corporations. This was over four percentage points higher than the lucrative oil and gas industries.
— from "It *was* a good year," *Financial Post* 7 April 79.

Why so many mergers?

The reasons for concentration of media ownership on a global scale are fundamentally the same as those for concentration in Canada. Indeed, company mergers take place so often and so quickly that it is difficult to keep up-to-date information on them. For Canada, the *Globe and Mail* reported that corporate mergers increased by 33% in 1978 alone! It furthermore suggested that if more precise figures were kept, they would probably also show that the value of assets involved in the mergers was up "considerably more".[71] The number and frequency of these mergers is closely related to the high level of profits in the communications industry. Despite "what you hear in the media" (!), the media and communications industries are one of the most profitable areas of investment that exist.*

The Senate Committee examined the charge that labour costs are the reason for newspapers doing badly and then being bought up by huge chains. They found that while publishing and broadcasting are subject to the same inflationary pressures as other sectors, "on an industry-wide basis both productivity and returns on capital are increasing faster than labour costs." *(Sen.*I:56)

The Committee found that retained earnings — that is, the profits which a corporation holds back and usually invests in expansion or in other corporations — were much higher in the daily newspaper business than in other manufacturing industries. This indicates both high profit levels, and a desire on the part of the owners to acquire still more companies:

> This underlines what we know already: that newspapers are less likely than other corporations to borrow or to issue new shares when they need extra money; usually they can finance expansions and acquisitions from their profits. (*Sen.*I:56)

The high profit levels prompt media owners to buy up still more companies, or develop still more sophisticated technologies: in order not to pay taxes on such high profits (such as the 180% cable TV profits), investors hold back, or "retain" these earnings and reinvest them elsewhere. For Canada (as in some other countries):

---

*Levels of profits in the cable TV business are almost beyond belief. In a ten-year period (1967-77), total pre-tax profits for cable in Canada increased by 2,411%! Even average profits in communications are sensational (see box this page). From 1972 to 1977 pre-tax profits were still an extraordinary 180%. CRTC (79) Special Report on Broadcasting in Canada, Vol 2, p. 7-7 and 7-8.

One of Roy Thompson's most memorable observations was that a TV broadcasting permit is 'like having a licence to print your own money.' . . . ownership of a daily newspaper often amounts to the same thing, except you don't need a licence . . . (*Sen*.I:47)

Under our tax laws, shareholders are taxed only on the earnings they receive as dividends. The remainder, the profits the company keeps in the treasury as retained earnings, aren't taxable until they're distributed. The effect is that large corporations which keep earning profits build up larger and larger reserves of retained earnings.[72]

When a company makes new acquisitions the money that was profit becomes a new cost and is therefore not taxed in the same way. Money then comes back to the investor from several sources: the original newspaper, say, and its affiliates and cable stations. Thus, while we speak of TV "networks", referring to their electronic hook-ups, we might also use the same image to describe media ownership: *profit networks* . . .

"In examining our books, Mr. Mathews promises to use generally accepted accounting principles, if you know what I mean."

And the larger they become, the easier it is for the media industries, like any giant company, to get huge amounts of credit (if they so wish) to finance still larger take-overs . . .

Here is a newspaper's description of Time, Inc.:

It was once simply the factory of words. Now the house that Luce built has added rooms for timber, shipping containers, pay-TV, food marketing information, real estate — even racquetball. A 'broad-based

communications company' is what it calls itself, but many people are not sure what to call it. One person suggests simply labelling it the money factory.[73]

Given such conditions, many competitors of the large media complexes have not been able to survive.

Decisions about new technological developments in the different spheres of mass media communications are made by the very firms that stand to gain by these developments. In the field of satellite and cable systems, the same firms that dominate the electronics, aerospace and media industries are important decision-makers:

On the list of the 20 principal owners of cable TV systems are Hughes Aircraft, Warner Communications, Gulf & Western, CBS, RKO, Transamerica, Time-Life, and General Electric. Among the most important distributors of pay cable TV are Warner Communications, Columbia Pictures, Time-Life, Hughes Aircraft and Gulf & Western.[74]

The global market

The world has become an integrated "global market" for the global corporation (and more recently, fundamentalist religion). This is how the President of one of the largest corporations in the world, IBM, describes the world:

For business purposes, the boundaries that separate one nation from another are no more real than the equator. They are merely convenient demarcations of ethnic, linguistic, and cultural entitites. They do not define business requirements or consumer trends. Once management understands and accepts this world economy its view of the marketplace — and its planning — necessarily expand. The world outside the home country is no longer viewed as a series of disconnected customers and prospects for its products, but as an extension of a single market.[75]

In an international context, Canada is a principal market for American situation comedies and news. According to the head of Columbia Motion Pictures and TV,

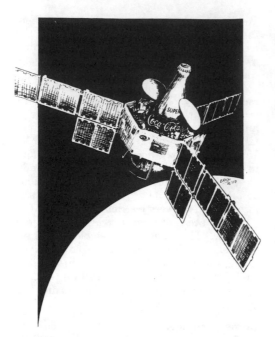

Certainly the best American customer [*sic*] today, the easiest customer, and best payer, is Canada.[76]

Canadians are part of the same information, news and entertainment "market" that people in India, Nigeria or Brazil are. The type of technology, and the power and ownership needed make the world what is known as a "seller's market". Used goods can be peddled

for as much as the market will bear. Thus, people all over the world watch *Get Smart*, a situation comedy from the 1960s, over and over again . . . up to five times a day in some cities and regularly in 67 countries.[77] *Bonanza* has an estimated weekly audience of 350 million.[78] These serials are older than the many millions of young people around the world who watch them. American business supplies local cultures the world over.

One might ask, what is wrong if Maritimers, Torontonians, Inuit, Brazilians or Nigerians all are watching the same TV programme?

To answer this question the meaning of the IBM President's statement above must be fully understood. A professor at the Massachussetts Institute of Technology explains in another way:

> The function that American international communications can serve is to provide people with things for which they are craving but which are not readily available to them . . . Another thing that people crave is simply to see what a modern way of life is like — seeing *commodities*, seeing how people live, or hearing popular music.[79].

The President of the Television Bureau of Canada described the interests that the new video technology would serve in this way:

> Be prepared to use it in whatever form it takes in the 1980s, because video-

---

. . . the broadcasting of popular music is not likely to have any immediate effect on the audience's political attitude, but this kind of communication nevertheless provides a sort of entryway of Western ideas and Western concepts, even though these concepts may not be explicitly and completely stated at any one particular moment in the communication.

Dr Joseph Klapper (CBS), to U.S. House of Representatives Committee on Foreign Affairs, 4 May 67. R. Barnet and R. Muller, *Global Reach* (1974), p.31. Emphasis ours.

Lee S. Bickmore, former chairman of the National Biscuit Company, believes the key to the global market is 'the tendency for people all over the world to adopt the same tastes and same consumption habits,' and he has some ideas to help that process along. Some time ago he told *Forbes:* 'Why, we plan some day to advertise all over the world. We might spend, say $8 million for an advertisement on a communications satellite system. It might reach 359 million people. So what we are doing now is establishing the availability of our products in retail outlets all over the world.' When we interviewed him four years later, he was talking of reaching 2 billion munchers someday. In projecting the Ritz Crackers box on TV screens around the world, he emphasised that *his company is selling more than crackers, 'We are selling a concept.'*

Dr Joseph Klapper (CBS), to U.S. House of Representatives Committee on Foreign Affairs, 4 May 67. R. Barnet and R. Muller, *Global Reach* (1974), p.31. Emphasis ours.

communication has become the dominant force in our market place.

It has already changed the social structure of the world, and will likely do so again . . . It will grow to become the single most effective medium that advertisers can use to reach consumers.[80]

Discussion/research

• The 1970 Senate Committee said Canadians should begin to consider the media as a public resource, like electricity, and give them effective regulatory bodies.
• "Knowledge is a non-material investment, which like investments in means of production must be made profitable."
— President, Philips Corporation.[82]
Discuss these divergent points of view.

6. Isn't there any good news?

The title of this chapter was *This message was brought to you by* . . . We now have an idea of who brings us our daily messages . . . what we know about our community, our country, our world.

Some conclusions
We have seen that the mass media in Canada and throughout the world are in fact controlled by very few groups and individuals. These same groups and individuals also sit on the boards of directors of food chain stores, banks, power corporations and oil companies.

We have seen that in the mass media, professional businesspeople, *not* professional journalists, have effective control of the media. That is, the businesspeople make the crucial decisions about overall direction of the media — for investments, for expansion in other industries, staff levels, cutbacks in other areas. These managerial decisions affect in the most profound way the content of the mass media.

Large corporate interests view the mass media primarily as a vehicle to reach a mass market: a large body of people who will *"buy"* things . . . their entertainment, their news coverage, their political commentaries, their world-view — and their commercial products. This fact has an enormous effect on the way we ourselves perceive our involvement in the world.

We have noted that the technology of mass media, by its very nature, concentrates power and decision-making in the hands of a few,

and limits public access to it. Decisions about the continued development of this advanced technology are made by the mass media's owners — those who have the most to gain by them.

These are some of the major trends in the media today. Multinational corporations create in our minds a picture of ourselves — and a picture of the "Third World". (These pictures will be examined in Capters IV and V.) We have seen that these trends are not unique to our country, but rather are global trends. Despite the apparent "information explosion" so often talked about, in fact our sources of information are very restricted.

"Isn't there any good news?" one might well ask. "The picture looks so bleak . . . I see the tremendous influence exercised by advertising, I learn that the media are in fact controlled by so very few. Everything I learn seems to make me feel that I am less and less in control of my life . . ."

Some good news
The picture would indeed look rather bleak if we neglected to note that many people do not accept that present trends in the mass media are definitive or irreversible. Within the media industries themselves, there are many who are raising some of the very questions raised here.

Also worthy of note is the experience of the internationally respected paper *Le Monde*, published in Paris. While not a community effort in the same sense as the others mentioned, it has however maintained considerable independence by remaining under the control of its editorial staff. Millions of dollars of advertising have been turned down in order to maintain a 3-to-2 ratio of news to advertising.* In turn, *Le Monde's* standards of excellence make it a publication in which the most distinguished scholars and others would aspire to see their articles appear.

There have also been hundreds of community groups that have created alternatives to the large media complexes. Co-operative radios, small newspapers, record companies, book publishers, theatre companies, film co-operatives, co-operative bookstores, research teams — all have sprung up and developed across the country. Like alternative energy groups, food or other co-ops, these initiatives prove that *many* people have the skills, intelligence and talent to carry out the endeavours hitherto considered the exclusive domain of

*This ratio is in sharp contrast to North American papers: the ratio of news to ads in the daily press now is estimated at 40% to 60% — almost an exact reversal of pre-World War II ratios in the press.

"Have you been listening to the 6 o'clock news again?"

"experts" or highly paid managers of one kind or another.

Though not *mass* media, they do prove that ordinary people can get together, plan and create products of quality, ranging from their own windmills to their own publishing houses or recording studios. Profit does not have to be one's final goal.

There is also some good news as regards "Third World" news coverage. In 1975 a news pool was created by the non-aligned countries, in order to attempt to counteract Western-dominated news sources. There is also the Inter Press Service, begun in 1964, for coverage of Latin American news,[84] as well as a number of other news pools. Such news pools naturally do not resolve the question of how fairly or accurately "Third World" journalists themselves report on their countries, but then neither does the predominance of "Western" coverage around the world.

While the above examples *in themselves* are not by any means simple solutions to the problems raised in this section on ownership, they do go a long way to show what is possible. They are proof of the determination of many people who will continue creating alternatives to what they consider unsatisfactory or unjust media control. There are references to these alternatives throughout this book and in Section VI.

We should like to suggest that *while the mass media are a powerful force, so is an aware group of people who have made intelligent decisions based on careful thinking and sound information.*

In the end, of course, whether any type of news is good or bad depends on what *you* decide is important to you.

Discussion/research

1. News and advertising have a lot in common. Think about it. You want your message to hit the market just like we want news to hit the reader — with considerable impact. In *Maclean's*, news and advertising have established a unique bond: readers buy us because they have an appetite for both . . .

   . . . You want to reach an affluent market. We've got it . . .

   . . . One year after our launch as a weekly newsmagazine *Maclean's* is unabashedly proud of success. *We've got the medium: you've got the message. We'll make it work.*

   — Ad for *Maclean's* magazine.[84]

   a. Discuss the meaning and implications of the point of view put forward in the above quotation.

   or

   b. In a research essay, examine in depth the content and form of *Maclean's* magazine's newsreporting and its advertising, bearing in mind the above quotation. (See John Sullivan, "A year of the New Maclean's", *This Magazine* 11:1, Jan-Feb 77.)

2. The minority, the ruling class at present, has the schools and press, usually the church as well, under its thumb. This enables it to organise and sway the emotions of the masses, and make its tool of them.

   — Albert Einstein.[85]

   As you know, Albert Einstein was the Nobel Prize-winning physicist whose discoveries include the Theory of Relativity, and the theoretical basis for nuclear fission. You possibly did not know, however, that such a distinguished scientist would hold such views about the suppresion of information in our society.

   a. Find out what Einstein's own views were on the use of nuclear fission for making weapons, and the history of his opposition to this use of nuclear power.

   and/or

   b. What is the role of the scientist in society? What *ought* to be the role of scientists in society?

   c. What is the role of the information media in communicating scientific information to society as a whole? What ought it be?

Further Reading

Packaging the news
James Aronson (1971) NY: International Publishers

Global reach
R. Barnet and R. Mueller (1974) NY: Simon and Schuster

The Washington connection and Third World Fascism
N. Chomsky and E. Herman (1979) Montreal: Black Rose Books

Don't blame the people
R. Cirino (1971) NY: Random House

The Canadian corporate élite
Wallace Clement (1975) Toronto: McClelland and Stewart

The corporate village
C. Hamelink (1977) ed., Rome: IDOC

La parole ça se prend
Institut Canadien d'Education des Adultes (1980), Montreal: ICEA

Les actualités télévisées: le monde recrée au service du pouvoir
Institut Canadien d'Education des Adultes (1979), Montreal: ICEA

Many voices, one world
Sean MacBride (1980) ed., report by the International Commission for the Study of Communication Problems, Paris: UNESCO

Canadian newspapers: the inside story
Walter Stewart (1980) ed., Edmonton: Hurtig Publishers

Who's in control?
United Church of Canada, Division of Church and Society (1978)

Audio/visual

Controlling interest
(16 mm colour film, 45 min.), on the world of multinational corporations, as corporate executives see it, and as working people see it. Available through DEVERIC, Halifax, DEC Toronto, and elsewhere in Canada.

Citizen Kane
(16 mm black & white film, 119 min.), director Orson Welles, available from Criterion Films, 1541 Barrington Street, Halifax, and elsewhere in Canada.

IV. Propaganda, bias and point of view

Chapter IV: Propaganda, bias and point of view

Introduction

> Trying to determine what is going on in the world by
> reading the newspaper is like trying to tell the time by
> watching the second hand of a clock.
>
> Ben Hecht[1]

Of the hundreds of international reports in the media, how many actually deepen our understanding of global issues? While the media's focus today may change from one particular country or "hot spot" to another, the *kind of coverage* they give in general does not change fundamentally. The media, as Mr Hecht says, are focusing on the second hand of the clock.

Of course, despite this limitation of the media, we all have a definite view of the world. We all watch TV or read the newspaper in order to find out what is going on in the world. No one could possibly verify all information for themselves in libraries before forming an opinion. That is why methods of analysing information are so important. If you know how to "de-code" mass media messages (Chapter II), you can make sound judgments about many issues even if you are not an expert in every field. Only when an issue becomes particularly important to you for some reason, will you need to determine whether you need to seek more information.

In this chapter, we shall look at an example from Canadian mass media coverage of one particular "hot spot" in the world. It illustrates how some of the methods of analysis in Chapter II can be applied to everyday news and information. This is done by way of example only: you must apply the general points made here to current issues in your own area. By way of example as well, we have included some information sources other than the mass media to show their usefulness in helping to build a clearer picture of any given issue.

Defining terms

Let us begin by clarifying some terms. In human communication, *all* the messages we receive will be the product of one of three types: someone's propaganda campaign; their biased presentation of information; or simply their point of view.

There are many different understandings of such terms as "propaganda", "bias" and "point of view". We propose the following distinctions.

Propaganda is information and opinions (especially prejudiced ones) that are spread to influence people in favour of or against some doctrine or idea. In general English usage, "propaganda" is a pejorative term, referring to campaigns of lies or untruths, though the word is not always used in this way. (For example, the word's Spanish cognate, *propaganda*, means both "advertising" and "propaganda".) However, because propaganda has negative connotations in everyday English usage, we will take this to be its meaning for our purposes.

The term's origins go back to early 17th century Italy, when the reigning Pope formed a committee of cardinals, the Congregation for the Propagation of the Faith*, to lead the Counter-Reformation in response to the Protestant Reformation. The work of this committee also included the spreading of Christianity to the foreign missions.

The invention of the printing press in the 15th century and the development of movable type resulted in the propagation of ideas in a manner unlike any that preceded it. This technological development allowed, for the first time in history, the spreading of ideas from one sender to a multiplicity of receivers, through mechanical means. Texts could be printed by a press rather than hand-written individually.

The next major development in propaganda's history would be found much later, in the 20th century, with the use of radio and moving pictures to sway large numbers of people. These inventions played key roles in the rise of Nazism in the 1920s and 1930s, and during and after World War II itself, propaganda techniques were used by both Allied and Axis powers.

Bias is defined as a tempermental or emotional leaning to one side. The term originates in the French *biais*, oblique or slant.

---

*propaganda, Italian, from Modern Latin, *Congregatio de propaganda fide*.

Point of view refers to the perspective from which a certain statement is made. Scientists or historians have a certain point of view when they carry out their work. This view is still subjective, since *all forms of human expression are subjective, by definition.* However, because this point of view is stated (and can be judged against "objective realities"), the validity of the point of view is open to examination.

Humans are complex, and therefore their language or actions seldom fall readily into simple categories. So too with the categories we have identified here. The lines between bias and point of view in particular can at times be hard to distinguish.

Nevertheless, some of the major characteristics of propaganda, bias and point of view do stand in sharp contrast to one another.

Distinguishing characteristics

Declared motive. One way propaganda, bias and point of view differ from one another is the extent to which the message emitter declares his/her motive in transmitting a message.

Propagandists usually mask their motives: "We Do It All For You" is a familiar slogan in North America. With the daily barrage of messages we receive, how many of us have the time or the inclination to reflect on such a claim, and consciously decide whether it is a true or false statement?

Determining the motives of the *biased* person, however, can be difficult as well. Often biased people simply do not recognise their own feelings or prejudices. We ourselves may not be able to see another's bias if it coincides with our own. However, if one's intentions or motives are honest, one will be able to clarify in whose interest one is speaking, when asked.

Finally, the person presenting a certain *point of view* will attempt to make explicit what interests s/he represents, and what assumptions s/he is working on.

Persuasive techniques used. Differing persuasive techniques are used for communications based on propaganda, bias or someone's point of view.

As a result of *propaganda* campaigns, people adopt attitudes and beliefs that have been suggested to them. The individual likely has never consciously thought about them. Most of us have had the experience at least once of meeting someone who has challenged our attitudes or ideas, and asked us *why* we thought a certain way. On these occasions one may not really have known the answer, and perhaps replied simply, "I never really thought about it." It is possible that some of our attitudes have been influenced by some form of propaganda. Through persuasive techniques, pleasure, humour or enjoyment; hatred or revulsion; pride, patriotism or strength; status; identity — any number of feelings and impressions are unjustifiably but effectively associated with specific images, commercial products or political messages.

The *biased* person may use any number of these techniques to persuade us, though perhaps not necessarily on purpose.

Last, those presenting a certain *point of view* will attempt to base their message on some form of reasoning — whether logical, aesthetic, moral or other. Someone can be said to represent a point of view rather than a bias if s/he strives to (a) identify his/her own interests; (b) open them to examination; (c) encourage discussion; and (d) take into serious consideration dissenting points of view.

Relationship to power. A third way in which propaganda, bias and point of view differ from one another is the relationship needed to power, in order to operate.

Propagandists must have access to political and/or financial, religious or military power. Being powerful enough to control technology — whether a printing press centuries ago or a TV network with satellite hook-up today — is central to the propagandist's success.* It determines how many people can be reached by the same message, and therefore how many people can be persuaded by it.

Biased people, however, do not necessarily have the same access to power or the mass media, although sometimes they do. One newspaper may be known to have a Tory slant in its news and editorials, another a Liberal slant, or a "pro-business", "pro-labour" slant etc.

Someone putting forward a particular *point of view* will be less likely to seek out the powerful to relay their messages for them. The idea or feeling they express will convince on its own merits.

*While the mass media of communication do not necessarily disseminate propaganda, propaganda today could not be successful without the mass media. Furthermore, one can see how easily they lend themselves to propaganda campaigns: *by their very nature,* the mass media *emit* messages to masses of people from very limited numbers of production and emission centres. The mass media are not designed to receive messages in the same way, to engage their audience in a dialogue about the content of their messages.

The distinctions we have made between bias, propaganda and point of view are intended to clarify the relationships that certain forms of communications engender: for example, one needs a great deal of power to mount a propaganda campaign; one needs none at all to express one's point of view. However, these distinctions so far have left aside the question of the *validity* of various positions put forward by propagandists, biased people, and those with a particular point of view.

It is important to distinguish between the *validity* (i.e., the truth, untruth, acceptability or unacceptability) of the positions put forward through various techniques of propaganda, bias, point of view, and the *means themselves*. The most detached, well-meaning scientist may hold erroneous views. A propaganda campaign may be truthful. A Canadian example is the "Participaction" campaign, whose media advertising claimed that you will be healthier if you are in good physical condition. Thus, the form (e.g. propaganda techniques) must be distinguished from the content (exercising is good for you).

In the case of the nuclear power debate, both pro- and anti-nuclear interests have used propaganda techniques in their campaigns.

Profiles of propaganda, bias, and point of view

	PROPAGANDA	BIAS	POINT OF VIEW
Relation to power	Necessary	Not necessary	Not necessary
Medium used	Mass media (plus any other appropriate combination)	Possibly mass media but not necessarily	Possibly mass media but unlikely
Audience	Large numbers	Possibly large numbers	Possibly large numbers
Declared motive	Intentionally disguised	Sometimes disguised, more often unclear; biased person may be *unaware* of the interests they are serving	Stated in communication; interests in presenting a particular point of view are evident
	Is conscious of the real interests s/he he represents	Can be unconscious of the real interests s/he represents	Person is conscious of the *real* interests s/he represents
Techniques used	Propaganda devices and faulty reasoning	Propaganda devices and faulty reasoning	Never propaganda devices (depending on quality of work . . . no faulty reasoning, etc.)
	Sources often disguised	Source may or may not be mentioned, but not necessarily intentionally	Sources stated
	Initial message given in such a way as to elicit an *uncritical* acceptance of point of view	Initial message given in such a way as to elicit an emotional or uncritical agreement with the biased source	Initial message given in such a way as to elicit a *critical* response

Here are examples of the kind of tone, vocabulary and reasoning used in the three fundamental positions discussed here — propaganda, bias and point of view. These are fictitious comments on the book you are reading at this moment:

| Kind of Language (examples) | "Everyone, from the man in the street to the university community and people in the media themselves, is fed up with a few individuals who have been knocking the media. One professor I spoke to said, "No patriotic Canadian would ever write such a thing!' He speculated that this book on the media was the 'sort of thing card-carrying communists and infiltrators would come up with.' Whether the group is communist or not, one thing is certain: they're stirring up a lot of trouble." | "This rag-tag clique of ivory-tower pseudo-intellectuals must have gone to their gurus of so-called 'independent thinking' to come up with the kind of laughable attempt at 'clarification of ideas' as one finds in their recent exercise of self righteousness, *Between the lines*. It is published by . . . ., probably on the verge of bankruptcy, and distributed by teachers and students naïve enough to still be crusading for 'social justice' in an age of lifeboat ethics." | "The table on this page is an attempt to summarise the distinguishing characteristics of point of view, bias and propaganda. However, it should only be considered a summary (partial at that). For more information, see the bibliography at the end of the chapter. **Discussion** 1. Where does *Between the lines* fit into this schema? 2. Have you seen any ommissions?" |

Both sides have also produced biased presentations on nuclear safety or its danger. And both pro- and anti-nuclear groups have found members of the scientific community whose points of view were "scientific" but who held diametrically opposed positions.[2]

Having now distinguished between the three ways in which messages are sent to us (through propaganda, bias or point of view), we will now examine a sample of Canadian mass media coverage of what was a "hot spot" for a very long time.

Discussion: Propaganda, bias and point of view

1. In the USSR, the human rights organisation Amnesty International is described as being "in a leading position among organisations which conduct anti-Soviet propaganda". In Brazil it is described as "an instrument of communist terrorism". In Iran during the Shah's rule, the organisation was described as an "espionage agency".[3]

   a. In your view, would denunciations from regimes with such divergent political systems enhance the credibility of a human rights organisation or detract from it?

   b. Obtain a copy of the booklet *Amnesty International in Quotes*, and choose a criticism of the organisation from a "Communist-bloc", or "Western" or "Third World" nation. Prepare a report on that country, and Amnesty International's research on it.

Cartoon from *La Manana*, Montevideo, Uruguay, 20 February 76, two days after Amnesty International launched a worldwide campaign against the use of torture in Uruguay. The signs read: calumny, lies, defamation. Source: Amnesty International 1975-76 Annual Report.

The first casualty

It has been said that the first casualty of war is truth.

In the 1970s, a war tore apart the country of Zimbabwe (Rhodesia) in southern Africa, although, like the Vietnam war, it was only termed a *war* by governments or the mass media in its final stages. Zimbabwe smouldered away for years, out of sight of the mass media usually, until an occasional incident would flare up there, whereupon daily bulletins would resume.

Zimbabwe is a rich country: asbestos, copper, iron and the strategically important chrome are some of its resources, as is its land, much of which has great agricultural potential. From 1890 till 1980 the territory, known as Rhodesia, was ruled by whites — colonists from Great Britain. Pressured by Britain and black nationalist movements to concede some power to the country's black majority, colonial Prime Minister Ian Smith proclaimed a Unilateral Declaration of Independence in 1965. The United Nations then imposed economic sanctions against the illegal government, and within the country, black nationalist movements took to armed revolt.

At the time the following article was written, three black politicians (Sithole, Muzorewa and Chief Jeremiah Chirau) had agreed to the Smith government's "internal settlement" of the question of black political representation. Among other things, whites retained their grossly unequal land allocations and had veto rights over all legislation. The black nationalist movements of ZANU and ZAPU had joined to form the Patriotic Front in opposition to the white minority government. The war continued.

In a sense, Zimbabwe is "history" now. No longer is it the news every night. This very fact can make an examination of it all the more interesting, as we now have the advantage of being able to look at how events were reported, in the light of history.

The following article appeared during one flare-up in that long war. It comes from *Weekend Magazine*, which at the time had a huge circulation — a supplement to many Canadian newspapers and delivered free to homes.

There were many thousands of casualties in the Zimbabwe war. Was the first of them the truth about what was going on there?

We ask you to read the following passage from *Weekend Magazine* December 2, 1978, as you might have done — casually, over Sunday breakfast . . .

The Bloody Road to Zimbabwe", *Weekend Magazine* 2 Dec 78

THE BLOODY ROAD
TO ZIMBABWE

**In Rhodesia blacks
outnumber whites by more
than 25 to 1. Majority
rule may soon become
reality, but as Jim
Christy discovered, so
too may all-out civil war**

O N MY FIRST MORNING IN
Salisbury I woke early, around 6
a.m., anxious to explore. I had
arrived the night before and experienced more than a little trepidation
as the plane made its descent. But it
was surprisingly easy getting
through customs. Though it was Friday night the streets were virtually
deserted save for security police pa-
trolling in twos, often with Alsatian
dogs. I did not expect to find that most
of the police are black and that bars,
hotels and restaurants in Salisbury
seem to be fully integrated. I did not
expect to find that blacks neither bow
and scrape nor cringe when you address them.

I was halfway through breakfast in
the Meikles Hotel when the radio announced the first news of the massacre.

cre at the Emmanuel Mission School. The mission, run by the Elim Pentecostal Church, is situated in the thickly forested Mountains of the Mist area of eastern Rhodesia, 15 kilometres southeast of Umtali and eight kilometres from the Mozambique border. The terrorists came during the night armed with Russian Kalashnikov rifles. They went into the dormitories at the school and told the black students who they were and not to make a sound. They left after making a political speech. Then they woke the nine missionaries—five of them women—and the four children and took them out to the playing field. The women were raped and, along with the men and the children, bayoneted to death and mutilated. One woman was hacked to death with an axe. Another, repeatedly stabbed and bludgeoned with a length of wood, somehow managed to escape to the bush. She would die a week later in a Salisbury hospital.

I T WAS GHASTLY AT THE EMMANUEL School. Blood left dried trails across the school grounds and had formed darkened patches on the soccer field. Hardened security police stood on the blood-stained grass and sobbed or turned away when someone emerged from the bush holding a piece of a human body.

I started back to Umtali, walking along the road through the woods to get the feel of the African countryside and reflect on what I had seen. I was in some of the most awesomely wild land in the world, and the greatest white hunter of them all, Frederick Selous, a friend of Theodore Roosevelt, used to roam this very bush.

Local villagers and Rhodesian troops oversee the remains of 17 black Africans—nine of them children—shot by terrorists

Now his name belongs to Rhodesia's elite anti-guerrilla corps, the Selous Scouts. After I had gone a mile or so an army truck pulled over and a middle-aged man leaned out of the window and asked, "What the hell are you up to?"

"Walking to Umtali."

He shook his head in disbelief. "Get in!"

He spent the 10-minute ride talking about the narrow limits of my intelligence and the odds against my making it to town. "There's a real war going on out there, friend."

T HE PERPETRATORS OF THE Emmanuel Mission massacre claimed to belong to ZANLA, also known as the Patriotic Front, which is led by Robert Mugabe and Joseph Nkomo. ZANLA is the armed branch of the Zimbabwe African National Union, whose leader, Ndaban-

ingi Sithole, is one of the black men bers of the executive committee of t transitional government. When Sit ole became part of the governmer Mugabe parted company with him. is Mugabe's intention to assume abs lute power in Zimbabwe as a result civil war. But in a statement issu from his Mozambique hideout M gabe disclaimed responsibility for t massacre.

His statement was similar to a co ment in London by the British forei; secretary, David Owen, who declar he had no reason to believe that t slaughter was not actually carri out by Rhodesia's own security for for reasons of propaganda. Both M gabe and Owen were suggesting, other words, that the Rhodesian ar had killed 13 people to discredit R ert Mugabe.

M UGABE HAS THE BACKING (Prime Minister James C; laghan of Britain. He is al supported by U.S. President Jimr Carter and United Nations Ambass dor Andrew Young. He is suppl with arms by Russia. He has Brit support simply because he oppos the same government that is anatl ma to Britain. He has Russian su port because he is ostensibly a Ma ist. If he comes to power he will beholden to the Soviets, who w then—so the Rhodesians argue— well on their way to dominating mineral wealth of southern Afi and the Cape shipping routes. He American support because Amer always chooses the wrong side. parently the American governme whose policy in Africa is based much on guilt as greed, feels it incu bent to oppose a government accu of racism.

BUT IT DOES NOT TAKE LONG in Rhodesia to discover that the supposed white totalitarian rule is a myth perpetuated by the press in other countries. Rhodesia was ruled until 1976 by one white man. He now shares the governing body—the executive council—with three blacks, a change he instigated. He has promised that beginning January 1 black's will have a majority in Rhodesia's Parliament. The deal worked out by Henry Kissinger in 1976 calls for free elections at the end of this year. Due to the threat of disruption by the guerrilla movement, however, Ian Smith has indicated that it may be impossible to hold them. Even if the elections aren't held, it is only a matter of time before blacks—whether moderates or extremists—rule Zimbabwe.

Discrimation has of course always existed in Rhodesia. Often it is hidden behind the claim that blacks are not capable of governing their country because most of them are backward and illiterate. What the whites really think is that Africans are inferior. White liberals in other countries who call for majority rule are afraid to admit that it is not a smooth transition from the kraal to the Parliament buildings. By not acknowledging this fact in order to avoid being accused of racism, whites outside Rhodesia are playing into the hands of people such as Mugabe and Nkomo who want absolute power and the "liberation of Zimbabwe."

What no one outside Rhodesia seems to realize is that Rhodesia is a test case. If Rhodesia cannot make a peaceful transition to black rule, no country in southern Africa can. Now Ian Smith, in his heart of hearts, may be a staunch racist. For all I know he has a plaster black man holding a lamp at the foot of his driveway. Maybe he enjoys sitting around with a toodle atop his head telling kaffir jokes to other men in topees. But whatever his motives, he has put his government on the line. One gets the feeling that all the Boers of South Africa would commit mass suicide before they would even consider doing the same thing. Political leaders who oppose Smith choose to ignore the implications of his move. What is certain is

Fearing terrorist attack, thousands of Africans have fled their villages and set up makeshift homes in the market square of Salisbury, Rhodesia's capital

that there is not much time left.

IN A BAR IN UMTALI I MET A black soldier named Philomon. He offered to drive me to Salisbury in his little Ford Anglia. He told me it would take a couple of days because of the 3:30 curfew on the Umtali Road. He was a short stocky man, a Matabele tribesman, dressed in a camouflage suit. He wore a floppy olive drab cap and around his waist was one of those cloth belts perforated with metal-rimmed holes for attaching accessories. The belt was empty save for a leather holster that held a machine pistol.

We drove northwest out of Umtali. Philomon was a defector from the ranks of Rhodesian guerrillas. When he discovered I was connected with a magazine he started to tell me his story. He had attended a mission school like Elim, he said. He had been an eager student and a top-notch soccer

player. "My dream was to go to a university but that looked quite impossible. There were some men who started coming to visit me at my home in Gwelo. All I knew was that they were interested in politics. One day they came and said I had been awarded a scholarship to go to university in the United States. I was very thrilled and happy. They told me I could leave in a couple of days when my escort would be ready to take me. I said that I needed a visa but they told me all that had been taken care of. We flew to Nairobi and got on another plane and then another.

WHEN WE LANDED FOR THE last time we were in East Germany. I never got to America. I spent a year at a Russian school where they gave me a little money each week and I learned Marxism, Russian language, communications, weaponry and such things as espionage techniques, plastic explosives, poisons, coding and de-coding and rudimentary torture. It was very good training.

"After my training I was brought back and crossed the border through the bush near Chipinga. They introduced me to a young kid. It was to be my responsibility to train him and organize a small cell of recruits in the area. Once I had formed an effective unit we were to begin activities such as blowing up bridges, like the one at Birchenough, while cars were on them.

"The young boy they had given me was 15 years old. He told me that he had been promised a good job and a car and white women once the party took over Zimbabwe. One day we

were near the ruins at Chibyumani. I told him to wait for me in camp. I told him I was going to stop a car, rob the driver and go to find groceries. I stopped a car and hitched a ride into Fort Victoria and joined the Rhodesian army."

We had passed the town of Odzi and were in the Mtanda Mountains. The Anglia strained as it climbed a long hill. In the distance we saw an army truck come over the rise, then another and another. "They will probably stop to warn us of the curfew," said Philomon.

The lead truck flashed its lights.

Philomon nodded and said, "I guess we'll have to spend the night in Rusape."

The first shots felt like gravel hit-

...teen people survived the crash of an...

ting the hubcaps. Before I realized what was happening the window on the driver's side was hit and an intricate web of cracks spread across the glass. The car swerved crazily into the path of the oncoming army trucks. I banged my head as I tried to get under the dashboard. Philomon kept driving across the road and into a ditch. We got hit two or three more times on the driver's side. Before we had bumped to a halt I had the door open and I tumbled out. Pilomon was right behind, falling on top of me and rolling over, cursing his pistol for being a pistol.

I looked at the woods behind us. "Jesus Christ!"

"What?"

"We're going to get it from there." Philomon let off a few rounds into the woods. "No," he said disdainfully, "they're too dumb to know about crossfire."

The soldiers were now exchanging fire with the terrorists in the woods. I had seen only one of them, a black man in a T-shirt and a red beret. I had seen him fire and run back into the bush. He seemed to gallop, stepping high over branches and rocks as he made for cover. He wore black-and--white high-topped sneakers.

Two of the soldiers crossed the road and crashed into the brush. A couple of others were firing submachine guns with drilled chrome barrels. The smoke escaped from the holes and

hung in the late afternoon air. I moved along the ditch away from the car and remembered all those movies where the GIs crawl through no-man's land on their bellies. Philomon followed me. We lay there hugging the ground. The shooting had diminished and sounded half-hearted now. "They weren't after us," Philomon said. "They knew the trucks would have to gear down coming over the hill."

When the soldiers came back out of the woods, Philomon and I got up from the ditch. He went over to the soldiers and they talked logistics. I kept looking around expecting to get hit any moment. "We saw five of them," one of the soldiers said, "but

we can't go and chase them becaus we have to patrol. We can't leave yo and the trucks here."

I shook hands with each of the so diers. One of them said, "Welcome t Zimbabwe, mate."

RHODESIANS, BLACK ANI white, live with the constan threat of terror. As Paddy Shields, a member of Parliament said at a news conference, "Rhode sians have been asked to endure more than the average person should b asked to take on in a lifetime." Ever time you step off the pavement yo have to be on the lookout for lan mines. I told a man in a bar I wa waiting to go out to the front. "Hel you want to go to the front?" h laughed. "I live in the suburbs. Com on out to my house." He wasn't kic ding. While I was in Rhodesia lan mines accounted for deaths in ever area of the country, including th suburbs of Salisbury.

It is only a surprise the first tim you see someone hand over his .303 the reception desk of a hotel. When checked in at the Meikles Hotel on m return from Umtali, I was wearing a army shirt, khaki trousers and fiel boots, and the woman at the receptic desk asked, "Where's your gun When I told her I didn't have one sh looked at me as if I were either nuts unpatriotic. Stores in Salisbury ad vertise that they have bomb-pro windows. You cannot go into ar place of business without having ba and parcels checked.

Particularly subject to guerrilla a tack is the town of Bulawayo in t southwest. It is a remote cattle settl ment on the edge of the Matopos, ghostly region of bare granite hil with starkly contrasting wooded va leys and the painted caves of ancie bushmen. Farmers heading to ar from town are prime targets for t rorist attacks. The resorts at Victor Falls on the Zambezi River at the e treme western tip of the country a virtually deserted from fear of a bush. Earlier this year 10 people or tour around the falls were gunn down as they crossed into Zambia

16 STEPS
to making Heinz carrots

Heinz food scientists and nutritionists are constantly working to ensure that every food ingredient we use and every infant food we make is carefully selected and thoroughly prepared and tested throughout our entire process.

Below, we have listed the steps we utilize in the preparation of Heinz Strained Carrots. Although the care and testing are a constant factor for all our other infant foods, each product is prepared and analyzed individually with the goal of maximizing the nutrient content of that product.

1. GROWING THE CARROT. Heinz Agriculture and Food Research Departments are constantly growing new varieties of carrots under different soil and climate conditions. In fact, we look at approximately 10 varieties in an average year. Scientific tests are used to check the general appearance, colour, texture and nutritional quality of these new breeds. On the basis of these tests, we choose the varieties we'll continue to grow and use.

2. GRADING. All the carrots used in our baby food must be Canada Grade #1 and at least 1½" in diameter. They must be a good healthy orange and have a natural sweetness to them.

3. INGREDIENT INSPECTION. All our carrots are carefully inspected to make sure they meet strict quality control standards.

4. STORAGE. While they're waiting to be made into baby food, carrots may be stored at a temperature of 40-50°F and 90% humidity for a time period of up to, but not exceeding, two weeks.

5. CLEANING. A four-stage process begins at this point. Carrots are first water sprayed. Then steamed to loosen the skin. Next, they move to a second washer which removes a very thin layer of skin. Finally, the carrots are inspected and trimmed by hand.

6. EQUIPMENT INSPECTION. Before actual manu-facturing starts, all our stainless steel equipment is spotlessly cleaned and inspected to pass stringent microbiological tests.

7. STRAINING. This process turns carrots into baby food. First, the carrots are diced. Then steam cooked and passed through a series of screens until they turn into a puree. AT NO TIME IN THE PROCESS ARE ANY ARTIFICIAL FLAVOURINGS, COLOURINGS OR PRESERVATIVES USED. SALT IS NO LONGER ADDED TO CARROTS OR ANY OTHER HEINZ VEGETABLES.

8. STEAMING. Once all the coarser particles have been removed, the puree is heated in a steam jacketed rotary cooker to allow each particle to receive the exact required temperature and time of cooking.

9. DE-AERATION. Since the straining process incorporated air into the carrots and air could, if left, cause a loss of vitamins, de-aeration removes the air.

10. ANOTHER INSPECTION. Once again, Quality Control has to pass judgement on the consistency, sweetness, colour and micro-biological safety of the carrots.

11. CONTAINERS. Before we fill them, all our jars are air-flushed for complete cleanliness.

12. FILLING. The strained carrots now go into jars and are capped with steri-seals locking in the freshness. From fresh product to fresh packed in only 8 minutes.

13. STERILIZATION. The sealed jars are retort sterilized and moved to the final inspection.

14. FINAL INSPECTION. If the carrots pass physical, chemical and microbiological tests, they're labelled and packed.

15. STORAGE. If not shipped immediately, the sealed and sterilized carrots are stored in our warehouse at controlled temperature.

16. SHIPPING. From us to your supermarket. The end of a process that guarantees that every jar of Heinz Baby Foods meets the exacting standards you'd set for yourself.

Good nutrition starts with Heinz.

Young recruits to the Zimbabwe African People's Un hideout near the Rhodesian border

...efuge for the Patriotic Front troops.

Farmers around Fort Victoria, 300 ...ilometres south of Salisbury, have ...rmed their own anti-cattle-rustling ...peration. Until the small group of ...rmers organized themselves, ter-...rists were stealing 300 cattle from ...e area each week. The stolen cattle ...re slaughtered for food or bartered ...r mealie-meal, the native dietry ...aple. Excess meat is smoked and ...idden in underground caches. A for-...er mercenary soldier from Toronto ...elped organize the group over a year ...go. He says it is a mounted unit ...ade up of local farmers from the po-...ce reserve. They are under the com-...and of a member of the regular ...rce. They use their own horses, but ...niforms, saddlery and FN rifles are ...rovided by the British South Africa ...olice. There is also a small foot pa-...ol of African police reservists under ...e command of one African police ...nstable.

One of the difficulties in combating ...e terrorist forces is lack of manpow-... Within 30 days of his 16th birth-...y, a non-African boy is required to ...gister for national service. Between ...e ages of 18 and 25 he must put in 1 ... years of full-time service and a fur-...er three years of "efficient part-...me service." All white males be-...ween the ages of 25 and 38 have to ...end at least half the year on active ...ty. This does not mean clerking or ...illing at an armory; they are sent ...to the bush, into operational areas. ...nscription for white men between ... and 50 was introduced last year. ...en in that age group are required to ...end up to 10 weeks a year on active ...ty.

BLACKS ARE NOT SUBJECT TO conscription, but black volun-teers make up the majority of the ...odesian army. Many are afraid to ...n the military or the security police ...cause of terrorist retribution. This ...ne fear keeps black children out of ...ool. A black joining the army or ...ntinuing his education beyond the ...vest level is called a "Tshombe," or ...d-out. Anyone who refuses to join ...e Patriotic Front may be forced into ...ning and spirited across the border ... the training countries—Mozambi-...e, Zambia, Tanzania or Angola. ...ne man I talked to had recently

been rescued along with 10 other blacks by a group of Rhodesian sol-diers. He had been captured near his home outside Bulawayo while on his way to work. His captors set the group on a forced march toward Binga on Lake Kariba. From there, they were told, boats would take them to Zam-bia and then on to Tanzania. After eight days of marching they were still only halfway to Binga. When the group reached the Tjoljo Road the ter-rorists stopped a bus and robbed the passengers. They commandeered the bus but ran into a military roadblock. After a battle during which two sol-diers and four terrorists were killed, the hostages were set free.

When I got back to the Meikles Ho-tel it was full of journalists who greet-ed each other effusively. "Darling! How are things in Fleet Street?" They had arrived in time to cover the funer-al at Umtali. It was scheduled for Thursday, and they cursed when it was postponed until Friday. They had to spend another idle day hanging around the ministry of information or drinking in the hotel lobby. A press plane flew them into Umtali and out again two hours later. They turned the funeral into a circus, colliding with each other and practically fall-ing into the newly dug graves to get shots of the caskets being lowered —all the photos, all the hard news from the latest "incident" in Rhodesia.

Discussion

1. What was your initial response to reading this article?

2. What incidents did the article describe? Record all the comments people make.

3. What are the main points of the article?

4. What was the political situation in Zimbabwe according to the article? Now, re-read the article more carefully. Refer to the *checklists* for careful thinking and other sections of Chapter II.

5. How would you classify this article? — As propaganda? Bias? Point of view?

6. If you analyse this passage in discussion rather than in writing, be sure to take good notes: you will likely cover many points which we have not covered in the textual analysis which follows.

Textual analysis of:

"The bloody road to Zimbabwe", Jim Christy
Weekend Magazine
(2 Dec 78 p. 7-11)

Note: This analysis is given by way of example only. Your work is to apply similar methods to more current issues.

Method of analysis

In examining this article, we studied the language used: tone, vocabulary, recurrence of certain words etc. We also examined the content and the reasoning underlying the messages being relayed. *Reasons*, we propose, can be logical, conscious and well defined. However, they can also be aesthetic or moral; they can be made at the level of the sub-conscious; they can be unknown to the person who has unwittingly been convinced by them.

We should therefore like to distinguish between *rational* and *non-rational* "reasoning". Rational reasons are ones that a person can think through and can explain in point form. People are accustomed to analysing these. Non-rational reasons, however, are feelings or intuitions one has about something. Non-rational reasons may be expressed in terms of admiration, wonder, repugnance, and so on. They can determine an attitude, which in turn

supports a more conscious argument (the "rational" reasons). Non-rational reasons are nevertheless reasons. They are elusive and difficult to identify, because of the plane on which they operate: people are generally not accustomed to analysing them. Yet if one wants to find out how opinions are formed — how impressions are created in people's minds —these factors must be identified and analysed. We have attempted to do so here.

We examined the *Weekend* article for statements based on verifiable evidence, and for statements which involved interpretation, speculation, or unsubstantiated claims.

It should be remembered, too, that in reading any given message or engaging in any form of communication, *the receiver (reader) is always implicated* in that communication. That is, the reader (or TV viewer) takes some position in relation to the message, agreeing, disagreeing with it, ignoring or registering information. At times this is done consciously, at others, it is done unconsciously. In the case of this article, for example, at no point does the author explicitly state that "Canadians should favour the lifting of trade sanctions against Rhodesia." However this very position can be inferred if one examines the unstated "reasoning" process we have just described.*

— But no further talk of method; let us examine the text.

Context

The feature of the *Weekend* issue was "Ian Smith of Rhodesia". The magazine carried a front-page drawing of Smith's head, with a revolver pointed at his eye. "The bloody road to Zimbabwe" followed upon another article of about the same length in words, entitled "Last of the few", which was a portrait of Smith, by Christopher Munion (included in appendix).

At the time, the white minority (4% of the population) ruled Zimbabwe despite an economic blockade. Slightly over a year after the *Weekend* article appeared, the Patriotic Front parties would be swept to victory in internationally supervised, free elections, winning 77 of a possible 80 seats.

Form

The article (original) measured approximately 175 column centimeters (2,500-2,600 words). Photographs took up about as much space (150 col. cm), or almost twice as much

---

*That is, lifting sanctions will be the best we can make of a bad situation, the reader infers.

space if one counted the full-page photo on the first page of the article. The title of the article and photo captions were in blood red. Page numbers refer to *Weekend* magazine page numbers.

Content: the message

The theme of the article is that the war in Zimbabwe is ghastly, and could worsen. A reign of terror exists. The main thesis is stated in the second sentence; "Majority rule may soon be a reality, but . . . so too may all-out civil war."

There are two terms to this proposition. The first — that majority rule may soon be a reality — has been established in the previous article on Smith by Christopher Munnion,[1] and is reiterated in this article on *WM* p. 9 col.1:

> Even if elections aren't held, it is only a matter of time before blacks — whether moderate or terrorists — rule Zimbabwe.

The massacres that have taken place are grim proof of what is likely to come.

In the middle of the article, we find the justification for past policies:

> Discrimination has of course always existed in Rhodesia. Often it is hidden behind the claim that blacks are not capable of governing their country because most of them are backward and illiterate. What the whites really think is that Africans are inferior. White liberals in other countries who call for majority rule are afraid to admit that it is not a smooth transition from the kraal to the Parliament buildings. By not acknowledging this fact in order to avoid being accused of racism, whites outside Rhodesia are playing into the hands of people such as Mugabe and Nkomo who want absolute power and the 'liberation of Zimbabwe'.
>
> p. 9 col.1

However, change will be inevitable, since blacks outnumber whites 25 to one.

What kind of change will come about? The author implies that if the kind of change comes about that the Patriotic Front guerrillas are fighting for, bloody, "all-out civil war" will ensue. This is because the Patriotic Front wants "absolute power". According to the author, the Patriotic Front has perpetrated horrendous massacres, and its tribal groupings

Ian Smith of Rhodesia

will fight amongst themselves, if given power. Finally, as the photo on the front page tells us, the whites will go down fighting such savage people.

In the passage just quoted, we find the statement:

> White liberals in other countries who call for majority rule are afraid to admit that it is not a smooth transition from the kraal* to the Parliament buildings.

What is the *message* conveyed here? The implication is that blacks would not know how to govern themselves: they are essentially tribal — cattle herdsmen. (The author incidentally presumes to describe the inner thoughts of "white liberals" around the world.)

However, after glancing at the atrocities committed by blacks, would not you, too, agree that "most of them are backward and illiterate"?

Let us examine the implicit reasoning in this article. It can be summarised thus:

Implicit reasoning

1. Blacks outnumber whites 25 to one. (Page 7 col. 4)

2. Therefore, change is inevitable.

---

kraal: A South African group of huts, or enclosure for cattle.

3. The *kind* of change will be a choice between the "moderates" and the "extremists". (p. 9 col. 1)

4. The Patriotic Front massacred the missionaries. (p. 8 col. 1)

5. The Patriotic Front want "absolute power".

6. Because the Patriotic Front want absolute power, and because (as the massacres and tribal fighting prove) it will not be "a smooth transition from the kraal to the Parliament buildings",

7. One might do well to support a "moderate solution". It is the only possible way to avoid further bloodshed.
(The previous article indicated one way in which Canadians could support a "moderate solution" — by lifting sanctions: p. 6 col. 4.)

This, then, summarises the author's implicit reasoning.

One might answer, "— But it was not a thesis with reasons for everything! It was an on-the-spot report!" Was it indeed?

Let us now examine more closely the reporting in the article. How much of what appears in the *Weekend* magazine article is in fact Jim Christy's eyewitness reporting? How much has come from other sources?

The article itself describes a massacre (p. 8 col. 1-4); gives an analysis of the geopolitical situation there (p. 8 col. 4) and some historical background (p. 9 col. 1). The author tells us how the Patriotic Front massacred the missionaries:

> The terrorists came during the night armed with Russian Kalashnikov rifles. They went into the dormitories at the school and told the black students who they were and not to make a sound. They left after making a political speech. Then they woke the nine missionaries — five of

Local villagers and Rhodesian troops oversee the remains of 17 black Africans — nine of them children — shot by terrorists

The terrorists came during the night armed with Russian Kalashnikov rifles. They went into the dormitories at the school and told the black students who they were and not to make a sound. They left after making a political speech. Then they woke the nine missionaries — five of them women — and the four children and took them out to the playing field. The women were raped and, along with the men and the children, bayoneted to death and mutilated. One woman was hacked to death with an axe. Another, repeatedly stabbed of wood, bludgeoned with a length managed to escape to the somehow. She would die a week later in a bush. hospital.
Salisbury

IT WAS GHASTLY AT THE EMMANUEL School. Blood left dried trails across the school grounds and had formed darkened patches on the soccer field. Hardened security police stood on the blood-stained grass and sobbed or turned away when someone emerged from the bush holding a piece of a human body.

them women — and the four children and took them out to the playing field. The women were raped and, along with the men and the children, bayonetted to death and mutilated. One woman was hacked to death with an axe. Another, repeatedly stabbed and bludgeoned with a length of wood, somehow managed to escape to the bush. She would die a week later in a Salisbury hospital.

It was ghastly at the Emmanuel School. Blood left dried trails across the school grounds and had formed darkened patches on the soccer field. Hardened security police stood on the blood-stained grass and sobbed or turned away when someone emerged from the bush holding a piece of human body.

p. 8 col. 1

... Grisly, horrific details. Yet what are the *facts* that the journalist himself can verify? Who did the eyewitness reporting? Who was able to identify a weapon, for example, as a "Kalashnikov weapon"? We then read the article more carefully ... Although the first impression one gets is that Christy was on the spot, this is not a correct impression. However, *first impressions are lasting impressions —* especially for the casual reader.

The verifiable facts

On closer examination, we found that, on the basis of what the journalist has written in this article, the following is what he himself can account for:

The author flew into Salisbury. The next morning, he heard a radio report of an attack on a mission. (*Page 7 column 4*)

Somehow, and at an unspecified time afterwards, he arrived at the mission, some 200 kilometers away, and saw (1) the bloodied schoolgrounds; (2) the soldiers weeping; and (3) someone emerge from the bush "with a piece of human body". (*p. 8 col. 1*)

He tried to walk back to the nearby town of Umtali, but was picked up by a Rhodesian in an army truck, who upbraided him during the ten-minute ride for walking in a war zone. (*p. 8 col. 2*)

In an Umtali bar the author met a black soldier who offered to drive him back to Salisbury. On the ride, the soldier described his time with, and defection from, the "Russians". (*p. 9 col. 2*)

As the two were driving, their car was caught in an ambush. After the incident, the author met the soldiers in the convoy, with whom he shook hands (*p. 10 col 1*) and exchanged greetings. ("Welcome to Zimbabwe, mate.") (*p. 10 col. 4*)

The author at some point attended a news conference with a Rhodesian M.P., and went to a bar where he talked to a man who offered to take him "to the front" — which, the man said, was in his suburbs. (*p. 10 col. 4*)

The story ends with the author returning to his hotel. (*p. 11 col. 4*)

These are the *facts* that the author puts forward. The rest of the article is *interpretation.* — Did you have that impression as you read the article? If you are like many people we asked to read this article, you had the impression that there were a lot more facts that Christy himself could substantiate.

The impressions

The author has left us with an *impression,* presenting much of what he has been told *as if it were fact* that he, by his presence there, could substantiate. (But surely the photographs are enough evidence of the horror . . .)

In a 2,500-word story, the author has witnessed one ambush. He has talked to two men in bars; has exchanged words with a hotel receptionist, several soldiers, talked to another man who is also unidentified; has attended a news conference given by a government official; and has talked to other journalists. His *eyewitness* reporting of "The bloody road to Zimbabwe" consists of one roadside incident in which vehicles are damaged (no casualties). The author says, "it does not take long in Rhodesia to discover that the supposed white totalitarian rule is a myth . . ." (p. 9 col. 1). On the basis of what he has written, it did not take him more than a few hours or days to reac his conclusions . . .

Yet the horror, the immediacy of the war is what we remember. The author has succeeded in making the reader think he can corroborate everything in the article. How has he created this impression?

The presentation

First and most important, the author has photographs, which we unconsciously assume "prove" his case: "A photograph cannot tell a lie."

The article is full of emotionally-charged words. By this we mean adjectives, nouns, verbs, figures of speech that *carry with them* the way a person feels about the thing s/he is describing. The linguist S. I. Hayakawa described them as "purr-words" or "snarl-words".

Of all the emotionally-charged words we found, none were favourable to the Patriotic Front guerrillas (understandably, since the author asserts that they carried out the massacre); eight were unfavourable to blacks or to the guerrilla movements; three were favourable to the established white order, and none were unfavourable to it. The "purr-words" for whites are much more evident in the preceding article ("The Last of the Few"), but here are

two examples from "The bloody road to Zimbabwe": "the greatest white hunter of them all, Frederick Selous." Selous' name, the author tells us, now belongs to Rhodesia's "elite anti-guerrilla corps".[5]

"Security" — a word heard so often that it is becoming transparent — is present every time the word "police" is mentioned. It is interesting to see how certain words are grouped: "security police"; "police constable"; "mercenary soldier". Making such distinctions in everyday Canadian speech would seem redundant: normally one would simply say "policeman" or "mercenary". In their context, the added qualifiers to the words create a distance between the actor and the action — they "soften" the message being relayed.

So far we have only referred to how whites have been portrayed in this article. How have blacks, and black guerrilla movements been described? Here are some of the "snarl-words" associated with them: The guerrillas are "terrorists"; they "massacre" women and children, and return to "hide-outs". Whether they are aligned with the white minority or they are fighting to oppose it, blacks in general are "tribal". The caption to the picture of a Rhodesian black soldier on the side of the Smith government reads:

Like a modern African chieftan, a member of Rhodesia's security forces stands at his post.

p. 9 col. 4

Such a statement, *outside the context of this article,* is patronising and racist. Here, however, in the context of a story of a massacre, it passes almost unnoticed.

How is racism itself seen in this article? The first mention of it is that the American government "feels it incumbent to oppose a government accused of racism" (p. 8 col. 4). The second mention of racism follows within paragraphs. Christy dismisses the charge of racism against blacks, saying that "the supposed white totalitarian rule is a myth perpetrated by the press in other countries." There then follows the key paragraph on why "moderate" solutions can be the only solutions and "discrimination" is not racism — the core, we have suggested, to his implicit, logical argumentation.

So, we are to infer, institutionalised racism does not exist in Rhodesia — only "discrimination". The discrimination is well justified (the massacres attest to this). Yet no reference

is made to any "objective realities" that could prove or disprove charges of racism — such as the existence of laws, customs, statistical information about income or nutritional levels.

But then maybe Smith himself personally *is* racist, the author speculates. Who can say? . . . This is where the word "racist" appears for the second time:

> Now Ian Smith, in his heart of hearts, may be a staunch racist. For all I know he has a plaster black man holding a lamp at the foot of his driveway. Maybe he enjoys sitting around with a topee atop his head telling kaffir jokes to other men in topees. But whatever his motives, he has put his government on the line.
>
> p. 9 col. 1

The message is: While Smith may or may not be a racist, what counts are his actions. And his actions have been conciliatory. At *his* instigations he has shared his power with the "moderate" blacks Muzorewa, Sithole and Chirau. (In the other *Weekend* article, we learned that Smith "elevated" two blacks on his ranch to manage his cattle and crops.)

Even though the privileged whites in South Africa "would commit mass suicide before they would even consider doing the same thing," Smith knows that "there is not much time left." (p. 9 col. 2). The "moderates" must get everyone's support in order to avert a bloodbath.

The reader is left not knowing whether the ruling Smith-Muzorewa government in Rhodesia is racist or not. After reading the article, one has no more *facts* about racism in Rhodesia than before. However, the reader is left with definite *impressions* of the situation in Southern Africa. It is that there will likely be a bloodbath, if the Patriotic Front gains "absolute power".

The casual reader might understandably infer that this confusion about whether or not Rhodesian society is racist comes from the fact that the situation there is indeed confused. Therefore who is to know for sure? — Those who are "on the spot", who have had first-hand experience, who are authorities on the question, should know. To the casual reader, the massacre, the exchange with soldiers, the ambush, were all seen and experienced by the journalist.

The *overall message* the reader gets, then, is two-fold:

• The implicit, "'logical" message is that we should make the best of a bad situation and

support the "moderates", for if we do not, it is reasonable to expect "all-out civil war."

• This implicit message has been prepared by, and is rooted in a second message, one based on an emotional appeal. This emotional message has been communicated to us (1) most importantly through pictures ("a photo cannot tell a lie"); (2) through selective inclusion and omission of information (see below); and (3) through a presentation of this information (language and organisation of the article) that elicits an emotional rather than a rational response.

Because of the strength of the reader's *emotional* reaction — repugnance at what s/he has read and seen — the reader tends not to give a critical, thinking response to the implicit logical arguments that the author puts forward. Because of the horror of the events depicted, it is difficult to remember to ask the questions of a detached observer: the reader is involved on an emotional level, not an intellectual level.

Under these circumstances — which may last no longer than the time it takes to flip past the pages and scan a page — we accept *without question* statements that we might examine much more carefully in a less emotionally-charged atmosphere.

The article's messages

Here are some of the article's specific messages:

Blacks are capable of the most obscene atrocities.

The Patriotic Front guerrillas are responsible for the murder at the mission.

This is only one example of what might come about with a PF victory . . . civil war.

With a Patriotic Front government in "absolute power", the ensuing carnage would be unthinkable.

We had better support Muzorewa and the "moderates" and hope for the best.

But if we had not been so shocked by what we had seen and read, we might have asked ourselves many questions. Here are some of them:

The article's messages:	Questions asked in a more detached setting:
Blacks are capable of the most obscene atrocities.	Are not whites capable of them as well?
The Patriotic Front guerrillas are responsible for the murders at the mission.	Just a moment! According to what sources? From the text it is impossible to tell who was an eyewitness.
	Why does the author not say who he talked to at the mission?
	The Patriotic Front are reported (incidentally) to have completely denied having had any part of the murder. The British Foreign Secretary is reported to implicate the Selous Scouts as the real perpetrators of the crime. Why was no spokesman from either group interviewed directly on this important point?
	Why are the denials of the Patriotic Front and British Foreign Secretary buried in the article in such a way that I only noticed them the second time I read the article?
This is only one example of what might come about with a Patriotic Front victory . . . civil war.	On what is the author basing such broad generalisations? (On the evidence of the massacre he has presented photos of? — But he was not there to know for sure who did it . . . Why did he not take any of his own pictures?)
With a Patriotic Front government in "absolute power", the ensuing carnage would be unthinkable.	
We had better support Muzorewa and the "moderates" and hope for the best.	Who are the people he calls moderates?

Distorting reality: "extremists" versus "moderates"

The author automatically labels groups as "extremist" and "moderate", making no attempt to justify this labelling. This technique is commonly used to legitimise the group one is supporting (the moderates), making one's own position appear to be the most reasonable of available alternatives.

The labels are given the force and meaning of *fact*, but with no corresponding reference to reality. According to the indications in the article, here is a schema of the Rhodesian reality:

Leftwing Extremists	Moderates		Right-wing Extremists
Fanatical blacks: the Patriotic Front, who the author says commit atrocities and who want "absolute power"	Muzorewa, Sithole and Chirau	Smith	Fanatical whites: ". . . all the Boers in South Africa . . . would commit mass suicide" before ceding power to black moderates, as Smith has done.

Majority of blacks: their allegiance could go either way

Ian Smith appears as the go-between for the black "moderates" and the white right-wing extremists. One thus has the impression that Smith has granted large concessions to the blacks, and that Muzorewa is a "moderate".

In describing the situation this way, the author persuasively implies that the allegiances of the majority will float from the moderates to the extremists, depending on such things as white support for the moderates and international recognition. This floating majority of the population could be anchored to the "moderates" as easily as it could to the "extremists", as long as the "moderates" are granted some concessions and have world support.

The article discussed neither the concessions Smith was to have made to the moderates, nor did it examine the moderation that the author claims is the characteristic of Muzorewa.

Even a brief glance at what powers were *not* conceded to the "moderate" blacks will show why the author would decide to ignore the question: judged against the concrete situation, claiming Muzorewa was a moderate would be ludicrous.

Muzorewa agreed to have no actual power over the police, the military and judiciary — virtually all the key powers of any nation. While in power, the "moderate" Muzorewa allowed the continued harassment, arrest by police and bombing from the air of the black population. The declared state of emergency, in effect since UDI in 1965, continued under the *Emergency Powers Act* and the *Law and Order (Maintenance) Act*. Dozens of regulations and directives controlled all aspects of Rhodesian life — from censorship of the press, to twenty-two-hour curfews, to summary arrest and execution of anyone the police or army might suspect. Under one of the emergency regulations in 1977 it became an offence to:

> communicate to any other person any rumour or report which is likely to cause alarm or despondency.[6]

If such facts were reported in an article, claims that whites conceded anything significant to the blacks, or that Muzorewa was a "moderate" would appear patently absurd.

The term "absolute power" must be scrutinized as well. By "absolute power" the author means control over the powers of the police,

military and judiciary. The Patriotic Front's insistence on controlling these key posts after internationally supervised elections is described as its wanting "absolute power". Such a statement would appear ridiculous if applied to our own country, but it does not occur to us to think in those terms while reading an article about terror and bloodshed.

By using the term "absolute power" in this way, the author has also found an extremely effective way of calling up in the mind of the reader a cluster of images that are unrelated on the level of reality, but that are nevertheless intimately related on another level of our consciousness. The term subtly reminds us of Lord Acton's well-known maxim, *Power corrupts, absolute power corrupts absolutely . . .* It conjures up the "absolute power" of, say, the insane and despotic Ugandan ruler Idi Amin . . .

The article also leaves aside the extent of support for the Patriotic Front amongst the population in Rhodesia. At the time the article appeared, it was estimated that 90% of the countryside was controlled by the Patriotic Front.[7] With this in mind, we propose a schema of the Rhodesian reality which fundamentally differs from the *Weekend* magazine model:

Patriotic Front	versus	Muzorewa, Sithole & Chirau
Majority of blacks support the P.F.		plus White minority

Subsequent elections are rather dramatic proof of the soundness of such a description of the situation there: 77 seats went to the Patriotic Front, and just three seats went to Muzorewa's party, despite a South-African backed campaign of over $8 million.

The author's description of international support for the Patriotic Front creates the *illusion* that everyone is helping Patriotic Front (ZANU) leader Mugabe, while no one is helping the beleaguered whites:

> Mugabe has the backing of Prime Minister James Callaghan of Britain. He is also supported by U.S. President Jimmy Carter and United Nations Ambassador Andrew Young. He is supplied with arms by Russia.
>
> p. 8 col. 4.

What exactly the American and British "backing" consists of is never explained: this is be-

cause there was none. However, the author has successfully created the impression that the West is, to use a South African expression, "soft on communism". The origin of Rhodesia's arms supplies (we might expect by now) is not mentioned.

Other techniques

A number of other persuasive techniques can be identified in the article.

Recurring words, cognates or related words

Certain words, when repeated often enough or reinforced with related words, have a barrage effect upon the reader: one's critical faculties cannot focus on every word that passes in front of the eye. The cumulative effect of these words helps to create a picture in the reader's mind (which is corroborated by the photos). None of the recurring words has

Review of propaganda techniques

We re-read the Weekend magazine article with the Reviews and Checklists from Chapter II in mind. The article contained elements of the following propaganda techniques.

Twisting and distortion

The war is depicted as one between blacks and whites. It was not; it was between a privileged minority — including blacks — and the majority of people, mostly all black. According to the article, within the black camp, blacks are simply aligned along tribal lines. This is also a distortion. John Stockwell, former CIA head of operations in Angola describes how this distortion can be used effectively in his book, *In Search of Enemies.*

Selective omission

In describing the situation in Zimbabwe, the author failed to mention many important points — total casualties, the amount of territory controlled by both sides, the living and working conditions for blacks etc. (see *Omissions* in this section).

Incomplete quotation

The reverse of an incomplete quotation is the quotation that makes the interviewer no more than a mouthpiece for the person "interviewed". This means that the speaker is neither challenged nor required to produce any evidence for the claims made. — If the author has quoted his sources accurately, then we can see that he did not ask any followup questions to some very important points (e.g. *WM*. p. 9, col 3 & 4).

Persuasive devices

Most important, *photographs* with cut-lines explaining them are used to illustrate the text. Without even reading the article, we have formed an impression of what happened. Other techniques include: *Testimonial* (the reader has the impression that this is a "first-hand" account of a massacre when it is nothing of the kind); *Glittering Generalities* (e.g., "He has American support because Americans always choose the wrong side"; Selous, "the greatest white hunter of them all . . ."); *Name-calling* (e.g., "terrorist"); *Innuendo* (e.g., "He told me that he had been promised a good job and a car and white women once the party took over Zimbabwe"); *Baseless speculation* (e.g., "so too may all-out civil war [become a reality]; "all the Boers of South Africa would commit mass suicide before they would ever consider . . ." Also, the author makes no reference to conditions, laws or institutions that would prove either way that the government is racist or not racist).

been defined in any way (e.g., what is a "moderate"?), yet a definite *impression* is left with the reader:

terrorist, terror	Russia, Russian
massacre, slaughter	Marxist, Marxism
hideout	security policy
absolute power	security policemen etc
tribesmen, tribal	moderates.

Qualifiers and grouping phrases

In Chapter II there were some examples of how a qualifier within a sentence can make the reader take a leap of logic that s/he would never take in other circumstances. For example, we would react in an extreme case if someone wrote,

Rightly or wrongly, child abuse is here to stay.

However, when the issue is further away from home, we are less directly implicated, we feel we are less informed about an issue and perhaps are less aware of the same leaps in logic:

the "supposed" white totalitarian rule

Either it is totalitarian or it is not. There was plenty of evidence available to show that the white minority regime was indeed a very harsh and cruel one. What evidence is there to cast any doubt on the matter? Such a qualifier casts doubt on the truth of any claim.

Other examples:

> *Even if* the elections aren't held, it is only a matter of time before Rhodesians, *black and white*, live in the constant threat of terror.
> . . . *whatever his motives*, [Smith] has put his government on the line.

Omissions

The article has included many claims that cannot be proven by the author himself, yet it omits a number of other points (in addition to ones already noted). If people really wanted to understand the situation there — not just have their own prejudices confirmed — they would not find the information they need in this article.

• If the article is a *war report*, why is there no mention of the following:

Overall casualties, for both sides, among combatants, and among non-combatants?

Overall inventory of where arms are coming from, for the minority government, and for the guerrillas? (It does mention that the guerrillas receive Russian weapons, but how many? What ratio is this to the total amount of arms received from all sources, for both sides?)

The amount of territory controlled by both sides?

(The article leaves the reader with the impression that the PF has imposed itself by force on black people. There is no hint that the PF must of necessity have widespread support from inside Zimbabwe in order to survive.)

The estimated size of forces? The number of refugees in neighbouring countries?

• If, however, the article is supposed to be a general *report on conditions* in the country, why is there no mention of the following:

Comprehensive press censorship in Rhodesia, including strict government control of journalists' movements? (The *Christian Science Monitor* reported that as many as 70 journalists critical of the Rhodesian government had been deported up to July 1978)[8]

Laws restricting the movement of blacks; working and living conditions for blacks, including housing, nutrition, etc.

The existence of "protected villages" and free-fire zones; the number of refugees? Reports of Selous Scouts' activities; reports of medical and administrative infrastructure set up by guerrillas in guerrilla-controlled land?

• If the article is describing *economic, social,* or *political conditions,* it would have to touch upon at least some of these areas as well.

• If the article is an *eyewitness report* of the war, why is there no mention of:

How the author knew exactly what happened at the mission and where he got his supplementary information?

Why he did not take his own pictures at the scene of the massacre? (It is reasonable to think that a journalist would know how to take pictures.)

• If the article is a *report on war victims,* why is there no mention of:

The total number of civilians killed by Rhodesian government forces, and total number of civilians killed by guerrillas? The total number of deaths related to curfew laws and arbitrary detention?

The killing, by Rhodesian forces, of large numbers of people in raids into neighbouring countries. In one raid, for example, 1,500 Zimbabwean refugees were reported to have been killed.)[9]

Checklist for careful thinking

We consulted the Checklist for careful thinking in our analysis, and these were some of our findings. What were yours?

What is the source?

The source of the major report of the massacre is unknown. The author is unsympathetic to the idea of the Patriotic Front having control of government.

What is the core of the message?

Bloody civil war will result if the Patriotic Front gains "absolute power".

What is presented in support of the point of view?

The massacre is the proof of the barbarity of the Patriotic Front and the implicit reasoning is that blacks (and the Patriotic Front) are barbaric and would engage in wholesale slaughter if they came to power.

How is the message being conveyed?

Through photographs.
Speculation, testimonial, glittering generalities, name-calling and innuendo are among the techniques used to convey the message.

Who stands to gain?

The "moderates" would gain and through them the business interests in Southern Africa that benefit from cheap labour and the wealth of natural resources. Discrediting the Patriotic Front and blacks in general would create an attitude favourable to the idea of real power (control of the economy, judiciary, police and armed forces) being handed over very slowly, and to the "moderate" Muzorewa, who would ensure that whites and foreign investors would remain in effective control.

Conclusions and questions

1. The article

The masked origin of the author's stories (a second- or third-hand account written as if it were an eyewitness report)*, name-calling ("terrorist" etc.), unnamed sources ("a man I talked to"), and in general the language and selective inclusion and omission of information lead us to conclude that the article *has the effect* of

a. clouding issues in Southern Africa; but at the same time

b. implicitly proposing "solutions" to the situation there which would maintain the status quo.

Whether or not this was the author's *intention* is another matter. At best, the article can be described as being biased, naïve and poorly researched.

2. The journalist

A responsible journalist would have identified the sources of his information — not made an account appear to be an on-the-spot report when it was not. A less biased reporter would attempt to moderate his language and substantiate at least some of his claims with evidence. A journalist with even a modicum of initiative would have taken his own pictures.

---

*By no means do we wish to imply that it is wrong to use other sources in writing an article or making a newscast (see Chapter I). It is wrong, however, to *disguise* one's sources.

3. The publisher

Most important, however, a principled writer or publisher would not publish an article until there were reasonable and probable grounds for finding the story to be true. This article was published, even though the truth of the Rhodesian government's account was highly contested at the time.

Under Canadian law, for example, a publisher would hesitate to print something that was strongly disputed or considered false by any of the main parties concerned — for fear of litigation if not for more ethical reasons. In the case of this article, the Foreign Secretary of Great Britain questioned the authenticity of the report of the massacre, and the Patriotic Front categorically denied that the guerrilla movement was responsible. In fact *both* named the Rhodesian government's own forces as likely perpetrators of the crime. (It had been proven that security forces and Selous Scouts had engaged in such activities in the past.) Such contention over the basic facts of a story would usually be enough to halt most publishers, if the issues were local ones. However this, with *Weekend,* was not the case: the aggrieved group had no real way of replying.

Weekend magazine chose to publish this article over others. Most of us would think that if a journalist or writer had an article published in a large-circulation magazine, s/he would have to be very good at their work. In analysing this article, we have seen that this is not necessarily the case. The deciding factor, rather, is whether or not the story will fit

In order to clarify the direct intention to manipulate the news, it is necessary to make an important distinction between Black, White and Grey Propaganda. According to a strict definition, White, Grey and Black Propaganda are terms which do not refer to the content, but rather to the attempt to hide the source. The *U.S. Army Field Manual of Psychological Operations* states: 'Propaganda is also classified on the basis of the identification of its source. White = identifiable. Grey = hidden. Black = deliberately attributed to another source. Grey, white and black do not refer to anything inherent in the content.' A second definition, offered by Marchetti in *The CIA and the Cult of Intelligence*, is 'telling the truth = white; mixture of truth and half-truth = grey; outright lies = black.' He adds, 'Disinformation is a special type of 'black' propaganda —usually supported by false documents.' It seems to me that the essence of disinformation is to introduce into 'the enemy's' communications system false information, which purports to be its own, in order to create confusion.

Fred Landis, "The CIA makes the headlines: psychological warfare in Chile," *Liberation*, March/April 1975

into the *general editorial policy*[10] of the magazine:

> The power of the press is the power of selection. Newspapers and broadcasting stations cannot dictate how we think and vote on specific issues; but their influence in *selecting* those issues can be enormous.
> (Senate Committee on Mass Media, 1970).

In its appeals to prospective advertisers, *Weekend* magazine said that it could sell their products very successfully (one of the proofs given was reader interest in the weekly polls the magazine conducted). In the December 1978 issue of *Weekend* magazine, what was being "sold" to the buyer (reader) on the level of ads — and also on the level of content of articles?

On the level of *content,* we have seen that, according to the author, the "moderates" in Rhodesia presented the only hope for a peaceful settlement there. This is the content of the article, the political or ideological "product" that *Weekend* "sold" to its readers that week.

On the level of *advertising,* what was being sold to the reader? Who advertises in the magazine?

While there were a number of advertisers in *Weekend* magazine, by far the largest was Rothman's. As you may remember, its full-page ads usually formed the back cover of the magazine: prime advertising space. Mentioning *Weekend's* advertisers is relevant because, as was seen in Chapter III, owners or advertisers can exercise a great deal of control over their publishers.

Rothman's is part of the giant Rothman's — Carling O'Keefe group. Rothman's is owned by South Africa interests. Rothman's of Pall Mall Canada holds 50.1% ownership of Carling O'Keefe, and the snakes and ladders of corporate ownership continue: Carling O'Keefe has franchises in both football (Toronto Argonauts) and hockey (Quebec Nordiques) . . .

We do not wish to speculate about the editorial intentions of *Weekend* magazine. However, we will refer back to an earlier discussion on the influence that owners and advertisers can have over the content of publications:

> In real life industrialists and department store managers do not pound on the publisher's desk and demand favourable treatment. They do not have to. An owner who lunches weekly with the president of the local power company will always grasp the sanctity of private ownership in this field more readily than the public-ownership ideas of a few crackpots. With the best of will, he may tell himself that his mind is open. Yet, as a businessman whose concerns are intimately bound up with those of other businessmen, he has a vested interest in maintaining the status quo.[11]

Using the Checklists from Chapters I and II, and referring to the definitions of propaganda, bias and point of view in this chapter, in which category would *you* place "The bloody road to Zimbabwe"?

One of the questions in our Checklists for careful thinking asks, *Who stands to gain?*

How would you answer this question, in reference to the *Weekend* article?

We have also included in the following section the point of view of other sources which give a different interpretation — and different information — about events during the same period. Does this information alter your point of view? Was "the truth" about what went on in Rhodesia the casualty of that war?

You must answer the questions.

Discussion/essay topics — Propaganda, bias and point of view

1. First impressions are lasting impressions — especially for the casual reader. With its short articles on a variety of topics, a magazine like *Weekend* is intended for the casual reader. But what if first impressions are *false* impressions? Do you think the mass media have a responsibility to give full and fair coverage of the issues they deal with?

    a. If so, how would you determine whether an issue was in fact being fairly treated?

    b. If you do not think the mass media have such a responsibility, does anyone have this responsibility in society?

2. In a 1980 study of American press coverage of another part of the world, El Salvador, the Columbia University School of Journalism found that an average of *eight out of 10 quotes* in the stories it reviewed came either from United States or Salvadorean government officials.[12] Discuss the implications of this form of coverage.

3. The first casualty of war is truth. Discuss the meaning, validity and implications of this statement.

4. There were two 'Reigns of Terror', if we could but remember and consider it; the one wrought murder in hot passions, the other in heartless cold blood; the one

Remember now , it must look like you do all the talking

lasted mere months, the other had lasted a thousand years; the one inflicted death upon a thousand persons, the other upon a hundred million; but our shudders are all for the 'horrors' of the minor Terror, the momentary Terror, so to speak; whereas, what is the horror of swift death by the axe compared with lifelong death from hunger, cold, insult, cruelty and heartbreak? A city cemetery could contain the coffins filled by that brief Terror which we have all been so diligently taught to shiver at and mourn over; but all France could hardly contain the coffins filled by that older and real Terror — that unspeakable bitter and awful Terror which none of us has been taught to see in its vastness or pity as it deserves.
— Mark Twain, writing about the French Revolution, in "A Connecticut Yankee in King Arthur's Court"

    a. Do you agree with Mark Twain's interpretation of the French Revolution? Why or why not?

    b. How might this interpretation be applied to the situation in Southern Africa today?

    c. What might be Mark Twain's view of media coverage of "Third World" news today?

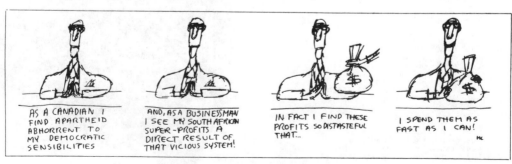

AS A CANADIAN I FIND APARTHEID ABHORRENT TO MY DEMOCRATIC SENSIBILITIES

AND, AS A BUSINESSMAN I SEE MY SOUTH AFRICAN SUPER-PROFITS A DIRECT RESULT OF THAT VICIOUS SYSTEM!

IN FACT I FIND THESE PROFITS SO DISTASTEFUL THAT...

I SPEND THEM AS FAST AS I CAN!

c. Rothman's-Carling O'Keefe empire in Canada

The purpose of this brief article is to provide an outline of the South African-based Rothman's empire and to document the extent to which its corporate tentacles extend into the Canadian economy in the form of consumer commodities.

Under the Rothman's Group of South Africa is Rothman's of Canada. The latter's dominant subsidiary is Rothman's of Pall Mall Canada Ltd. This company, in turn, controls Carling O'Keefe Ltd. through 50.1% interest. The following list documents the subsidiaries of Carling O'Keefe Ltd.:

BENNETT BREWERIES LTD.
CALGARY BREWING AND MALTING CO. LTD.
O'KEEFE BREWING CO. LTD.
CANADIAN BREWERIES AND TRANSPORT LTD.
THE CARLING BREWERIES LTD.
WILLIAM DOW BREWERY LTD.
DORAN'S NORTHERN ONTARIO BREWERIES LTD.
DORAN'S BEVERAGE CO. LTD.
JORDAN VALLEY WINES LTD. (83.8%)
   JORDAN WINES LTD.
   VILLA WINES LTD.
   CHALET WINES LTD.
   GROWERS WINES LTD.---which owns:
      BEAU SEJOUR VINEYARDS LTD.
      CASTLE WINES CO. LTD.
      CASTLE WINES OF CANADA LTD.
      REGAL IMPORTERS LTD.
CENTURY IMPORTERS LTD.
STAR OIL AND GAS

Rothman's of Pall Mall Canada Ltd. also controls a number of additional companies:

ALFRED DUNHILL OF LONDON LTD.
FILTROMAT OF CANADA LTD.
LARUS AND BROTHER CO.
ROCK CITY TOBACCO CO. LTD.
ROTHMAN'S HOLDINGS CANADA LTD.
TURMAC TOBAKMAATSCHAPPIJ CANADA LTD.
ROTHMAN'S INVESTMENS LTD.

Rothman's-Carling O'Keefe products are readily identifiable in the Canadian consumer market. In order to educate Canadians with the commodities that bear the mark of apartheid and exploitation of the black majority in Southern Africa, we list here the wines and beers produced by these South African controlled companies that are sold in Alberta.

DESSERT WINES

Jordan Branvin Port
Villa Berry Cup
Jordan (Alta.) Port
Jordan Branvin Sherry
Ste. Michelle Beau Sejour Rich Red
Ste. Michelle Beau Sejour Rich White
Ste. Michelle (Sask.) Beau Sejour Sherry
Jordan 4 Aces Sherry
Jordan Gold Seal Sherry
Villa Cream Sherry

RED TABLE WINES

Jordan (Alta.) Belfontaine
Jorden (Alta.) Claret
Jordan (Alta.) Red Dinner
Jordan (Alta.) Still Rose
Jordan (Alta.) Valley Red Table
Jordan (Ont.) Rubi Rouge
Jordan (Ont.) Valley Still Rose
Ste. Michelle (Sask.) Beau Sejour Red Dry

WHITE TABLE WINES

Jordan (Alta.) Sauterne
Jordan (Alta.) Valley White
Jordan (Alta.) White Dinner
Jordan Valley Pink Champagne

SPARKLING WINES

Jordan (Alta.) Baby Bear
Jordan (Alta.) Lonesome Charlie
Jordan (Alta.) Sparkling Sangria
Jordan (Ont.) Cold Turkey

BUBBLING WINES

Jordan Valley Crackling Rose
Jordan Crackling Cold Duck
Villa Crackling Cold Duck

CARLING O'KEEFE BEERS

Alta 3.9
Black Label Lager
Bohemian Maid
Calgary Export Lager
Carlsberg Lager
Cascade Pilsner
Golden West
Heidelberg
O'Keefe Old Vienna Lager
O'Keefe Extra Old Stock Malt Liquor

Source: Free South Africa Committee Edmonton (1976)
Millions against millions

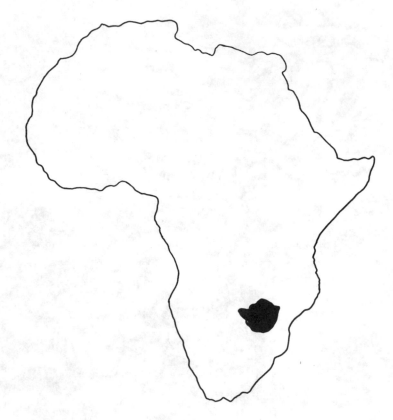

The other side of the story

One of the principal characteristics of propaganda and the mass media of communication is that they are *unidirectional* — one-way forms of communication. The receiver has no effective way of replying to them, challenging their arguments or disagreeing with the messages they relay. Also as was seen in Chapter III, a very small segment of society is making the decisions which exclude most people from significant access to the media (e.g., prime-time TV, feature articles in high-circulation magazines). In these circumstances, groups who do make the headlines are often reduced to trying to "counter" unfavourable or inaccurate coverage of them.

For this reason, we present here some examples of sources other than the mass media which were available at about the same time that the *Weekend* magazine article entered the homes of thousands of Canadians. There is a brief indication of what kind of sources they are. Unlike the *Weekend* article, all these sources were generally very critical of the white minority's privileged position in Zimbabwe and Southern Africa in general. The examples given are now of course from the past; *however, for whatever "hot spot" in the news as you read this, there are similar, alternative sources of information.*

In the *Weekend* article, it was said that

> Rhodesians have been asked to endure more than the average person should be asked to take on in a lifetime.

Here is another side to the story. We ask you to consider, while reading the following passages from alternative sources, *which* Rhodesians in fact endured more than one should be asked to take on in a lifetime.

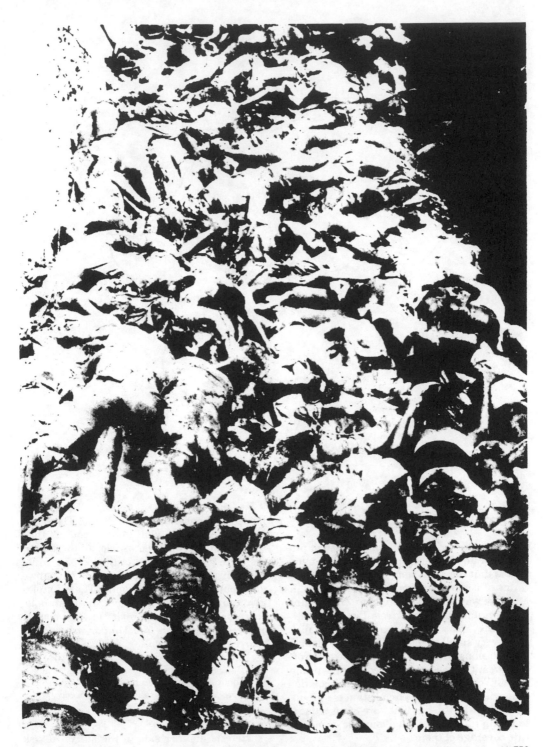

South African forces attacked a Namibian refugee camp at Kassinga in southern Angola, May 4th, 1978. In this one raid, 759 refugees were massacred, and 200 more were kidnapped. Those released have reported that the 200 prisoners have been subjected to brutal torture and mutilation, including the loss of eyes, ears, fingers and genitals. Coverage of such atrocities committed by the "security forces" rarely if ever appears in the commercial press.
Sources: Counter Information Services, Anti-report No. 21: Buying Time in South Africa; and International Defence and Aid Fund for Southern Africa.

Rhodesia: the propaganda war was excerpted from a book by the same title, published by the Catholic Commission for Justice and Peace in Rhodesia, and the Catholic Institute for International Relations (CIIR) in London, England. The Commission's director, Bishop Donal Lamont, was an outspoken critic of the white minority regime. Later, the Rhodesian security forces would raid and destroy the Commission's printing presses.

Rhodesia
The Propaganda War

This latest report from the Catholic Commission for Justice and Peace in Rhodesia highlights the extent of the propaganda war being waged by the Rhodesia Front regime. It also illustrates the contradictions of the propaganda campaign—to assuage white fears on the one hand and on the other to terrorise the black population in an attempt to isolate the guerrillas. As support for the nationalist cause has increased, the propaganda has become increasingly strident. It takes several forms—displaying the mutilated corpses of guerrillas and distributing photographs of them accompanied by threats, warning the black population that if they co-operate with the guerillas they will be killed. The latest element in the psychological warfare is the mass distribution of crude leaflets depicting guerrillas as 'mad dog terrorists', responsible for killing, rape and spreading venereal disease. At the same time the government has issued regulations which make it an offence to publish or distribute anything which may contribute to the spreading of alarm and despondency. Whilst the regime is thus actively engaged in spreading alarm and despondency among black Rhodesians, it is going to inordinate lengths to prevent white Rhodesians from knowing the truth of their situation.

International coverage of the war in Rhodesia is at best mediocre. There is a dearth of foreign correspondents inside the country so that several newspapers have to rely on the same reporter writing under different names. Foreign correspondents have to be careful not to be too critical of the Rhodesian regime. Those who are too critical either have to leave the country or are deported. Recently the BBC correspondent Brian Barron has been refused an extension of his work permit because when he reported on a massacre of 23 blacks in north-eastern Rhodesia he said "Well, we only have the Rhodesian security forces version of the massacre..." Few journalists are permitted to enter the operational areas and those who are allowed to do so are subject to censorship. As a result, most reporters are dependent on government statements and few have any opportunity for rounded background investigation. In consequence the realities of the war are distorted.

This report includes an analysis of the Rhodesian regime's policy of rounding up rural Africans into "protected villages". It is estimated that these villages now contain half a million Africans in conditions of great hardship. This inhuman policy has gone largely uncriticised in the media. Indeed Rhodesian propaganda presents these villages as havens of safety and welcomed by the local people.

It is clear that some of the atrocities of the war are committed by the Rhodesian security forces. Indeed the judgement of many missionaries on the spot is that the army is responsible for the bulk of the terrorising, brutality and killing of civilians. Rarely, if ever, is this conveyed in the international press. One incident described in this report tells of the killing of 35 civilians, most of them women and children and the serious wounding of another 31 by the security forces. The initial report of this incident in London's largest evening newspaper, the *Evening News*, stated "guerrillas kill 34". According to the first report in the *Evening News* "Security chiefs (said) the civilians were lined up and shot with automatic weapons". In later editions the story had altered to the "killed in crossfire" account which also appeared in other British newspapers. The security forces, who claimed they were merely engaged in a normal follow-up operation of nine guerrillas, described the incident as "an unfortunate set-back". Eventually the truth of what had happened was conceded but dismissed as "unfortunately inevitable in fighting of this nature". (*Rhodesian Herald* Editorial, May 11 1977.)

The fact is, far from protecting black civilians, the Rhodesian security forces place little value on their lives. In view of such incidents it is understandable that nationalists accuse the Rhodesian security forces of shooting anything black that moves. Nor is it surprising that the control of the army and police is a crucial factor in any negotiations for a settlement.

Evidence of the kind of lawlessness which is being legitimised by the Rhodesian government is continually emerging. In the most recent example, the Rhodesian Minister for Justice and Law and Order, Hilary Squires, assured white vigilante groups that they would be indemnified against any legal repercussions if they killed anyone whilst recovering stolen cattle (*The Times*, July 28 1977). Statements from the Rhodesian government about the importance of maintaining law and order in the 'interim period' sound hollow under such circumstances.

Propaganda attempts to isolate guerillas

The rural psychological campaign conducted by the Smith government in Rhodesia took a new twist in April with the publication of a series of propaganda leaflets designed to discredit the guerillas. Unlike previous campaigns which warned people of the punishment they would face if they assisted the nationalist soldiers, the new leaflets attack the guerillas directly and portray them as "mad-dog communist terrorists."

The one page leaflets contain a drawing and an English text on one side, with the same text in Shona and Sindebele on the reverse side. Nine have been issued so far. They are handed out to more than half a million people living in the country's protected villages, distributed at rural schools and are posted on shops and public buildings in the rural areas.

All nine bear the same basic message: Guerillas are communist terrorists and communists embody all that is evil. The leaflets accuse the "murdering mad-dogs" of every conceivable crime—kidnapping children, starving and beating recruits, infecting

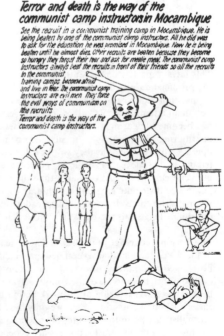

Terror and death is the way of the communist camp instructors in Mocambique

See the recruit in a communist training camp in Mocambique. He is being beaten by one of the communist camp instructors. All he did was to ask for the education he was promised in Mocambique. Now he is being beaten until he almost dies. Other recruits are beaten because they become so hungry they forgot their fear and ask for mealie meal. The communist camp instructors always beat the recruits in front of their friends so all the recruits in the communist training camps become afraid and live in fear. The communist camp instructors are evil men they force the evil ways of communism on the recruits

Terror and death is the way of the communist camp instructors.

men with V.D., shooting old men and young girls,
engaging in every kind of brutality. "Terror and
th is the way of the communist terrorists" is the
me running through the leaflets which read like
ndard one primers.

They must think we're stupid," commented one
n after seeing the leaflets. Another said, "We
w the so-called terrorists. They are our sons,
thers and relatives. We know the government
s lies about them."

nother man crumpled the leaflets in his fist and
lared scornfully, "They're nonsense. They show
foolish the government is." Someone else
led and said, "We use them to light our fires."
st feel that at least they are an improvement over
vious propaganda which showed gory
tographs of the mutilated bodies of dead
rillas.

our of the nine leaflets single out the
U/ZANLA forces which are headed by Robert
gabe. All nine mention Mozambique and the "evil
munist camp instructors" there. The word
nmunist' or 'communism' appears in almost
ry line and is used seven or eight times in each
et.

he leaflets try to convince people that the
ration movements are not an authentic national
e, but are tools of communist agents outside the
ntry. They also seem geared to diminish the
ularity of ZANU and its leaders. They are very
ch in line with the directives for a national psy-
logical campaign which were issued by the
AC (Psychological Action) Secretariat last
ober and recently revealed by David Martin in
Observer. These directives spell out the strategy
e used to sell a negotiated settlement to various
ps of the population. According to these
ctives, the propaganda aimed at rural Africans
ld seek to isolate the guerilas from the general
can population and it is stated very explicitly:
sons who now persist in causing unrest and
orting terrorism can now be identified as the
ny of all Rhodesians because they wish to
ose a foreign military dictatorship and are there-
agents of a foreign government (use Mozam-
e as an example—communist terrorists)."

he new psychological warfare seems to be a last
effort to defeat those who would demand
ificant changes in the economic and social
ctures of the society. No such changes are en-
ged by the present regime. The directives clearly
e that despite negotiations the national aim
ains the same and "Therefore no dramatic
ges will take place to the existing pattern of
and everyone, black and white, must be
uraged to participate in maintaining normality
the preservation of order." The propagandists
also instructed, "Emphasise that this is an

achievement for moderation and responsibility and
a defeat for terrorism, Marxism and extremism;
therefore it is not in any sense a sell-out or a
capitulation.

While the guerilla forces may be winning on the
battlefield, therefore, they are to be denied the
victory at the conference table. The propaganda
depicts them as the enemies of the people who want
to "destroy the people with sickness and death so
that their evil communist masters may come from
their hiding places in Mozambique and steal the
country from the people."

It is doubtful whether many Africans believe such
propaganda. Most say that the government is
wasting a lot of time and money producing useless
pieces of paper. Rather than destroying the image of
the guerillas, the government publicity makes them
greater heroes in the eyes of the rural majority.
August 1977 ∎

The following document, *Zimbabwe: winning hearts and minds* was produced by TCLSAC (Toronto Committee for the Liberation of Southern Africa). A support group for Southern African independence movements, TCLSAC is financially sustained by memberships and donations, and has no political party affiliations. It raises some funds for Southern Africa, and carries out an education programme and support work in Canada. The article included here appeared in *TCLSAC Reports*, the group's newsletter, and was adapted from an American pamphlet, as noted on the last page of the article. (The Washington Office on Africa is an independent research body funded by major churches in the U.S. and some labour unions.)

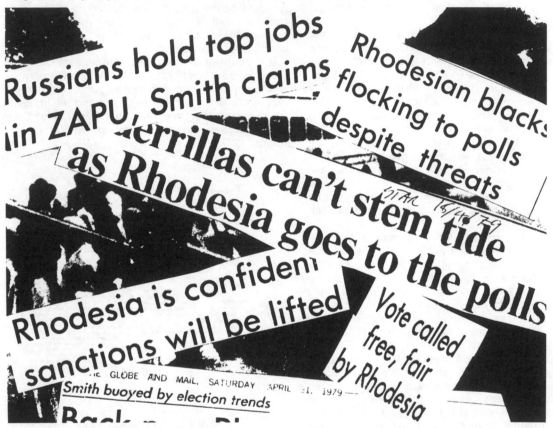

Zimbabwe: Winning Hearts and Minds

Each time another white person is killed in Rhodesia, western journalists vividly depict a scene of bloodshed and brutality and inevitably blame the incident on the liberation forces of the Patriotic Front. When this occurs, the illegal regime scores a propaganda victory, using the event to discredit the guerillas and to win support for its war effort, and, since April 24th, to gain international recognition for its internal settlement and "elected" government.

For instance, when Pentacostal missionaries and their children were killed near the eastern border on June 23rd, 1978, the regime flew foreign journalists to the scene of the slayings, allowing them to photograph freely, and to send back stories without censoring the gory details. This was quite a contrast to the massacre of 22 Africans by security forces two weeks previous when even the statements of two members of the interim Executive Council were censored. It also far

overshadowed the coverage of a massacre only 24 hours earlier when Rhodesian troops raided a refugee camp 33 kilometers inside Mozambique, killing 17 refugees and 2 UN Food and Agriculture Organization volunteers from Belgium.

The statements of the liberation forces, if used at all, are reduced to a few sentences and buried in the middle of an article. Most Canadian and US media simply repeat the regime's accusations that the guerillas are on the rampage against whites and the church. This process reinforces racist images which make it easy to believe stories depicting Africans as brutal barbarians. It bolsters the regime's contention that it is fighting to preserve Christianity and civilization against the attacks of "murdering mad-dog communist terrorists."

The media thus tend to act as both judge and jury - to pronounce a verdict instead of giving their audience the evidence needed to form their own conclusions.

SELOUS SCOUTS: REAL TERRORISTS

The Canadian and US media have given scant coverage to the Selous Scouts, an elite counter-insurgency unit in the Smith army which impersonates guerillas and commits atrocities in order to discredit the authentic liberation forces. Their activities make it extremely difficult to tell which side is in fact responsible for any atrocity. In the eyes of the African people, the Scouts are the real terrorists and would not shrink from murdering missionaries if it would serve their cause. The Commission for Justice and Peace in Rhodesia had gathered significant evidence linking the Scouts with the death of seven missionaries at St. Paul's Mission in February, 1977 as well as to several major massacres of African civilians which had been blamed on the guerillas:

All but one of the priests to whom I spoke stressed that their African congregations were convinced that the killings were being carried out by the Selous Scouts... The (former) Bishop of Umtali,

Rt. Rev. Donal Lamont recounted... "I had a visit from one of my African clergy who reported that he was terrorized by European members of the security forces. They said to him: 'You'd better watch out. One dead missionary is as good as 100 dead terrorists to us'."
David Martin in London Observer, March 13, 1977

A thirteen man section of Selous Scouts posing as guerillas arrived at Nyadiriri kraal... On their arrival, Lytton, the section commander, interrogated Mr. Nyadiriri... After torturing him for two hours without obtaining any useful information, Lytton... ordered his band to shoot down the innocent man... Three days later the (Rhodesian Broadcast Corporation)... report was as follows:
"Terrorists arrived at Nyadiriri Kraal and demanded food. Mr. Nyadiriri refused them food and the murderers gunned him down with their Soviet automatic rifles."
Account of Wonderful Mukoyi, captured Selous Scout, Zimbabwe News, July-December, 1977

MISSIONARIES: FRIENDS OF PF

Missionaries who have stayed in rural areas have generally formed a working relationship with the liberation forces in their region. Some church personnel provide food, shelter and medicine to the liberation army. It is therefore much more likely that missionaries would be viewed as enemy targets by the Smith regime than by the guerillas. The church, as a rule, does not report the presence of guerillas, a crime that carries a maximum penalty of death. It is missionaries who have witnessed and exposed torture and ill-treatment of African civilians by the security forces.

Several church people who have been killed were firm supporters of the Patriotic Front. One of the first victims, Bishop Adolph Schmitt, was a life-long friend of Patriotic Front leader Joshua Nkomo. The Pentacostals who were the most recent victims were re-

portedly cooperating with the liberation forces in their area. On the other hand, missionaries of churches which support the regime, such as the Dutch Reformed Church and the Anglicans, have never been touched.

The campaign against the Roman Catholic Church by the Smith regime is deliberate and calculated because of the stiff resistance which that Church has put up against the injustice and mass murder of people... Smith, in an attempt to cover up these atrocities, has accused us of committing them... The truth is that the white missionaries are being sacrificed by the Smith regime on the mistaken belief that the gullible Western world will believe his side and see justice in his cause and injustice in ours.

> Robert Mugabe, President of ZANU
> U.N. Conference on Zimbabwe and
> Namibia
> Maputo, Mozambique, May 16, 1977

It is a wicked lie for anybody to suggest that freedom fighters are molesting or killing missionaries... Those who have left the country because they could not stand the oppressive system in our country, or because they feared for their lives, must know that they will be needed in a free Zimbabwe. We shall take trouble to bring them back to continue to perform their invaluable service.

> Joshua Nkomo, President of ZAPU
> Lusaka Radio, September 1977

THE PROPAGANDA WAR

Propaganda has been a powerful weapon in the Smith arsenal. The regime publishes numerous pamphlets depicting Rhodesia as a happy multi-racial society beset by communist invaders from without its borders. A national psychological campaign was launched in Oct. 1976 to sell the idea of an internal settlement and to depict the liberation movement as Marxist, terrorist and extremist. This pervasive propaganda provides the government with

a plausible motive for blaming the missionary killings on the guerillas:

> In Rhodesia the news media are completely controlled by the regime. Only a censored version of the killings (or any other aspect of the war) reaches the outside world. Journalists who have been critical, or even skeptical, of official Rhodesian propaganda have been promptly deported, over 70 of them to date.
>
> Christian Science Monitor, July 11, 1978

WHY WE HEAR ONLY ONE SIDE

The Smith regime goes to inordinate lengths to conceal the real situation in Rhodesia from the outside world, and even from its own citizens. Since the white minority regime seized power illegally in 1965, Rhodesia has been in a declared State of Emergency. Such laws as the Law and Order (Maintenance) Act curtail freedom of the press as well as freedom of speech, particularly with regard to the conduct of the war. It is a crime to publish anything "contrary to the interests of public safety or public order," or anything likely to "cause fear, alarm and despondency." Since January of 1978, all reports relating to the war must pass through the hands of government censors. The penalty for violating the new press restrictions is a $700 fine or one year imprisonment or both.

Journalists' access to information is also severely limited. On arrival in Rhodesia journalists are informed that they are forbidden to enter operational areas without government permission and escort. This includes almost the entire country except for the cities of Bulawayo and Salisbury.

They are also forbidden to visit the government's "protected villages," in which one-third of the rural population is restricted. Because of the racial segregation enforced by the Land Tenure Act, it is also difficult for white journalists to visit African townships or to talk to Africans without drawing the attention of the police. Reporters are usually

tailed by the Special Branch of the police and their hotel rooms are often searched.

The government also controls journalists by issuing them work permits for a limited period of 29 days. If their reporting is not acceptable to the regime they will not be granted an extension.

During briefings by military personnel, journalists are fed the regime's side of the war and also discouraged from talking with Africans. They are indoctrinated with the stereotype of Africans as hostile, anti-white, and tribally oriented. With this kind of introduction it is small wonder that many correspondents are forced to rely on gossip which circulates among journalists who gather at the Quill Club in Salisbury's Ambassador Hotel.

THE EYE OF THE BEHOLDER

North American media coverage of Zimbabwe is also biased because of the structure of the media itself. Reuter, UPI and AP are the major sources of foreign coverage for most papers. None have reporters based in any of the front-line states where they would hear the Patriotic Front's version of the war. In contrast,   the agencies have bureaus in Salisbury where they are inundated with the Smith regime's propaganda. Individual reporters who cover Africa for the major big-city papers and magazines generally have to cover almost all of the continent. They can only spend a few days at a time in Rhodesia, and seldom have time to establish African contacts and get an in-depth reading of the situation.

The highly concentrated corporate owrership of the media is not interested in sympathetic portrayals of movements with socialist objectives. It is therefore not surprising that reporters or editors do not get encouragement to write stories that break stereotypes or challenge assumptions that the Patriotic Front is the enemy. This same factor helps to explain why evidence of US support for the minority regime – the continued violations of sanctions, the supply of oil from US subsidiaries in South Africa, the 500 mercenaries in Smith's army –

is often ignored. The combined effect of Rhodesia's propaganda, encouragement of racist biases and the corporate interests of US media help to explain which stories on Zimbabwe will continue to "stop the presses". Canadian media, as exemplified by Toronto's Star and Globe, are only marginally less blatant in their propaganda war against Zimbabwe.

OUT FROM UNDER THE MEDIA'S BIASES

How can we avoid taking on the same biases about Zimbabwe that are expressed in major media from which we get most of our information?

1. Learn to read and listen critically

Next time you read an account of a massacre, an attack on the church, or an assessment of political developments in Rhodesia, refer back to this article to help evaluate what you read.

2. Alternative media

To escape the limitations of the establishment media, seek out other sources of information. Magazines such as International Bulletin, In These Times, Seven Days and The Guardian can round out your information about southern Africa. Good sources of in-depth information on southern Africa include:

Southern Africa
156 Fifth Ave., Room 707
New York, N.Y. 10010

TCLSAC REPORTS
121 Avenue Rd
Toronto, Ontario
M5R 2G3

Reprinted from brochure published by:
Washington Office on Africa
110 Maryland Ave., N.E.
Washington, D.C. 20002 ∎

These are some of the questions from *Zimbabwe Quiz,* prepared by the International Defence and Aid Fund (IDAF).

Information on starvation, working conditions, police detentions and Security Forces brutality had for years been distributed by such groups as IDAF, Amnesty International, major churches, humanitarian organisations and human rights groups.

What is urban life like for the Africans?

The townships are overcrowded and in many cases are squalid slums. In many there is no domestic electricity, water has to be fetched from a tap in the street and sanitary facilities are very primitive. Few entertainment and recreational facilities exist (except municipally-owned beerhalls) and schools and other social services are inadequate. The townships are designed strategically: water and electricity can be cut off in the event of strikes or political demonstrations.

In Salisbury there is a small township called Marimba Park where a small number of African families own European-style houses; it is regularly inspected by overseas visitors.

Why do Africans remain in the urban areas if life is so bad there?

For several reasons. Firstly because it is the only place where there is a chance of earning a living; nearly all the country's industry and commerce is in the urban areas. Secondly the Tribal Trust Lands are so poor and overcrowded that they cannot support even their present population. Thirdly, because the whites need cheap African labour, they have introduced a system of laws and taxation which forces Africans to enter into the cash economy and work in the whites' industry and trade. Finally many Africans are now urban-born and have no other home.

Is segregation applied to schools in Rhodesia?

Yes. There are separate schools for each racial group, Africans, Coloureds, Asians and Europeans.

Is this segregated education equal for all races?

No. The standard for Africans is much inferior.
● School is compulsory for all European children but not for Africans. In fact 60% of African children have to leave school before the end of their primary education and only 0.2% reach the VIth form.

● There is extreme overcrowding in African scho double sessions have become common practice because of shortage of classrooms, schools and teachers.

● In the year 1972-3 the regime allocated R$20.1 mil for the education of 69,901 European, Asian and Colou school children; the amount allocated for 788,071 Africans R$21.8 million.

● Whilst the parents of European children pay little or school fees, African parents have to pay for stationery, m text books and also to contribute to school funds. This probl is particularly acute in secondary education where many r schools of necessity are boarding schools. For most par the fees are almost prohibitive.

What happens to immigrants or foreigners who disa with the policies of the regime?

They can be deported. These powers have been used e sively against journalists, missionaries and university lect The regime can also declare a person a prohibited immi and thus prevent him from entering the country.

The 1970 Citizens Act enables the regime to depri their citizenship persons who obtained it by registration not by birth). By use of these powers the regime has been to deport some of its own citizens.

Fig I. Land Allocation & Population.

Europeans

Land: 45 million acres
Population: 273,000

Africans

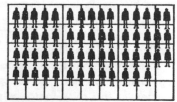

Land: 45 million acres
Population: 5,800,000

Key: Each figure represents 100,000 pe
Each square " " 1 million ac

1e 1970 Citizens Act enables the regime to deprive of
citizenship persons who obtained it by registration (i.e.
·y birth). By use of these powers the regime has been able
·port some of its own citizens.

3. Employment by Race, 1973

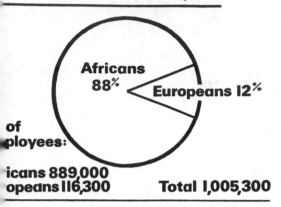

of
ployees:

·icans 889,000
opeans 116,300   **Total 1,005,300**

Africans and Europeans receive equal pay in
desia?

The average income per employee for Europeans during
was R$3,901. For African employees the average income
R$359. The gap between average European and African
s has increased from R$2,809 in 1970 to R$3,542 in 1973.

4. Earnings by Race, 1973

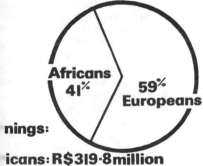

nings:

·icans: R$319·8 million
opeans: R$453·9 million
al: R$773·7 million

African wages sufficient to live on?

A poverty datum line unit at the University of Rhodesia
ated the income required for families of various sizes to
 the poverty datum line (i.e. minimum subsistence level).
e unit found that in January 1974 in Salisbury the average
y had six members who would require an income of over
 per month. In fact over 90% of Africans employed in
 and mines were earning less than R$70 per month.

Can Africans join trade unions?

The rights of Africans to organize in trade unions are restricted
by complex legal constraints. The major items of legislation are
the Masters and Servants Act of 1901 and the Industrial
Conciliation Act of 1934 as amended. The Law and Order
(Maintenance) Act of 1960 as amended also contains numerous
powers which are used to regulate trade union activity.

The Masters and Servants Act which governs the employment of domestic servants and agricultural workers (over 53%
of the total African workforce) denies them the right to form or
join trade unions. Under the Act workers who are disobedient
or neglectful can be fined or imprisoned.

The Industrial Conciliation Act was amended in 1959 to
allow certain categories of workers, mainly in manufacturing
and trade, the right to form or join trade unions. Under the
Act conditions are laid down for the registering of trade unions
and the resolving of industrial disputes through a system of
industrial councils and industrial boards. The Registrar of
Trade Unions is vested with wide arbitary powers including
the right to refuse to register a trade union. The system of
industrial councils and boards is similarly weighted heavily in
favour of the government and employers.

The Act, whilst allowing for multi-racial unions, provides
for the establishment of racially segregated unions and even in
the multi-racial unions voting rights are defined so as to guarantee white workers' domination. The Act also makes the establishment of general unions, i.e. unions catering for workers in
several industries, illegal.

The overall effect of this legislation is to make it virtually
impossible for African trade unions to function. In 1971 it was
estimated that only 5.2% of the total urban African workforce
was represented by registered trade unions.

Are African workers allowed to strike?

Rhodesian labour and security laws make it virtually impossible
for African workers to hold a lawful strike. The Masters and
Servants Act, which governs the employment of domestic
servants and agricultural workers, makes any act of disobedi-
ence an indictable offence. It is a criminal offence for anyone
to be involved in strike action in " essential services " which are
defined so broadly that few areas of employment are not
included.

Many other restrictions exist. The Law and Order (Maintenance) Act makes it illegal to picket, controls the organisation
of trade union meetings and even makes it an offence, with a
penalty of ten years' imprisonment "to boo. . . anyone who has
not joined a strike with you ".

In practice many trade unionists have been detained or
restricted, the Unlawful Organisations Act has been used to
ban trade unions and the police have brutally suppressed
strikes by African workers.

Is unemployment a problem in Rhodesia?

Yes. It is estimated that tens of thousands of urbanized
Africans are unemployed. This huge reserve of labour allows
employers to pay starvation wages with the sure knowledge
that if their workers strike, they can simply be replaced. ∎

These secret Rhodesian government documents were discovered and reprinted in the Mar/Apr 78 issue of *Zimbabwe News,* the official bulletin of the Patriotic Front (ZANU). The entire document appears to have been reproduced (a section appears below). The documents were neither introduced nor commented on by the magazine, although the issue was devoted to the "Enemies of the People", and the headline above the document was: "The régime's strategy for perpetuating colonialism".

Rhodesian Government secret Papers

Confidential (7)

PSYAC SECRETARIAT
P.O. Box UA 350
Salisbury

Directive of
national psychological campaign

Situation:

1. Following the recent proposed political changes, sections of the Rhodesian Population have become confused and require a clear interpritation of Government policy. Our enemy ·vill try to capitalise on the situation. Maximum effort is, therefore, required by all government agencies to help clarify the position and counter enemy propaganda.

2. An immediate result of the detente exercise in December 1974, was that the terrorists said that the government has surrendered. Intelligence from the locals dried up und our success in the terrorist war suffered a serious set back. Recently we have managed to regain the lost ground and a further setback now cannot be permitted.

Mission:

3. To direct Government agencies on psychological action tasks to be implemented on a national scale.

Execution:

4. *General Outline:* The material to be disseminated has been prepared for various target groups. In the operational area certain groups are to be detailed with the security forces, Internal Affairs and other persons. Responsibility for the implementation of the campaign in

other areas will be determined by PSYAC. PACC/ Sensor teams will co-ordinate, activities assess and evaluate reaction report and take recommendation to PSYAC.

Operational Areas:

5. *Security Forces:*
(a). *Dissemination:* Security forces unit commanders are to disseminate to all ranks under command using the information at appendix

c. Where applicable, Security forces may disseminate information contained in other appendices when in contact with the various target groups.

b. The Senior army and police officers at Sub JCC's are responsibie for the overall SP co-ordination in their area.

Confidential
Appendix "A"

Target groups (African): TTLs, Chiefs, Headmen, Kraal Heads, APA Farmers, Co-opted employees, Council Staff, Rural Businessmen and Local African Employees, European Farm Labourers, Women's Clubs and Young Farmers Clubs

1. It has been agreed, there will be a change in the form of government in Rhodesia. The most important change is that shortly there will be a Council of State with equal representation, leading to a new constitution. This provides an opportunity for black Rhodesians to participate in a responsible fashion in national and local government and in the decision making processes. Initially these African representatives will be nominated.

2. What does this mean to the black Rhodesian? It means persons who now persist in causing unrest and supporting terrorism can now be identified as the enemy of all Rhodesians, because they wish to impose a foreign military dictatorship and are, therefore, agents of a foreign government – (use Moçambique as an example – Communist terrorists).

3. Therefore, anyone who continues with criminal acts of terrorism is an obstacle to peace and increased prosperity. These people will be rooted out and destroyed, but this costs money, which would otherwise have been used for African development. For example your roads and bridges, clinics, schools Increased development in the African areas leads to greater job opportunities.

4. Our best course is clear, we must all help in destroying these criminals as quickly as possible so that we can take advantage of peace to live normal lives and thereby increase prosperity.

5. What is peace and prosperity?

(a) *Peace* No more interference in your traditional customs and way of life by terrorists. E.G.

i. Rape/seduction of wives and daughters.
ii. Atrocities on your people e.g Murder, mutilation and landmines.
iii. Demanding of food and money.
iv. SF will no longer have to interrupt your normal life in their search for terrorists.
v. No pressure to get your children to join this pointless and dangerous cause. ■

Interview with a Patriotic Front leader

This is a small part of an interview with Joshua Nkomo, one of the leaders of the Patriotic Front, called a "terrorist" by the Smith regime. It appeared in the 25 April 79 issue of the New York *Guardian*. The newspaper's masthead describes the paper as "an independent radical weekly."

"Question: *What sort of society are you fighting for?*

Answer: We are a people with a past — and our past must be preserved and be influenced also by systems elsewhere which appear to us to be systems that take the human element into consideration as the decisive factor. The socialist system does this, unlike the capitalist system that regards human beings as objects of profit.

You are wanted when you are useful for profit purposes as a labourer and when you lose your ability to produce you are forgotten and discarded and nobody wants to know where you will go to. We are talking of things that have happened in Zimbabwe. We have had people going to Johannesburg to work there in the mines — as soon as they are affected by silicosis they are abandoned, sent back home, nobody is told to find out how they will survive.

In our mines in Zimbabwe when people get affected by dust or contract tuberculosis, they are immediately turned out of the houses they occupy to give way to others who are strong and can work.

You cannot go on with that sort of thing. We regard human beings as important — a society, an organised industrial society, a socialist society is what appeals to us, that's our way.

Question: *The Patriotic Front backs a nonracial society for Zimbabwe?*

Answer: We have said there is a war going on. We have called upon people of all colours — races in fact — to rally to the call of the Zimbabwe revolution. All of the people who have chosen to make this country home are welcome."

Discussion/essay topics

1. In a writing assignment, prepare a short, fictitious "eyewitness" account of an event,

— as seen by a white Rhodesian;

— as seen by a black Rhodesian. Base your account on research into the country's life and society at a particular point in history (i.e., very recent past? five years ago? ten years ago?)

2. Prepare a similar "eyewitness" account for another part of the world or here in Canada.

3. Starting in the late 1970s, the mass media began to give wide coverage to the situation in Afghanistan. On one day, however, a news story appeared with this headline: "Reconstituted reality: faking Afghan war coverage." Look up the story in the 9 February 1980 edition of the *Globe and Mail*. With this article in mind, analyse news coverage of Afghanistan.

4. Study media coverage of a country or issue that is currently in the news.

5. Prepare a detailed review of a National Geographic television special or Via Le Monde/CBC's *Lost Kingdoms*. Be specific in your reference to the commentary, the images presented, any camera or other techniques you can identify, and the general impression left with the viewer.

6. One often hears "informed sources" quoted in newscasts. How does one qualify as an "informed source"' Who is the source, and who informs the source? Are there any circumstances in which a journalist would be justified in quoting unnamed, "informed sources"? When would this not be justified?

Further reading

Southern Africa stands up
Wilfred Burchett (1978) New York: Urizen Books

The great white hoax: South Africa's international propaganda machine
Julien Burgess et al. (1977) London: Africa Bureau

The first casualty: the war correspondent as hero, propagandist and myth-maker
Phillip Knightley (1975) New York: Harcourt Brace

An African abstract
Dennis Lewycky and Susan White (1979) Winnipeg: Manitoba Council for International Co-operation

In search of enemies: a CIA story
John Stockwell (1978) New York: W.W. Norton & Co.

Investment in oppression: Canadian responses to apartheid
Taskforce on Churches and Corporate Responsibility (1979) Toronto: TCCR

Audio-visual

Namibia: a trust betrayed
(28 min. fillm, 16 mm colour) A clear historical documentary, from the time of the settlers to the present day. Produced and distributed by the United Nations; also available through the United Church.

South Africa: white laager
(54 min. film, 16 mm colour) This film examines South Africa's siege mentality, which has persisted since white colonial pioneers fought from within a circle of covered wagons known as a "laager". Reveals the thinking of South Africans, and how they have come to form their attitudes and opinions. Available through Villon Films, 4580 Prince of Wales, Montreal, Quebec H4B 2L3

Film and literature lists

Here are three excellent sources of up-to-date information and background documents.
The Africa Fund
198 Broadway, New York, N.Y.
10038 U.S.A.

IDAF International Defence and
Aid Fund for Southern Africa
P.O. Box 1034 Station B
Ottawa, Ontario K1P 6R1

South African Education Project
Division of World Outreach
United Church of Canada
85 St. Clair Avenue East
Toronto, Ontario M4T 1M8

V. `Underdevelopment`: case studies

Chapter V: "Underdevelopment": Case studies

Introduction

Third World.
Underdevelopment.
Underdeveloped countries.

What things come to mind when you hear these words?

Many people think of a poor country. The popular image we have is that in the "Third World" there is only misery; the land is parched and is good for nothing, and there is no food for the people. Diseased children grow up in filth, poverty and illiteracy. The country we imagine is grossly overpopulated, and the brutality of daily life becomes so commonplace that only the most unbelievable of atrocities is considered significant.

While there are some inequalities, like the very rich in India, in this imaginary country, this is almost understandable, given the swollen populations, the primitive facilities, the fact that almost everyone is illiterate, almost no one has any technical know-how, and the general population has no experience in governing themselves. Every once and a while in this hypothetical country, the teeming masses swell up in revolt over something, and thousands of screaming, howling mobs are seen, direct by satellite, on your television screen.

From Iran, Nicaraugua, Vietnam or the Philippines, the message: *"The natives are restless."*

These pictures stored in our minds are inaccurate and misleading Yet one book, or even ten, could not possibly disprove every false impression we have about the "Third World", and provide the corresponding "counter-information". This is why you, the reader, must examine these images, and look for the facts yourself, beyond the stereotypes. Only you can dispel for yourself the many false impressions of others (and perhaps even of yourself) that are created by the mass media.

In this chapter we shall examine briefly two areas of underdevelopment. Our intention is to demonstrate the need for careful thinking (and independent research, if necessary) if one wishes to have an informed opinion about what is going on in another country, in one's own country, or indeed in one's own life.

The following case studies are by no means exhaustive samples of mass media and other images of underdevelopment. However, we do hope they demonstrate the importance of the cautionary statement, "Don't believe every-

thing you hear." The material presented here ought to be subject to the critical analysis that we encourage for all sources of information.

Like a camera or the human eye, the mass media must focus on certain images and exclude others. What images do the mass media highlight? Which ones do they exclude? Why?

Discussion

1. Draw up a complete list of sources of information on the "Third World" that you encounter in your daily life. (They may be ads for charities, but also cartoons, ads for consumer products, TV shows — any reference to the countries that are part of the "Third World".)

2. Prepare composite pictures of the "Third World" from these sources.

3. Call forth all that you know of the country of Brazil. Are there ads, any television shows, consumer products or other things that are associated with this country?

"Before we demand that Parliament protect our industry against cheap foreign imports manufactured at slave-labor wages, I'd like to remind you, sir, that we own 67 percent of those foreign factories!"

"Underdevelopment"
Case Study #1: Brazil

Brazil spreads over almost half of the South American continent. This country is the fifth largest in the world (after the USSR, Canada, China and the US). It borders on all but two South American nations (Chile and Ecuador) and accounts for half of South America's population. Its coastline is more than 7,400 kilometres long.

Far from being poor, Brazil is a "Third World" country with immensely rich human and natural resources. It is estimated that 50% of Brazil's population is under the age of sixteen, and 62% under twenty-four. The Brazil-Canada Chamber of Commerce[1] notes:

> **Industry:** Brazil's economic development has been marked by a heavy emphasis on industrialization. Today Brazil produces a wide range of sophisticated products and is importing technology which will make it possible to produce an even wider range in the future.

> **Agriculture:** Despite the rapid growth of Brazil's industrial sector, agriculture is still the mainstay of the Brazilian economy. About 40% of the population lives on the land, and in 1977, 70% of Brazil's export revenue came from agricultural products, with coffee and soybean accounting for about 31%.
> Because of its fertile soil and favourable climate, Brazil can grow practically all known varieties of grain, fruit and vegetables, and is virtually self-sufficient for food requirements, except for wheat.

In 1977, Brazil was the world's second largest agricultural exporter, after the United States, with sales of US$8.4 billion, including processed foods.

> **Forests:** One half of Brazil is covered by forests and its timber resources are second only to those of the USSR.
> However, only about 20% of its forest land is now being used. Major forest areas of the Amazon tropical rain forest, the coastal sub-tropical rain forest along the eastern seabord, and the Parana pine forests of the temperate southern highlands . . .

> **Mineral Resources:** Brazil is rich in mineral resources, having one-quarter of the world's reserves of iron ore and large quantities of manganese and bauxite (aluminum). Other minerals existing in smaller but significant quantities are lead, potash, copper, tin, precious stones, salt and shale. The mineral wealth potential has not been fully explored, primarily because of the vast unsurveyed areas where exploration and prospecting are difficult.
> The completion of the 5,000 km Trans-amazon Highway, running east and west about 300 km south of the Amazon River and stretching from the Atlantic to Peru, is opening up the large Amazon basin area. This is expected to increase the contribution mineral wealth will make to the national economy.

> **Petroleum:** In 1977 Brazil imported about 80% of its crude oil requirements. This heavy reliance on foreign sources for oil (which provides half of Brazil's energy) was largely responsible for the country's serious balance of payments deficits in 1974, 1975 and 1976.

"It's More Practical to Divide the Profits among 2,000 Generals than among 100 Million Brazilians"

The "Economic Miracle"

Since the military coup of 1964, and especially since 1968, most free-enterprise economists have deemed Brazil's economic performance as the "Economic Miracle". Until 1975, the country maintained the phenomenal economic growth rate of 10% annually. Steel and cement production jumped yearly, and automobile production soared to the point where today there are more Volkswagen beetles produced in Brazil than in Germany. By all the standard indicators of economic success, Brazil has reached an economic "take-off" point.

Fabulous amounts of foreign investment and loans poured into Brazil. According to a report for the U.S. Senate Subcommittee on Multinational Corporations, "private foreign investment plays an important, if not pivotal, role in the Brazilian model of economic growth."[2]

Money has poured into Brazil — from all over the world, including Canada.

How has this "economic miracle" been described by the financial media? Here are some headlines:

OPPORTUNITIES ABOUND FOR
INCREASED TRADE, BUT CANADIAN
COMPANIES ARE MISSING THE BOAT
Financial Post
18 Oct 75

"The trade opportunities", we learn in the article, "are staggering".

MINERALS GALORE
Financial Times
25 Oct 76

AMAZON REGION HEADS TOWARDS
SECOND BOOM
Financial Times
10 May 75

BRAZIL SITS PRETTY ON
HOME-GROWN OIL
Latin America Review
7 Sept 77

SOYBEANS TAKE SPOT IN BRAZIL
Express & News
4 July 73

There may be some problems in this country, but basically they are under control:

BRAZIL TURNS BACK CLOCK TO BEAT
GOVERNMENT FOES
Globe & Mail
4 July 77

The article accompanying this last headline described changes in the constitution that would ensure continued power of the military government.

Obstacles to development in this country may include the inhabitants of a region:

INDIANS HALT AMAZON ROAD
Braz. International Bulletin
Winter 75

But solutions can be found:

QUICK INTEGRATION IS BRAZIL'S AIM
Manchester Guardian
9 Jan 77

So, development of Brazil's incredible riches continues on its inescapable course:

CIVILIZATION IS SLOWLY ADVANCING
ON MYSTERIOUS, HOSTILE AMAZON
Financial Post
6 December 75

What is this "mysterious, hostile Amazon"? What is this dark, unknown country?

For some, Brazil is the land of the Economic Miracle. For others, it is a land of dreams. This land of dreams is full of life, danger and adventure, with impossible wealth, incredible promise, forbidden fruit . . .

The Dream

"She sighed . . . and then felt her heart turn a somersault as those double doors suddenly swept open again. Their dark panels framed one of the tallest men she had ever seen, lithe and erect, wearing kneeboots of leather moulded to the strong calves of his legs. Tan breeches were belted into a flat, athletic waist, and a fine white linen shirt covered his broad chest and a pair of wide shoulders. The neck of the shirt was open against a tawny-skinned throat, and as Jaine's gaze rose to the man's face she knew instantly why Laraine had been fascinated and then terrified by this man.

Her cousin had thought she could enslave him and bend him to *her* caprices, and then had discovered that he placed no woman upon a pedestal but made of each one a captive of his dominating personality. The woman whom he married — for whatever reason — would be his total possession and subject to *his* will. Never would she be allowed to run almost free on the end of a long and tolerant leash.

Just in time Laraine had realised this . . . but Jaine, the onlooker and not the participant in romantic affairs, knew the kind of man he was the moment she set eyes on his face. Compelling and magnetic were overdone expressions, but in his case they applied in full. His eyes were as tawny as sherry, but the lines beside them were as incised as if shaped by steel on stone. There was nobility in his brow and in the strong facial bones . . . it was strange that she should think this distinguished and striking man capable of diabolic behaviour . . . yet that impression struck her at once.

From his black brows to his gleaming boots he was dangerous and she, a loveless, lonely fool in dread of losing what little she had of Madge's affection, had entered his house . . ."[3]

The dream is filled with the promise of immense wealth — and someone who is menacing, attractive. If you have not already guessed, this is the dream of Brazil of Harlequin Romances. The heroine has set eyes on the lord of a million acres of Brazilian territory. The unedited passage quoted here is from a Harlequin novel on Brazil, promoted with a full-page ad in *Weekend* magazine, and given out free by Harlequin.

Why is such a passage included for serious study of the "Third World"?

First, there are many economic ties between Canada and Brazil, though most Canadians are unaware of them. One of these ties is Harlequin, Canada's largest publisher.[4] A Canadian multinational corporation, Harlequin recently added a Brazilian operation, Editors Arlequim S.A., to its world-wide holdings. Through its major shareholder, Torstar Corporation, Harlequin is linked with other major mass media outlets in Canada. Brazilians, Japanese, Fijians, and Filippinos now join Canadian women in dreaming about themselves, and the world, through romance.

Our image of Brazil remains for the most part at the level of a Harlequin romance . . . or a Maxwell House commercial or travel brochure for tourists. — Possibly our image of Brazil will be created in part by the financial page, where the headlines quoted earlier appeared. In the general public's mind, Canada's significant ties with Brazil are vaguely apparent, at best. Yet for Brazil, Canada's involvement there is extremely important: of the twenty largest foreign investors in 1973, the first was not American or European, but Canadian.[5]

Another reason for including the Dream image of Brazil is that, up to this point in our study of the mass media, Canada has appeared to be principally a *consumer* of American mass culture (Chapter II), not a producer of mass culture. *Canada is now a major exporter of mass culture as well,* in large part, thanks to Harlequin.

"Welcome to the wonderful world of Harlequin," says a subscription letter, inviting the reader to buy books that "will carry you away to distant lands". You will have travelling companions who will reveal "their exciting lives, their innermost emotions to you." The dream world of Harlequin *informs* the reader about the "Third World"'. Yet however misleading these dream-pictures are, they remain alive and indelible in the mind of the reader. The Harlequin picture of Brazil is one of the many pictures of the "Third World" that we see through the mass media — lands filled with swarthy, prodigious lovers, high intrigue,

immense wealth, and mute, "uncivilized" savages:

> Mark could never decide what had taken him to this small Polynesian island . . . for Joanna, in civilized England, the changes were even greater.

So reads the promotion for another Harlequin, entitled *Little savage*.

Romance and adventure

Romance and adventure are two extremely powerful themes affecting the way we think —precisely *how* they do so is a matter of continued study. On a conscious plane, we may know perfectly well that a novel is fiction and that a film is an illusion. However, the "willing suspension of disbelief" so central to enjoying a novel or film has certain consequences. In the case of great poetry, theatre or other artistic statement, it is this very suspension of disbelief that allows us to see the *"truth"* in their messages. Yet during an aesthetic — or emotional experience (e.g., seeing photos of a massacre, as in Chapter IV) — we are intellectually at a vulnerable point. Ideas and images can enter our minds through one gate (entertainment), but can eventually find their ways down the corridors to other, inner entryways that are unguarded, where we store the data with which we form attitudes and opinions.[6]

Unless we return to the same ground, after the initial impact is passed, to decide whether the same statement is "true" in other ways as well, we may accept uncritically many ideas that otherwise might be rejected as untrue or at least discounted because they were unverifiable.

The Dream versions of the "Third World" create false pictures of rich and poor. They encourage people to dream . . . but with these images, our dreams and fantasies are based on *distorted images of reality.*

The Dream also promotes a booming tourism industry that fulfils just enough of these dreams so that we never really have to awake from our reverie. A look at advertisements for travel and cruises will illustrate this point.[7] The Dream pictures leave out the millions of people who live, work and die producing the wealth of a country. They do not describe the situation of the vast majority of people around the world.[8]

In describing the James Bond film *Moonraker,* which takes place partly in Brazil, its director commented,

> This is the most fantastic advertising that Brazil could have.[9]

Because Brazilian censors would not allow any unfavourable picture of Brazil to be shown, the director commented that "they don't have to worry because we only show the beautiful part." He also noted that tourism in Egypt jumped dramatically after *The Spy Who Loved Me* was released, much of which was filmed in that country. In the case of the *Moonraker* one can clearly see how the very subject matter and characters of mass culture twist reality. As the film director says,

> James Bond is a creature of luxury and he doesn't hang around in favelas.

Favelas are Brazilian slums.

It is difficult to make sense of all these pictures of the "Third World". How does the Harlequin or James Bond picture relate to the pictures of starving children with bloated stomachs in an ad for charity? How do these pictures relate to images on a TV screen of howling mobs in front of an embassy?

There is another kind of Dream — the traveller's dream. It is the dream of nostalgia; but a dream that in fact is photographed in living colour:

> VANISHING CULTURES AND LIFESTYLES
> Now is the time to get
> to know these peoples
> and their ways . . .
> before their cultures
> disappear under the
> inexorable wheel of
> progress.

So tells us the publicity for a 12-volume set of coloured photos and commentary, promoted by a company, The Friends of History.[10]

Only by spending years in travel and study could you get to know so many fascinating peoples, from so many remote corners of the world. "Hundreds of brilliant full-color photographs, accompanied by lively, highly-readable text, take you on an unforgettable trip around the world", the Friends tell us. "You'll meet these colourful folk and share the most intriguing details of their daily lives, all in the comfort of your own armchair."

From the comfort of your own armchair, also, you may learn that a certain area has rich deposits of oil; that another has important mineral deposits; uranium; tin . . . From the comfort of your armchair you will agree that it has been "fascinating" to have been able to "share the moments, big and small" of the people whose days are numbered on this earth . . . .

The Nightmare

The following article, *THE AMAZON: Multinationals and Native Extermination,* has been reprinted from the Inter-Church Committee on World Development Education.

THE AMAZON:
Multinationals and Native Extermination

It is estimated that upon the arrival of the Portuguese in 1500 there were between 1.5 and 3 million natives in Brazil. At the end of the last century, there were still 1.0 million, but in 1963 their numbers had dropped to 200 thousand. This dramatic decline, which many scientists have denounced as "genocide", continues. In 1967, their numbers were reported at 100 thousand and, in 1968, at only 80 thousand.

Furthermore, anthropologists have recognized the extinction of 87 indigenous tribes in Brazil in the last 50 years, and that 57 out of the existing 143 tribes are now rapidly disappearing.

What are the causes of this enormous tragedy? Perhaps if we follow more closely what has happened to one of the most important indigenous nations in Brazil in the past decade, we shall be able to understand the roots of this situation.

The Example of the "Cintas Largas"

Before and during the first centuries of Portuguese colonization, the indigenous population lived, by and large, close to the seashore because of the more convenient climatic and environmental conditions. But they were continuously forced inland by the aggressive policies of the European settlers, who constantly attempted to enslave them and conquer their lands. The result was that they were decimated and finally pushed into the most uninhabitable regions of the hinterland — especially into the Amazon, an area of difficult access to the white man until recently.

For innumerable generations, the Cintas Largas (Wide Belts) was the indigenous nation which dominated the hinterland on the Western border between the Brazilian provinces of Mato, Grosso and Rondonia. Conflicts had been avoided until 1963 when the Billington Mining Company, a subsidiary of Royal Dutch Shell, moved into the area and, not by chance, a series of incidents began.

The arrival of the Billington Mine followed the development of the Brazilian/U.S. Geological Survey, which indicated the existence of large concentrations of cassiterite in the area (the largest known in the world). These developments produced a wave of speculators and adventurers into the area, which started to push the indigenous population off their lands. As the Cintas Largas resisted, a systematic policy of extermination was carried out against them.

Massacres followed in 1964/65 and were reported upon by the international press: "Sticks of dynamite were dropped from the air on the Indians' villages, and survivors were machinegunned later on" (*The Times,* London, January 27, 1970). The *National Geographic* (September 1971) reported: "Indians were shot on sight. I know several Cintas Largas with bullet scars. Poisoned foods were left temptingly on trails". Even the Brazilian newspapers recognize that "until this day the Cintas Largas refuse to take sugar because the first time they received it from the white men, it was purposefully poisoned and killed a whole village" (*Jornal do Brasil,* July 19, 1974). According to the *Toronto Star* (June 28, 1972), ten years after these massacres, the perpetrators of these crimes -- one of whom was pictured in several European newspapers cutting a Cintas Largas woman in half while hanging from a tree   had yet to be brought to trial.

After these events resulted in wide international repercussions, the government decided to establish a reserve for the Cintas Largas, which was called "Parque Nacional de Aripuna". In 1970, there were between three and four thousand natives living in 22 different villages on the reserve. In this same year, the Billington Mine already had control of 720,000 acres of land under various stages of exploration, prospecting and negotiation.

In December 1971, the Cintas Largas carried out a last act of rebellion against the colonizers, killing two white men and burning a governmental Indian post station. The Brazilian Minister of Interior blamed the incident on the Indians' resistance to staying on the reserve and their "nomadic inclinations" and "geographic ignorance"![2] But other facts proved the situation to be very different.

Shortly afterwards, news reached the public that since March 1971, the government had concluded its joint Geological Survey of the country and had declared the Rondonian territory a major mining development region, not only for tin (cassiterite), but also diamonds, lithium, gold and other strategic minerals. Thus started the negotiations for mineral leases with numerous national and multinational companies. Governmental plans for the area included construction of a regional branch of the Transamazonian Highway and the opening up of credits for white "colonizers". One of the big companies attracted to prospect these newly-discovered riches was the Cia. Estanifera do Brasil, a local subsidiary of the multinational W. R. Grace and the Patino Group.[3]

Of course, no mining operation of such magnitude could be started without convenient access to a skilled labour market which the indigenous people could not and would not provide. Therefore, 500 families were settled inside the Indian reserve, and a diamond prospecting company was also established in the area, marking a distinctive move by the government towards abolishment of the reserve. The process which followed resulted in the disruption of the indigenous life of the Cintas Largas with all its terrible consequences.[4]

In November 1972, a French physician visited the reserve of Aripuna to investigate the health conditions of the Cintas Largas. His report presented frightening results and appealed for immediate action from the International Red Cross. He said, for instance, that one of the tribes which had been "pacified" only two years before, was in extremely grave condition — they were being decimated by tuberculosis, infections and, above all, starvation. In the six months previous to the writing of the report, more than 25 per cent of the tribe had died. If such a tragedy happened to this particular tribe, one can easily imagine the situation of the other villages which had been on the reserve for a longer time, to the point of being forced to rebellion in 1971. The physician stressed the fact that the Cintas Largas could no longer live in their environment due to the invasion of the mining companies which, with the support of the governmental agencies, had disrupted natural life, burnt forests, and killed animals.[5]

More recently, Fr. Iasi, a Roman Catholic priest in charge of missionary work to the Indians of the area, denounced the selling of 120 thousand hectares of land for new white settlers inside the reserve, as well as the construction of two new roads which will cross and divide the original reserve in every direction bringing the National Park to an end.[6]

The governmental Director of the reserve even declared in an interview in 1972: "In less than four years the Cintas Largas' lands have been divested, epidemics have started, and many of the people have already taken the first miles in the road that will lead them to misery, hunger, prostitution for their women, and the end. . ."[7]

The Rush for the Riches of the Amazon

The fate of the Cintas Largas is just one example of what is happening all over the Amazon basin since the Brazilian government opened its doors to the penetration of the multinational corporations. Another striking example has been the Parque Nacional do Xingu which was the first and largest indigenous reservation. Ever since its inauguration in 1961, the area has been diminishing steadily to the point where it has now been crossed by the Transamazonian highway — the consequences of which have already been considered in the case of the Aripuna reservation.[8]

Not by chance, the companies responsible for the building up of the Transamazonian highway in the area have decided "for engineering reasons" upon this change in the original plans of the highway. They are the same companies responsible — in association with foreign capital — for the development of the huge cattle ranches located in the lush pasturelands which will produce for export.

Rewriting History

Source: NACLA (1974) Guatemala

U.S. AID has distributed through Central America 10 million copies of school textbooks such as the one in this picture. In the third grade textbook (published in 1969) there is a discussion of the arrival of the Spanish to Latin America.

"The Indians lived where there was gold but did not know its value. A Spaniard came looking for gold. The Indians showed him where it was. The Spaniard, to show his gratitude, taught the Indians to read and write. He also taught them to believe in one God. The Indians, in turn, were grateful to serve him. Thus, they lived happily in their village mining gold and cultivating the land. Then other Spaniards came and attacked the village. The Indians fled. The son asks, 'Why did the Indians not return?' 'Because they found a place to live better,' answered Mama. They realized that they had found a very beautiful place. The Indians felt grateful to those who made them flee." *Source: ROCAP Book Program, Grade 3, Book 2.*

Little by little, the Amazon is unveiling its treasures and attracting the pillage of world capital. The air-photographic mapping conducted by the Brazilian/U.S. Geological Survey has already publicized great discoveries. And, in 1970, a new Project Radar Amazon (RADAM) began and is being carried out in great detail and technological sophistication in order to locate the more profitable mineral concentrations.

In addition to confirming the above-mentioned discoveries in Rondonia, this programme also detected one of the largest concentrations of iron ore in the world -- in the Carajas Mountains in the state of Para. In this same province the third largest world reserve of bauxite was discovered. And the Amazon has already become the third largest producer of manganese and

other strategic minerals, 90% of which are exported to the U.S.A.

The question then arises: "who benefits from these riches"? Certainly not the native peoples who are being exterminated, together with their natural environment. Neither does the huge majority of the Brazilian population whose miserable income does not allow for participation in the consumption markets. Those who benefit are thus only a tiny elite of shareholders, bureaucrats, businessmen and military who, both in Brazil and abroad, represent the interests of the big multinational corporations.

The Brazilian government has already approved 400 huge farming projects in the area whose high technological level and access to external markets imply a varied degree of association with the international corporations. The biggest enterprises are directly operated by the foreign corporations which tend to diversify their investments in every respect.

A very clear example of this trend is given by the Daniel Ludwig Corporation, an American-based company which owns 2.4 million acres in the State of Para (about the size of Holland). Its main economic activity in the area is the bauxite mine of Monte Dourado. But it is also starting to produce on a large scale timber and cellulose, rice, sugar cane, palm oil, and choice cattle meat — everything, obviously, for export to Europe or North America. Denouncing of

Giant companies like Brascan have invested heavily in Brazil, as have Canadian chartered banks and other institutions. Brascan is owned by the Bronfman family. This family now controls or has major interests in Seagrams, Labatt's (14 brands of beer), London Life, Toronto Blue Jays, Montreal's huge Place Ville Marie; half a dozen of the country's largest shopping centres, much of downtown Calgary and 20% of the Continental Bank of Canada; products like Habitant soups, Laura Secord, Catelli pasta . . .

What *motivates* such businessmen? What is important to them? What drives them to expand; to take over more and more companies . . . to gain power over the lives of literally hundreds of thousands of people? Is it some mysterious, "inexorable wheel of progress"? Here is what Peter Bronfman says of his own and his brother's ambitions:

"Edward and I have always wanted our major position to be in a public company, to give our children maximum liquidity so they could act at will. If they wanted to build a house in Hawaii they could do it. Brascan is really the fulfilment of that goal."

(*Maclean's* 9 Jl 79)

> **We are going to create a policy of integrating the Indian population into Brazilian society as rapidly as possible. We think that the ideals of preserving the Indian population within its own habitat are very beautiful ideas, but unrealistic.**
>
> — Brazilian Minister of the Interior, 1974, quoted in J. Molyneux *World Prospects* (1979) Scarborough: Prentice-Hall, p. 360.

the use of slave labour on this property has attracted international public opinion to the point where even the military government conducted a formal investigation of the charges.[10]

The riches of the Amazon are being divided among the big mining corporations. U.S. Steel bought the concessions for the Carajas Mountain iron ore reserves; Bethlehem Steel is the major miner and purchaser of Brazilian manganese; Patino, W. R. Grace and others we have already mentioned; Royal Dutch Shell is also prospecting copper, nickel, zinc, tin and other minerals through its Mineracao, Rio Xingu in the river of the same name. Timber is also controlled by international companies such as the Georgia Pacific which is the biggest American producer of plywood. Alcan a Canadian spin-off of Alcoa, already has $90 million in the State of Para. And the list is growing every day...

The Brazilian military partners are in charge of providing the needed infrastructural developments to make possible the practical aspects of this international penetration. Besides the Transamazonian highway, which is in fact an overall system of connections inside the Amazon basin, the government is also building ports for all major economic exports.

The port of Itaqui, in the province of Maranhao, will serve U.S. Steel's exports; the port of Santarem, in the Amazon River, has been modernized to channel the productions of Alcoa's and Ludwig's concessions; Imperatriz, in the Tocantins River, will serve the diamond and manganese mines; Porto Velho in Rondonia, the extensive tin concessions; Itaitub, in Para, is being constructed just north of the tin and gold deposits, etc.

The Native Peoples: "An Obstacle to Development"

In December 1973, the Brazilian government formalized by decree what had already become long-established practice: "The government reserves itself the right to penetrate into the native people's territories whenever it may consider these territories of higher interest for the country, and a need for progress and development ..."[11]

This legislation consecrates the practice of annihilation of people and expropriation of land of the indigenous peoples in Brazil, and officially confirms

that they will never be safe or in a place of their own in this country, for even the reservations granted by the government itself can at any moment be confiscated.

And to what "higher interest" are these native rights sacrificed? To the interests of "progress and development", that is, the progress and development of the multinational corporations. "The progress of the Amazon will not be stopped because of the Indians" declared the Minister of the Interior (Jornal do Brasil, August 18, 1973). And a high official of the National Organization of Assistance to the Indians (FUNAI) said that "the total integration of the native populations is necessary through their absorption as manpower" (Jornal do Brasil, May 14, 1972).

The Roman Catholic Church, together with representatives of the native peoples themselves have already stated that the indigenous peoples of this country should have:

- Their reservations in definitely demarcated lands, to be respected by public and private agencies;
- Medical assistance to help them to face the problems of contagious diseases resulting from contact with white men;
- Technical assistance for their participation -- to the extent that they themselves decide — in the economic systems to be developed in their regions;
- The right to choose their own patterns of relationship with the white men without economic, social or cultural pressures towards their assimilation.

But the Church itself is aware that these aims can only be achieved in a different context:

"The change of the (governmental) indigenous policy would imply a complete change in the Brazilian political model which values the products more than the producers, the profits more than the workers, the GNP more than the people's income, and the national progress more than the very lives of the people..."[12]

Footnotes

1. Data from the New York Times, August 2, 1974, and Veja, S.Paulo, April 15, 1970.
2. Jornal do Brasil, April 25, 1972.
3. The Economist, September 2, 1972.
4. Jornal do Brasil, December 17, 1971.
5. Jornal do Brasil, November 21, 1972.
6. Jornal do Brasil, August 14, 1974.
7. Jornal do Brasil, March 13, 1972.
8. New York Times, March 5, 1972.
9. O GLOBO, Rio de Janeiro, July 20, 1971.
10. Opiniao, Rio de Janeiro, May 13, 1974.
11. "Sobre o Estatuto do Indio" by the (R. Catholic) Indigenous Missionary Council, Brasilia, April 1974.
12. "Y Juca Pirama — The Indian, the one who must die", document by the Bishops and priests who work among the native peoples in Brazil, December 25, 1973. ∎

Some of the most vocal opponents to the Brazilian dictatorships have been the churches of Brazil. The Archbishop of Recife, Dom Helder Camara, a Nobel Peace Prize nominee, was one of the signatories of the following document. He was forbidden to *all* the press, under a banning order.[11]

The text that follows is an abridgement of a document released in May 1973, by bishops, archbishops and provincials of the religious orders of Northeastern Brazil (one of the poorest regions in Latin America, with a population of almost 30 million inhabitants). The publication of this document was prohibited in Brazil, by order of the Brazilian military government. The complete text may be obtained by writing to the Inter-Church Committee for World Development Education.

I HAVE HEARD THE CRY OF MY PEOPLE

I have seen the affliction of my people
and have heard their cry because of their oppressor
I know their suffering.

(Ex. 3:7)

These words from Exodus, spoken by God to Moses, are a fitting expression of our feelings in these days.

Before the suffering of our people, humbled and oppressed for centuries, we feel called by the Word of God to take up a position, a clear position on the side of the poor, a position taken in common with all those who commit themselves to the people for their true liberation.

As ministers of liberation, we have need now more than ever before for continuous conversion in order to serve better; we need to listen to the cry of the man of the Northeast, crying for this ministry of liberation, pleading with us to share his "hunger and thirst for justice".

This man's march towards liberation challenges our society and enters into conflict with its criteria of profits and luxury, with the distortion of statistics and other official data aimed at justifying the "institutionalized violence" in which we live.

It is thus in deep consciousness of our pastoral and prophetic function that we are going to talk in this challenging hour.

We will begin with official data, the findings of scientific surveys, so that our judgment in the name of God will not be based on superficial impressions or subjective attitudes. Our point of view is that of man, the whole man and all men. It is that of God who, making himself man, transformed man in Christ, the measure of all things.

The De Facto Situation in the Northeast

On the basis of technical information and statistical data released by official organisations, one may conclude that the Northeast of Brazil has indeed retained the elements which brought international fame to the region: oppression, misery, injustice. The situation has even worsened, without any prospect, at this moment or in the immediate future, of a meaningful commitment on the part of the government to transform this reality.

Underdevelopment continues to be the most important characteristic of the Northeast.

Per Capita Income

The annual per capita income in the Northeast is about 200 dollars, i.e. about half of the per capita income of Brazil in general.

Only 3.3% of the income-earning population earned more than 500 cruzeiros a month (70 dollars) and only 0.86% earned more than 1,000 cruzeiros (i.e. 150 dollars).

These statistics on the per capita income give us an approximate idea of the de facto situation.

But in spite of their generality, concealing some extreme inequalities at the human level, do they demonstrate that man is really the measure of all things?

Labour

Unemployment and underemployment reach alarming rates in our region. Of the work-age population, 23% are unemployed or underemployed.

Nutrition

Hunger in the Northeast has taken on the characteristics of an epidemic. Surveys conducted in cities in different parts of the region have yielded the following results as to percentages of intake as measured against scientifically recommended standards (= 100%):

Calories	56%
Proteins (total)	81%
Calcium	74%
Vitamin A	4%
Vitamin C	54%

This general situation is still more acute and serious in particular areas of our region, such as areas where sugar cane is the only crop grown.

Undernourishment, which leads to reduced physical stature as was ascertained by surveys, also includes among its effects the phenomenon of

a great number of mentally deficient persons in the region.

In 1972, tests were conducted in three municipalities in the Mata region of Pernambuco to ascertain the IQ of 109 children.

The average IQ registered was between 72.4 and 78 which, on the Terman scale, indicates retarded intelligence.

Housing

A publication of the department of Human Resources of SUDENE (Superintendency for the Development of the Northeast), February, 1970, estimates that the Northeast lacks 2.3 million housing units, and the figure is growing.

To the insufficient number of houses must be added the low quality of housing and the poor health conditions.

An official survey during the first quarter of 1970 reveals that out of 5 million houses in the Northeast in that year, 76% did not have running water, 73% did not have indoor plumbing and more than 75% of these houses had no electricity.

These statistics — or simply familiarity with our cities — reveal a truly alarming situation and expose, in the sphere of housing, the gap between the rich and the poor.

Education

Of all persons above 5 years of age — i.e. those who should be in school or have been through school — about 60% are illiterate, according to the 1970 census.

According to an official publication, 20% of the population of the Northeast is of school age but, as of a few years ago, the Northeast had a primary education network able to cope with only half this number.

Primary teaching is gravely affected by the serious lack of school buildings, equipment, teaching material and pedagogical resources. The percentage of non-professionals varies, according to the particular State, from 50% to 75%.

In higher education, there was a change: the number of graduates went from 16% in 1961 to 15% in 1970.

Health

In February, 1970, the Department of Human Resources of SUDENE stated that "the population of the Northeast continues to have very low health standards and high percentages of fatal diseases, in line with the per capita income".

Schistosomiasis is a disease caused by worms which live in undrained ditches, lakes, etc. Almost invisible, they enter animals or humans through the skin and lodge in the intestines; tissue damage eventually causes death. The skin of its victim's face turns yellow; his abdomen becomes swollen and distended. According to estimates, along the coastal plain from Rio Grande do Norte to Bahia, it affects 90% of the population. Another 500,000 persons in a region of 12 million inhabitants, are victims of Chagas disease, a fatal disease carried by an insect.

It is estimated that there are 100,000 tuberculous persons in the region and that there are 30,000 new cases each year.

Contagious diseases account for 22% of deaths.

Infant mortality is very high. In the Northeast as a whole, the average is 180 per 1,000 live births.

Health services available in the region cannot cope with the huge problems just mentioned. On the average, there is one doctor for every 5,000 inhabitants; in the cities, this average is higher: 1 for every 1,250 inhabitants. In the same year, the Northeast had 1.9 hospital beds for each 1,000 inhabitants.

With poignancy, João Cabral de Melo, the poet of the Northeast, has depicted the drama of the Northeasterner:*

> And if our common name is Harsh,
> equal in life in every way
> We die an equal death
> The same Harsh death
> The death of one who dies
> Of old age before his thirties
> Of entrapment before his twenties
> Of hunger a little every day.

What has caused this situation?

The facts outlined above may, in the eyes of some, seem to indicate that the masses who, on the human level, suffer the consequences of an unacceptable social structuration should resign themselves to the situation, admitting that change is impossible. Is then underdevelopment the fate of the Northeast? To say that oppressive conditions are due to fate or preternatural forces is incompatible with Christian anthropology. Fatalism is a valuable tool in the hands of those who profit from false conceptions of society imposed on the people; it deters men from identification of the true causes of oppression.

The effects of the system are felt most heavily in the Northeast, whose archaic social and economic structures are responsible for the degree of poverty in the region.

Nevertheless, the Northeast is an example of the Brazilian economic policies, whose model of growth necessitates alliance with foreign capital, thus creating those policies characteristic of dependent capitalist systems.

The most important consequence of this option is change in the goals of national development. Since it became a function of the operation of foreign capital on national soil, development began to be defined in terms other than those of the interests of Brazilian society. Development began to be defined in relation to the profit realizable by foreign

---

(Morte e Vida Severina) [There is a nuance here which does not immediately carry over into English: the word translated as "harsh" — *severino* — is also a very common *name* in Northeast Brazil; it thus lends itself to a collective usage, refering to all Northeasterners, all condemned to the same fate. — ed.]

corporations and their associates in our country. This explains why one of the former priorities in the policy of national development — the elimination of regional disparities — had to be sacrificed.

The new economic policy required also that all economic, social and political institutions be submitted to a profound revision in order to adjust to the conditions for supranational capital expansion in our country.

Rights and Freedom Suppressed

In view of this, the national executive power invested itself with the prerogatives of absolute power. The sum of the measures it promulgated resulted in the negation of values and rights which had been won at great cost and incorporated into Brazilian institutional life, especially in the field of democratic freedoms. The Constitution itself was subjected to a higher power: Institutional Act No. 5, which places in the hands of the Executive the total and supreme power of decision over any question according to its own judgment. The autonomy of other powers was prejudiced in favour of the Executive. Political parties lacked autonomy to make decisions. The channels through which the will of the people was expressed were suppressed. The president of the Republic and the governors of the States exercise their prerogative without the basis of a mandate.

The inviolability of the home, the writ of habeas corpus, the privacy of correspondence, the freedoms of the press, assembly and expression, are rights which were taken away from the people. The liberty to form labour unions and the right to strike were taken from the working class.

When such conditions of oppression and injustice meet with resistance, the violation of human rights escalates in acts of still greater violence. Official terrorism established control through espionage and secret police, in a growing state domination over the private life of the citizens, frequently resorting even to such extremes as torture and assassination.

Brazilian Miracle?

In the economic field, the greatest offensive ever conducted in Brazilian history in favor of the inflow of foreign capital is now under way. The government is anxiously pushing through measures to assure the profits sought by the capital being invested here. Not only are public savings being prodigally spent to implant infra-structures opening up the conquest of resources and markets, but also all eventual risks due to possible future political changes are being forestalled by agreements guaranteeing investments, which, if they are broken, will bring the country under sanctions by foreign tribunals.

This new economic policy was put into practice with such impetus that in a few years' time results were obtained which supposedly demonstrated its intrinsic validity. Since 1968 Brazil has attained a GNP growth rate of about 10%. The policy has suc-

ceeded to such a point that, in economic circles, its authors are being credited with employing miraculous forces.

On the one hand, the "Brazilian miracle" has never gained the people's faith, devotion and hope; on the other hand, it has resulted in privileges for the wealthy and punishment for those already sacrificed; it came as a curse upon those who had not asked for it.

The imbalance is still more glaringly revealed in the fact that the 1% richest group of the Brazilian population raised its share of national income from 11.7% to 17%, while half of the population with lower income saw its share reduced from 17.6% to 13.7%. In 1970, in other terms, a certain 1% of Brazilians earned more than did half of the entire Brazilian population.[*] What is very serious is that such an income concentration was made possible because the buying power of wages was brutally lowered. Between 1961 and 1970, the decrease of the real wage (calculated on the basis of the minimum wage in Guanabara) was about 38.3%. During the same period, the increase of average real productivity was 25.6%[**]

Institutionalized Violence

The socio-economic, political and cultural situation of our people is a challenge to our Christian conscience. Undernourishment, infant mortality, prostitution, illiteracy, unemployment, cultural and political discrimination, exploitation, growing discrepancies between rich and poor, and many other consequences point to a situation of institutionalized violence in our country.

The rich become always richer and the poor always poorer in the enclaving process of economic concentration inherent in the system.

On the other hand, the necessity of repression in order to guarantee the smooth functioning and security of the capitalistic system becomes always more imperative. Repression has expressed itself in many ways: curtailing of the constitutional prerogatives of the legislative branch of government; the depoliticalization of rural and urban trade unions; the elimination of student leadership; the establishment of censorship; persecution of workers, peasants and intellectuals; harassment of priests and members of active groups of the Christian churches — all this in various forms of imprisonment, torture, mutilation and assassination.

The burden of this tragedy, which falls more heavily on the Northeast, far from being the ineluctable result of natural deficiencies, is, now more than ever before, the consequence of a process fixed by the will of men committed to international capitalism. This made possible the construction of an unjust society and the maintenance of its crushing

---

[*](see João Carlos Duarte, *Aspectos da distribução de renda no Brasil em 1970*).
[**](source: *Conjuntura Econômica*, FGV, Sept. 1971 and *Anuário Estistico do Brasil*, IBGE).
Institutionalized Violence

How can one balance these books . . .

Balance sheet: Credit

"Already by 1966 global corporations accounted for some 64% of the total net profit in the five major dynamic sectors of the Brazilian economy (rubber, motor vehicles, machinery, household appliances, and mining). But by 1971 that share was up to 70%. By 1961 global companies owned 100% of automobile and tire production and 59% of electrical appliance manufacturing. Ten years later, foreign ownership in the latter two industries increased to 67% and 68% respectively. Fifty-five global firms received 66% of the net profits of the 100 largest private enterprises in Brazil in 1971, and the 45 largest local companies received 34%."

R. Barnet (1974) *Global Reach,* NY: Simon & Schuster, p. 147

Modern Brazil: Two views of Sao Paulo (pop. 10 million) which is . . .

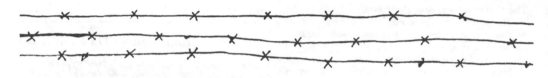

Photos: *LAWG Letter, Vol. IV No. 2*

. . . Brazil's largest city: the Favelas or shanty towns.

Balance sheet: Debit

"It should be noted that only 30% of Brazil's potential labour force earns any money at all; the remaining people — the marginals — try to scrape a living as best they can. If they beg or steal, it is for food . . ."

J. Molyneux (1979) *World prospects,* Scarborough: Prentice-Hall p. 360

"Although brutal and violent arrests of political prisoners have diminished, Amnesty International is concerned at increasing reports of the torture and ill-treatment of people — adults and minors — suspected of ordinary crimes. Church, legal and newspaper sources maintain that electric shock treatment and other methods of torture are inflicted as a matter of routine on petty criminals and delinquents. The purpose of such treatment is often to force suspects to confess to crimes they have not committed. In October 1976, for example, in the remote province of Mato Grosso, in the small township of Riberao Bonito, a priest, Father Joao Bosco Piendo Burneir, was shot by police when he went to protest about the torture of two women in the local police station. It is difficult to estimate how common such practices are since the victims, naturally, rarely file complaints. However, some idea of the extent can be got from the examination of police figures for the number of people detained on suspicion alone in Sao Paulo in the first two months of 1977. There were 28,000 of them."

"Brazil", *Annual Report,* Amnesty International (1977)

weight in order to defend, nurture and increase its privileges. The injustice created by this situation has its foundation in the capitalistic system of production which necessarily produces a class society characterized by discrimination and injustice.

International capitalism and its allies in our country — the dominant class — impose by the media of communication and education a dependent culture. They use this to justify their domination and dissimulate the oppressive system which sustains them. At the same time they attempt to lull asleep vast strata of the population, aiming at the formation of a type of man resigned to his alienation. The present model of economic growth, whose results remain of no use to working and oppressed classes, aims at emptying our people of true global objectives for the transformation of society.

The historical process of class society and of capitalistic domination necessarily leads to a fatal confrontation of classes. Even though this fact becomes clearer every day, it is still denied by the oppressors — and is confirmed by their denial. The oppressed masses of workers, peasants, and underemployed know this and deepen their growing liberative consciousness.

The Government and the People

The present model of economic growth, whose results are worthless for the oppressed working class, aims to deviate our people from the global objectives of the transformation of the society. *whose*

Massive propaganda, the utilization of soccer as a means of expressing patriotism, manoeuvrings to give an illusion of economic progress, such as sports lotteries, do not succeed in dulling the consciousness of the people who know how to identify the true results of the "miracle".

The absence of freedom, the violence of repression, the injustices, the impoverishment of the people, and the alienation of national interests in favour of foreign capital cannot be signs that Brazil has found the road to its historical self-assertion as a nation.

The confirmation of Brazil's true calling to greatness will come from the capacity we have to use our vast material and human resouces for the building up of a society based on our truly Christian traditions and humanistic values, entitling us to play our part together with the people in the construction of a world in which all antagonisms of religion, class and race, and international aggression and exploitation, have been overcome.

The Church in the World

The Church cannot remain indifferent before all that has been exposed. We know that we will not be understood by the many who, because of their self-centred interests, cannot or do not want to understand even evident facts.

For obvious reasons, they transform faith into a theory about our personal relations with God, without interfering in social and political action among men. They use it as an ideological tool, to defend groups and institutions which are not at all at the service of man and are thus opposed to God's design.

Regretting the erroneous thinking of many well-meaning Christians in this regard, Pope John XXIII observed: "the inconsistency between religious faith in those who believe and their activities in the temporal sphere, results — in great part if not entirely — from the lack of a solid Christian education".

We have to recognize in a spirit of true humility and penance that the Church has not always been faithful to its prophetic mission, to its evangelical role of being at the side of the people. How many times, involved in the mesh of evils existing in this world, the Church, in a sad deformation of the evangelical message, has played the game of the oppressors and received favours from those who hold the power of money and of politics against the common good?

We are convinced that this is the hour for an option for God and for the people. This is the time for fidelity to the mission. It is certain that the price of such a choice has always been persecution.

The Gospel is calling us, Christians and all men of goodwill, to become engaged in this prophetic undertaking.

Letter from Manoel Da Conceicao

Manoel da Conceicao is a leader of the Rural Workers of Vale do Pindare, a union supported by 100,000 peasants in the Northeast. He has been arrested and tortured twice. The following letter was written in December 1972 and smuggled out of a prison in Rio de Janeiro. It is unknown whether or not he is still alive.

"I am threatened with death if I denounce the crime that was done to me. I spent four months facing heavy tortures in the 1st Army Barracks of Rio de Janeiro and later in the Navy Secret Service – CENIMAR. Six times I was taken to the hospital practically dead. The beatings were so bad that not a place was left on my body that wasn't black and blue, blood vessels broke under my skin, and all my hair fell out.

They tore out my fingernails. They perforated my penis and my testicles with a needle until they came to resemble a seive. They tied a rope to my testicles and dragged me on the terrace, then hung me upside down. They chained my wrists and hung me on a bar, took off my artificial leg and tied up my penis so I wouldn't urinate. They left me without food and drink and on only one leg. They gave me so many electric shocks that my ear drums burst and I am impotent.

They nailed my penis to a table board and left me nailed 24 hours. They threw me into a pool, tied up like a pig; I almost drowned. They put me in a cell that was completely dark. I spent 28 days urinating and defecating in the same place where I lay down to sleep. They gave me only bread moistened with water. They put me inside a rubber box, turned on a horn so that during eight days I didn't eat or sleep and I almost went crazy. They injected my blood stream with "truth serum". I went out of my mind and became crazy, knowing nothing of my situation while I was being questioned.

They lay me down on the floor and threatened to tear out my guts through my rectum with a piece of metal that had three corners with three rows of saw teeth.

There are dozens of other things, but it is enough for now. After doing all this with me, they took advantage of a false I.D. card and denied that I am Manoel da Conceicao, for I didn't have any document to prove this. They figured that once I have been here twelve months and the people have forgotten about me the government could order them to put me in a helicopter and drop me into the high seas. This was a promise made every day. Their main objective is to isolate me from the people. My life once more is in the hands of the Brazilian people. And only the people have the right to judge my actions."

Source: *This Magazine* Jan-Feb 75, "What's Canada Doing in Brazil?" by Tim Draimin and Jamie Swift

Christian hope, which points to a new mankind, reconciled with itself and united with the Universe, does not allow us to remain inert, passively awaiting the hour of the restoration of all things. It demands an unremitting and active presence, capable of eliciting, in the course of history, the signs of Resurrection, the outlines of the new mankind of the future.

Brothers, the assurance given by Jesus in his eschatological discourse, is an incomparable strength for us in this hour of darkness laden with promise:

> *Revive and lift up your head*
> *because the time of your liberation*
> *is at hand.*

Hélder Pessoa Câmara,
  Archbishop of Olinda and Recife, Pernambuco
José Lamartine Soares,
  Auxiliary Bishop of Olinda and Recife
Severino Mariano de Aguia,
  Bishop of Pesqueira, Pernambuco
Francisco Austregésilo Mesquita,
  Bishop of Afogados da Ingazeira, Pernambuco
Walfrido Mohn, OFM,
  Provincial of the Franciscans of Recife
Hidenburgo Santana, SJ,
  Provincial of the Jesuits of the North, Recife
Gabriel Hofstede, CSSR,
  Provincial of the Redemptorists, Recife
João José da Motta e Albuquerque,
  Archbishop of São Luis, Maranhão
Manoel Edmilson da Cruz,
  Auxiliary Bishop of São Luis
Rino Carlesi, FSCJ,
  Prelate of S. Antônia de Balsas, Maranhão
Pascásio Rettler, OFM,
  Bishop of Bacabal, Maranhão
Francisco Hélio Campos,
  Bishop of Viana, Maranhão
Antônio Batista Fragoso,
  Bishop of Cratéus, Ceará
José Maria Pires,
  Archbishop of João Pessoa, Paraiba
Manoel Pereira da Costa,
  Bishop of Campina Grande, Paraiba
José Brandão de Castro,
  Bishop of Propriá, Sergipe
Timóteo Amoroso Anastácio, OSB,
  Abbot of the Monastery of São Bento, Bahia
Tarcisio Botturi, SJ,
  Vice-Provincial of the Jesuits of Bahia ∎

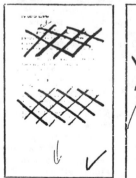 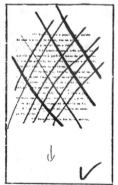

The censor at work: pages of a short story by Dalton Trevisan, *Uma barata leprosa* ('The Leprous Beetle'), as 'passed' by the censor.

The preceding article was prepared by the Inter-Church Committee on World Development Education. A major source of alternative information about other parts of the world are the major Christian churches — Anglican, Roman Catholic, Lutheran and United. Through their missions they receive information about the "Third World" that has often been vehemently denied by governments, but subsequently has been proven to be true.

It is interesting to note that, for having published these and similar reports, Church members of all denominations have been labelled as being "left-wing" or even "communist"': *the truth of the information they present is not discussed.**

Social control through censorship

The suffering of so many people seems almost unbelievable to most Canadians. We do not see it in the financial pages of newspapers, or in romance novels or adventure films. The ugly side of Brazil is kept hidden from the mass media — even within Brazil itself. This remarkable feat can be attributed to the *interaction of two modes of repression* — torture, and censorship of the press:

> Censorship kept accounts of torture from appearing in the press, while the threat of torture (compounded by harassment of journalists, bombings of newspaper offices, summary arrests, and other forms of intimidation) kept the press in line. Both were standard practices of the regime, and both were based on a common ideology.
>
> Known as the doctrine of 'National Security and Development', that ideology holds as one of its basic tenets that modern Western society is permanently at war with communism and other subversive forces. Only with these enemies kept perpetually at bay can economic development occur. In taking on this war, particularly against internal subversion, the Brazilian state was therefore acting in the best interests of the nation.
>
> . . . By excising news of social conflict, one could create a falsely peaceful image of society. This image of political stability, enforced by the military, lured foreign investors to Brazil. Logically enough, Brazil's famous 'Economic Miracle' took place during the period of harshest repression, from 1968-73.[12]

---

*See Chapter II, Attacking the Person, Not the Argument.

The following article on censorship of the press describes what one journalist saw in Brazil. (John Wicklin's "The long shadow of censorship" was the second part of a two-part feature, titled "Brazil: everything is booming but democracy", in *Atlantic Monthly,* August 1979.)

The Long Shadow of Censorship

The military police censor, working over the proofs of the weekly newspaper of the Archdiocese of São Paulo, came upon a quote: "You shall know the truth, and the truth shall make you free."

"Who wrote that?" he asked the editor. "It's not attributed."

"St. John—he was quoting Jesus."

"I still don't like it." He struck it out.

In Rio de Janeiro, the news director of Rede Globo, the country's major television network, received his daily call from a colonel in the Federal Censorship: "There are troop movements near the Uruguay border. You are not to carry any reports about them." The news director obeyed.

At the editorial office of *Veja,* Brazil's largest news magazine, a story arrived by telex from the bureau chief in Brasilia, reporting on corruption among high government officials. Almost immediately, the colonel in charge at the headquarters of the Federal Police telephoned the editor and said, "You can't publish anything about corruption in Brasilia." The editor realized that the military censors were plugged into *Veja*'s telex lines.

In São Paulo, Wladimir Herzog, thirty-eight, a leading journalist and news

director of the country's biggest public television station, was called in for interrogation by army officers about his contacts with the left. That day, he died in their custody.

These incidents occurred during the recently completed five-year term of Ernesto Geisel, fourth general to serve as President of Brazil since the military revolution. The public furor over Herzog's death four years ago led to a change in tactics of suppression in Brazil. To the displeasure of conservative generals in the government, Geisel ruled out the harsh measures of arrest, interrogation, torture, and death that had been used to keep journalists, priests, and academics in line.

Within the last twelve months, the government has stopped the copy and page-proof censorship that had been imposed on the more outspoken newspapers. About six months ago, censors' phone calls to news publications and television news departments were apparently halted.

Many papers, especially those in the more liberal south, burst forth with long-pent-up criticism of the government, the governing Aliança Renovadora Nacional (ARENA) party, and the army, which has ruled the country since its generals overthrew a progessive

president, João Goulart, in March 1964. As the end of his term neared, Geisel, an authoritarian who had not permitted personal opposition even from his military colleagues, began talking about an *abertura*—an "opening" to democracy and eventual restoration of civil rights denied the people under the continuing "state of emergency." Liberal newspapers and the Movimento Democrático Brasileiro, the only opposition party permitted by the regime, picked up the word *abertura* and tried to further the idea. Ominously, hardliners in the army warned that, despite all this talk of an opening, the people should expect no rapid return to democracy.

On March 15 of this year, Geisel handed the government over to another general, João Baptista de Oliveira Figueiredo, former head of the National Intelligence Service. Figueiredo announced that he would "implant democracy in Brazil in a year and a half, at the maximum." This pledge came a week after Vice President Walter Mondale, following a meeting with Figueiredo in Brasilia, told the head of the governing party that he was "much impressed with the climate of a democratic opening in Brazil."

I was in Brasilia the day Mondale was there, and the feeling I got was not the same as his. In reporting on the subject during two months in the country, I came to believe that the *abertura*, particularly in freedom of speech and press, was more apparent than real.

*Entertainment, cultural, and public affairs programs on television remain under censorship. A TV station must display on the screen before each program a certificate saying it has passed the Censura Federal.

*Movies must be submitted to the Censorship for approval of content and for a government ruling on the age a person must be to see the film.

*Theater scripts must be sent to Brasilia for a censor's stamp on each page; two censors must attend the dress rehearsal, to make sure that the actors' gestures and looks do not change the meaning of the approved lines.

*Book manuscripts must be approved in their entirety by the Federal Police before the books can be published.

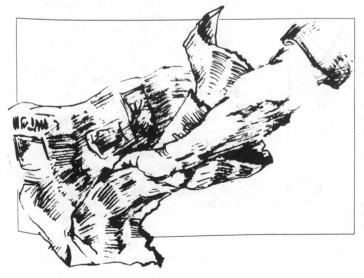

BRAZIL

*And a close look at the lIfting of prior censorship of the printed press shows that restrictions have merely been shifted to two other areas—enforcement of the national security laws and the use of economic pressures to make the publications conform.

"The government has a thousand ways of pressuring newspapers," said Julio Mesquita, director of *O Estado de São Paulo*, the most prestigious paper in Brazil. This being true, self-censorship has become the price of survival, except at such financially powerful publications as *O Estado*, which has the money to withstand litigious and economic attacks. (When the paper wanted to build a large new building, the government refused to permit any Brazilian bank to lend it mortgage money; after a long delay, the management was able to finance the building through the First National Bank of Boston. A smaller paper might not have been able to find such financing.)

O Estado, with a circulation of about 250,000, has never willingly accepted prior censorship, the kind that is exerted by phone calls from the colonels. Therefore, censorship was imposed on it by force: a resident censor was planted in the newsroom to strike from copy and proofs anything he thought his military superiors would disapprove. At first, the morning daily tried to leave blank spaces in place of deleted material. But this was not allowed. So the paper printed epic poems in place of the censored passages. Its afternoon edition, *Fôlha da Tarde*, printed recipes, which occasionally made inventive use of puns on "ingredients" to indicate the names of government officials mentioned in censored stories. Thus, a story about Laudo Natel, then governor of São Paulo state, became "Lauto Pastel" ("Rich Pastry") in the substituted recipe.

When I asked Mesquita and other editors why Geisel had lifted prior censorship of newspapers and yet retained it in television, his explanation was that newspapers in Brazil talk to a literate elite; television talks to the illiterate masses. No more than 10 percent of the country's 120 million people read newspapers, but more than half of them have daily access to a television set. Television reaches into the shanty towns where live the poorest of the poor, and into the homes of low-income agricultural and industrial workers. These are the people who can be influ-

enced for or against the regime, so the regime believes; the educated elite who edit the papers for the educated elite are already against the government. So, Geisel reasoned, why have a hassle over direct press censorship from newspaper and magazine editors and the academics, when they have no real power to influence the general populace?

Editors mentioned another factor: President Carter's campaign on human rights. Modern Western industrial nations, including the United States, value freedom of the press as a central indicator of a country's standing in civilized society. In 1977, the U.S. State Department angered the Brazilian regime by submitting a report to Congress that criticized the country's record on freedom. But now Geisel could say that he had restored freedom of the press, and thus had brought Brazil back into the club of civilized nations.

Officials of the new administration justify continued censorship of television programs, theater, and films by calling them "cultural, not political." It is done, according to a presidential decree in 1970, to protect the public from broadcasts and films "offensive to the morals and good customs" of the Brazilian people. Surprisingly, several editors said they felt there was some justification for this kind of censorship. Roberto Civita, editorial director of Editora Abril, the largest magazine publishing house in Brazil and the publisher of *Veja*, said: "I think this makes sense. There must be a line drawn somewhere about everything." Who draws the line? An independent "code office" might be better than having the government do it, he said, "but someone has to do it."

By all accounts, however, the government has used the "morals and good customs" rationale to edit out of television and films any political ideas it disapproves. Indeed, at the time the decree was published, the minister of justice explained that the object was "to combat the insidious efforts of international communism to impose free love and dissolve the moral fiber of society."

For the most part, the country's intellectual leaders have vigorously opposed censorship of any kind.

No law has ever been passed by the Brazilian Congress establishing *political* censorship of news, in print or on the air. In theory, such censorship is prohibited by the constitution. Rather, political censorship was imposed under the "emergency" dictatorial powers given to the president in 1968 by Institutional Act No. 5. This act, aimed at

the anti-government urban guerrilla movement, gave the president the authority to dismiss Congress and elected officials, jail citizens without giving cause in political cases, overrule the courts, deprive citizens of their political rights for up to ten years, and rule by decree. All this in the guise of protecting "national security."

Although the academics, priests, and students who led the urban guerrillas were soon hunted down and killed, the Act remained in force for ten years, until Geisel allowed it to expire on January 1, 1979. Before he did, however, he had the Congress, over which he had assumed control, pass a bill that would give him and succeeding presidents "emergency" powers similar to those under IA 5, except that they must be renewed every six months.

Prior censorship was one of the most formidable tools of IA 5 for suppressing dissent, and it was systematically applied. The Federal Police, a military force reporting to the Ministry of Justice but usually controlled directly from the president's office, set up a Division of Censorship of Public Entertainment. Censors are trained at the Federal School for Censors in Brasilia. Secret guidelines have been laid down for them by successive military regimes, but these have never been revealed to editors and writers. The result has been a suppression at worst vicious and at best capricious.

One target of censorship over the years has been Cardinal Paulo Evaristo Arns of São Paulo, a leader of Roman Catholic Church opposition to the regime's violation of human rights. From the beginning, the Censura let the Cardinal know it did not want him to discuss social concerns on the archdiocesan radio station. He did not comply, and on October 30, 1973, the station's license was abruptly suspended. *O São Paulo*, his weekly newspaper, was placed under resident censorship. Sermons by the Cardinal and social pronouncements by the Pope were deleted in the proof stage; the paper was forbidden even to mention the name of Dom Helder Camara, another outspoken opponent of the regime who is Archbishop of Recife and Olinda.

To avoid having a resident censor imposed upon it, *Fôlha de São Paulo*, which vies with *O Estado* as the leading newspaper in the city, decided to accept the telephoned edicts of the colonels on news it was not to touch. But under the editorship of Claudio Abramo, a respected journalist of the left, it often published editorials and commentary denouncing government suppression. For this, Abramo was jailed briefly on several occasions. Then, in 1977, after a

BRAZIL

columnist wrote a satirical piece about an army hero, the military told the owner of the paper it wanted Abramo out of the editorship. Abramo was promptly given another position. The amount of dissenting "op-ed" comment has been cut back, but the paper remains critical of the government.

Television has shown none of the independence newspapers have shown. Rede Globo, the network with the largest audience, has cooperated with government censorship virtually without protest. The management in Rio believes that money can be made without freedom of speech. "In Brazil, TV is a government concern," a spokesman told me. "At any time, they can end the concession. We must be more cautious than the newspapers. Our eight P.M. news can change the views of 40 million people—so this gives TV more responsibility to see that this new process of *abertura* runs normally."

Normality, at Globo, includes submitting for government approval twenty episodes at a time of all television novellas, the nighttime soap operas that are standard popular fare. (One novella on youth problems was recently vetoed, reportedly because the government did not want to acknowledge that there *were* youth problems.) Until January of this year, news stories also had to have government approval. Now, self-censorship prevails. During the strike of 154,000 auto workers in São Paulo, which the Figueiredo government immediately declared illegal, the regime let it be known that it would not look favorably on extensive coverage by television. As a consequence, Roberto Marinha, who owns most of Globo stock, personally edited news coverage of the strike, to see that it stayed in bounds.

News on public television gets less attention from the government than does commercial TV because its audience is small. Even so, TV Cultura, the modern broadcasting operation funded by the State of São Paulo, submits even segments of home study courses for censorship, if they relate to political or social subjects. The staff has internalized the warning given them by the death of Wladimir Herzog.

"Vlado," as he was known, was a left-leaning liberal whose views angered the ultraconservatives in the Second Army garrison, headquartered in São Paulo. The Department of Internal Operations ordered him to present himself for

questioning on Saturday, October 25, 1975, at the "Tutóia Hilton," where several dissidents had been tortured to death. Another journalist, waiting in the anteroom to be questioned, testified later in court that he had heard shouts exchanged between the interrogator and Vlado, and then the interrogator ordered equipment for torture. Shortly after that, he said, Vlado's shouts ceased. Late that afternoon, the Second Army issued a statement that Vlado, having confessed to membership in the Communist party, hanged himself in his cell. Cardinal Arns, the head of the journalists' union, and professors at the University of São Paulo, where Vlado taught part time, called the statement a lie.[1] More than 30,000 students boycotted classes at the university; thousands attended an ecumenical service the Cardinal conducted in São Paulo Cathedral for Vlado, a Jew. His death became a *cause célèbre* in the press of Brazil and around the world. On this story, the censors backed off.

President Geisel saw the developing situation as a threat to his regime. He warned General Ednardo D'Avila Melo, commandant of the Second Army, that he would brook no more "suicides" at the Tutóia Hilton. Two months later, a laborer died there under similar circumstances. Geisel promptly dismissed General Ednardo and replaced him with a less conservative general, signaling to the rest of the army that he was dissatisfied with the repression. Since then, no suspicious deaths of political prisoners have been reported. Claudio Abramo told me he thinks that so long as papers are free to report such acts, the army will not be able to resume torture and murder.

The big question in Brazil, however, is whether the army hard-liners, who no longer look on President Figueiredo as a dependable member of the *apparat*, will permit further liberalization in the areas of free speech and press. Within the new administration, officials themselves are arguing about how far it is proper—and safe—to go with the "opening" to democracy.

At the Ministry of Justice in Brasilia, I asked the chief of cabinet, Dr. Syleno Ribeiro, whether the ministry was committed to an *abertura*.

"What some people call *abertura*," he said, "is merely the process of continuing the perfection of our national insti-

tutions that began when the country gained its independence in 1822." A woman lawyer sitting in as the ministry's counsel on human rights commented, "There is no opening in Brazil because, since the Revolution, our institutions have never been closed."

After these remarks, I realized that my questions on the future turn of events were not going to be answered in this interview. Ribeiro suggested that I write out my questions and said, "By tomorrow noon, at your hotel, you will have the answers, written by the minister of justice himself." The answers never came.

The minister, Petronio Portela, was at the time involved in a public exchange over censorship with Eduardo Portela, the new minister of education and culture. One official of the new government had pointed out that only two countries censor books—Brazil and the Soviet Union. Petronio's predecessor, Armando Falcão, had prohibited or burned 500 books during the Geisel years. Books, said Petronio, should be censored by "fitting persons" in the Ministry of Education and Culture, not by the Federal Police. Eduardo, a Rio professor and former literary critic, agreed that books should not be censored by the Federal Police, but neither did he want to take the responsibility for censorship. Eduardo is part of the government, his chief of cabinet told me. "If the government thinks we will have to have some kind of censorship, then of course we will accept it," she said. "But it will be done by the Ministry of Justice."

In the end, the decision on all forms of censorship will be made by President Figueiredo. And he finds himself in a dilemma. On one horn, journalists, academics, and leaders of the opposition party are determined that there shall be no turning back from the concessions to freedom they won from Geisel. On the other, old-line generals don't want to permit open criticism of the army. They fear that, should a democratic civilian regime win control of the government, they are in danger of being made to account for past excesses at a Brazilian "Nuremberg trial." "Before we are allowed democracy," said one disgruntled editor, "the last general must die in bed."

The fear is reflected in the prosecution of *Veja*, now under way in the Supreme Military Tribunal. In February, the news magazine published two investigative reports by Antônio Carlos Fon which gave times and places in which dissidents had been tortured and killed, the names of army officers who committed the torture, and the names of colonels and generals responsible for

---

[1] Last October, a justice in a civil court ruled that Vlado had been incarcerated illegally, that the subsequent investigation by the army did not substantiate the army's claim of suicide, and that Vlado's widow and two children must be indemnified for his death while in army custody.

permitting it to happen. The army prosecutor brought charges that the articles were "subversive in the extreme." Their sole intent, the indictment said, was to "turn public opinion against constituted authorities," a crime punishable under the national security laws. If convicted on charges brought by the military, Fon can be sent to jail for five years.

I asked a source involved with his defense why the military, which is inseparable from the government, had decided to prosecute *Veja* at a time when government leaders were talking about an opening to freedom.

"What I think the military is saying," he replied, "is this: We are not going to stand trial for what happened between 1968 and 1976. *Veja* is as good a place to give that message as any—it's big and it's middle-of-the-road. If you say it to *Veja*, it's clear to everyone."

Since he has not intervened, Figueiredo, whose whole life has been devoted to the army, apparently wants the message to be conveyed. If the prosecution is carried out, it will be an exception to what is reported to be his official strategy: avoid confrontation with the major organ of the press, but prosecute vigorously publications of the alternative press. This is an obvious bow to the army extremists who are angered by the probing of these dissident papers. Actions for violations of the national security laws are now in process against *Pasquim*, a satirical weekly in Rio; *Tribuna da Imprensa*, a Rio daily; *Reporter*, a Rio monthly; *Resistência*, a monthly in Pará, and *Movimento*, an investigative weekly in São Paulo.

The attack on *Movimento*, an influential journal of 25,000 circulation set up four years ago with contributions from journalists and professors, is a good example of how the government uses the security laws and economic pressure to discourage opposition in the press.

I talked with Antônio Carlos Ferreira, its "responsible director" (the Brazilian title for top editor), on the second floor of 'a nondescript house in a middle-class section near the Cemetery of São Paulo. In the rooms around us, I saw men and women in faded jeans who looked interchangeable with reporters, editors, and production people on any alternative paper in the United States. The pressures on them have not been subtle. Three times the paper has been removed from the newsstands by government officials, even though the censors had approved the contents. Ferreira has been questioned many times by the Federal Police. "Certainly, our phones are tapped and certainly, we are being followed," he said. And now he is being called to answer charges in the Supreme Military Tribunal. The accusation, in effect, is that he endangered national security by writing about arguments within the ARENA party over Geisel's choice of Figueiredo to succeed him. Ferreira, a man in his thirties who has a wife and two small children, was matter-of-fact about his prospects.

"I will be given a hearing before four military officers and one civilian judge," he said, "and then I will be sentenced to prison."

"Is that decided in advance?"

"Sure—they're the military, aren't they?"

"Can you appeal?"

"Yes, but I will be in jail."

Besides an interim editor, *Movimento* will have to find a new printer, inasmuch as the government has warned customers of its present printer not to patronize the company if it continues to print *Movimento*. Banks have been ordered to give the paper no credit and major companies warned not to advertise in its pages, Ferreira said. Most have complied.

Every day new examples turn up to suggest that freedom in Brazil has a long way to go.

*Twelve radio stations have been fined for failing to carry *Voz do Brasil*. Each night from 7 to 8 P.M., the government requires every AM and FM station in the country to carry *Voz*, a badly produced propaganda program touting the "miracle" of the country's advance as a major power. All over the country at 7 P.M., the people turn off their radios.

*The Brazilian Post Office refused to transmit a telegram of support from students of the University of Londrina to students of the University of Salvador (Bahia). Instead, postal officials turned the names of the signers over to the Military Police.

*In Curitiba, the Federal Censorship prohibited a children's play, *O Robo de Bobby*, from being seen by children under fourteen. The reason given: the play mentioned the words "worker" and "strike."

*The government fined TV Guanabara in Rio $2000 for broadcasting an interview in which the governor of the state was criticized.

*In May, retired General Hugo Abreu was jailed for twenty days by the army for publishing a book "damaging to the armed forces." Abreu, a former top government official, had opposed Figueiredo's nomination as president.

According to one of the country's leading academics, the auguries for wider freedom are not good. "People who read the liberal newspapers in Rio and São Paulo think there may be an opening to democracy," he said. "We who live in Brasilia think there will be a closed military regime for many years to come."

—JOHN WICKLEIN

REPORTS & COMMENT CONTRIBUTORS

John Wicklein is a journalist and educator who last wrote for this magazine on cable TV (February 1979). ∎

Brazil as the "Third World"

Brazil's dependence on foreign capital, its production of cash crops for export, its political system which encourages foreign investment (which provides the foreign exchange needed to buy the goods it has grown to depend on) makes this country resemble most others in the "Third World".

Most "poor" countries are huge exporters of primary products — from copper to cocoa to sugarcane to carnations. When you wheel your shopping cart around a supermarket, you find pineapple from the Philippines or South Africa, tinned corned beef from Argentina, tea from Sri Lanka (Ceylon). Food, metals, minerals, fibres, oil — all these products flow out from the "Third World" to our supermarkets, cities and industrial parks.

In Brazil, as in most other underdeveloped countries, land is used to grow products for profit and for export — not food for its people. Coffeee, the second most valuable commodity in world trade, is the economic lifeblood of fourteen underdeveloped countries. According to Roger Revell, director for the Centre for Population Studies at Harvard, one out of every ten cropped acres in the world is planted with non-nutritious cash crops such as cotton, tobacco, rubber, coffee, tea, jute, etc. The non-food acreage is comparable to all the tilled land in Europe![13]

Why would an underdeveloped country grow products for export rather than food for local consumption? The answer lies both in the history of underdeveloped countries, and in today's global economic structure. Over 300 years ago, colonial powers established plantation systems in countries they had subjugated throughout the world. The sole purpose of the plantations was to produce wealth for the colonizers, not food for people. In her book, *Diet for a small planet*, Frances Moore Lappé notes that this fact explains why most of the crops selected had no nutritional value, and highlights the appropriateness of the name these crops would later be given: *cash* crops. "Land that grows money," Lappé writes, "can't grow food."

The country with a cash-crop economy is dependent on an international market for foreign exchange with which it then must purchase its manufactured goods, its technology — and, in many cases, food). This international market does not treat producers well. Since 1952 the poor world has increased the volume of its agricultural exportation by more than 33%; for this effort, it has received a gain

in cash income of only 4%.[14] In 1960, El Salvador could buy one tractor with earnings from 165 bags of coffee. By the early 1970s, it needed 316 bags of coffee to buy a tractor.[15]

Changing the agricultural system of an underdeveloped country from cash crop to food production for domestic consumption takes years, and capital — in order to finance research into the best use of soil; to recondition the soil; to obtain different agricultural equipment; and to build a domestic distribution system for that food.* Most important, though, it takes the political will of the people of a country to bring about such a change — and they must have the power to effect that change.

Yet in most of the "Third World", arable land is owned by a tiny percentage of the population. Overall in Latin America, 7% of all landowners possess 93% of the arable land, according to a study by Robert Carty of the Latin American Working Group.[16] In most

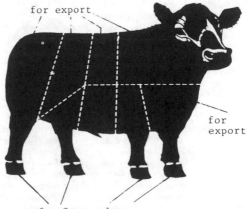

for export

for export

for Guatemalans

cases as well, this small minority is aligned with multi-national corporations. Together they control the capital; both profit enormously from the present situation. Barnet and Mueller point out that

> It is good business to grow high-profit crops for export rather than to raise corn, wheat and rice to support an indigent local population.[17]

Growing carnations on one hectare of land in Colombia will bring 1,000,000 pesos a year, while wheat or corn bring only 12,5000 pesos.[18]

---

*The roads and railways in underdeveloped countries lead from areas of production to ports and other exit points, not other areas within the country.

The *profit* that can be made on such items — not interest in nutrition, or an individual store manager's desire to cheer up our homes with pointsettias at Christmas and lillies at Easter — is what determines what we can buy in the Dominion Store, Safeway or IGA here at home. Barnet and Mueller conclude that

> The policies of global corporations feature increased production of luxury items such as strawberries and asparagus. But the money does not flow to the hungry majority, and those who used to subsist on local fruits and vegetables now find them priced beyond their reach.[19]

At a meeting of international nutritionists sponsored by the New York Academy of Sciences, Brazil was singled out as a country which was not benefiting from this kind of agricultural "progress". To a pro-military agronomist who said, "the rest of the world is better off because Brazil can export more than 10 million tons of soybeans a year," it was pointed out that the argument was not convincing when Brazilians themselves had nothing to eat. Forty percent of Brazil's population suffers from malnutrition.[20] Between 1960 and 1970, 6,300,000 peasant farmers in Brazil had to leave rural areas to join the ranks of the unemployed in and around the cities.[21] Food riots erupted when crops for export, like soybeans, replaced food such as black beans and potatoes (those staples rose in price by 400%

and 300% respectively). Milk became unavailable as dairy cattle were slaughtered to be exported as hamburger meat. Though Brazilian children under five constitute less than one-fifth of the population, they account for four-fifths of all deaths.[22]

A Brookings Institution study of world nutrition noted that while beef production in Central America increased dramatically during the 1960s, the per capita consumption of meat in those countries either increased marginally or declined. Costa Rica was a dramatic example: there, meat production increased 92% from the early 1960s to 1970, but per capita consumption *went down* 26%. The reason for this, the author noted, was that meat is

> ... ending up not in Latin American stomachs but in franchised restaurant hamburgers in the United States.[23]

This situation does not have to result in North Americans feeling guilty about enjoying a meal or admiring gorgeous plants — in themselves, good things. It can, however, lead many to seek out and support those who are working to change these conditions, and to challenge the priorities of those in power who continue to profit from the suffering of others.

Discussion/research

Commenting on an exchange with Bolivian potato farmers, a New Brunswick potato farmer came to some conclusions about underdevelopment in general:

> I have come to realise that underdevelopment isn't simply a lack of capital, but a dependence planned and implemented by those driven by greed.

The one major difference he had found between the two countries was that farmers in Canada are kept in place through loans, limited buyers and other forms of economic dependence, while in Bolivia farmers are kept in place through outright military suppression.

a. Prepare a discussion of this statement, based on information you have gathered on Brazil.
   or
b. In a research paper, discuss this statement, referring to land use policies, agriculture, fisheries policies and resource management in a "Third World" country and in Canada.

Source: NACLA

Since World War II great efforts have been made to attract overseas investors. This advertisement appeared in the Brazilian magazine Visao.

Miracle, Dream or Nightmare?

The situation in Brazil is extreme, but in essence it is no different than most "Third World" countries. Its connections with the "First World" and Canada in particular are multiple; the stakes for some very rich Canadians — and for most Brazilians — are very high.

The media present a grossly distorted image of this country — as they do of the "Third World" in general.

For the academic and business-world press, Brazil is a country which gets more than average coverage. This is because of the high Canadian investment in the country. This coverage can be divided into two distinct types:

Brazil as a wealthy, or potentially wealthy, country with obstacles that impede the kind of economic growth it is capable of (obstacles such as social unrest, native rights, nationalist sentiment); and

Brazil as a potentially wealthy country but with historical and existing policies and institutions which have tended to concentrate wealth in a few hands at the expense of many, with a little help from powerful foreign friends.

Both points of view share a common assumption: Brazil's wealth. However, the first point of view supports the interests of those who want to see this wealth exploited as rapidly as possibly while the latter speaks to those who would support a shift in emphasis to a fairer distribution of Brazil's wealth through changes in: land ownership, foreign control of industry and use of technology better suited to the Brazilian situation. The former point of view speaks to that portion of the population of Brazil (and wealthy investors which deal with Brazil) which controls most of the wealth. The latter point of view speaks to the portion of the population which is in the majority — about 80%.

Whether Brazil appears to you as The Economic Miracle, The Dream or The Nightmare will depend on what is important to you.

Discussion/research

1. Why do companies invest in the "Third World"? What are the effects of this investment?

What kinds of governments are common in "Third World" countries?

What form of government does Brazil have?

2. What are the results of foreign investment in Brazil?:

Resource development: land? food production?

Is the health and education of people improved?

Who benefits from foreign investment?

3. The following are "causes of underdevelopment" that have been suggested by many people.

   a. Rank these "causes" in order of importance, and mark the ones you judge to be untrue (or not causes but symptoms of underdevelopment):

   poor land and natural resources
   lack of education
   international trade policies and practices
   feelings of apathy and hopelessness

exploitation and domination by others
the colonial past
the indifference of others
overpopulation
hunger
wealth and power concentrated in the hands of a few
dependency on other countries
no job opportunities
lack of personal initiative
multinational corporations and lending institutions
unrest caused by revolutionaries

   b. If you find that some causes of underdevelopment have not appeared on this list, add them.

   c. Discuss in small groups, and take notes on the reasons given for various choices.

4. Where is the *"Free World"*? What countries would you include in the "Free World"? For what reasons?

5. If a person has visited or even lived in another country, does that make them an expert on that country? When we form judgments, what role should direct experience play?

Case Study #2:
Atlantic Provinces

In this second case study, we shall look at underdevelopment here at home.

Everyone has heard about the problems of overpopulation, poverty and malnutrition in the "Third World". Living in Canada, we can sometimes have trouble imagining what life is really like in underdeveloped countries, let alone know why conditions are like that there. In Canada, it seems that most people — especially young people with good educational opportunities — are able to live fairly comfortably.

Perhaps this is why we sometimes hear Canadians suggest that if the people of underdeveloped countries were more like ourselves — if they were only ambitious; worked harder; controlled their population growth . . . then perhaps their problems could be solved. Others believe that it is simply a lack of fertile land, water or other natural resources that is to blame, and that the rich industrialised countries ought to solve the problems by contributing relief in the form of food shipments and technical advisers. Yet others say that such foreign aid leads to the corruption and the prevalence of military dictatorships and totalitarian régimes in the "Third World". Still others say it is something inherent in the make-up of "Third World" people that results in the poverty, and that in any case it does not bother them as much as it would us, because they are used to it.

One is often left confused by such diverging views. Only a careful study of the conditions in other countries can begin to explain how and why underdevelopment occurs, why it continues to exist, and what can be done about it.

However, it is also useful to consider an example of underdevelopment closer to home. This is easier than you may think at first, because underdevelopment is not confined solely to the "Third World". Seemingly prosperous, technically advanced countries like Canada also suffer from underdevelopment.

What is underdevelopment?

What does Atlantic Canada have in common with an underdeveloped country like Brazil? People here do not go hungry, everyone has housing of some kind, few are visibly impoverished . . .

Some economic characteristics of underdevelopment

Underdevelopment is an economic and social condition that affects all major aspects of life in a country or region. Yet in an underdeveloped country, not everyone is harmed by this set of circumstances. As in Brazil, in an underdeveloped area, there is always a small percentage of people, both inside the country and outside, who benefit from underdevelopment.

In the economic sphere, one of the principal characteristics of underdeveloped countries is their *dependence* on exporting products. In many cases, these are raw or semi-finished materials. This export will in turn generate the funds needed to import the goods that cannot be produced locally. The manufactured goods cannot be produced locally because these underdeveloped areas lack the finance capital and technology to produce them. An underdeveloped country or region creates products for market elsewhere, and it imports finished products from elsewhere.

The underdeveloped country's primary producers typically have little control over the prices they receive for their products. A notable exception are the oil-producing countries which are members of OPEC . In most cases, the buying prices for raw products — whether bananas, fish, copper, coffee, pulpwood or potatoes — are generally determined by the buyers, not the sellers. (For example, the price of potatoes paid to New Brunswick farmers averaged $4.40/hundredweight in 1965, while nine years later in 1974 it averaged $2.27; over a ten-year period average prices declined by 1% each year, even as costs escalated.[24])

An underdeveloped region depends on shipping out its unprocessed goods to export markets; yet underdeveloped countries or regions often attempt to overcome this dependence by diversifying their economies, and attempting industrialisation.

In their bids to attract or hold on to investment and industry, underdeveloped areas may try to assure investors of a "favourable investment climate". Such a climate can be found anywhere that high rates of return (profit) can be made on investments. Conditions favourable to high profit levels include the following:

low costs:

• cheap labour

• favourable tax laws;

• infrastructure like roads, rails and other services already built and in place;

• relaxed or non-existent pollution or safety regulations;

• low-cost utilities such as electric power or communications systems; and

additional incentives:

• power rate subsidies;

• municipal or other tax exemptions;

• employment incentive grants;

• interest-free loans and grants, etc.

When these conditions are present, companies are able to realise high profits, and therefore are willing to invest.

Social characteristics of underdeveloped areas

However, underdeveloped areas that experience these economic conditions also very often experience social upheaval as a result.

The low wages, lack of social benefits that normally would be paid for by taxes, (hospitals, schools, etc.) and other conditions eventually result in social unrest. This unrest is then met with varying responses. Depending on the underdeveloped area, a country may declare martial law; or in another area, the legislature may simply alter its labour, pollution or other legislation to accommodate the industry being attracted.

Some indications of the break-down in society include:

• increased rates of alcoholism;

• widespread use of mood-altering drugs;

• increase in family problems (including violence in the home, neglect, divorce, etc.);

• growth in numbers of fundamentalist religions or cults.

Migration is another social characteristic of underdeveloped areas. People are constantly on the move, going "down the road", travelling across provinces — or continents — looking for work. From Turkey workers travel to Germany; from the Northeast of Brazil they go to São Paulo; from the bantustans of South Africa or neighbouring countries men travel to Johannesburg. From the Maritimes they went to Boston, then Toronto, and now they journey to Edmonton . . .

Which came first?

When we consider these aspects of underdevelopment it is often difficult to distinguish between the causes of this situation and the circumstances which developed as a result. Only careful study of the history of each underdeveloped area and its people will begin to answer this basic question. However, we propose certain working hypotheses which you can test for yourself, examining Nova Scotia's primary, secondary and tertiary sectors, and finding out something of its rich past. *Note: this section will not be complete until you have examined the information in a number of the publications and audio-visual materials listed here.*

The aim of this work is not necessarily to prove or disprove simplistically and definitively the working assumptions we propose; rather *its aim is to invite you to begin your own, continuing process of thought and research. If the proposed working assumptions are found to be inadequate, then better ones must take their place.*

Working hypotheses

For this section, we propose these working assumptions: *first,* that underdeveloped countries or regions may differ in the degree of their underdevelopment but not, fundamentally in kind. *Second,* we propose that the Maritimes can be defined as an underdeveloped region, in the sense described above. The *Checklist on development* (page 235) and the articles in this section expand on these points.

Method of analysis

Having set out certain working assumptions for you to use and test, we shall suggest certain sources of alternative information that are not normally found in business (or even academic) studies of the Atlantic region. They are listed at the end of this chapter.

The analysis they put forward applies to the Atlantic provinces as well as it does to the "Third World". It could be summed up by a statement that is made in one of the slide-tape shows:

> Western Europe did not go into the world and find underdeveloped countries — she created them.

Underdevelopment in Canada

In Canada, underdevelopment is usually called "regional disparity". This refers to the great difference between some regions of Canada and others — with regard to income levels, unemployment levels, levels of investment and so on.

It is a commonplace to call Alberta and the Western provinces the "haves" and Nova Scotia and the other Atlantic provinces the "have-nots". The general meaning this conveys is that the West of Canada is supposed to have the natural resources, the capital investment for industry and the jobs; while the East's resources are supposed to be depleted, its industries failed, and its people out of work. Although this is partially true, this schema does not describe the situation satisfactorily. Among other things, it does not explain how this situation has come to pass. It does not explain why long ago the Maritimes were booming, and now they have "gone bust".

The following article was prepared by the
Development Education Centre, Toronto.

Underdevelopment in Canada
Notes Towards an Analytical Framework

Section I
Basic Concepts

This paper has been prepared as part of a collection of articles on the
subject of Underdevelopment in Canada. While assembling this collection, we became increasingly aware of the need to integrate our understanding of the particular issues raised into some kind of analytical
framework. Hence this article does not attempt to summarize all the
different aspects of underdevelopment in Canada today. It does not aim to
be comprehensive. Rather, our purpose is to outline and illustrate an
approach to the study of the topic. This approach is presented largely in
historical and economic terms, as the context within which political questions can most fruitfully be discussed.

The articles collected in this file indicate the extent of foreign domination over the Canadian political economy, and also the extent to which
poverty and injustice exist in a country which has generally been considered wealthy and "developed". By implication, the articles suggest that
a self-generated development which benefits the majority of Canadians
can only be attained through a restructuring of economic and political ties
with the United States, and of class relations within the country.

This collection, then, challenges the image of Canada as an autonomous
and developed nation. It stresses three related issues: foreign domination
of the economy, regional disparities in living standards, and class divisions in Canada's social structure. It is on this basis of dependence,
unequal growth, and class relations that we are studying underdevelopment in Canada.

Some basic concepts are essential for this study. The process of unequal
and dependent development is generated in a *hinterland* nation or region
by the channelling of its natural, financial and human resources to another
centre, a *metropole*. The hinterland is integrated into the process of
development of the metropole in a way which distorts and limits the
growth of the former's productive forces. Through the same process
which makes the hinterland dependent, the accumulation and concentration of wealth in the metropole is promoted. The processes of dependent
and uneven growth which evolve in the hinterland are well summarized in
the phrase "the development of underdevelopment".[1]

This process occurs both among nations and among regions within each
nation. For example, the uneven growth within Canada, which has generally been described by the term "regional disparities" might better be
called, in this context, *internal colonialism*.[2] This stresses that the basis of
"disparities" lies in the power relations which operate between the central Canadian metropoles (Toronto and Montreal) and the rest of the
country.

These relations also operate at the provincial and local levels. In this
sense, it could be said that Vancouver operates as a metropole in relation
to the B.C. interior, from which minerals and lumber (natural resources)
and labour (human resources) are drawn on terms that progressively
enrich the city at the expense of its hinterland.

The conventional view of underdevelopment is of an area with a subsistence economy, desperately low levels of income, and poor education,
health and housing standards. These are features of many underdeveloped
societies in the "Third World" (Africa, Asia, Latin America and the
Caribbean). But these present living conditions are the consequences of
history, of an international system of power relations which began with
colonialism and continues to operate today through the monopoly

capitalist system. It is by analysing the operation of this system that underdevelopment in Third World countries as well as in Canada, can best be understood.

Because in Canada the extreme deprivation usually associated with underdevelopment is not nearly as acute as in Asia, Africa and Latin America, the image of Canada as an autonomous, developed nation has been widely accepted. Statistically, Canada has one of the highest living standards in the world. Consequently, many Canadians have grown accustomed to looking outside Canada for examples of underdevelopment. This tendency has been reinforced by information from international relief agencies, church mission programmes and government "aid" projects.[3]

But the relative wealth of Canada has obscured the connections between our own situation and that of people in the Third World. We think that study of these connections is necessary for an integrated understanding of Canada's particular position in the international power system.

In our view, Canada's position is not simply that of metropole, nor simply that of hinterland. It is not simply that of a central capitalist country, nor simply that of a peripheral, or Third World country. Canada shares some of the characteristics of both the central and peripheral capitalist nations.

On the one hand, Canada's relative wealth and pattern of income distribution resembles that of the central capitalist nations—the US, Western Europe, and Japan. On the other hand, some features of Canadian development more closely resemble those of peripheral capitalist nations like Brazil. The most obvious parallel here is in the degree of dependence on foreign capital and technology. The opening words of the Gray report on *Foreign Direct Investment in Canada* put the case clearly:

> *the degree of foreign ownership and control of economic activity is already substantially higher in Canada than in any other industrialized country and is continuing to increase.*[4]

This contradictory pattern of development allows Canada to play a dual role in the international political economy. On the one hand, Canada is a neo-colony to the United States, and on the other hand, a neo-colonizer of some parts of the Third World, notably the Caribbean.

In the continental structure, Canada's role is largely that of resource hinterland and additional marketplace for the US economy. American domination of Canada is a primary source of Canadian underdevelopment. But because Canadian-American relations do not operate in a vacuum, an integrated approach to this question must locate Canada in a broader international context than that of North America alone. The Canadian banks are a case in point: while they have financed much of the American takeover of Canadian industry, they are also extending their operations into control of the finance sector throughout the Commonwealth Caribbean.[5] It is in the context of this dual role in the international system that we would analyze the internal dynamics of underdevelopment in Canada.

One outstanding feature of this internal dynamic is the imbalance in economic power between central Canada and the hinterland *regions* of the nation. Another is the stunted or "truncated" growth of the manufacturing *sector* relative to the resource extraction and service sectors of the economy.[6]

In analyzing these contradictions, we would stress the importance of class relations in each region and in the country as a whole. Underdevelopment cannot be analyzed simply in terms of metropole/hinterland relations, for this would suggest that all classes in the hinterland have a common interest in restructuring relations with the metropole.[7] And it is clear that underdevelopment in Canada has operated to the benefit of some groups at the expense of the majority. The interests of the most powerful financial and industrial groups in Canada are tied to those of the US metropole, and they have accumulated their wealth within the limits set by uneven and dependent development.

We suggest then, that a critical analysis of underdevelopment in Canada should turn on two axes: metropole/hinterland and class relations. It is the

interaction of these two sets of forces that has defined Canada's particular historical experience, and the range of possible alternatives for future development.

Section II
Historical Roots of
Canadian Underdevelopment

"Underdevelopment is not a condition 'natural' to certain peoples or parts of the world. Neither is it ordained by the gods. It is the consequence of history." [8]

The present dynamics of underdevelopment in Canada grow out of a particular history. The pattern of external dependence, regional fragmentation, and class conflict was established at the time of the European conquest when military and cultural intervention severely disrupted the Indian societies of the St. Lawrence system.

The existing agrarian and trading patterns, in many cases very sophisticated, were destroyed either by outright force or by the more subtle methods of incorporating the native peoples into a political economy structured by the conquerors. This process brought on

such a rapid shift in the prevailing Indian culture as to lead to wholesale destruction of the peoples concerned by warfare and disease. The disappearance of the beaver and of the Indians necessitated the extension of European organization to the interior. [9]

The colonization of Canada took place as part of the global expansion of the European economies. It occurred after the Spanish and Portuguese conquest of Latin America, but before the consolidation of European dominance over Asia and Africa. In the search by the European powers for sources of raw materials, places to settle surplus population, and markets for goods processed at home, Canada came to satisfy particular needs.

Initially, in the sixteenth century, the French established a pattern of export of codfish and beaver furs, the first of a series of raw materials which Canada has supplied to external metropoles. Control over the economic life of New France was shared between ecclesiastical and feudal lords in partnership with merchants linked to trading interests in the mother country.

After the British conquered New France in 1759, they extended European control westward, largely to serve the expanding fur trade. Dominant among the British settlers were a few traders, mostly centred in

Montreal, who were later to become the nucleus of the Chateau Clique in Lower Canada and the Family Compact in Upper Canada. Thus Canada first entered the international economy as a colony—in a position of dependence. Furthermore, it was absorbed region by region—in fragments.

Fragmentation of Canada as a political and economic unit, then, was a fact long before American control over the nation became consolidated. It has its roots in the gradual colonization of different regions at different historical times. The St. Lawrence-Great Lakes system, for example, was integrated into the international economy long before white settlers displaced the native peoples from most of the Prairies. Thus it was possible for capital to be accumulated and power concentrated first in Montreal and later in Toronto. It was held by that fraction of the ruling class whose interests were primarily located in land speculation, trade, and commerce with Great Britain rather than in directly productive enterprises inside the colony.[10]

Hence a pattern of internal colonialism was established, fragmenting the Canadian economy to serve external metropoles through expansion in particular sectors and regions of the country.

After the founding of the Hudson's Bay Company in 1670, power in the regions west of Quebec was increasingly concentrated in its hands. The sweeping financial concessions and legal powers it exercised meant that the imperatives of the fur trade shaped patterns of settlement and employment, cultural relations between the white and Indian populations, and class relations among the white colonizers themselves. In testimony given by an employee to the British House of Commons in 1749, it is noted:

> *that the Indians bartered their furs for brandy, tobacco, blankets, beads and other goods; that the servants of the Company were absolutely forbidden to trade for themselves with the Indians; that he had seen one employee beaten merely for going to an Indian tent to light a pipe; and that these punishments were inflicted at the arbitrary will of the Governor of the Company.*[11]

The fur trade is a classic example of "staple" production, i.e. the orientation of regional economic and political life around a relatively unprocessed good designed for export to external metropoles. It is an organization of production which has recurred throughout Canadian history.

In different regions, and at different periods, a variety of staples have played the central role in Canada's economy—fur, fish, timber, wheat, minerals, and oil. For our purposes, the main point of interest is what causes the shift from one staple to another.

The shifts in production from one staple to another, from fur and fish to timber, or from wheat to minerals and oil, reflect changes in the structure of demand for those products in the external metropoles. But these shifts were also the result of particular development choices made internally, by fractions of the domestic ruling class.

The interaction of external and internal forces can be illustrated by analysing a particular historic period which defined much of subsequent Canadian development—from Confederation in 1867 to the implementation of John A. MacDonald's National Policy by the end of the century.

The core of the National Policy was the construction of the CPR, a railway to open the Prairies for settlement and serve as the backbone of an east-west mercantile network. The need for this network had become clear during the two decades before Confederation. The repeal of the British corn laws in 1846 and the end of the Reciprocity Treaty with the US in 1854 effectively eliminated the option of preferential access to the markets of the external metropoles.

As the links with both the British and American metropoles had been loosened, it became possible, and indeed necessary, to implement a plan for some sort of independent national development. John A. MacDonald's "national dream" would open the west to Montreal commercial

capitalists, with the support of British financiers, while a high tariff wall was designed to keep out American competition for these interests.[12]

The capital and labour necessary to carry out this project were accumulated at the expense of east coast shipping interests and the emerging industrial groups of east and central Canada. Indeed, the present distribution of power and wealth between central Canada and the Maritimes has its roots in this period, when the possibilities for self-sustained and diversified economic growth in the east were choked off.

After the decline of the traditional Maritime shipping and fishing industries in the early nineteenth century, there was a burst of investment in primary and secondary iron and steel, in textiles, and in sugar refining, promoted and financed by a system of independent Maritimes banks. But by 1900, Maritimes banks had been destroyed by the expansion of central Canadian banks into the area, draining savings from the Maritimes, and cutting off the financial resources needed for further industrial development. These savings went, not to central Canadian industry, but into building grain production and trade on the Prairies—which would be transported by the CPR.[13]

Thus the industrial underdevelopment of the Maritimes occurred simultaneously with the expansion of staple extraction on the Prairies. Both

trends reinforced the control of central Canadian financial institutions over national economic development, and stunted the potential for self-sustaining industrial growth in the country as a whole. The underde-velopment of Maritime industry, then, is part of the process which kept Canadian capital concentrated in primary resource extraction sectors and in commercial/financial sectors, leaving the secondary manufacturing sector open to the later takeover by American capital, which proceeded to organize regional economies along north-south rather than east-west lines.

In this way, Canada's dependent role in the international political economy defined the range of historical options open to ruling groups within the country. And while differences in interests among regional and sectoral fractions of the ruling class produced conflict over how these options should be carried through, it was working people who bore the real burden of it. The indentured labourers who constructed the railroad, the Indians who were starved off the Prairies to make way for it, the farmers who paid both inflated land prices and freight rates, and the taxpayers across the country who carried the enormous public debt incurred by it—all these people built the Montreal merchants' "national" dream, and shared the price with the Maritime workers who were pushed to the periphery of Canadian development.

At this point in the discussion, we feel it would be useful to illustrate that this dynamic of uneven and dependent development in Canada is not historically unique. Rather, the pattern we have just outlined of the "development of underdevelopment" through shifts in staple production and particular development choices, has many counterparts in the peripheral capitalist nations.

By reference to such parallels, it is possible to define structural similarities in the development patterns of countries outside the major capitalist metropoles. An instructive example in this regard is that of Brazil. Let us explore it, for this contradictory form of development has been fruitfully analysed by Latin Americans with a general approach similar to that which we are suggesting for study of Canadian underde-velopment.

The shift in staple booms from one region to another is a recurring theme of Brazilian economic history. In Brazil, the sequence of booms ran roughly as follows: sugar in the Northeast in the 17th century, gold in the interior province of Minas Gerais in the 18th century, coffee in the Sao Paulo region in the 19th and 20th centuries, and minerals in the Amazon area today. Along the way, there have been other, smaller booms which determined the shape of regional development on a smaller and more temporary basis—rubber and cacao being the most significant of these.

An approach to this case can be illustrated from the first of the booms, the golden era of the sugar plantations in the Northeast. The large sugar enterprises made up "possibly the most profitable colonial agricultural business of all times",[14] according to one observer. Yet the enormous wealth that it yielded to the Portuguese and to a local slaveowning aristo-cracy was short-lived. It never provided the basis for autonomous, self-sustained growth in the region.

When newer and more efficient plantations in the West Indies came into full production at the end of the seventeenth century, they were able to supply cheaper sugar to the European metropoles. The economic structure of the Brazilian northeast, totally reliant on this staple for its prosperity, began to decay.

The inability of Brazilian sugar to compete on the international market after 1700 had a variety of causes. Primary among them was the fact that drainage of profits back to Brazil left the local planter aristocracy with limited capital resources to use in intensifying and modernizing production. The decline of sugar was accelerated by the shift of capital and migration of labour, not into diversification of agriculture in the Northeast, but rather into a gold rush, a new boom, in Minas Gerais. The Northeast itself was left to stagnate on the periphery of the Brazilian economy, to the point where by the twentieth century it had become the poorest region in all Latin America.

The themes of this example are familiar enough to students of Canada. The export of staples to external metropoles, the shifts in staple booms which result in "regional disparities", mass migrations of working people in order to survive—these historical experiences are common among the peripheral capitalist nations, and have their parallels in Canada.

These two sketchy illustrations—the Brazilian Northeast in the 17th century and the Canadian Maritimes in the 19th century—cannot of course be seen as direct and mechanical comparisons. We do not mean to suggest that Canada is a Third World country, nor that the process of underdevelopment in these two countries has been identical.

Yet development and underdevelopment are two integrally related parts of a single global process. Both Canada and Brazil have participated in this process. And it seems clear that to understand how the central or metropolitan capitalist nations have managed to "finance" their growth, it is necessary to study the drainage of human and natural resources from the peripheral capitalist nations of the Third World. In this way, we are led to consider the distorted pattern of growth generated in the world's hinterlands, and to compare them with structures in Canada.

The process of development has particularities in each nation, and these must be considered in their specific historical context. But uneven and dependent growth is an integral feature of international capitalism, and is not unique to Canada.

Section III
Underdevelopment in Canada Today

> "...to build a model of an underdeveloped economy as a closed system is totally misleading. To isolate an underdeveloped economy from the general context of the expanding capitalist system is to dismiss from the beginning the fundamental problem of the nature of the external relationships of such an economy, namely, the fact of its global dependence." [15]

In the case of Canada, the nation's global dependence is primarily defined through its relations with the United States. The main instrument of American control in Canada is direct investment by US corporations. This form of investment can be distinguished from the way that British capital operated in Canada in the last century. British investment largely took the form of loans, or what is technically termed, portfolio investment. The objective of this investment was to obtain high and stable returns on capital without necessarily seeking control. Direct or equity investment of American-based corporations, however, implies ownership and control over the firms themselves, establishing branch plants of American parent companies in Canada. "Unlike loan capital, equity capital is not distant, passive and self-liquidating. It is, on the contrary, present, active and self-perpetuating." [16]

The overall extent of American investment in Canada is exposed by the Gray Report on Foreign Direct Investment in Canada, published by the

Federal government in 1972. The Gray report calculated the share of foreign-owned firms in the profits of all industries in 1968 as 41.3%. The definition of "foreign-owned" firms used in the report simply implied ownership of over 50% by nonresidents of Canada, which effectively ignores the fact that control is often exercised by groups holding far less than 50% of the stock.

The Gray Report shows 81% of total foreign capital invested in 1967, to be US in origin, although in the past few years the share of European and Japanese capital has undoubtedly increased. This investment is concentrated particularly in the manufacturing sector of the economy, where, again according to Gray, it controls 58.1% of total assets, rising to over 90% in petroleum and rubber products. Gray calculates however, that foreign ownership amounts only to 2.7% of assets in public utilities, 12.8% in financial services, 8.9% in transportation and 1.0% in communications.[17]

American domination, then, is not uniformly distributed among all sectors of the economy. While these statistics can vary according to the

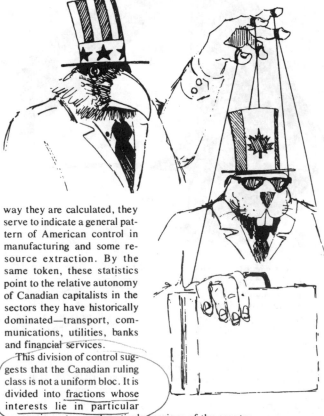

way they are calculated, they serve to indicate a general pattern of American control in manufacturing and some resource extraction. By the same token, these statistics point to the relative autonomy of Canadian capitalists in the sectors they have historically dominated—transport, communications, utilities, banks and financial services. This division of control suggests that the Canadian ruling class is not a uniform bloc. It is divided into fractions whose interests lie in particular economic sectors and particular regions of the country.

In many cases, these divisions do not prevent fractions of the ruling class on both sides of the border from co-operating. A case in point is the mammoth James Bay project, begun in northern Quebec in 1971. Here the Bourassa government is drawing on Rockefeller and Rothschild financing[18] and the bank savings of Canadians in order to generate electricity for the northeastern United States, and to open the region to American and Canadian mining interests like Hanna, Inco and Noranda.

As usual in Canada, the alliance of foreign and domestic banks, foreign and domestic mining corporations, and foreign and domestic utilities, has been co-ordinated through the state. Hydro-Quebec, a nationalized util-

ity, is issuing the bonds which guarantee funds for construction of the project. Meanwhile, government officials have been handling the P.R. necessary to gloss over the displacement of seven thousand Cree Indians, the destruction of the regional ecology, the 22% increase in costs of electricity by 1975 to Quebec citizens, and the increased imbalance of the Quebec economy in favour of resource extraction.[19]

Whatever the divisions among the interests of regional, sectoral, national, and international capital, the substantial conflicts here are with the workers on the project, the native peoples displaced by it, and the consumers who must ultimately pay for it.

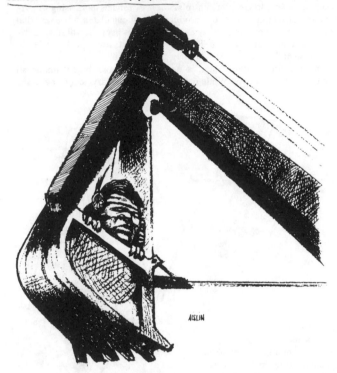

AISLIN

One case in which the divisions among fractions of the ruling class seem to be more significant is that of oil resources in western Canada. There, the major oil multinationals—Exxon, Gulf, Texaco, and Shell,[20] have effective control over Alberta government policy. However, Ottawa continues to respond to different interests, particularly those of industries in Ontario and Quebec which require cheap energy supplies. In this case, the lines are drawn between one region (Alberta), and another (central Canada); between one sector (oil) and another (manufacturing). An irony of little comfort to Canadians is that both Alberta oil and central Canadian manufacturing are largely under the control of major US corporations. These debates over energy taxes, royalties, pipelines, and national petroleum corporations, are revealing a series of divisions not only within the Canadian ruling class, but also between it and the American ruling class.

In Canada, then, we are dealing with a highly complex situation: a heterogeneous ruling class, a heterogeneous working class, a regionally fragmented economy, and a set of contradictory but integrally related roles in the international power system. It is in this context that current debates over dependence and unevenness in Canada can be critically analysed. We would focus attention on the domestic and international class forces behind particular "development projects".

Instructive examples in this regard are the refinery and port at Point Tupper on the Canso Strait of Nova Scotia, and the Sukunka coal mining operations in the Peace River area of British Columbia. In analysing such

projects, we would first consider the relations of the project with Canada's external metropoles—the major or central capitalist powers. In the case of Point Tupper, the corporation in control is Gulf Oil, of Pittsburgh, Pennsylvania, and the crude oil refined (or laundered) on the Canso Strait is destined for the American market. In the case of the Sukunka coalfields, production is aimed at meeting the energy needs of Japanese industry.

Next, we would consider the relations of the projects with Canada's hinterlands—the peripheral capitalist nations of the Third World. In the case of the Point Tupper refinery the crude oil is brought in from Angola, an African territory under armed Portuguese occupation. Canada is the world's largest importer of Angolan oil, bringing in more than two million tons a year—over one third of total Angolan production. Gulf pays taxes on this oil to the Portuguese government and thus finances the war against the Angolan people to the tune of about $50 million a year. Canada's role then, is one of "larceny by proxy"[21] as we draw cheap oil from Angola on behalf of a major American multinational, and finance the colonial occupation of Southern Africa. In this project, the link between American domination of Canadian industry and Canadian participation in the underdevelopment of the Third World is clear.

In the case of the Sukunka coalfields, the major corporate interests involved are those of Brascan (formerly, Brazilian Traction, Light and Power), whose head office is located in the Commerce Court, in the heart of our very own (?) Toronto. Brascan's investment in Sukunka is essentially financed by the enormous profits (nearly $100 million annually) which are drained from its hydroelectric utilities and manufacturing subsidiaries in Brazil.[22] In this way, surplus drawn from a Third World or peripheral capitalist nation is used to extract Canadian non-renewable resources for Japanese industry at an initial projected rate of 2 million tons per year. Once again Canada is linked to the underdevelopment of a part of the Third World in the interests of continued capital accumulation on a world scale.

These examples indicate how two economic mechanisms, trade and investment, operate to the detriment of Third World nations, and the enrichment of certain fractions of the Canadian ruling class. Clearly, however, this pattern of private capital accumulated in Canada is based on the distorted development of Canada itself.

Both these projects reinforce Canada's role in the international division of labour, as a supplier of raw materials, or staples, to more powerful, industrialized metropoles. Both projects will severely disrupt the regional ecology, through the contamination of air and water and the destruction of land. Both are capital intensive projects, and therefore offer relatively few jobs to people in the regions.[23] And, in both cases, as in the James Bay example previously mentioned, crucial financial and political support has been provided by the provincial and federal governments.

In Point Tupper, grants and loans from public funds have provided more than half the cost of the $18.7 million port facilities at the Gulf refinery. Those facilities are to be used exclusively by Gulf. Further infrastructure was built with federal DREE grants. In Sukunka, 40% of the invested capital is to be supplied by the NDP government of British Columbia, which is also assuming the costs of railway and other infrastructural needs.[24] Financing for these projects follows the classic pattern which made possible the completion of the original "National Dream"—the Canadian Pacific Railway—socialize the costs but keep the profits private. In this, as in other respects, it is clear that a major perpetuator of uneven and dependent development in Canada has been the State.

But these two examples, of course, are not unique. A similar pattern recurs in the cases of Canadian-based mining corporations like INCO which has a huge operation in the Sudbury region of northern Ontario, and large holdings in Third World countries—Guatemala and Indonesia.

In fact, INCO is the world's leading producer of nickel and Canada's largest producer of copper. Founded in 1902 by American steel interests, particularly those connected to the Morgan banking empire, it entered gradually into partnership with Canadian interests, notably those around the Bank of Montreal complex. By 1973 more than 50% of shares were

owned in Canada, and the number of Canadian workers employed in the major operation at Sudbury had begun to decline. The corporation is increasing exploration and production in the Third World. Contracts have been signed with the governments of Guatemala and Indonesia, two of the most brutal military regimes in the Third World.[25]

Ownership of INCO is now shared between American and Canadian capital. Ownership of Brascan is shared among American, Canadian and European capital. Ownership of Gulf Oil is almost exclusively American. Yet in spite of nationality, there are similarities to be found in the way all three operate.

One common feature is the heavy reliance of all three corporations on the Canadian state to finance foreign as well as domestic operations. Canadian tax money is funneled to private enterprise at the international level, through a variety of mechanisms—by tying aid, by granting export credits and by insuring foreign investments.[26] In these ways, the federal government's international policies complement the domestic policies of supporting uneven and dependent development at home.

In some cases, these corporate beneficiaries are acting mostly as a "funnel" for other foreign capital in the Third World. In others there is a fairly substantial relative autonomy of Canadian interests. At this international level, then, we again find divisions which parallel the sectoral and regional fractions within the Canadian ruling class previously mentioned. This distinction would need to be analysed in specific cases.

Among the Canadian-based corporations to study in this respect are several in the mining sector, such as Falconbridge (in the Dominican Republic, Namibia, etc.), Alcan (in Jamaica, South Africa, Indonesia, Brazil etc.) Cominco and Noranda. In the manufacturing sector we could look at Massey-Ferguson, Bata Shoes, and Micro-Systems International. In the financial sector we could analyse the operations of Canadian banks such as the Royal, the Nova Scotia and the Commerce, and their associated insurance companies. In the sector of transport and tourism, we could consider the Caribbean operations of Air Canada and the Commonwealth Holiday Inns, or the Latin American projects of Canadian Pacific Airlines and Hotels.

While analysis of these corporations may help to complete the economic picture of underdevelopment in Canada, there are other levels of social process which must be incorporated into any comprehensive theory. Those other levels of social process would include the political, the cultural, and the ideological.

In the course of this discussion, we have touched on a range of political questions. While the full political implications of the economic complexities which we have outlined are beyond the scope of this preliminary working paper, we would suggest specific issues be explored:

1. Canada's foreign policy is heavily dependent on direction from the United States. This political fact is rooted in the economic relations we have previously been describing. Participation of Ottawa in NATO, NORAD, and in defense-sharing agreements, has effectively ceded military control over our territory to the United States, even though

Canada has the distinction of being the fifth largest arms producer in the world, with the highest per capita output of military hardware —quite a record for a peacekeeper.

This effective integration into a continental military machine has repeatedly placed Canada in the position of safeguarding U.S. interests. Canada's role in the International Control Commission in Indochina and in the Middle East peacekeeping forces are two of many possible examples of this.

However, there does seem to be a certain relative autonomy of Canadian foreign policy in areas where U.S. interests are not threatened. One case in point is Ottawa's recent decision to slight a NATO ally by granting humanitarian aid to the liberation movements in southern Africa.

2. In relation to government domestic policies, it would be necessary to study the competition between fractions of the Canadian ruling class for control of the state apparatus. We have already discussed some of the complexities in the debate over oil and energy policy. Also, significant divisions in the class have surfaced over both priorities and patronage in the DREE programme.

A more localized case of struggle for control over the state is to be found in Quebec, where the separatist Parti Quebecois is proposing

social reform and nationalist measures in opposition to alliances of big capital, both Quebecois and English Canadian, merged in support of the Liberal Party.

3. The resolution of many of these contradictions hinges on the potential of the working class to mobilize itself and act on them. Outside Quebec, where cultural unity is building class solidarity, there seem to be many barriers in the way of that potential being realized.

   In large measure, those barriers have their foundation in the fragmentation of the political economy as a whole. Thus contact among different sectors of the working class, in resource extraction, light and heavy manufacturing, and services, has been limited. Similarly, the organization of the economy along north-south lines has restricted contact among different regions. And the division between Canadian and American unions has further militated against class unity. With such a heterogeneous working class, a fully coherent political response to ruling class development strategies has yet to emerge across the country.

4. In a society which operates more by persuasion than by coercion, one of the most difficult and urgent struggles against underdevelopment is at the level of consciousness of ideology. Given the internalization of values and attitudes which reinforce the present structures of uneven and dependent development, critical analytical work is essential if present power structures are to be transformed.

We hope that in the course of further work on these or related issues, people will refine the analytical framework outlined above.

Our approach to Canadian political economy continues to rely on two basic analytical concepts—metropole/hinterland, and class relations. It is in study of these sets of social relations that a dynamic and comprehensive theory can evolve, as an instrument for transforming the present structures of underdevelopment in Canada.

FOOTNOTES

1. This phrase was coined by the economic historian, Andre Gunder Frank. It is taken from his analytical work on Chile and Brazil. Our use of it here is drawn from his book *Capitalism and Underdevelopment in Latin America,* (N.Y., Monthly Review Press, 1969)

2. The term "internal colonialism" has been drawn from Pablo Gonzalez-Casanova's article, "Internal Colonialism and National Development", in *Latin American Radicalism,* I.L. Horowitz, Josue de Castro, and John Gerassi, eds., (N.Y., Random House, 1969)

3. This was perhaps clearest in the case of the Nigeria-Biafra war, during which posters of starving children consolidated the image which many Canadians had of deprivation as far distant from Canada.

4. Herb Gray, *Foreign Direct Investment in Canada*, (Government of Canada, Ottawa, 1972), p. 5.

5. For overall analysis of foreign investment in one West Indian economy, see Norman Girvan, *Foreign Capital and Economic Underdevelopment in Jamaica*, (Jamaica: University of the West Indies, 1971)

6. Among those who have drawn attention to this imbalance in the Canadian economy are Mel Watkins and Jim Laxer. For particular reference, see *(Canada) Ltd. The Political Economy of Dependency*, Robert Laxer, ed., (Toronto: McClelland and Stewart, 1973). This point is also emphasized by Herb Gray, op.cit., p. 6.

7. The view that all classes have a common interest in restructuring relations with the metropoles has been the basis of many populist strategies undertaken by the governments of different Latin American nations. Among those worth mentioning here is the particular case of Peru. The nationalist military regime there has focused public attention on "el imperialismo yanqui" as the major cause of underde-

velopment in Peru while using repressive measures to maintain class inequalities within the country.

8. This quote is from the educational sheets, *The Time is Ripe . . . The Stage is Set . . .*, published by the Development Education Centre, Toronto, 1971.

9. H.A. Innis, "The Fur Trade", in *Approaches to Canadian Economic History*, Easterbrook and Watkins, eds., Carleton Library Series, No. 31, (Toronto: McClelland and Stewart, 1971).

10. See Gary Teeple, "Land, Labour and Capital in pre-Confederation Canada" in *Capitalism and the National Question in Canada*, Gary Teeple ed., (Toronto: University of Toronto Press, 1972)

11. Gustavus Myers, *A History of Canadian Wealth*, (Toronto: James, Lewis, and Samuel, 1972), p. 43.

12. Cy Gonick, "Foreign Ownership and Political Decay", in *Close the 49th Parallel*, Ian Lumsden, ed., (Toronto: University of Toronto Press, 1970), p. 61-62.

13. This analysis is fully developed by R.T. Naylor, in a Ph.D. thesis entitled *Foreign and Domestic Investment in Canada: Institutions and Policy, 1867-1914*, written for Cambridge University in 1973.

14. Celso Furtado, cited by Andre Gunder Frank, in op.cit., p. 154.

15. Celso Furtado, "The Brazilian 'Model' of Development" in *The Political Economy of Development and Underdevelopment*, Charles K. Wilber, ed., (N.Y., Random House, 1973), p. 297-298.

16. Cy Gonick, op.cit., p. 57.

17. See Herb Gray, op.cit., p. 5, p. 22.

18. See Kari Levitt and Jean-Pierre Fournier, "Rio Tinto Zinc to benefit from James Bay Development Project", *Le Devoir*, April 10, 1973.

19. Canadian Association in Support of the Native Peoples, *A Brief Guide to the James Bay Controversy*, (Ottawa: CASNP, 1973), p. 9.

20. Bank of Montreal, *Guide for Oil and Gas Operators in Canada*, (Calgary, Alberta: Bank of Montreal, 1972.)

21. This phrase is drawn from an article by the Toronto Committee for the Liberation of Portugal's African Colonies, "Gulf Oil (Canada) Ltd. and Angola: Larceny by Proxy", in *This Magazine*, Vol. 7, No. 4, January, 1974. Information on the Point Tupper development project is drawn largely from this article, and another by Mike Beliveau, "Canso, Cabinda and the 'We Hurry' Boys: The Gulf Oil Story", in Round One, No. 2, February, 1974. The basis of Gulf operations in both Cabinda and Canso has of course changed a good deal since early 1974, and Angolan crude is no longer processed at Point Tupper.

22. A list of Brazilian subsidiaries, plus details on Brascan's past and present operations can be found in Project Brazil, "The Brascan File", *The Last Post*, Vol. III, No. 2, March, 1973.

23. In the case of Point Tupper, less than 150 workers are employed by the refinery, of whom only 20 are from the Canso region. See TCLPAC, op.cit.

24. Information on the Sukunka Project comes from Brascan submission to the Ontario Securities Commission, microfiche file number 73-14, re "Transfer of Canadian Assets", p. 4, dated October 9, 1973. Plans for Sukunka have changed substantially in 1974, and the future of the project was still unclear at the end of 1975.

25. This information on Inco is taken from *Business Week*, the *Northern Miner*, and annual reports of the company itself. It will be included in a dossier on Inco to be published by the Development Education Centre in February, 1976.

26. Analysis of Canadian aid policy can be found in *Canadian Aid: Whose Priorities?*, a study of Canadian aid projects in Latin America, from the Latin American Working Group, Toronto. Research on trade policy is being undertaken by Project GATT-Fly, an inter-church group located in Toronto. Current information on this subject can also be found in the monthly magazine, *Canada Commerce*, published by the federal department of Industry, Trade, and Commerce. ∎

Discussion/research

1. In the preceding article, it is stated that

> . . . development and underdevelopment are two integrally related parts of a single global process. Both Canada and Brazil have participated in this process.

Do you agree or disagree with this statement? On what basis?

2. Conduct a survey into your area:

a. How many people are working in each of the three major sectors of our economy — primary sector (agriculture, fishing, resource extraction) — secondary (industry and manufacturing) — tertiary ("service" sector).

b. Within each sector, what kind of work is being done?

c. What are the numbers of men and women, old and young, in each of the jobs?

d. What are the popular images of each kind of work?

e. What do people themselves say about their work? Conduct interviews with some people working in your area.

3. Definitions: Gross National Product. What does this term mean? What is a "marginal work force"? What is considered "unemployment"? "Underemployment"? How does Statistics Canada define unemployment? How does the Unemployment Insurance Commission (Employment and Immigration Canada) define unemployment?

4. Technological change: If there is one topic that seems to get people angry faster than almost any other, it is the Post Office. What would you say is the basis for the strong opinions most people have about the Post Office?

a. Conduct a survey of public opinion on the Post Office (cause of the problems, how to resolve them, etc.). Then review the book *Joe Davidson* (by J. Davidson and J. Deverell, 1978 James Lorimer Press).
For the people you interviewed, what were the main issues? For the people in the book, what were the main issues?

'*Modernization, Perkins, means goodbye to long hours, goodbye to working conditions, goodbye to sweated labor . . . in short, Perkins, goodbye.*'

b. After presenting this information clearly, state your own position. (If you are unable to do so on the basis of the information you already have, outline the questions you would need to have answered before being able to state your position.)

5. The workplace: We have certain "images" of old people and young people, but also of workplaces. —What kind of person is appropriate for what kind of setting? *Why?*

Produce a skit about working at McDonald's. (What might happen, for example, if the Canadian cook Madame Benoit found herself working in McDonald's?)

6. The following explanations have been given as the causes for "regional disparity" in the Atlantic provinces. Discuss the validity (or inadequacy) of these explanations of the causes of underdevelopment in the Atlantic region:

a. "The Atlantic provinces simply don't have enough natural resources to generate economic development. Our resource base is too limited."

b. "Too many of our people have left the region in the last hundred years, especially the young, the skilled and the educated. This means we have lost an essential human resource."

c. "We don't have enough businessmen with imagination, ambition and organisa-

tional talents, and a willingness to take risks. We just don't have enough entrepreneurs."

d. "We are a poor region and we cannot solve our problems on our own. We don't have enough local capital to invest in economic development here."

e. "It's our own fault. In general we are not smart enough, ambitious or hardworking enough to generate economic development."

f. "We don't have enough foreign investment. If we could attract more investors from outside, they would give us the economic development we need."

g. "Our local market is too small. There are not enough customers and consumers within the region to support many industries."

h. "We got a bad deal at Confederation. We were against it, and we have suffered ever since."

i. "There is not enough government spending in the region. Ottawa spends millions of dollars to build up the economy of Central Canada but ignores the East."

7. In an essay, discuss the validity (or inadequacy) of one or several of the above explanations of the causes of underdevelopment in the Atlantic region. (Suggested resources: those already listed in this section; and *Canadian Dimension* Vol. 12 No. 2, pp 18-21.)

Survey of opinions

8. On a separate sheet of paper, record your opinions regarding the statements below. Record, for each statement made, whether you (1) agree; (2) disagree; (3) are undecided.

AT LEAST OUR KIDS WILL HAVE JOBS !!!

9. On a separate sheet of paper tally your group's results. For each statement, note the number and the percentage of those who (1) agree; (2) disagree; and (3) are undecided.

a. Most poor people live in big cities.

b. Generally, poor people don't care as much about their children as middle-income people do.

c. Most poor people in this country live in the Maritimes.

d. Usually people in the Maritimes have as many opportunities as everyone else; they just don't take advantage of them.

e. The poor do not really mind bad housing, unemployment and being on welfare because they are used to such conditions.

f. Only about one in 20 families can be considered poor today in Canada.

g. The prices in poorer parts of Canada are lower than in the wealthier regions.

h. Most poor people spend more money on liquor and beer than middle- or upper-income people do.

i. Children in poor regions have practically the same opportunities to make good as the children of middle- and upper-income families in the wealthier parts of Canada.

j. Cape Bretoners are by nature contentious militants.

10. Write the Canadian Council on Social Development in Ottawa for information about poverty in Canada; or review Ian Adams (1971) *The real poverty report,* Edmonton: Hurtig.

There was once a factory which employed thousands of people. Its production line was a miracle of modern engineering, turning out thousands of machines every day. The factory had a high accident rate. The complicated machinery of the production line took little account of human error, forgetfulness, or ignorance. Day after day, men came out of the factory with squashed fingers, cuts, bruises. Sometimes a man would lose an arm or a leg.

Occasionally someone was electrocuted or crushed to death. Enlightened people began to see that something needed to be done. First on the scene were the Churches. An enterprising minister organized a small first-aid tent outside the factory gate. Soon, with the backing of the Council of Churches, it grew into a properly built clinic, able to give first-aid to quite serious cases, and to treat minor injuries. The town council became interested, together with local bodies like the Chamber of Trade and the Rotary Club. The clinic grew into a small hospital, with modern equipment, an operating theatre, and a full-time staff of doctors and nurses. Several lives were saved. Finally, the factory management, seeing the good that was being done and wishing to prove itself enlightened, gave the hospital its official backing, with unrestricted access to the factory, a small annual grant, and an ambulance to speed serious cases from workshop to hospital ward.

But, year by year, as production increased, the accident rate continued to rise. More and more men were hurt and maimed. And, in spite of everything the hospital could do, more and more people died from the injuries they received.

Only then did some people begin to ask if it was enough to treat people's injuries, while leaving untouched the machinery that caused them.

Economic aid

One of the solutions to the problem of underdevelopment has been economic aid of one form or another. Overseas aid has been given to other countries, and within our own country the federal Department of Regional Economic Expansion (DREE) is one example of a donor of "aid" to "poorer" parts of the country. DREE provides grants to businesses starting up or expanding in economically depressed areas.

How does economic "aid" fit into the process of underdevelopment? The following article, entitled *Aid: the new Trojan Horse,* suggests that foreign aid to underdeveloped countries in fact contributes to their continued underdevelopment rather than to their betterment.

Aid: the new Trojan Horse was produced jointly by the Development Education Centre and the Canadian Catholic Organisation for Development and Peace.

ID: THE NEW TROJAN HORSE

anadian government aid programmes in the eloping countries are growing dramatically. In 3-74, funds for official development assistance rose 15% over the previous year. Canadian "aid" often gested as a way to meet the emergency conditions ited by the "widening gap" between rich and poor. le some aid programmes do improve the living ditions of people in Third World nations, their act cannot be understood unless we examine the n "aid". Governments giving "aid" have specific rests which they attempt to protect and further. Aid grammes at present reflect those interests.

ne present way in which aid is offered often hinders development efforts of many Third World peoples. aid which the rich nations "give" to the poor is far n disinterested. This was made quite clear in the t recent foreign policy statement made by the adian government:

t (development assistance or aid) is an important d integral part of the general conduct of Canada's ternal relations, particularly with the developing untries . . . It provides an initial source of financing r export of Canadian goods and services to the less veloped nations and provides Canadians with the nd of knowledge and experience which helps pport the expansion of Canadian commercial terests overseas."

(International Development,
Foreign Policy for Canadians.)

In this next social program, shall we say we support the concept and reduce our role or announce a sweeping reorganization and kill the damn thing?"

In other words, aid is not "given". It usually comes with strings attached. These strings are ways of making sure that the donor governments and the businesses they represent will benefit directly from the aid. This statement may seem harsh, but it is borne out by looking at the history of aid programmes.

a) Background: Aid and the Cold War

After the Second World War, the United States inaugurated the Marshall Plan to help reconstruct the devastated countries of Europe. This plan also had the goal of stopping the spread of Soviet Communism in Europe. During this period, and throughout the Cold War, the West, through its foreign policy, sought to contain Communism in all parts of the world.

It was in this context that Canada instituted its first and largest aid programme — the Colombo Plan. Under this programme, which was started in 1951, the Canadian government allocated over 1½ billion dollars to Canadian and American allies in Asia. Lester Pearson summed up the political goals which lay behind this programme.

"Communist expansionism may now spill over into Southeast Asia as well as into the Middle East . . . If Southeast and South Asia are not to be conquered by Communism, we of the free democratic world must demonstrate that it is we and not the Russians who stand for national liberation and economic and social progress."

Lester Pearson, in *A Samaritan State*

The use of aid as an instrument of foreign policy continued on into the sixties. As former President John Fitzgerald Kennedy explained:

"Foreign aid is a method by which the United States maintains a position of influence and control around the world, and sustains a good many countries which would definitely collapse or pass into the Communist block."

John Fitzgerald Kennedy, 1962.

And, more recently, former Prime Minister Edward Heath stated to the British House of commons:

"There are bound to be some political considerations — there always have been — involved in the use of development aid. The criteria will remain the same."

Edward Heath, 1970

b) Aid as a Political Weapon France/Guinea

The use of aid to "buy allies" can be turned against countries withdrawing from alliances. In this way, France has used aid as a politcal weapon. When Guinea, a former French colony in West Africa chose total independence rather than associate status with France in 1958, the French withdrew their entire aid

"I pledge allegiance to the flag of the country that gives me the best deal."

programme. As they left, they took with them valuable records and statistics on Guinea, and everything from telephones to wire cable.

Had the French really been inspired by humanitarian rather than political or economic motives, the independence of Guinea would not have resulted in such retaliatory measures.

U.S.A./Canada/Chile

A more recent example is the use of aid in the economic blockade of Chile under the elected government of Salvador Allende. During the six years preceding Allende's election the Inter-American Development Bank, (IDB), of which Canada is a voting member, funnelled $190 million worth of credit to Chile. When Allende was elected, he nationalized Chile's major copper mines, until then American owned. The IDB cut off all loans to Chile, and aid from Canada and the U.S. for non-military purposes dried up almost completely.

Allende denounced these actions in his speech to the United Nations General Assembly on December 4, 1972:

"From the very first day of our electoral triumph, on September 4, 1970, we have felt the effects of a large-scale external pressure against us which tried to prevent the inauguration of a government, freely elected by the people, and has attempted to bring it down ever since. This action has tried to cut us off from the world, to strangle our economy, and paralyze trade in our principal export, copper, and to deprive us of access to sources of international funding."

The Canadian government, through its Ex[port] Development Corporation (EDC), vetoed sev[eral] requests from Allende's government for machinery [for] the lumber industry, and spare parts for ot[her] industries. Only after Allende was killed in the blo[ody] coup of September 11, 1973, did the EDC agre[e to] finance the purchase of $5 million worth of Cana[dian] aircraft and parts to the new military regime. [And] within months of the coup, the IDB pledged $[?] million to the new military rulers.

Just as Chile was unable to defend its interes[ts in] the face of political pressure from the more pow[erful] nations, other Third World nations have been unab[le to] resist the influence which the rich exert through [their] aid programmes.

In this context, we should have the greatest res[pect] for governments of countries like Tanzania who h[ave] done all they could to refuse aid which has ult[erior] motives. President Nyerere has said:

"Those who give loans . . . must do so because [they] wish to take part in man's human development [not] because they wish to control our young s[tate?] Tanzania is not for sale."

c) Aid as an Economic Instrument

More subtle than the political strings on aid ar[e the] economic ones. Eugene R. Black, a former Preside[nt of] the World Bank, an international lending agency, explained how aid promotes the business [and] commercial interests of the donor countries [and] particularly those of the U.S.

Humpty-Dumpty world-view

"The question is," said Alice, "whether you **can** make words mean so many different things." The question is," said Humpty Dumpty, "who is to be master. That is all."

The North-South Dialogue encourages certain forms of foreig[n aid] but not others. Is this "aid" really aid? For that matter, is the dialo[gue a] dialogue? Perhaps buried in the Brandt Commission report is the [rea]son why Australia and New Zealand are part of the "North", [while] other countries, which also were once called **colonies**, are still p[art of] the "South".

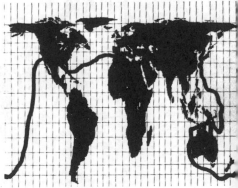

Map on cover of the Brandt North-South report. Subtitle of the report is "A Progra[mme] for Survival".

oreign aid provides a substantial and immediate arket for U.S. goods and services; foreign aid imulates the development of new overseas markets r U.S. national companies', foreign aid orientates ational economies towards a free enterprise system which U.S. firms can prosper."

)A

he same principles apply to Canadian aid pro-ımmes, which are primarily administered through Canadian International Development Agency)A). See Strategy for International Development peration 1975-80 Information Canada No. E94-975.

lanadian aid to the developing nations is not nply a gift, and CIDA should not be regarded as a aritable body." (Paul Gerin Lajoie)

ıteral Aid

ur bilateral aid programme, which channels money ı the Canadian government to governments in the d World, stipulates "that recipient nations must at least two thirds of the aid to buy goods and ices produced in Canada." That is, bilateral aid is

Most of the money never actually leaves the ıtry but is funnelled directly to Canadian ınesses to pay for the goods and services needed in "hird World.

ferring to the bilateral aid programme, Mr. Gerin-ie said:

Ve know that 80-90% of this money is currently ing spent in Canada on Canadian goods, mmodities and services . . . 7,564 contracts have en placed with Canadian firms in the past three ars."

March 12, 1973

ıe aid which is said to be of primary help to the ient country is more often than not conditioned so it acts primarily as a stimulus to growth in the ır country.

rough this type of aid recipient nations are forced ıy goods and services from sources which are not

ONCE UPON A TIME THERE WAS TEA, SUGAR, FLOUR, RICE, POTATOES, MEAT, COFFEE . . . .

Chris Welch, Introduction to Chile.

"I'll give to you and you'll give to me and true international love will blossom."

— John Crosbie, as Finance Minister on CBC Food Show 25 Mar 79

necessarily the cheapest ones available. For example, in 1971 Canada lent Botswana $20 million to construct hydroelectric facilities and finance the purchase of Canadian turbines, generators and transmission line. In the following year Botswana was forced to borrow a further $10 million to meet the increased costs of the Canadian equipment.

Tied Aid

Tied aid also forces Third World nations to use the costly services of technical personnel from the donor nation. These consultants, engineers, architects, etc. are paid at the rates which prevail in their home countries. This means that a disproportionately large amount of aid granted is returned to the donor nation via its personnel. To look again at the Canadian case, out of CIDA's total official development assistance of $431 million in 1971-72, $77 million was paid out in professional fees. This figure does not include the amount spent on maintaining overseas volunteers in these countries.

EDC

Another arm of the Canadian government involved in lending money to other countries is the *Export Development Corporation. (EDC)* The EDC, a corporation owned and operated by the Canadian government, was established to increase Canadian exports by lending money to foreign buyers. Such loans are tied to the purchase of Canadian goods. Although it might appear that the EDC is helping to finance companies in the Third World which are badly in need of capital, a closer look often reveals that those corporations which receive loans are simply subsidiaries of Canadian or American firms abroad.

A particularly noteworthy example of EDC loans to Canadian based corporations in underdeveloped countries was the recent loans to Exmibal of Guatemala and P.T. International Nickel of Indonesia. Both companies received $17 million from the EDC. Both are controlled by the International Nickel Company of Canada (INCO), based in Toronto. While Guatemala and Indonesia got the machines and the debt, Canadian companies got the contracts to produce the machines and the taxpayers put up the money.

Multilateral Aid

Canada's *multilateral* aid programme funnels development assistance through international institutions such as the World Bank, the International Monetary Fund, the Inter-American Development Bank and various United Nations organizations like the Food and Agriculture Organization (FAO). "Multilateral aid is mediated through such international bodies rather than being arranged directly between two governments."

Multilateral aid could lessen the economic and political constraints on aid and allow for more flexibility than does bilateral aid. However, most of the multilateral agencies are controlled by the donor nations. While their policies may not simply represent the interests of an individual donor, they do represent the overall interests of the rich, industrialized nations rather than those of the recipient nations.

a) The World Bank

The International Bank for Reconstruction and Development, or the World Bank, is an example of this. Control is determined by the amount of money a country puts into the Bank. Thus the U.S. and the U.K. have more voting power than all the underdeveloped countries put together. Furthermore, the president of the World Bank has always been an American, thus further ensuring American control over the Bank's priorities.

India

This is clearly seen in the case of India which had difficulty in obtaining a World Bank loan in the mid-fifties. The Bank insisted that, as a pre-requisite for obtaining credit, India had to abandon restrictions it had placed on foreign participation in its economic development. India at first refused, in an attempt to maintain some control over its own economy. However, when its foreign debt began to rise dramatically, India was forced to agree to the terms of the World Bank loan and open up the most profitable sectors of its economy to foreign capital. In this way a loan which was originally sought as aid eventually turned out to be an instrument whereby foreign investors could make profit from an already poor country.

Argentina

A more flagrant example of the way in which the World Bank conditions its "aid" is seen in Argentina. In 1967 the Bank insisted that Argentina dismiss 70,000 railroad workers to curb inflation before authorizing a loan to the country.

"The World Bank is not a 'development institution' its primary goal is the maintenance of economic stability, a pro-western outlook in the government underdeveloped countries and the preservation of present international trade and investment relati ..."

Bruce Nissen, "Building the World Ba

b) The International Monetary Fund (IMF)

The IMF offers temporary relief from immedi debts or lack of foreign currency with which to goods. It does this by making new loans, re-schedul old loans, and supplying credit for the importatio consumer goods. The IMF has enormous power as international credit agency. This power over underdeveloped countries in particular, lies in th economic weakness and need for foreign exchange.

The IMF encourages foreign investment encouraging governments to impose policies like a strike legislation, tax benefits to foreign corporati and guarantees that profits will not be prevented f leaving the country. The Fund also demands t governments cut inflation by drastically reduc "non-productive" programmes like health, welfare, housing. These are the kinds of specific measures wl a country must implement if it is to receive tempor relief from the IMF.

While these conditions make the investment and l climate better from the point of view of the Fund, t have drastic effects on the local people. They lea large increases in unemployment, and the failur small, local businesses which cannot compete with larger foreign companies.

Indonesia

A case in point is that of Indonesia. After the mili coup of 1965, the regime accepted the conditions wl the IMF attached to its loans. As a result of this, a l number of native industries were forced xo close de because of competition from foreign (mostly Japan

I'll give to you . . .

Bilateral aid: Funds are tied to the purchase of Canadian goods (at least 80%) as well as governed by a regulation stipulating that 66⅔% of all goods procured under the programme must be Canadian. Therefore, in 1971-72, of all CIDA funds, 70% ($260 million) were spent on Canadian food, commodities, machinery and technical services.

— from "Feature: bulk of aid spent in Canada" Information Division of CIDA, March 1973.

s imported on credit. Many people consequently heir jobs. In 1968, 20,000 government employees fired in order to cut back government spending. ew debts which the military took on in accepting MF's "temporary relief" were so large that one ess magazine warned:

e Indonesian economy has won a reprieve from kruptcy but can expect eventually to be strangled ts foreign liabilities just after the economy starts et off the ground after the present five-year plan Do donors really intend to force Djakarta into kruptcy in the long run?"

Far Eastern Economic Review, June 4, 1970

er Multilateral Institutions

tilateral institutions such as the various agencies United Nations present an alternative to the type disbursed by the IMF and the World Bank. Third l nations do have better representation in such ies as the Food and Agriculture Organization but budgets remain restricted and aid through agencies is often confined to emergency relief. ermore, the influence of the rich nations in U.N. ies is still very significant as they are the largest cial contributors to the international organi-.

reen Revolution: A Case in Point

of the most highly publicized aid programmes in years has been the "Green Revolution". This

programme concentrates on improving food crops through the introduction of new, high-yielding strains of wheat, rice, and other grains. These "miracle" grains are dependent on heavy applications of fertilizer and carefully controlled irrigation to be successful. The approach is a product of Western technology — researched, developed, and applied by the Rockefeller and Ford Foundations. It is presented as a package to farmers in the Third World, and has been applied from Mexico to India.

The problem with this approach is that it is expensive and therefore only wealthy farmers can obtain the credit necessary to become "Green Revolutionaries". This leads to poorer farmers being forced off the land into employment as poorly paid rural labourers or becoming part of the mass of unemployed in the already over-crowded urban slums. One recent report indicated that in 1969, at the height of the optimism over the Green Revolution approach to the food problem, there were 40,000 eviction suits filed against poor farmers in the Indian state of Bihar and double that number in the state of Mysore.

This high-profile project, in which foreign aid has played an important part, has worsened the pattern of land distribution in the Third World. It has increased the amount of land held by the already wealthy and has benefitted those regions already most developed by increasing their crop yields. At the same time, the poorer areas have been neglected for lack of the funds needed to implement the imported solution. The Green Revolution has thus contributed further to the distorted development and the imbalanced distribution of land where it has been applied.

"Aid only" as a solution to the hungry people in the Third World, can create more problems. Famine continues on in places like India and Bangladesh where the project was most enthusiastically applied. Given this record, it must be said that the Green Revolution failed to attack the roots of the problem of hunger in the Third World. It was the rich man's solution to the poor man's problem.

Military Aid

"The assurance of stability, which depends in part on adequate training and equipment of security forces, is a pre-requisite for balanced economic and social development."

Paul Martin, Canada's Former External Affairs Minister

A major proportion of aid to the Third World is for military purposes. Frequently in the press, there are notices of major arms sales to poor countries, most of which are financed with loans or grants considered to be foreign aid.

Military shipments used to be a major part of Cold War politics, but now are aimed at combating local unrest and "subversion" from within poor countries. In the years immediately following World War II, the United States and Europe perceived the Soviet Union as the major threat to their military and economic interests. However, the fall in 1959, on Cuba's Bastista regime, a major recipient of U.S. military support, prompted a major policy shift. It indicated that the desire of people within Third World countries for basic redistribution of land, income, and resources, represented a threat to the interests of the industrialized countries.

"The basis for military aid to Latin America abruptly shifted from hemispheric defence to internal security, from the protection of coastlines and from anti-submarine warfare to defence against Castro-Communist guerrilla warfare."

Edwin Lieuwen, "The Latin American Military"

Given this shift in policy, the United States has allocated a large proportion of aid funds to strengthening military and police forces in Third World nations where its interests are greatest. For example, between 1950 and 1969, Latin America received $1,357.2 million in military assistance whereas Africa, which has far less U.S. investment, received $325.2 million. These amounts were, of course, far exceeded by the amounts spent in Asia, where the Americans were actively involved in several areas of conflict.

Throughout the Third World, there has been a wave of military coups, since the early 1960's. Today, the military governments in Asia, Africa, and Latin America far outnumber the civilian ones. This growth in the number of military regimes is not unconnected to the boom in arms shipments and military training from the industrialized countries.

Military aid incorporates the worst features of foreign aid as presently structured. The money hardly ever leaves the donor nation, as it is spent on defence production. Military aid perpetuates technological and political dependence and does little to further the real development of Third World peoples. It often maintains an unjust and repressive status quo and makes it difficult for the poorest people to make their demands heard without fear of harsh reprisal.

Conclusion

"Oh miserable citizens, what is this great madness?
Do you believe that the enemy has sailed away?
Or do you think that any gift of the Greeks lacks deceit?
Is that what Ulysses is famous for?
Either the Greeks, shut in, are hidden in this wood,
Or this machine was built against our walls,
To look into our homes,
And to come upon the city from above,
Or some deception lies hidden.
Do not trust the horse, Trojans,
Whatever it is, I fear the Greeks even bearing gifts."   *Aeneid, Virgil, 36 B.C.*

Much of what is now called "aid" is little more than a cover for commercial and political interests in the Third World. Recent years have seen a sharp increase in the amount of aid flowing from the rich nations to the poor. However, in the same years the gap has continued to grow between the developed and the underdeveloped worlds. Aid as it is now offered makes the countries of the Third World more and more *dependent* upon the donor countries, while not confronting the basic problems of illiteracy, malnutrition, social inequalities, disease, and unemployment.

If aid programmes are to be truly meaningful, they must be far more than instruments of the rich nations' economic and political interests. For aid to be truly humanitarian, it must be based on a principle of sharing of the world's resources and the ability to utilize them. They must be based on a principle of *partage* (or sharing) in which the coercion of the weak by the strong has no place. This sharing, of course, involves more than charity. For aid programmes to encourage

. . . and you'll give to me

"The inflation figures also conceal the polarization: the price of *feijoa* (the staple black bean) rose 400 percent in 1973 as a result of a blight and the increased production of soya beans for export; potatoes rose 300 percent in the same period; and milk is unavailable because cows were slaughtered for beef to export."

— Halliday and Moulineux, "Brazil: the underside of the Miracle" *Ramparts* Apr 74.

"For every $1 that the US contributes to international financial institutions that give aid, the recipients spend $2 to buy goods and services in the US. For every $1 paid by the US into the World Bank alone, $9.50 flows into the nation's economy in the form of procurement contracts, operations expenditures and interest payments to investors in the bank's bonds."

TIME magazine, 26 Mar 79

development in the Third World, must not be si ways of exporting our surplus goods. We must reco] that many models of development exist in the 7 World.

As people concerned about development and s justice we need to confront inequalities at hom(exploitation abroad which have allowed to the pr our "high standard of living". In doing so, w(discover common interests and common needs those expressed by Third World people. Ther relations with the Third World are those of partner common struggle. ∎

Checklist on development

What is a developed country and what is an underdeveloped country? This checklist suggests a framework with which you can study other countries and our own.

Social

What are the social aspects of life in the country? What conditions exist in the following areas:

Health: What types of illnesses are most common? Diseases? What health care infrastructure is there?

Housing: What types of housing are most common? Are they available to both rural and urban dwellers?

Education: What is the rate of literacy? What percentage of the population goes to school? How many finish school? Is the curriculum appropriate?

Nutrition: Is the country self-sufficient in food production? What are its staple foods? Does it produce cash crops or food for human consumption?

Employment situation: What kinds of work do people do? Are many people self-employed? What is the rate of unemployment? Underemployment?

Population: What is the country's size, density, growth rate, life expectancy, infant mortality rate, . . . ?

Economic

What are the characteristics of the economy? What are the critical factors for generating wealth in the country? (e.g. minerals? cash crops, manufacturing industries, service industries?)

Who benefits most from the wealth generated? (e.g. the general population? internal élites? external sources such as large companies? other countries?) What is the Gross National Product? What is the per capita income? Is the country's wealth evenly distributed?

Is there a comprehensive economic program for the country? Does industrial activity fit into the overall scheme or does it tend to be ad hoc? What does the country import and what does it export? Who are its trading partners? What is the country's balance of payments?

Is the technology being developed appropriate for the country?

What is the economic outlook for the future?

Political

Is there a history of colonial domination?

Describe the basis of the political system which exists. Is the country stable politically? What is the extent of popular support for the government? What is this country's position in relation to the "super powers"?

Describe the struggle for independence. What evidence is there of genuine political and economic independence?

Cultural

Is there a healthy local culture? Who participates in it and what forms does it take? How do cultural activities fit in with other aspects of daily life? (e.g. do women participate as equally as men? Does everyone participate?)

Is there any evidence of disruption of traditional cultural values and practices? What has caused this disruption?

What attempts are being made to preserve the cultural heritage?

Based on: CUSO-DEVERIC Schools Project

Conclusions: Where is the "Third World"?

After examining the case studies of Brazil and the Atlantic provinces, is it possible to say "underdeveloped *countries*" exist? What is the "Third World"?

With these two case studies, we have tried to identify some of the major characteristics of underdevelopment. We have seen that *pockets* of underdevelopment exist everywhere — even in a country like Canada, considered one of the richest countries in the world.

Throughout this book, the term "Third World" has appeared in quotation marks. This has been done purposefully — in order to set off the term, to make the reader take notice of the words, and be wary of them. Quotation marks remind the reader that an abstract term like "Third World" is no more useful than the concept it represents.

Just as we must listen for oversimplifications or distortions when we hear that "the average person" does such-and-such, so must we realise that the term "Third World" can make us think that the problem of underdevelopment is somewhere else — far away — instead of being close to home. While convenient and useful, the term "Third World" should not mask reality but help us to understand it better: and the reality is that a great gulf exists between a very few with wealth and the power to make fundamental decisions, and the vast majority — most of us in Canada and the "Third World" — whose lives are affected by these few in control.

It is in this sense that the First and Third Worlds are one and the same system.

"*I don't like 6% unemployment either, but I can live with it.*"

Gloom

After a study of one region of Canada, in some ways the picture can begin to look even more depressing. Where are the solutions? Unemployment, underemployment, large migrations of people from one place to another, abuse of resources, pollution, dependency on outside investment, social ills such as alcoholism — all of these problems seem as chronic here as they do in the "Third World".

Doom

In the *Economic aid* section it was shown how outside "aid" can be like the Trojan Horse — destroying society, but from the inside. Far from improving conditions in a country or in an area of "regional disparity", aid and government incentive programmes usually cost recipients more than if no aid had been given at all.

Money itself is no easy solution to the problem of underdevelopment — whether it is in Canada or in the "Third World".

What to do about underdevelopment

A cynical response to the question of underdevelopment would be to laugh, yawn or say "So what?".

This cynical response assumes that events and conditions surrounding individuals will not affect *them:* "I'll get by somehow and survive on my own. You can bet Number One is going to succeed no matter what." There is not much more one can say to cynics (they usually have all the answers). However, daily newscasts of massive layoffs and rising prices are obvious reminders that the destinies of all peoples are linked. Someone who denies this is doing so against considerable evidence to the contrary.

On the other hand, a naïve response to the situation would be to say "Let's think positively. There's too much negativism these days anyway!" A good example of this kind of

thinking can be found in the slogan seen in the *Chronicle-Herald* Nova Scotia's largest-circulation newspaper: "What will *you* do today for Nova Scotia?" This implies that there are individualistic answers to the huge problems facing the whole of society. It tells you that you, individually, are responsible (or not responsible) for society's problems — and that you, *individually*, are going to have to figure out how to solve them in your own personal life.

"Thinking positively", to our knowledge, has never cleaned up an oil slick; has not preserved farmland from the advance of a highway — whether in Brazil or Nova Scotia. "Thinking positively" has never brought back any industries that have moved to other countries; it has not prevented nuclear accidents; it has not brought back to life miners who have been killed by unnecessary accidents or disease.

However, in itself, thinking positively about problems is *good:* the trouble only comes when people are misled into thinking that

simplistic or individual actions can solve society's problems.

In the Maritimes, in Latin America, Southern Africa and throughout the world there are people who are indeed "thinking positively", in a productive way. Many people of different walks of life — farmers, fishermen, workers, young people, old people — are working to improve conditions in their communities. However, their voices are seldom heard. We never see them in their work.

If you examine the messages of the mass media carefully, you can see how easily the media can misrepresent the lives, struggles, aspirations and hopes of peoples throughout the world. A caricature of a people or an issue, a trivialisation or distortion of their concerns can have enormous impact on the way people understand certain issues, and even how they understand themselves. This is why analysing communication, especially mass communication, is so important.

While there is no one simple answer to the question of what to do about underdevelop-

"A lesson to remember: the development of a country is brought about by the people."

"I always hated those bastards on welfare. . .Now I am one!"

ment, we propose that in your own thinking and research, you try to use the tools for analysis that are included in this book. These "decoding devices" should help you to look beyond the stereotypes, to see what lies beyond them — to *"read between the lines"*.

There, between the lines, a whole world exists. There is a glimpse of it in Chapter VI.

To think clearly. To "think positively". After finding out where your *real* interests lie, then it will be time to work towards solving some of the "world problems" that you have seen affecting your life and your community.

Discussion

1. What are some of the "World Problems" today
— in your own life?
— community?
— Canada?
— the world?

If you had this discussion at the beginning of the book and you recorded it, check back now and see if people's ideas have changed — if some people now put more emphasis on one area than another, or if they see more links between problem areas.

2. Having identified what the problems are, *what are some of the solutions?* You could organise discussion in a debate style for this topic.

Further Reading

Brazil

Report on allegations of torture in Brazil
Amnesty International (1974) London: Amnesty International

Global reach
R. Barnet and R. Mueller (1974) NY: Simon and Schuster

Let me speak!
Domitila Barrios de Chungara (1978) NY: Monthly Review Press

"The development of underdevelopment"
Andre Gunder Frank (1966) *Monthly Review* Vol. 18, No. 4

Cruel dilemmas of development: twentieth-century Brazil
Sylvia Hewlett (1980) Basic Books

Index on Censorship
especially Vol 8/No 4 on Brazil; Bi-monthly, $18/yr indiv.; 205 East 42nd Street, New York N.Y. 10017.

Latin American and Caribbean Labour Report
Latin American Working Group (LAWG) monthly, $7/year indiv. Bulk
orders available; P.O. Box 2207, Stn. P, Toronto, M5S 2T2

LAWG Letter
Bi-monthly, $10 indiv.

**Population Target: the political economy of population control in
Latin America**
Bonnie Mass (1976) Toronto: Latin American Working Group

Report on the Americas
North American Congress on Latin America (NACLA) 151 West 19th
Street, 9th floor, New York, NY 10011; Bi-monthly, $13/year indiv.

The Atlantic Provinces

**Of dust and time and dreams and agonies: a short history of
Canadian people**
Pat Bird (1975) Toronto: Canadian News Synthesis Project

**Paradises in the sun: tourism in Prince Edward Island and the
Caribbean**
Mary Boyd (1976) Toronto: Inter-Church Committee for World
Development Education

Round One
Development Education Resource Services (DERS) pamphlets,
c/o 5803 Cunard Street, Halifax, Nova Scotia, 75¢ copy. #4 Nova
Scotia versus Big Gypsum; #5 Point Tupper: the price of development;
#5 New Forest in Nova Scotia; #7 Farmers, Feds and Fries: potato
farming in the Saint John valley. (Several other relevant pamphlets are
out of print but may be available through the public library: issues on
Tourism in PEI, Michelin Tires, etc.)

**Out of work: why there's so much unemployment, and why it's
getting worse**
Cy Gonick (1978) Toronto: James Lorimer & Co.

Resources and development in Newfoundland
Sean MacCutcheon (1975) OXFAM Centre, 382 Duckworth Street,
St. John's, Newfoundland.

**Work and technological change: case studies of longshoremen and
postal workers in St. John's**
Brian O'Neill (1981) St. John's: NAFE-TEN DAYS committee,
PO Box 2252 Station C, St. John's

Now that we've burned our boats ...
People's Commission on Unemployment in Newfoundland and
Labrador (1978) St. John's: Newfoundland and Labrador Federation of
Labour

**Regional disparities: why Ontario has so much and the others can't
catch up**
Paul Phillips (1978) Toronto: James Lorimer & Co.

Audio-visual
Brazil

Except where otherwise noted, the following resources are available
through the DEVERIC Lending Library and other similar lending
libraries across Canada.

BRAZIL: The price of a development miracle
(20 min. slide/tape show)

Dependency by design: the roots of colonialism in Latin America
(20 min. slide/tape show)

Controlling interest
(16mm colour film 45 min.)

BRAZIL
CBC *Ideas* series, March 1980. Requests should be made to CBC
Radio.

Land: a new priority
(16mm colour film 50 min approx) Requests should be made to the
National Film Board.

Atlantic provinces

Farming on the Margin: agriculture in Nova Scotia
(20 min. slide/tape show)

Finest Kind: the 1939 Lockeport, N.S. Lockout
(30 min. video tape)

Inshore/offshore: the Atlantic fishery
(20 min. slide/tape show)

The Steel Show: Sydney Steel
(20 min. slide/tape show)

**Worlds without Work: unemployment in Newfoundland and the
Third World**
(20 min. slide/tape show) Requests should be made to the St. John's
OXFAM Centre, 382 Duckworth Street, St. John's Nfld.

VI. Do not adjust…

Chapter VI: Do not adjust . . .

Communication and modern world problems

Communication and Modern World Problems

Having examined with a critical eye our main sources of information — the mass media — there now must be mention of some of the other sources of information that do exist. Information gleaned and analysed from these other sources, in addition to what you can judge to be truthful in the mass media, will allow you to come much closer to understanding what is really going on in another part of the world or in your own community.

This chapter ends with a list of information sources to explore when you work on other issues in the future. The list should become quite literally "open-ended": it should be added to as you encounter new information. It should also assist you in developing a method of looking critically at the things you encounter in everyday life. By knowing how to separate fact from opinion, how to recognise faulty reasoning or appeals to bias or prejudice, you should be prepared to act intelligently in everyday life, on the basis of independent thought. We think people's ability to do so is an indicator of true democracies and truly advanced civilisations.

And, while we may speak of "modern world problems", the point is to work towards *solutions*. For this work, the Further Reading and Resources sections, as well as other references in the book, could be starting points.

1. The analysis

Is there such a thing as the "plain truth", or are there only hundreds, even thousands of equally valid interpretations? Is everything relative?[1] This book has encouraged you to develop a healthy scepticism towards all sources of information. But does this fact mean that, in the final analysis, individuals are left with *no* reliable information with which to form judgments? Does this mean that everything remains forever suspect and open to question?

There are many people who have held such a view, including eminent scholars, playwrights and scientists. A number of them have chosen the same image to describe their process of discovery. According to their view, we study a person's character, a particular mystery, an historical or present-day event

'Heads we believe the research study, tails we don't.'

from many angles and varying depths. Each new discovery is described as being one more layer peeled off an onion. We keep peeling, delving further into our subject, peeling off more layers and coming closer to the centre. And yet as we go further and deeper, it seems that we know less and less. In the end, we have nothing, for there is no core to the onion. The onion has vanished.

We propose a different view. Rather than using this metaphor to describe the process of investigation, we suggest that a more satisfactory one is the oscillating line — originally introduced by the French historiographer Henri Marrou.

We begin at the surface of a question, with a preliminary working hypothesis. Next, we submerge ourselves, as it were, in the empirical evidence, "les réalités". Re-surfacing from this stage of the research, we (i) examine our initial working hypothesis and (ii) propose a new one (hypothesis xy). If our first one was basically sound, our new one will be a modification of the first. If not, we will start with another, and try again.

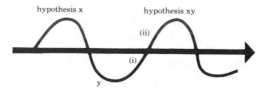

Then, going back to our sources, we will find further basis for our theory, or for a slightly different one. So, as a given problem is studied in greater depth, we will in fact come closer to a correct understanding of it. The

process could continue forever — for knowledge is never static or definitive, but is a progression. Yet just as surely as our hypotheses will become more refined if we follow the method properly, so we will approach more closely the truth.

Marrou's view of historiography (the writing of history) is, in our view, an extremely important contribution to the history of thought — a "quantum leap" from the generally accepted understanding of the "scientific method".

We hope it receives wider discussion and application.

We can affirm, then, that there does exist such a thing as "the truth". The path leading toward it may be long and difficult — occasionally resembling more closely a labyrinth or mine field than a path. It is perhaps arrogant to think that anyone could ever actually reach the end of the path and find "The Truth". As long as you live, however, you will be on some path.

We should like to end the *analysis* part of this book with the following statement about "objectivity" in the field of journalism:

> If one man argues one way, we seem duty bound to get somebody, whether he's right or wrong, who will argue the opposite. They balance each other off, and leave the impression that the truth lies somewhere half-way in between. The method is misleading in most cases, because truth is where it is and not between anything.

Essay

"Every nation has the government that it deserves."
— Joseph de Maistre (1754-1821), Letter on the subject of Russia, 1811.

Discuss.

Postscript: the experience

This book has been about analysis. It will be successful to the degree that you are able to make good use of the methods and information presented in it — to "read between the lines" of any communication; to sort out what is fact, what is opinion; and to distinguish between what is true and what is untrue.

The success will be seen in how people deal with each other in their daily lives, as well as in how they handle any of the more specialised areas of "current events". The content of this book cannot be tested like others; cannot be "crammed for" just before the exam.

Because we live in North America, however, our careful thinking and independent research often seem to uncover only *bad news*. We may learn, for example, that such-and-such causes cancer; that so many people's health and lives are endangered by such-and-such; that the *real* motives of a person or company we once respected are in fact very questionable; that our needs and even our self-image are manipulated by advertisers and marketing experts. We have seen that the poor and the powerless are seldom granted the dignity of presenting their side of the story, on their terms, in their way.

Your priorities in life determine whether you consider certain news good or bad. It takes work — and it can be very hard —to determine what your view of the world is. It can be even harder to know where your *real* interests lie. And only you can discover this.

In the next few pages, however, we hint at what you might find if you were to explore the culture of other peoples, if you were to hear the voices of others, in other places, nearby or far away. You might agree with us that the wealth, depth and keenness of their expression would be comparable to our own (if indeed we knew it well . . .). We hope, finally, you will agree with us that there is another side to the story. One has only to want to hear it.

TOUCH

When I get out
I'm going to ask someone
    to touch me
    very gently please
    and slowly,
    touch me
    I want
    to learn again
    how life feels.

I've not been touched
for seven years
    for seven years
    I've been untouched
    out of touch
    and I've learnt
    to know now
    the meaning of
    untouchable.

Untouched — not quite
I can count the things
that have touched me

One: fists
At the beginning
    fierce mad fists
    beating beating
    till I remember
    screaming
    Don't touch me
    please don't touch me.

Two: paws
The first four years of paws
    every day
    patting paws, searching
    — arms up, shoes off
    legs apart —
    prodding paws, systematic
    heavy, indifferent
    probing away
    all privacy.

I don't want fists and paws
I want
    to want to be touched
    again
    and to touch,
    I want to feel alive
    again
    I want to say
    when I get out

Here I am
please touch me.
    — Hugh Lewin, imprisoned 7 years, South Africa

I CAME BACK.

No God, Its not the same.
The Black child is.
His her face.
His her pearly teeth.
His her knotted kinky hair.
His her "not you elder!"
and the games they play are different.

Now three jumps,
back to back,
side to side,
Three this way.
No, three that way.
God, what's going on.
I was away "only" ten months.

Three this way,
into squares like remote control
that reminds me
of the electric button
that switched the steel door
into my oblivion
only this time
three or two Black children played
a new game.

God. I came back.
Days I gave up.
My living grave
my death.

Four walls and the keys
rattle into steel doors
into grill gates
into four dirty walls
dirty stenchy grey blankets.
And eternal toilet.

God. Am I back.
To the Black child
forever at play in the streets
and to touch his Amazon-like
crop of hair as though viewed from the sky.
But what had I done.
Black child tell me. Please.

God. I want to relove
this child for ten months in retrospect,
twenty four hours 281 days
dark months of brutality.
How many kisses of love to the day
I would have smothered
like I have seen other
fathers do.

And torture Black child.
I loved you through it all.

God. I'm back.
              2nd after detention. 2:30 p.m.

— *Molefe Pheto, South Africa, detained 281 days, 271 of them in solitary confinement.*

BOY ON A SWING

Slowly he moves
to and fro, to and fro,
then faster and faster
he swishes up and down.

His blue shirt
billows in the breeze
like a tattered kite.

The world whirls by:
east becomes west,
north turns to south;
the four cardinal points
meet in his head.

     Mother!
Where did I come from?
When will I wear long trousers?
Why was my father jailed?

— *Oswald R. Mtshali, South Africa*

These poems are anonymous. Their authors are prisoners in the Penal de Libertad (Free-dom Prison, as a betrayal of language would have it), the main prison for political offenders in Uruguay. They were written on cigarette papers and have been smuggled out of the concentration camp.
Source: Index on Censorship, October 1980

Nº 5
SI VIERAS
LAS CONTRADICCIONES QUE HAY
EN EL EJÉRCITO
SI HUBIERAS ESCUCHADO
CÓMO DISCUTÍAN
ALFERES, CAPITAN
MIENTRAS ME DABAN

Nº 6
A VECES LLUEVE
Y TE QUIERO
A VECES SALE EL SOL
Y TE QUIERO
LA CÁRCEL ES A VECES
SIEMPRE TE QUIERO

Nº 7
¿ME OÍS?
YO DIJE Q. TE CONOCÍ EU UN
BAILE
QUE NOS PRESENTÓ PEDRO
¿ME OÍS?
YO DIJE Q. FUE DIEGO

Sometimes it rains
and I love you
sometimes the sun appears
and I love you
prison is sometimes
always I love you.

SIZWE BANSI IS DEAD

The theme of *Sizwe Bansi is Dead* reflects the cruel absurdity of repression in South Africa. Sizwe Bansi is a rural black, who, like so many others, comes to the city in search of work so that he and his family may live. But to live he must die, figuratively: since the regulations will not allow him to stay in the city, he is forced to abandon his own identity and assume that of a dead man. The dead man, whom Sizwe and his friend Buntu stumbled across in the street after a night of drinking, had been fortunate enough to possess a pass book with special provisions allowing him to live and work in the city. In South Africa every black over the age of 16 must at all times carry his or her pass book, a sort of internal passport containing information on the bearer's personal and employment history, and stipulating where he or she is entitled to reside. In the play, by stealing the dead man's pass book and assuming his identity, Sizwe is able at least to eke out the subsistence-level existence of a black urban worker in South Africa . . .

The dialogue between Sizwe and Buntu reveals many of the unbearable features of life for a black South African. For example, both must be separated from wives and children . . . Life seems meaningless, and Sizwe says,

'I wish I was dead, I wish I was dead.'

In the course of the play, Sizwe addresses himself to the audience, saying,

'What's happening in this world, good people?
Who cares for who? I am a man.'

For people who do care about the basic rights of others, the Centaur Theatre production of *Sizwe Bansi is Dead* is an informative, entertaining and well-acted performance.

— From a review of Athod Fugard's play, Sizwe Bansi is Dead

Many small bands of Indian people, in the Amazon Basin, have been moved in recent years, to a central area called the Xingu reservation. This approach to dealing with the genocide and other atrocities against Indian people in Brazil, by prospectors and other invaders greedy for Indian land, is the brain-child of two men, the Villas-Boas brothers. Initially, these men had the usual "iron-clad" guarantees from the Brazilian Government, that the Xingu reservation, at least, would not be invaded in any way. However, after many small bands of Indian people had come to the "haven" that the Xingu reservation was supposed to be, the Government of Brazil built a highway through the reservation . . .

This is a pre-highway song that attempts to be the Indian eye view of a man who is about to begin the long trek to Xingu.

David Campbell is a songwriter, poet and singer of Arawak Indian ancestry, who was born and raised in Guyana, South America, and now resides in Canada. — Development Education Centre, Toronto.

XINGU

The red sun rises high
Come rise and go with me
Pack your warishee with all that you can carry

Come, capui, we must go to Xingu
That's what the people say
Leave our river and trees for Xingu
Xingu far far away

We will not last here long
They say that if we stay
Strange men will come here soon
And take our lands away

Come, capui, we must go to Xingu
That's what the people they say
Leave our river and trees for Xingu
Xingu far far away

Will he who takes us there, to Xingu to start again
Like his brothers before him bring us only rain

Come, capui, we must go to Xingu . . .

Today we leave our home for Xingu, far far away,
But one day we'll be strong
We'll rise and fight that day.

Come, capui, we must go to Xingu . . .

— *David Campbell*

ON MY WAY TO WORK

On my way to work
I think of you.
Through the streets of the town
I think of you.
When I look at the faces
Through steamy windows
Not knowing who they are, where they go . . .
I think of you.
My love, I think of you.
Of you, compañera of my life
And of the future,
Of the bitter hours and the happiness
Of being able to live
Working at the beginning of a story
Without knowing the end.

When the day's work is over
And the evening comes
Lengthening its shadow
Over the roofs we have made
And returning from our labour
Discussing among friends
Reasoning out things
of this time and destiny,
I think of you.
My love, I think of you.
Of you, compañera of my life
And of the future,
Of the bitter hours and the happiness
Of being able to live,
Working at the beginning of a story
Without knowing the end.
When I come home
You are there
And we weave our dreams together . . .

Working at the beginning of a story
Without knowing the end.

— *Victor Jara*

Victor Jara was a Chilean poet and musician who died four days after the CIA-backed military coup d'état in Chile in 1973. Before his death in the Santiago stadium, his hands were broken in torture.

Jara used his artistic abilities in support of the working people of Chile. He became a well-known figure during the flourishing of culture and popular movements under the elected socialist government of President Salvador Allende. This song to his beloved compañera *was also a song of love to his countrymen, with whom he was building a new society. It was translated by his wife, Joan Jara.*

To fight for national culture means
in the first place to fight for the
liberation of the nation, that material
keystone which makes the building of a
culture possible. There is no other fight
for culture which can develop apart from
the popular struggle.

Franz Fanon, The wretched of the earth

Those who profess to favour freedom,
and yet deprecate agitation,
are men who want crops
without ploughing up the ground.
They want rain without thunder and lightening.
They want the ocean without the awful roar of
its waters. This struggle may be a moral one;
or it may be a physical one; or it may be both
moral and physical; but it must be a struggle.
Power concedes nothing without a demand. It never
did, and it never will. Find out just what people will
submit to, and you have found out the exact amount
of injustice and wrong which will be imposed upon
them; and these will continue until they are
resisted with either words or blows, or with both.
The limits of tyrants are prescribed by the
endurance of those whom they oppress . . .

Frederic Douglas
Negro slave
August 4, 1857

How can we tell you the size
of our dream?

Today
our Revolution
is a great flower
to which each day
new petals are added.

The petals are the land
reconquered,
the people freed
the fields cultivated
schools and hospitals.

Our dream has the size
of Freedom.

— *Mozambique*

*With the Arusha Declaration of 1967, the govern-
ing party of Tanzania laid down principles of economic and social development that were to build on
traditional African society rather than colonial or neo-
colonial societies. Mass urbanisation, industrialisation, élitism and dependence on foreign investment
and aid were to be avoided.*

*Whether or not this programme is succeeding in
Tanzania is an important question. It is also important, however, to know what thoughts animated the
original movement for economic, social and cultural
independence.*

. . . The growth must come out of our roots, not through the
grafting on to these roots of something that is alien to them. This
is very important, for it means that we cannot adopt any political
'holy book' and try to implement its rulings with or without
revision. It means that our social change will be determined by our
own needs as we see them, and in the direction that we feel to be
appropriate for us at any particular time.

Inherent in the Arusha Declaration, therefore, is a rejection of
the concept of national grandeur as distinct from the well-being of
its citizens, and a rejection, too, of material wealth for its own sake.
It is a commitment to the belief that there are more important
things in life than the amassing of riches, and that if the pursuit of
wealth clashes with things like human dignity and social equality
then the latter will be given priority . . . With our present level of
economic activity, and our present poverty, this may seem to be an
academic point; but in reality it is very fundamental. So it means
that there are certain things which we shall refuse to do or accept,
whether as individuals or as a nation, even if the result of them
would give a surge forward in our economic development.

From the Arusha Declaration, Tanzania

JAMES BAY

Panamerican highway
Through Native land sea to sea

James Bay Hydro-electric scheme
Branch of the same old tree.

Cowboy didn't you hear
A story that's old and true

If you live by the gun
The gun's gonna get you too.

Men of cold blood rape the land, rape her with fire and steel,
Ride over Red man, fish and fowl, break up the ancient wheel
But I want you to know, what you build now will fall some day,
There's a curse on your head, your children will have to pay . . . .

Your great grandfather stole the land, from MicMac, Mohawk and Cree,
Nothing's really changed since then, in the land of the brave and free
And your empire grows, as you build without asking why,
Taking green from the earth, taking blue from the morning sky.

Tall are your towers in the sky, wide are your man-made lakes,
Princes of Plastic did you say, taking is what it takes?
And there always must be, broken lives so your power can grow,
For you're sent from above, and don't reap the sad seeds you sow . . .

Cowboy didn't you hear
A story that's old and true

If you live by the gun
The gun's gonna get you too.

— *David Campbell*

*The Panamerican highway crosses South America (see the Brazil case study, Chapter V).
Many Indian tribes were exterminated in order to build the highway.*

The American Indians are the
original ecologists. The way they lived
for centuries was in total harmony with their
environment. I think the concept of an ecological
balance is relatively new to our own society.

It has a lot to do with respect. Respect for
life. Respect for Creation. If you respect your
own life, you can respect the life of another.

It's easier to ignore the threats posed by the
nuclear power industry if there's nobody you feel
responsible for. I suppose the person who made
it possible for me to focus on this issue was my
son. I want my son to be able to have his own
children without being afraid that the increased
levels of radiation in the environment could cause
them to be born deformed.

We're going to have to think about what we need
and what we want. About what's important.

— *Jackson Browne*

There is a pervading sense of discouragement
and frustration among the people of this country
who feel powerless as individuals to bring about
change. There are, however, ways in which all of
us as individuals can contribute to finding a
solution to this problem.

. . . We can join together to raise the consciousness
of this country to a level where people will no longer
tolerate the tragedies which have taken place.

— *The Doobie Brothers*

These and many other recording artists have organised to oppose nuclear power developments. They are members of MUSE, Musicians United for Safe Energy. Revenues from their album and film, No Nukes, fund pro-solar energy groups.

The liberation of women
does not come through
men making concessions
to women, but through
constant organised struggle
by women, through their
effective contribution at
the political, social and
productive levels.

The Organisation of Omani Women

The colonial policies of the
Spanish fascists destroyed
the civilisation of our
people. Our objective is to
rediscover the progressive
elements in our traditions
and in alliance with the
progressive forces of today,
build a civilisation that
assures the liberty and
the rights of everyone.

— *Polisario*

. . . A people armed with a progressive culture is
a people well along down the road to success in
any liberation struggle.

The liberation process for us has two sides.
We are talking about an oppressed Black people
in this country. We are talking about an oppressed
Black people in Africa, Southern Africa. And
unless the two of us come together to understand
the cultural aspect of our existence as a weapon in
our hands which we can use to advance our cause on
this and the other side of the ocean, then we are
not understanding the struggle which we ought to
be fighting . . . in which we *are* fighting.

— *Mtshane Ncube, Patriotic
Front (ZAPU), June 29,
1979, at a benefit concert
with Bob Marley and the
Wailers*

To Think and Speak

Nobody can live alone. Nobody can
live without communicating with others,
without saying what he thinks, what he
wants, and what he feels.

Parents talk to their children; a
brother to his sister; a boy to his
girl friend.

Nobody can live without thinking,
without feeling, without wanting.

To speak is to think aloud;
to speak is to make others hear what we
think ourselves.

Reading exercise from Guinea-Bissau

Discussion/essay

1. Discuss any one of the following examples of cultural control.

- The régime of the Shah of Iran (1953-79) banned the works of Lewis Carroll (*Alice in Wonderland, Through the Looking Glass*), because they were considered "subversive" and "communist-inspired".

- In South Africa's infamous Robben Island prison, the poet Dennis Brutus titled his works *letters* rather than *poems*, because it was illegal for a banned person to write poetry, though it was legal to write letters.

- In pre-Independence Eire (Ireland) the "wearing of the green" was outlawed.

- In the Maritimes, speaking Micmac or Acadian in some schools was strictly prohibited.

- When slaves were brought to America, they were forbidden to use traditional African drums and other instruments, under pain of beatings and even death.

- After the 1973 military coup d'état in Chile, a traditional Indian musical instrument, the *charango* was banned.

Why would authoritarian régimes think it necessary to control cultural forms of communication?

2. What is the relation between controlling a society and controlling a culture? Who should have control? For what reasons? Who does have control of culture in our society? Give specific references.

3. "An artist might elect to fight for freedom or slavery." — Paul Robeson. Discuss.

4. In the Roman Empire, the ruling emperors made two important provisions for conquered peoples under their control — "Bread and Circuses".

Discuss the meaning and implications of the word "entertainment'.

5. Review one of the chapters of *Them and us in literature* by Paul O'Flinn (1975 London: Pluto).

2. Resources

The ultimate reason for learning and studying about the world is to benefit from its bounty and its beauty, and to contribute to it as well. In order to do this, people must gain control of their own lives. This book has made a start at compiling the necessary tools for critical thinking, with which you can better understand the world.

Only you, the user, can decide to do more than "survive" in this world; only you can carry this work further.

The most important resource is yourself. If you, your friends and the people who share your interests apply the methods of analysis outlined in this unit and take careful notes you will surely have the most valuable tools you will need. The following are some suggestions that can be revised and updated as you make new discoveries.

This list is a beginning. By no means exhaustive, it does however give an idea of the number of centres, groups and publications which you are unlikely to hear about through the commercial media. You are even less likely to find any of the publications in your drugstore or corner grocery.

Because they are, for the most part, community-oriented rather than profit-centred, their perspective can be critical of present structures and trends in our country and world-wide. They are often operated for free by people in their spare time: hence the particular publication listed may no longer exist as you read this (though others will). While of course no one publication is perfect, we can recommend them as very worthwhile sources of alternative information. (Sources recommended in other parts of the book generally have not been repeated.)

This list has an international development focus; it does not indicate the very important, related work of other groups — **labour, native groups, environmental groups, women's** and **solidarity groups, independent film, theatre** and **cultural groups.**

You can make those connections by getting involved in your own community.

Basic tools   Though they are generally not thought of in these terms, there are three things that should be considered as indispensable as radios in most homes. Everyone should have their own **good dictionary** — one with accurate and interesting illustrations and entries. Similarly an **up-to-date atlas** is worth the money it will cost you. There are economic and social atlases, ones that show migration or agricultural or industrial production . . . Knowing the capital cities and where the borders are represents only a tiny part of what you can find out from an atlas. And, you should buy **index cards** and always have them on hand. Why they are so useful is that you can use the information you have noted down on them over again, in different ways. Write only on one side; put one idea or quote on one side of each card. What you hear and see every day *is* worth noting down. Though unglamourous, these are essential tools.

Libraries   Many other basic reference books can be used at the library. Arrange to take a tour of any library you don't already know or use. If you can, arrange to go at times when library staff are not busy. They are a wealth of information. You can consult **encyclopaedias** for articles on your area of interest; **newspaper and periodical indexes** list many major stories covered in the newspapers . . . which you then can look up and read. Libraries should have **Hansard,** the official record of debates in the House of Commons, as well as other government documents and business publications. Even if you live in a rural area, there may be library services which you are unaware of. Write to the one in the community closest to where you live for more information.

Alternative bookstores   Hundreds of books not readily available in commercial stores may be available here. The partial list includes Onion Books in Saskatoon, Liberation Books in Winnipeg, Development Education Centre (DEC) and Student Christian Movement (SCM) Bookstore in Toronto, Octopus Books in Ottawa, and Red Herring Bookstore in Halifax. They take special orders and will mail books to you.

Reports   Government reports, company annual reports, business publications, information from embassies etc. will provide you with the official positions of government and industry. This is an important factor to take into account when researching from a critical point of view.

Subscriptions/newsletters

The following are some of the sources of information which you may find useful.

Alternatives Articles on resource use, pollution, energy, conservation and wilderness. Makes the vital connections between environmental issues and wider issues in Canadian society. Quarterly, $10/year. Trail College, Trent University, Peterborough, Ontario K9J 7B8

Amnesty International publishes extensive research documents on human rights and conditions in most countries in the world. Its annual report summarises country situations and its work throughout the world. A monthly *Bulletin* comes with membership; suggested contribution is $25, subject to your ability to pay. For a list of publications write to P.O. Box 6033 Station J Ottawa, Ontario K2A 1T1

BBC The British Broadcasting Corporation has films and audio-visual resources for rent and sale. Manulife Centre, 55 Bloor Street West, Suite 510, Toronto, Ontario M4W 1A5

CBC Radio news and current affairs shows include Canada Watch, The House, Ideas, Maritime Magazine, Open Circuit, Our Native Land, Quirks and Quarks, Shoptalk, Sunday Magazine, Sunday Morning. CBC television shows dealing with current affairs include the Fifth Estate, Man Alive, the Nature of Things and Science Magazine. Transcripts are sometimes available. Write for the CBC Learning Systems catalogue or the Radio Programme Guide, P.O. Box 500, Station A, Toronto, Ontario.

CCSA Bulletin From the Canadians Concerned for Southern Africa Committee, Box 545, Adelaide Street Station, Toronto, Ontario M5C 2J6

Canadian Civil Liberties Union Updates on Canadian human rights issues. Newsletter comes with membership, $10. 229 Yonge Street, Suite 403, Toronto, Ontario M5B 1N9

Canadian Dimension Features articles with a critical perspective: on labour, women, health and safety, plant closings, food prices, politics, economics. An important Canadian resource. 8 issues/year, $14 ($9 students, $7 pensioners). Suite 891, 44 Princess Street, Winnipeg, Manitoba R3B 1K2

Central America Update An excellent news digest and information bulletin put out jointly by the Latin American Working Group (LAWG), the Jesuit Centre for Social Faith and Justice and the Community Information Research Group (CIRG) 6 issues/year, $8 individuals. P.O. 2207 Station P, Toronto, Ontario M5J 2T2

Connexions supports networks of grass-roots organisations across the country through publishing abstracts from recent publications and descriptions of groups active in the areas

under study. Issues have focused on Militarism, Health, Racism, Women, Atlantic Canada. 5 issues/year, $12, 427 Bloor Street West, Toronto, Ontario M5S 1X7

Dollars and Sense makes the "dismal science" of economics lively and relevant. Technological change, social service cutbacks, trade wars are some of the many issues covered. Monthly, except June/August, $10/year. 38 Union Square, Room 14, Somerville, MA 02145, U.S.A.

GATT-Fly's regular newsletter and mailings highlight important research into Canada as a world trader and exporter, and the role of international financing in world underdevelopment. Topics include Canada's food industry, the national debt, textiles, Order a list of these indispensable resources, and subscribe to the *GATT-Fly Report*, 5 issues/year, $10 individuals. 11 Madison Avenue, Toronto, Ontario M5R 2S2

S. A. RAID INTO MOZAMBIQUE

IDAF The International Defence and Aid Fund for Southern Africa publishes excellent documentation on South Africa, Namibia, Zimbabwe, Angola, Mozambique. Its May/June 80 issue of *Focus,* for example, was one of the few publications to give coverage to the newly independent Zimbabwean government's release of 17,600 of the estimated 22,000 prisoners in that country. Order a catalogue and subscribe to *FOCUS,* P.O. Box 1034 Station B, Ottawa, Ontario K1P 5R1

AFRICA

& ARGENTINA

Index on Censorship is an excellent source of first-hand testimony, reference material on current human rights questions, political and social analysis, and an outlet for actual banned manuscripts. Reports on "East", "West" and "Third World" countries. It includes poetry, prose and essays. Features have included: the Nuclear Cover-up; the Commitment of the Latin American Writer; Count Me Out of the Soviet Writers' Union; Press Censorship in Brazil. 6 issues/year, $18, 205 East 42nd Street, New York, N.Y. 10017 U.S.A.

ICCHRLA Newsletter gives important background on the human rights situation in Latin America, from the point of view of the major Canadian Churches. It reports on public church statements and the results of fact-finding missions to Latin America. 40 St. Clair Street East, Toronto, Ontario M4T 1M9

LAWG Letter Produced by the Latin American Working (LAWG), this publication provides excellent information on such issues as militarism, foreign investment in Latin America, Canadian and other foreign aid. Issues are sometimes country-centred (Peru, Guatemala, Panama) or problem-centred (Economic Relations and Human Rights). Quarterly, $10 individuals. P.O. Box 2207 Station P, Toronto, Ontario M5S 2T2

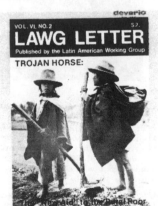

Latin America and Caribbean Labour Report Also published by LAWG, the *Report* monitors trade union issues, and provides invaluable background documentation (e.g., how the Agrarian Reform of El Salvador's President Duarte was used to identify and murder elected leaders in the countryside). Monthly, $7 individuals, P.O. Box 2207 Station P, Toronto, Ontario M5S 2T2

Merip Reports focus on the political economy of the contemporary Middle East, and the role of imperialism, class and national struggles in the region. 9 issues/year, $14. 1470 Irving Street N.W. Washington DC 20010, U.S.A.

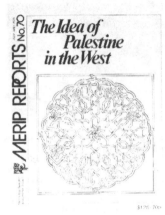

Mother Jones features well-researched exposés on many contemporary issues (e.g. the dumping of chemical, pharmaceutical and technological products on the "Third World"; Inside the Nuclear Industry; the New Rights). Monthly, $15 year. 1886 Haymarket Square, Marion, Ohio 43305, U.S.A.

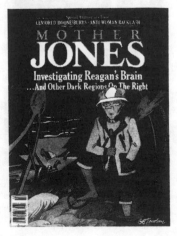

Multinational Monitor provides news and feature stories on the activities of multinational corporations around the world — their impact on society, and what labour and citizens' groups are doing about them. It sometimes has a country focus (Phillippines, Australia, El Salvador) or an issue focus (food production and aid). Monthly, $15/year. P.O. Box 19312, Washington D.C. 20036 U.S.A.

NACLA Report, by the North American Congress on Latin America, provides indispensable research on the political and economic forces at play in Latin America. Well-written articles and beautiful graphics on issues such as: Causes of Jamaican Migration; International Finance; Peru; Argentina; El Salvador: Why Revolution; Roots of Labour Militancy in Peru; Latin America and the Changing World Economy. Monthly, $13/year. 151 West 19th Street, 9th Floor, New York, N.Y. 10011, U.S.A.

NFB National Film Board catalogue films may be borrowed for free. P.O. Box 6100, Montreal, Quebec H3C 3H5

New Internationalist has both "Third World" and "Western" coverage, and a contributing Canadian editor. It is an excellent source of up-to-date information with clear illustrations and photos, and short, readable articles. Monthly, $15/year, 175 Carlton Street, Toronto, Ontario M5A 2K3

New York Guardian is an "independent radical news weekly". As far back as the Korean war and later during the Vietnam war, it gained a reputation as a newspaper that would tell the truth about what was going on elsewhere and at home. Weekly, $23/year. 33, West 17th Street, New York, N.Y. 10011, U.S.A.

Ploughshares Monitor examines Canadian military politics and expenditures, arms sales and other related issues. Original research you will not find elsewhere. You may be surprised to discover the real role of Canada in international militarism. Bi-monthly, Institute for Peace and Conflict Stud-

ies, Conrad Grebel College, Waterloo, Ontario N2L 3G6

Project North is a project of the major churches in Canada. It gathers and circulates up-to-date information on Northern Development and Native Peoples. Designed to provide informed support of native groups in Canada. Write to 154 Glenrose Avenue, Toronto, Ontario.

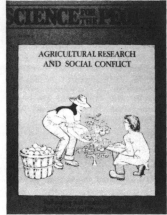

Science for the People is intended for people seeking a "radical and progressive view of science and technology". Special issues have provided excellent information on such issues as technological change, the food industry, the politics of cancer and cancer research. Bi-monthly, $14/year. 897 Cambridge MA 02139, U.S.A.

Southern Africa In addition to providing excellent coverage of political and economic matters, this magazine also examines social issues such as the role of women in newly independent Zimbabwe, and has a poetry section. High-quality photos complement articles of the same calibre. Monthly, except July/August, $10/year. 17 West 17th Street, New York, N.Y. 10011 U.S.A.

Taskforce on Churches and Corporate Responsibility monitors the practices of Canadian corporations, and speaks in shareholders' meetings on behalf of the major Canadian churches (who hold shares in the companies). The newsletter describes corporate activities, and ways in which concerned Canadians can act. *Investment in Oppression: Canadian responses to apartheid* originally published by the YWCA, is an important book to order. $6/year for the newsletter. 600 Jarvis Street, Toronto, Ontario M4Y 2S6

TCLSAC Reports are put out by the Toronto Committee for the Liberation of Southern Africa. They include information and suggestions on ways of showing direct support to popular movements in Southern Africa. Monthly, $15 or $8/year for unemployed people. 427 Bloor Street West, Toronto, Ontario M5S 2X7

This Magazine The title always confuses people ("*What* magazine?"), but it is one of the few in Canada that give a place for teachers to discuss Canadian issues from an analytical as well as practical point of view. Deals with many Canadian and international topics, including labour, art, poetry, reviews, and schools. An important, readable, and thought-provoking magazine. Bi-monthly, $7.50/year. 70 The Esplanade, 3rd Floor, Toronto, Ontario M5E 1R2

United Church of Canada publishes useful background papers on a number of social issues. Its *Issues* series has dealt with Prisons in Canada, Corporate Ownership, Human Rights; the *South Africa Education Project* sends out regular information on South Africa and Canadian involvement there. 85 St Clair Street East, Toronto, Ontario

Information centres/sources

You can write to the following centres for their catalogues and for any newsletters they may have. Many have books, periodicals, films and slide shows that you can borrow.

Arusha Centre
#106 - 223 12th Avenue SW
Calgary, Alberta

Canada-Asia Working Group
11 Madison Avenue
Toronto, Ontario M5R 2S2

Centre Video Educatif
C.P. 124
Bathurst, N.B.

Cross Cultural Learner Centre
533 Clarence Street
London, Ontario N6A 3N1

Cross Cultural Communications
Centre
1991 Dufferin Street
Toronto, Ontario

CUSO Development Education
151 Slater Street
Ottawa, Ontario

Development and Peace
67 Bond Street
Toronto, Ontario M5B 1X5

Development and Education Centre
(DEC)
121 Avenue Road
Toronto, Ontario M5R 2G3

DEVERIC
Development Education Resource &
Information Centre
P.O. Box 3460
Halifax, N.S. B3J 3J1

Global Community Centre
94 Queen Street S.
Kitchener, Ontario N2G 1V9

IDEA Centre
418 Wardlaw Avenue
Winnipeg, Manitoba R3l 0L7

IDEM/DIEM
Development Education Resource
Centre
7017 Sherbrooke Street West, Apt 16
Montreal, Quebec

IDERA Centre
2524 Cypress Street
Vancouver, B.C. V6J 3N2

International Centre
Queen's University
Kingston, Ontario K7L 3N6

International Education Centre
St Mary's University
Halifax, Nova Scotia

Ontario Public Interest Research
Group
University of Waterloo
Waterloo, Ontario N2L 3G1

One Sky Cross-Cultural Centre
134 Avenue F South
Saskatoon, Saskatchewan S7M 1S8

Ottawa-Hull Learner Centre
78 Daly
Ottawa, Ontario

OXFAM-CANADA
251 Laurier Avenue West
Ottawa, Ontario

Scarboro Foreign Mission Society
2685 Kingston Road
Scarboro, Ontario M1M 1M4

Ten Days for World Development
600 Jarvis Street
Toronto, Ontario M4Y 2J6

YMCA International Development
Programme
36 College Street
Toronto, Ontario M5G 1K8

Of interest to educators

The resources already listed might be supplemented by the following.

Amnesty International

Flaws in the pattern: human rights in literature (1978) A resource for Canadian teachers. Includes sections on *Animal Farm, Nineteen Eighty-four, Macbeth;* **Human Rights, Past and Present** (1978) for history teachers. Also prepared by Canadian members, this book contains sections on a number of areas, including the Holocaust, and Canada's War Measures Act. Write to Amnesty International, P.O. Box 6033 Station J, Ottawa, Ontario M4W 1A5

Book and Periodical Development Council

C*ns*rsh*p: stopping the book banners (1978) This is a short, well-documented and practical guide for citizens, especially teachers and librar-

MMMM....
EDUCATIONALLY
EXCITING,
BUT WE ARE
RUNNING A
SCHOOL YOU
KNOW

ians. One page has an incomplete list of books banned at various times and places: *Tom Sawyer, The Bible, Richard II, The Odyssey,* and the *Critique of Pure Reason* figure among others. The editors note that the "it-could-never-happen-here state of mind is a gift of victory to every censor in the land." Write to the Book and Periodical Development Council, 86 Bloor Street West, Ste. 215, Toronto, Ontario M5S 1M5

CUSO

Development Education: How to Do It (1980) A guide designed for the many CUSO committees across the country, but of interest to others as well. For this and other resources, write to CUSO Development Education, 151 Slater Street, Ottawa, Ontario.

OXFAM-CANADA

Land, People and Power: the question of Third World land reform (1977) by Jane Craig. This book discusses the agrarian crisis and three case studies: Guatemala, India and China. Also OXFAM-AMERICA's **El Salvador Land Reform 1980-81 impact audit** (1981), by L. R. Simon and J. C. Stevens. **Perspectives on World Hunger** (1981), by the St. John's, Nfld. OXFAM Committee, is an excellent guide to the central questions in the food and aid debate. Les-

son plans and audio/visual suggestion. Write to OXFAM-CANADA, 251 Laurier Avenue West, Ottawa, Ontario K1P 5J6, or to one of the many OXFAM committees across the country.

Teaching as a subversive activity by Neil Postman Charles Wiengartner (1969), Harmondworth: Penguin

Classrooms of resistance by Chris Searle (1975), London: Writers and Readers Publishing Co-operative

Critical teaching and everyday life by Ira Shor (1980), Montreal: Black Rose Books

Leader's Kits by Ten Days for World Development for the February days of study and action for world development. Write to 600 Jarvis Street, Toronto, Ontario M4Y 2J6

This Magazine, bi-monthly magazine, $7.50/year, 70 The Esplanade, Toronto, Ontario, M5E 1R2

The problem exists in the classroom because it exists in the world, Susan Wayne editor. Toronto: Co-operative Schools Group on Development Education. Write to DEC, 121 Avenue Road, Toronto, Ontario M5R 2G3

Working teacher, quarterly magazine, $5/year, by and for teachers. Box 36534 Station B, Vancouver, B.C. V6R 2G0

Appendices

"*I miss the room I used to live in; I had the
impression of knowing so much more . . .*"

Appendices

For Chapter I:

For Chapter III:

For Chapter IV:

THE UNIVERSAL DECLARATION OF HUMAN RIGHTS

Preamble

Whereas recognition of the inherent dignity and of the equal and inalienable rights of all members of the human family is the foundation of freedom, justice and peace in the world.

Whereas disregard and contempt for human rights have resulted in barbarous acts which have outraged the conscience of mankind, and the advent of a world in which human beings shall enjoy freedom of speech and belief and freedom from fear and want has been proclaimed as the highest aspiration of the common people.

Whereas it is essential, if man is not to be compelled to have recourse, as a last resort, to rebellion against tyranny and oppression, that human rights should be protected by the rule of law,

Whereas it is essential to promote the development of friendly relations between nations,

Whereas the peoples of the United Nations have in the Charter reaffirmed their faith in fundamental human rights, in the dignity and worth of the human person and in the equal rights of men and women and have determined to promote social progress and better standards of life in larger freedom,

Whereas Member States have pledged themselves to achieve, in cooperation with the United Nations, the promotion of universal respect for and observance of human rights and fundamental freedoms,

Whereas a common understanding of these rights and freedoms is of the greatest importance for the full realization of this pledge,

Now therefore, the General Assembly proclaims

This Universal Declaration of Human Rights as a common standard of achievement for all peoples and all nations, to the end that every individual and every organ of society, keeping this Declaration constantly in mind, shall strive by teaching and education to promote respect for these rights and freedoms and by progressive measures, national and international, to secure their universal and effective recognition and observance, both among the peoples of Member States themselves and among the peoples of territories under their jurisdiction.

Article 1

All human beings are born free and equal in dignity and rights. They are endowed with reason and conscience and should act towards one another in a spirit of brotherhood.

Article 2

Everyone is entitled to all the rights and freedoms set forth in this Declaration, without distinction of any kind, such as race, colour, sex, language, religion, political or other opinion, national or social origin, property, birth or other status.

  Furthermore, no distinction shall be made on the basis of the political, jurisdictional or international status of the country or territory to which a person belongs, whether it be independent, trust, non-self-governing or under any other limitation of sovereignty.

Article 3

Everyone has the right to life, liberty and security of person.

Article 4

No one shall be held in slavery or servitude; slavery and the slave trade shall be prohibited in all their forms.

Article 5

No one shall be subjected to torture or to cruel, inhuman or degrading treatment or punishment.

Article 6

Everyone has the right to recognition everywhere as a person before the law.

Article 7

All are equal before the law and are entitled without any discrimination to equal protection of the law. All are entitled to equal protection against any discrimination in violation of this Declaration and against any incitement to such discrimination.

Article 8

Everyone has the right to an effective remedy by the competent national tribunals for acts violating the fundamental rights granted him by the constitution or by law.

Article 9

No on shall be subjected to arbitrary arrest, detention or exile.

Article 10

Everyone is entitled in full equality to a fair and public hearing by an independent and impartial tribunal, in the determination of his rights and obligations and of any criminal charge against him.

Article 11

(1) Everyone charged with a penal offence has the right to be presumed innocent until proved guilty according to law in a public trial at which he has had all the guarantees necessary for his defence.

(2) No one shall be held guilty of any penal offence on account of any act or omission which did not constitute a penal offence, under national or international law, at the time when it was committed. Nor shall a heavier penalty be imposed than the one that was applicable at the time the penal offence was committed.

Article 12

No one shall be subjected to arbitrary interference with his privacy, family, home or correspondence, nor to attacks upon his honour and reputation. Everyone has the right to the protection of the law against such interference or attacks.

Article 13

(1) Everyone has the right to freedom of movement and residence within the borders of each state.

(2) Everyone has the right to leave any country, including his own, and to return to his country.

Article 14

(1) Everyone has the right to seek and to enjoy in other countries asylum from persecution.

(2) This right may not be invoked in the case of prosecutions genuinely arising from non-political crimes or from acts contrary to the purposes and principles of the United Nations.

Article 15

(1) Everyone has the right to a nationality.
(2) No one shall be arbitrarily deprived of his nationality nor denied the right to change his nationality.

Article 16

(1) Men and women of full age, without any limitation due to race, nationality or religion, have the right to marry and to found a family. They are entitled to equal rights as to marriage, during marriage and at its dissolution.
(2) Marriage shall be entered into only with the free and full consent of the intending spouses.
(3) The family is the natural and fundamental group unit of society and is entitled to protection by society and the State.

Article 17

(1) Everyone has the right to own property alone as well as in association with others.
(2) No one shall be arbitrarily deprived of his property.

Article 18

Everyone has the right to freedom of thought, conscience and religion; this right includes freedom to change his religion or belief, and freedom, either alone or in community with others and in public or private, to manifest his religion or belief in teaching, practice, worship and observance.

Article 19

Everyone has the right to freedom of opinion and expression; this right includes freedom to hold opinions without interference and to seek, receive and impart information and ideas through any media and regardless of frontiers.

Article 20

(1) Everyone has the right to freedom of peaceful assembly and association.
(2) No one may be compelled to belong to an association.

Article 21

(1) Everyone has the right to take part in the government of his country, directly or through freely chosen representatives.
(2) Everyone has the right of equal access to public service in his country.
(3) The will of the people shall be the basis of the authority of government; this will shall be expressed in periodic and genuine elections which shall be by universal and equal suffrage and shall be held by secret vote or by equivalent free voting procedures.

Article 22

Everyone, as a member of society, has the right to social security and is entitled to realization, through national effort and international cooperation and in accordance with the organization and resources of each State, of the economic, social and cultural rights indispensable for his dignity and the free development of his personality.

Article 23

(1) Everyone has the right to work, to free choice of employment, to just and favourable conditions of work and to protection against unemployment.
(2) Everyone, without any discrimination, has the right to equal pay for equal work.
(3) Everyone who works has the right to just and favourable remuneration insuring for himself and his family an existence worthy of human dignity, and supplemented, if necessary, by other means of social protection.
(4) Everyone has the right to form and to join trade unions for the protection of his interests.

Article 24

Everyone has the right to rest and leisure, including reasonable limitation to working hours and periodic holidays with pay.

Article 25

(1) Everyone has the right to a standard of living adequate for the health and well-being of himself and his family, including food, clothing, housing and medical care and necessary social services, and the right to security in the event of unemployment, sickness, disability, widowhood, old age or other lack of livelihood in circumstances beyond his control.
(2) Motherhood and childhood are entitled to special care and assistance. All children, whether born in or out of wedlock, shall enjoy the same social protection.

Article 26

(1) Everyone has the right to education. Education shall be free, at least in the elementary and fundamental stages. Elementary education shall be compulsory. Technical and professional education shall be made generally available and higher education shall be equally accessible to all on the basis of merit.
(2) Education shall be directed to the full development of the human personality and to the strengthening of respect for human rights and fundamental freedoms. It shall promote understanding, tolerance and friendship among all nations, racial or religious groups, and shall further the activities of the United Nations for the maintenance of peace.
(3) Parents have a prior right to choose the kind of education that shall be given to their children.

Article 27

(1) Everyone has the right to freely participate in the cultural life of the community, to enjoy the arts and to share in scientific advancement and its benefits.
(2) Everyone has the right to the protection of the moral and material interests resulting from any scientific, literary or artistic production of which he is the author.

Article 28

Everyone is entitled to a social and international order in which the rights and freedoms set forth in this Declaration can be fully realized.

Article 29

(1) Everyone has duties to the community in which alone the free and full development of his personality is possible.
(2) In the exercise of his rights and freedoms, everyone shall be subject only to such limitations as are determined by law solely for the purpose of securing due recognition and respect for the rights and freedoms of others and of meeting the just requirements of morality, public order and the general welfare in a democratic society.
(3) These rights and freedoms may in no case be exercised contrary to the purposes and principles of the United Nations.

Article 30

Nothing in this Declaration may be interpreted as implying for any State, group or person any right to engage in any activity or to perform any act aimed at the destruction of any of the rights and freedoms set forth herein. ∎

Atlantic Canada media ownership

How does Atlantic Canada fit into the larger pattern of media ownership in Canada?

The Senate Committee noted that "conventional wisdom still cherishes the image of the 'independent' owner-editor, a tough but kindly old curmudgeon who somehow represented the collective conscience of his community. If this image ever had validity, it hasn't now." (*Sen.*I:5). This observation has particular relevance to Atlantic Canada today, where one can still have the impression of being separate and different from the rest of Canada, since there are many local newspapers and media outlets. In fact, however, our region has the dubious distinction of having within it what has been called "the greatest regional concentration of mass media ownership in Canada" (*Sen.*II:86) — in New Brunswick. While the New Brunswick situation is the most extreme example of media control in Canada, the other Atlantic Provinces fit into the same general pattern of a very few people controlling the media.

Newspaper, television and radio ownership patterns are similar to others across the country: the most powerful stations are typically group-owned, with a sprinkling of small independent stations. The extent of overlapping ownerships between print and electronic media is difficult to determine, because companies do not have to disclose this information. It is however possible to get some idea of the situation from the information that is made public.

Among the influential local media owners, one finds in Nova Scotia the industrialist R. B. Cameron, well known for his Sydney Steel connections and less well known for his holdings in Fundy Publications Ltd; Halifax business executive David B. Joudrey and Halifax lawyer J. Thomas MacQuarrie, who are both directors of Fundy Group Publications and Kentville Publishing. The late Lawrence F. Daley, a lawyer, had interests in Maritime Broadcasting, Halifax Herald and Dartmouth Free Press; Hon. Garnet Brown (NS Min. of Recreation), A. Irvine Barrow and Charles V. Keating (former President of Loto Canada) have large interests in cable television.

In New Brunswick the Irving family dominates all aspects of media ownership. In Newfoundland, local media owners are well-known and wealthy families: the Crosbie family with interests in Robinson and Blackmore Printing and Publishing; the Jamieson family with its

EJ 3/2/77 p4

Good grief! This balance sheet won't do — why damn it, a child could understand it."

radio station chain, Arthur Lundrigan with interests in the Humber Valley radio chain . . .

Corporate disclosure: snakes and ladders

If you are interested in knowing exactly who owns a particular newspaper or company in your area, you may have a great deal of work ahead of you. You must try to make your way through a complex network of investment companies, joint ventures and holding companies to find out who the owner might be. At the end of your searching, you could well find that you still only have the names of the directors of the company — not who owns or has controlling interest in it.

Canadian law obliges the very large corporations and all broadcasters to disclose information about their operations, but it does not deal with relatively small-scale companies, such as the owners of a few newspapers, publishing companies, printers or distributors — however important the impact of these media might be on an area with a small population like the Atlantic region. Referring to the lack of information about the operations of media corporations, the Special Senate Committee on Mass Media noted:

> We are confronted with a delicious irony: an industry that is supposed to abhor secrets is sitting on one of the best-kept, least discussed secrets, one of the hottest scoops in the entire field of Canadian business — their own balance sheets! (*Sen.*I:63)

It was in these conditions of corporate secrecy, then, that any information has been assembled about ownership of the media in the

Weekly Newspapers — Nova Scotia
by circulation

Town/City	Name	Circulation	Owned/controlled by
Bridgewater	South Shore Telecaster	16,460	**Group** (F.G.P.)
Kentville	The Valley Telecaster	15,454	**Group** (F.G.P.)
Sydney	Cape Breton Highlander	13,473	
Dartmouth	Dartmouth Free Press	13,000	**Group links** (H.H./DFP)
Antigonish	The Antigonish Casket	12,212	Church
Yarmouth	The Vanguard	10,498	**Group** (F.G.P.)
Digby-Middleton	The Mirror	9,400	**Group** (F.G.P.)
Kentville	Kentville Advertiser	8,902	**Group** (K.P.)
Port Hawkesbury	The Scotia Sun	7,700	
Windsor Junction	The Grapevine	7,000	
Bridgewater	Bridgewater Bulletin	7,571	
Shelburne	Shelburne County Telecaster	5,875	**Group** (F.G.P.)
Amherst	The Citizen	5,500	Cumberland Pub. Ltd.
Shelburne	The Coast Guard	4,300	**Group** (F.G.P.)
Windsor	The Hants Journal	5,675	**Group** (K.P.)
Sydney	MicMac News		
Springhill-Parrsboro	The Springhill & Parrsboro Record	4,500	
Lunenburg	Progress-Enterprise	4,448	
Liverpool	The Advance	4,205	Advance Pub. Co.
Greenwood	The Argus	3,800	
Digby	The Digby Courier	3,850	
Oxford	Oxford Journal	3,107	
Berwick	The Register	2,725	Berwick Pub. Ltd.
Bridgetown	The Monitor Weekly	2,285	
Annapolis Royal	The Spectator	1,878	
Yarmouth	The Light-Herald	1,850	**Group** (F.G.P.)
CFB Cornwallis	The Cornwallis Ensign	1,500	
Arichat	The Richmond County Record	1,300	
Yarmouth	Courier de la Nouvelle-Ecosse	3,200	
		181,568 Total	

Source: Atlantic Year Book 1979
Groups: F.G.P. = Fundy Group Publications; H.H. = Halifax Herald; D.F.P. = Dartmouth Free Press; K.P. = Kentville Publishing

Atlantic region and in Canada. The information is to the best of our knowledge accurate and the most recent available. We encourage you to make notes and add or alter information where appropriate.

New Brunswick

The Irving family of Saint John completely owns four of the five English-speaking dailies in New Brunswick, and controls the fifth:

Saint John Telegraph Journal	100% ownership
Saint John Evening Telegram	100% ownership
Moncton Daily Times	100% ownership
Moncton Transcript	100% ownership
Fredericton Gleaner	controlling interest

It has been suggested that significant influence is exercised over the sixth daily as well, the French *l'Evangeline*, through extensive advertising (*Sen*.II:62).

Also controlled by K.C. Irving Limited are:

Moncton Publishing Co. Ltd

Moncton Engraving Ltd

Brodier Co.

University Press of New Brunswick

Unipress Ltd.

Brunswick Books (wholesalers and suppliers of books and magazines).

Irving Oil Co. Ltd. (including nine wholly-owned subsidiaries and part interests in three other companies) and Irving Pulp and Paper are some of the other Irving holdings (Royal Commission on Corporate Concentration Study #16:5). Statistics Canada's *Intercorporate ownership* listed more than 80 companies as part of the Irving conglomerate, and even this list did not include two publishing companies (that put out two newspapers), and one printing firm.[1]

Irving, through New Brunswick Publishing Company and New Brunswick Broadcasting Co., controls all private television stations and the province's major English-language radio station in Saint John, CHSJ. The head of the Canadian Newspaper Publishers' Association declared to the Special Senate Committee on Mass Media that

> Mr Irving has in effect created a private empire in New Brunswick, complete with its official press —print and electronic. (*Sen*.I:70)

However, it was only revealed at the end of 1979 that this empire had belonged to a still larger empire since 1973 — one of the largest oil companies in the world, Standard Oil of California. For six years, the company of the local boy who had "made good" had been 49% controlled by this American oil and agribusiness giant.

Outside of the Irving media interests, there remain only the rest of the radio stations. The Neill family owns one of the two most powerful private radio stations — CFNB/Fredericton, through Radio Atlantic (1970) Ltd. Another powerful transmitter, CFBC/Saint John, is controlled by three men — James H. Turnbull, James A. MacMurray and Robert Lockhart. In addition to controlling CFBC-AM and -FM in Saint John, these three shareholders, together with an associate of MacMurray, C. William Stanley, control 62% of the cable system servicing Saint John (through Fundy Cablevision Ltd.), and 55% of Miramachi Cable Ltd. serving Chatham and Newcastle. Mr. MacMurray controls 55% of the two cable systems servicing Edmundston, St Basil, St Jacques and Clair (Edmundston Cablevision Ltd.).

Two men, Jack Schoone and Irving Zucker, control the next most powerful private radio transmitter, CFQM/Moncton, and CKNB/Campbellton, CKCW/Moncton, CFAN/Newcastle and CJCW/Sussex, as well as a station in P.E.I., CFCY. Mr. Schoone is a resident of Moncton and Orillia, Ontario, and Mr Zucker is a resident of Hamilton, Ont. They own ten AM and two FM stations there.

"Mr Fortier: Do you buy anything that is for sale?

Mr Irving: If it is a reasonable buy and providing I have the money.

Mr Fortier: When you are dealing, do you treat the acquisition of newspapers any differently than you treat the acquisition of other commodities?

Mr Irving: Well, I don't. You have to select your commodities.

Mr Fortier: Well, I think it is for you to do that.

Mr Irving: All right. So far as a good commodity itself, I deal with all good commodities and I put the newspaper business in the same category."

— Exchange between Mr K. C. Irving and Senate Committee Counsel Fortier, Special Senate Committee Proceedings, No. 5, p. 41.

Of the remaining four English private radio stations in New Brunswick, one is a company with stations in Nova Scotia (Bathurst Broadcasting), two are owned by the same company (Edmundston Radio) and the last appears to be independent and is owned by two people, James Ross of Fredericton and Geoffrey Rivett, with Donald J. Stevenson as a director as well.

Nova Scotia

Of the seven daily newspapers in Nova Scotia, three belong to the giant Thomson Newspaper chain (*Cape Breton Post*, New Glasgow *Evening News*, Truro *Daily News*), with a combined circulation of 51,541. Two are owned by one family, the Dennis family (the *Chronicle Herald* and the *Mail Star*, c.c. 128,275). The last two are independent, with a combined circulation of roughly 12,700 (*Bedford-Sackville News* and the Amherst *Daily News*).

For a small province, Nova Scotia has many newspapers. Of the 30 weekly newspapers in the province listed in the 1979 Atlantic Year Book, the largest eight accounted for approximately 60% of the total circulation. All but two of these eight had group connections. Of the two remaining independents (the *Cape Breton Highlander* and the Antigonish *Casket*), one was owned by a church.

Fundy Group Publications puts out the following:

Bridgewater
South Shore Telecaster 16,460 *weekly*

Kentville
Valley Telecaster   15,454 *weekly*

Yarmouth
Vanguard   10,498 *weekly*

Digby/Middletown
Mirror   9,400 *weekly*

Shelburne
*Shelburne County
Telecaster*   5,875 *weekly*

Shelburne
Coast Guard   4,300 *weekly*

Yarmouth
Light-Herald   1,850 *weekly*

Yarmouth
Farm Focus   12,500 *twice/month*

Yarmouth
Sou'wester   11,000 *weekly*

Yarmouth
Viking (tourist public.) 200,000 *yearly*

When he bought Fundy Group Publications, industrialist R. B. Cameron is reported to have made the offhand comment, "I'm just interested with the results on the books."[2] Mr Cameron, a resident of New Glasgow, is also President of Tidal Power Corporation, Cape Breton Heavy Water Ltd, Deuterium of Canada Ltd., and R. B. Cameron Ltd. He is Chairman and Chief Executive Officer of Maritime Steel and Foundries Ltd, Chairman and President of Cameron Contracting Ltd., a Director of the Bank of Canada, the Royal Bank, Dover Mills Ltd, and the Canadian Geriatrics Research Society.

Kentville Publishing produces the *Kentville Advertiser* and *The Hants Journal*, and has a huge printing and publishing concern. Who owns Kentville Publishing Ltd.? Under present laws in Canada, this information does not have to be disclosed to the public. However, it is thought that Kentville, too, forms part of R. B. Cameron's holdings. By law, companies are obliged to make public their boards of directors. Both Fundy and Kentville have on their boards of directors accountant David B. Joudrey and lawyer J. Thomas MacQuarrie.

As for television, there is one private TV broadcasting network in Nova Scotia, the ATV network. The Atlantic Television System Ltd. has licences for TV throughout the province. CHUM of Toronto controls 50% of the vote through Mr Allan Waters, President and General Manager of CHUM in Toronto and President of Radio CJCH 920 Ltd. in Nova Scotia (see Newfoundland below also).

Nationally, Mr. Waters is a director of CTV Television network, the Canada Development Corporation and Royal Trust. CHUM's subsidiaries include National Security Systems Ltd., Telephone Store Ltd (90%) and the Ottawa Football Club. Another 30% of ATV is controlled by Celtic Investments Limited, which owns three radio stations as well. Celtic is owned by J. Marven Nathenson, Norris N. Nathenson and Mrs. Shirly Tutty. Another 11% is owned by Frederic Sherratt Ltd. Mr. Sherratt is President of ATV System Limited, and Vice-President of Radio CJCH 920 Ltd.

IF YOU FIND MISTAKES IN THIS PUBLICATION, PLEASE CONSIDER THAT THEY ARE THERE FOR A PURPOSE. WE PUBLISH SOMETHING FOR EVERYONE, AND SOME PEOPLE ARE ALWAYS LOOKING FOR MISTAKES !!!

The importance of cable television warrants an entire chapter; space does not permit us to treat it here. However, since it is one of the fastest-growing and most lucrative investments that can be made, and since it has a far-reaching impact on those who receive it, we hope that research will be initiated in this area. Here, for example, are the owners of the two principal cable stations in the Halifax-Dartmouth area:

Halifax Cablevision shareholders	*% vote*
A. Irvine Barrow	45%
Hon. Garnet Brown*	45%
J. Keith Lawton	5%
Donald D. Anderson	5%
	100%

Dartmouth Cable tv	*% vote*
Charles V. Keating	50%
Hon. Garnet Brown*	25%
Charles Henry Reardon	25%
*N.S. Minister of Recreation	100%

CJCH. Radio CJCH 920 is 100% owned by CHUM, with Mr. Allan Waters of CHUM its President and Mr. Sherratt its Vice-President. *Maritime Broadcasting.* CHNS, CHNX-SW, CHFX-FM. The largest of the multi-media complexes, Maclean-Hunter, owns 90% of Maritime Broadcasting. Halifax lawyer, the late Lawrence F. Daley was Maritime's President, as well as Vice-President of the Halifax Herald Ltd. and its legal counsel for some time. He was also Secretary of the board of directors of Dartmouth Free Press. For some time he was President of New Brunswick Broadcasting Company (owned by the Irvings), and one of Irving's principal legal advisers. Outside these media interests, Mr. Daley was a director of L.E. Shaw Limited, First Maritime Mining Limited, President of S. Cunard and Co. Ltd. and a member of the advisory board of the Royal Trust Company.
CFDR. Dartmouth Broadcasting owns this second most powerful private radio station. Charles A. Patterson controls Dartmouth Broadcasting. He is a former Toronto Star journalist and prominent member of the Liberal party.
Other. It is worth noting that the Truro stations of CKCL-AM and -FM are owned by the Colchester Broadcasting Company. Vice-President of the the Truro firm (Colchester) is Neil McMullen, who is also shareholder in Bathurst Broadcasting. Mr McMullen is listed as the licencee of five other stations in Nova Scotia — the third largest radio transmitter — CKWM-FM/Annapolis Valley, CKDY/Digby,

CKEN/Kentville, CKAD/Middleton and CFAB/Windsor. He is holding all five of these on behalf of a company to be incorporated . . .

Prince Edward Island

Prince Edward Island has three daily newspapers. Two, the *Guardian* and *Patriot*, are in the Thomson newspaper chain. The third, the Summerside *Journal Pioneer*, is owned by Sterling Newspapers Ltd, a chain of nine regional daily newspapers and two semi-weeklies in the West of Canada. Sterling's president, and the PEI paper's president, is none other than Conrad Black, one of the most powerful financiers in Canada. He heads the Journal Publishing, thus linking Canada's smallest province, famed for its red roads and children's story books, with some of the largest of Canadian corporations.

Mr Black is Chairman of Dominion Malting Ltd; President of Western Dominion Investment Co. Ltd; Director of Argus Corp., Canadian Imperial Bank of Commerce, Eaton's of Canada Ltd, Longman Canada Ltd, The Ravelston Corp., and Confederation Life. His holdings put him in charge of Dominion Stores, mining companies and hundreds of other related and unrelated companies.

There is no private television station in PEI (see page 133 on U.S.-beamed stations). CFCY radio station is owned by Eastern Broadcasting of New Brunswick. Eastern's

"Whenever I'm in the dumps, I just sit back and think of my $150 million."

principal owners, Messers Schoone and Zucker, own five AM and one FM station in the Maritimes and ten AM and two FM stations in Ontario, where they live. CHTN is equally owned by W. A. MacRae, and A. E. MacLennan and A. K. Scales; CJRW by Mrs Lois E. Schurmann and family.

Newfoundland

Two of the three daily newspapers in Newfoundland are owned by the Thomson Newspaper chain (the St John's *Evening Telegram* and the Corner Brook *Western Star*). In 1970 the Thomson chain bought these two papers from the Herder family, which still owns the third daily, the St John's *Daily News*.

Of the eight weekly papers in the province, seven are put out by one company, Robinson and Blackmore Printing and Publishing:

Carbonear	*The Compass*
Clarenville	*The Clarenville Packet*
Corner Brook	*Humber Log*
Gander	*Gander Beacon*
Lewisporte	*The Pilot*
Port-aux-Basques	*The Gulf News*
Salt Pond, Burin	*The Southern Gazette.*

Who, then, owns Robinson and Blackmore? As we have noted, that information does not have to be revealed to the public, but here are its directors:

Andrew C. Crosbie	President
A. H. Crosbie	Vice-President
Doyle C. Roberts	Managing Director
Lewis H. M. Ayre	
Wilfred Ayer	
Albert Perlin.	

Brother of Tory Finance Critic John Crosbie, Mr. Andrew Crosbie is Chairman of Am-

Daily newspapers - Atlantic Region by circulation

Name	Town/City	Province	Circulation	Owned/controlled by
Chronicle-Herald	Halifax	NS	128,275	one family
Mail-Star	Halifax	NS	c.c.	one family
Telegraph Journal	Saint John	NB	63,759	Group (I.)
Evening Times	Saint John	NB	c.c.	Group (I.)
Evening Telegram	St John's	Nfld	49,348	Group (T.)
Times	Moncton	NB	45,029	Group (I.)
Transcript	Moncton	NB	c.c.	Group (I.)
Cape Breton Post	Sydney	NS	30,971	Group (T.)
Gleaner	Fredericton	NB	22,380	Group (I.)
Guardian	Charlottetown	PEI	21,863	Group (T.)
Evening Patriot	Charlottetown	PEI	c.c.	Group (T.)
L'Evangeline	Moncton	NB	17,992	
Evening News	New Glasgow	NS	11,675	Group (T.)
Journal-Pioneer	Summerside	PEI	11,413	
Daily News	St John's	Nfld	10,072	Group (T.)
Western Star	Corner Brook	Nfld	9,825	Group (T.)
Bedford-Sackville News	Bedford	NS	9,250	
Daily News	Truro	NS	8,895	Group (T.)
Daily News	Amherst	NS	3,537	

Circulation figures are from the 1979 Atlantic Year Book.
T. = Thomson; I. = Irving; c.c. = combined circulation

bassador Manufacturing Company, Ambassador Manufacturing Company (Ontario) Ltd., Charles Cusson Limitee, Eastern Provincial Airways, Eastminster Assurance Agency Ltd., Maritime Central Airways Ltd., Viking Construction Ltd.; President and Director of the Avalon Lounge Ltd., Crosbie Realty Ltd, Crosbie Services Ltd, New Lab Pre-engineered Structures Ltd, Northern Express Ltd, Robinson and Blackmore Printing and Publishing Ltd., Robinson and Blackmore Holdings Ltd., Wabush Enterprises Ltd, Chimo Shipping Ltd, Crosbie and Company Ltd., Crosoils Ltd, Holdings Corp. Ltd, St John's Development Corp. Ltd.; Director of the Bank of Montreal, Domac Enterprises Ltd, Trinity Brick Products Ltd, Colonial Cordage Co. Ltd, Nfld. Steamships Ltd, Yellow Fish-Un Ltd; Member of the Advisory Board, Central and Nova Scotia Trust, and Past President, Newfoundland Board of Trade.

Mr Alexander Harris Crosbie of the same Crosbie family, is President of A.H. Murray & Co. Ltd, Colonial Cordage Co. Ltd, President of Bold Lumber Co. of Ontario, and Past President, Newfoundland Board of Trade.

Mr Lewis Ayre is Chairman of Ayre and Sons Ltd, Ayres Ltd, The Newfoundland Telephone Company Ltd, Job Bros. & Co. Ltd, Holiday Lanes Ltd, Northatlantic Fisheries, Blue Buoy Foods Ltd, Maxmax Ltd; Chairman J. Michaels Fashions Limited; Director of Colonial Cordage Co. Ltd, Director of Newfoundland and Labrador Hydro, George G.R. Parsons Ltd, the Bank of Nova Scotia, Dominion Stores Ltd, Robinson Blackmore Holding Ltd, Hollinger Mines Ltd, Labrador Mining & Exploration Co. Ltd, Jannock Corporation, Clayton Construction (1965) Ltd; Clayton Refrigeration & Diesel Ltd; Member of the Advisory Board, Canada Permanent Trust Company; Past President Newfoundland Board of Trade.

All of the twenty-eight private TV outlets throughout Newfoundland are owned by Geoffry W. Sterling, President of Newfoundland Broadcasting Co. Ltd.

Mr. Sterling's company also owns ten radio stations in the province. He owns 100% of CKGM and CHOM-FM in Montreal through Maisonneuve Broadcasting and CKW; and 100% of CJOM-FM in Windsor, Ontario through Radio Windsor Ontario Ltd.

Former Federal Liberal MP Don Jamieson owns the Radio CJYQ 930 system of 5 stations; they are controlled in trust by Lloyd Hudson of St John's and Allan Waters of Ontario (President of CHUM Ltd.).

Four people own the 10-station Humber Valley Company system: Arthur Lundrigan, George Hillyard, Edna G. Murphy and Noel F. Murphy.

Research

1. A 1970 report showed that fewer than two in five Canadians knew the names of local media owners. Conduct a survey of your area.

2. The information in this book will be dated to some extent, even as it is printed — just as published information was dated when we put this book together. However, we uncovered very little startling new evidence in our research (apart from information about the American ownership of Irving). The general trends noted here, in all likelihood, will continue as they have in the past.

You may wish to update and improve the information. For newspapers and other print media, you can try to find out what you can from the publishers themselves. The Provincial Registry of Joint Stocks lists all companies incorporated in your province, noting directors of the company. Your regional library is a very useful resource.

For broadcasters, the Canadian Radio-television and Telecommunications Commission (CRTC), lists all owners and other information.

3. A case charging Irving with monopoly practices was brought against Irving by the Anti-Combines Branch of the Department of Consumer and Corporate Affairs. In the New Brunswick Supreme court, the trial judge found that a "complete monopoly" had been established. However, a court of appeal reversed the Irving conviction. Here is part of the decision:

It is clear from the above wording that the trial Judge was using the word monopoly therein in the ordinary sense or dictionary meaning and not in the restricted connotation of the word as defined in the Combines Act. I concur that K.C. Irving Limited created a complete monopoly in the dictionary meaning of the word with the final acquisition of the controlling interest in the 'Daily Gleaner'. I differ from the trial Judge, however, in his statement that when a monopoly (as defined in the dictionary) occurs, detriment in law results. Whether the one ownership businesses

have operated or are likely to operate to the detriment of or against the interest of the public is a question of fact not of law and a question which must be decided against the appellants* in this case before they can be found guilty; further it must be found against them beyond any reasonable doubt. If any presumption of detriment to the public arises out of the acquisition of a number of businesses by one individual, which I do not accept, that inference is rebuttable. The Combines Investigation Act is restrictive legislation limiting common law rights and should be strictly construed. I find nothing in the Act to create any such presumption or prima facie* case.

a. Put in your own words what the judge is saying.

b. Once this is done, discuss the meaning of this decision. What are its implications? *How can you "prove" Irving monopoly is operating against the public interest?*

appellants n. — those appealing the ruling (i.e. Irving)
prima facie adj. — having every appearance of proving a fact though it may not constitute certain proof.

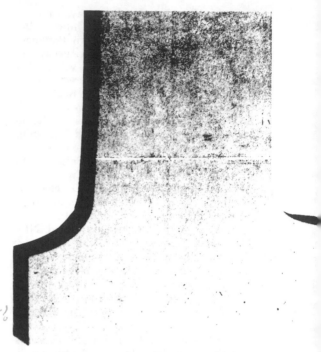

News and advertising have a lot in common. Think about it. You want your message to hit the market just like we want news to hit the reader – with considered impact. In Maclean's, news and advertising have established a unique bond: readers buy it because they have an appetite for both. We're offering you a top-notch medium for reaching readers with an eye for messages of consequence. We work well together.

Maclean's has been a weekly newsmagazine for one full year. We've been through a lot of changes, and we'll go through many more. It's just part of wanting to provide this country with the best in news journalism. Our endorsement by readers and advertisers sums it up.

Number One. Among the leading newsmagazines of the world, Maclean's has the highest domestic penetration of all. At 9% in Canada, Maclean's outranks Time in the U.S. at 6%, Der Spiegel in Germany at 5%, L'express in France at 3%. That's a good indication of the popularity of print in this country. And how Canadians like to get the news.

Number One. This year, as in 1978, Maclean's will lead all Canadian consumer magazines in total revenue. That's pretty solid endorsement from both readers and advertisers.

Number One. A year ago we took the plunge and became a weekly newsmagazine. We saw the need. And the possibilities. Canadians in 649,082* households are saying yes to our world-class coverage of news from a Canadian perspective. Each week. That's over thirty-three million copies across the land during our first year!

You want to reach an affluent market. We've got it. We reach 27% of managers and professionals in Canada, 25% of all Canadians earning more than $25,000 a year, 35% of all Canadians with a university education.† If you're positioned in Maclean's, you're reaching for the top.

One year after our launch as a weekly newsmagazine, Maclean's is unabashedly proud of success. We've got the medium; you got the message. We'll make it work.

*ABC Publisher's Statement-Average Canadian circulation, period ending Dec. 31, 1978.   †PM

CANADA'S WEEKLY NEWSMAGAZINE

Maclean's

FP Sp. Report Se.

Maclean-Hunter: "784,000 Business Prospects"*

One of the largest of the multi-media complexes, this company describes its audience as "business prospects". With just one of its publications, *Maclean's* magazine, reaching an average total paid circulation of 639,468, Maclean-Hunter is doing a lot of business:

Consumer Magazines
L'Actualite
AudioScene Canada
B.C. Outdoors
Canada & the World
Canadian Yachting
Chatelaine (English & French editions)
Chatelaine's New Mother / Mere Nouvelle
Financial Post Magazine, The
Flare
Home Decor Canada
Maclean's
Pacific Yachting
Photo Canada
Teen Generation
Business Publications
Batiment
Benefits Canada
Building Supply Dealer
Le Bureau
Bus & Truck Transport
Canadian Advertising Rates & Data
Canadian Automotive Trade
Canadian Aviation
Canadian Building
Canadian Controls + Instruments
Canadian Datasystems
Canadian Driver / Owner
Canadian Electrical Wholesaler
Canadian Electronics Engineering
Canadian Grocer
Canadian Hotel & Restaurant

Canadian Interiors
Canadian Jeweller
Canadian Machinery & Metalworking
Canadian Packaging
Canadian Photography
Canadian Premiums & Incentives
Canadian Printer & Publisher
Canadian Pulp & Paper Industry
Canadian Research
Canadian Secretary
Canadian Travel Courier
Civic Public Works
Creativity
Design Engineering
Drillsite
Drug Merchandising
Educational Digest
Electrical Contractor & Maintenance Supervisor
L'epicier
The Financial Post
Flour Covering News
Food in Canada
Forêt et Papier
Hardware Merchandising
Heavy Construction News
Home Goods Retailing
Industrial Product Ideas!
Investor's Digest of Canada
Marketing
Materials Management & Distribution
Medical Post, The
Men's Wear of Canada

Modern Power & Engineering
Modern Purchasing
Office Equipment & Methods
Oilweek
Le Pharmacien
Plant Management & Engineering
Quebec Industriel
Quincaillerie-Matériaux
Revue-Moteur
Shopping Centre Canada
Sporting Goods Canada
Style
Transport Commercial
Western Fisheries
Annual
Automotive Service Data Book
Canadian Industry Shows & Exhibitions
Canadian Special Truck Equipment Manual
Chatelaine Mere Nouvelle
Chatelaine's New Mother
Directory of Directors
Fraser's Canadian Trade Directory
Fraser's Construction & Building Directory
L'Hospitalite
Materials Handling Handbook & Directory of Buying Services
The National List of Advertisers
Real Estate Development Annual
Survey of Industrials
Survey of Funds
Survey of Markets
Survey of Mines & Energy Resources

CARD JULY 80.

In addition to these publications, Maclean-Hunter's diversified operations include radio, television, cable-TV, production of shows and exhibitions, business forms, personal radio paging, book distribution and book publishing. Here are some of Maclean-Hunter's subsidiaries:

Maclean-Hunter Cable TV Ltd. (99%).
(seventeen cable stations in Ontario, including four in Metro Toronto.)

(commercial TV stations in Calgary, Drumheller, Banff, Brooks, Burmis and Lethbridge; radio stations in Calgary, Chatham and Kitchener.)
  Maclean-Hunter Communications Ltd. (100%)
  Metro Home Theatre Inc., Detroit (100%)
  CFCN Communications Ltd., Toronto
99% owned by Maclean-Hunter Ltd.
TV stations:
  CFCN, Calgary, Lethbridge and Medicine Hat, Alta.
  Radio stations:
  CFCN, CJAY-FM, Calgary
  CHYM AM & CKGL-FM, Kitchener, Ont.
  CFCO, Chatham, Ont.
Other interests:
  Paul Mulvihill Ltd. (49%)
  Stephens & Towndrow Co. (80%)
  Newsradio Ltd. (80%)
  CFCN Communications Ltd. (99%)
  Design-Craft Ltd.
  National Book Centre of Canada Ltd.
  Macmillan Co. of Canada
  Telephone Communicators Canada Ltd.
  Maclean-Hunter Ltd. (Britain)
  Maclean-Hunter Publishing Corp. (U.S.)
  CKEY Ltd., Toronto.
  CKOY Ltd. (Ottawa radio stations

CKOY-FM and CKBY-FM)
  Maritime Broadcasting Co. (70%)
(Halifax radio stations CHNS-AM, CH-FX-FM, CHNX-SW).
  Data Business Forms Ltd.
  Special Interest Magazines Ltd.
  The Educational ABC's of American Industry, Inc.
  Maclean-Hunter B.V.
50% owned:
  Trans Canada Expositions Ltd.
  KEG Productions Ltd.
  Quality Service Programs Inc.
  Tarifmedia SA, Paris
  Media Daten,
  Verlagsgesellschaft mbH, Frankfurt.
  Media-Daten, Oesterreichisches Gmbh, Vienna.
  Media-Daten, Zurich.
  Dalie Tariffe Pubblicitarie SpA, Milan
  Corena Ltda., Sao Paulo.
Owned by subsidiaries:
  Maclean-Hunter Holdings Ltd.
  International Exposition Services Inc. (50%)
Maclean-Hunter Cable TV Ltd., Toronto
99% owned by Maclean-Hunter Ltd.
Operates 16 cable-TV systems serving 23 Ontario and U.S. communities.
Subsidiaries:
  Peterborough Cable Television Ltd. (75%).
  Suburban Cablevision New Jersey (84%).

FP 22 Sept 79

*Ad in *Financial Post* special report on the media, "Who owns whom" Sept 79.

Thomson Newspaper Chain

"Raise your sales with the zesty Thomson market!", enjoins this newspaper giant.* Founded by Canadian-born Lord Thomson of Fleet, this chain's chairman and principal owner is his son, K. R. Thomson, who lives in Canada and is also joint chairman of the International Thomson Organisation. It controls more than 119 papers in North America, and several British and South African publications as well. Here are some of the Canadian holdings of Thomson:

Dailies:
Barrie Examiner
Belleville Intelligencer
Brampton Daily Times
Cambridge Daily Reporter
Charlottetown Guardian
Charlottetown Evening Patriot
Chatham Daily News
Corner Brook Western Star
Cornwall Standard-Freeholder
Guelph Daily Mercury
Kamloops Daily Sentinel
Kelowna Daily Courier
Kirkland Lake Northern Daily News
Moose Jaw Times-Herald
Nanaimo Daily Free Press
New Glasgow Evening News
Niagara Falls Review

Orillia Daily Packet & Times
Oshawa Times
Pembroke Observer
Penticton Herald
Peterborough Examiner
Prince Albert Daily Herald
St. John's Evening Telegram
St. Thomas Times-Journal
Sarnia Observer
Simcoe Reformer
Sudbury Star
Sydney Cape Breton Post
Thunder Bay Times-News/Chronicle-Journal
Timmins Daily Press
Truro Daily News
Vernon Daily News
Welland Evening Tribune
Woodstock Daily Sentinel-Review

Weeklies:
Bathurst Northern Light

Collingwood Enterprise-Bulletin
Dunnville Chronicle
Elliott Lake Standard
Georgetown Herald
Hanover Post
Leamington Post
Yorkton Enterprise

Tri-weekly:
Trenton Trentonian & Tri-County News

Semi-weeklies:
Midland Free Press
Orangeville Banner
Swift Current Sun

(source: FP 22 Sept 79)

Thomson now owns FP Publications, which was listed as owning the following:

F.P. PUBLICATIONS LTD., Toronto.
Private company. Owners: John W. Sifton estate 22.5%; Bell Foundation 22.5%; Newsco Investments Ltd. (holding company for the Webster family) 22.5%; R. S. Malone 7.5%; Starlaw Investments 25%.
Malone, chairman of F.P. Publications, was formerly publisher of the Toronto Globe & Mail. Webster and Starlaw investments have extensive business interests outside publishing.
Owns daily newspapers in Quebec, Ontario, Manitoba, Alberta and British Columbia. Holds 3% of the class A shares of Selkirk Holdings Ltd.
Daily newspapers:
Calgary Albertan
Lethbridge Herald
Montreal Star
Ottawa Journal
Toronto Globe & Mail
Vancouver Sun
Victoria Daily Colonist
Victoria Daily Times
Winnipeg Free Press
Weekly:
Free Press Weekly Report on Farming, Weekend Magazine.
Job printing:
Montreal Standard Ltd.
Ronalds-Federated Ltd. (51.6%).
Subsidiaries (wholly owned):
F.P. Publications (Western) Ltd.,
F.P. Publications (Eastern) Ltd.

(source: FP 22 Sept 79)

FP Publications has interests in 2 cable companies —
Clement, *Corp. élite*, p. 312.

*Ad, Canadian Advertising Rates and Data October 1979

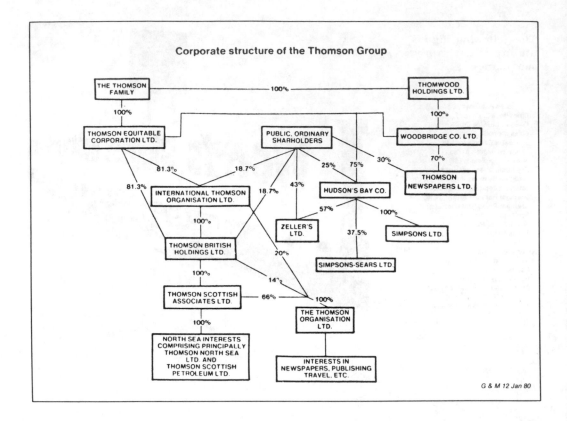

Corporate structure of the Thomson Group

G & M 12 Jan 80

Southam Inc.

Southam now operates the second-largest newspaper chain in Canada, with 14 dailies and a combined circulation of 1,267,000 at the end of 1978. It owns 39 business publications (daily, weekly and monthly), 26 other publications (including guide books, manuals, directories and yearbooks), 14 services, 49 shows and exhibitions, Canada's largest book retailer (Coles), and what is reported to be the largest bookstore in the world (Coles in Toronto). Here are some of Southam's publications:

Consumer Magazines
Canadian Pool & Patio
Business Publications
Administrative Digest
Canadian Architect, The
Canadian Chemical Processing
Canadian Consulting Engineer
Canadian Doctor
Canadian Footwear Journal
Canadian Forest Industries
Canadian Industrial Equipment News
Canadian Mining Journal
Canadian Office Products & Stationary
Canadian Petroleum
Canadian Plastics
Canadian Sales Meetings & Conventions
Canadian Transportation & Distribution Management
Canadian Travel News
Daily Commercial News & Construction Record
Electrical Equipment News
Electronics & Communications
Engineering & Contract Record
Equipment Finder
Executive
Genie Construction
Gifts & Tablewares
Health Care
Health Care Digest

Heating, Plumbing, Air Conditioning
Laboratory Product News
Modern Medicine of Canada
Medecine Moderne du Canada
Operation Forestières
Oral Health
Plomberie, Chauffage et Climatisation
Pool Industry Canada
Pulp & Paper Canada
Shop
Southam Building Guide
Water & Pollution Control

Annual
Administrative Digest Business Directory
Buyers' Guide to Process Equipment Controls & Instrumentation
Canadian Architect Yearbook, The
Canadian Forest Industries Directory
Canadian Mining Manual
Canadian Plastics Directory & Buyers
Canadian Ports & Seaway Directory
Canadian Shoemaking
Chemical Buyers Guide
Dental Guide
Electronic Procurement Index of Canada
Genie Construction Annuaire
Heating, Plumbing, Air Conditioning

Operations Forestieres Annuaire
Plomberie, Chauffage et Climatisation
Guide de l'Acheteur
Pulp & Paper Canada Annual & Directory
Water & Pollution Control Directory
Yardsticks for Costing

Daily newspapers:
Brantford Expositor
Calgary Herald
Edmonton Journal
Hamilton Spectator
Medicine Hat News
Montreal Gazette
North Bay Nugget
Ottawa Citizen
Owen Sound Sun-Times
Windsor Star

(source: CARD July 80)

The following figure
among Southam's
subsidiaries:

Canadian Publishers Co.
Coles Book Stores Ltd.
Coles Publishing Co.
Coles the book people! Inc.
Journal of Commerce Ltd.
McLaren, Morris & Todd Ltd.
M.M. & T. Holdings Ltd.
Les Publications Eclair Ltee
Southam Business Publications Ltd.
Southam Communications Inc.
Southam Farwest Printing Ltd.
Southam Press (Ontario) Ltd.
Southam Printing Ltd.
South-Times Publishiing Ltd. (75%)
Trans Ad Ltd.
Videosurgery Ltd.
Associates (50% owned):
Avcor Audio/Visual Corp.
Pacific Press Ltd.
Panex Show Services Ltd.
Pentacle VIII Productions Ltd.
Southstar Publishers Ltd.
Trans Canada Expositions Ltd.

Torstar Corp.

"The Star is the largest advertising vehicle in Toronto," an ad for the Toronto Star tells us.

Apart from magazine supplements, interests include newspaper with the largest circulation (500,000 daily) in Canada, eight suburban and small-town weeklies Toronto area, book publishing, controlled-circulation magazines and commercial printing operations.

Daily newspaper:
   Toronto Star.
Weekly newspapers, all 100%-owned by Metrospan Printing & Publishing Ltd.;
   Mississauga Times
   Oakville Journal REcord
   Etobicoke Advertiser/Guardian
   Mirror
   Aurora Banner
   Richmond Hill Liberal
   Woodbridge/Vaughan News
   Bolton Enterprise
Subsidiaries:
   Comac Communications Ltd. (95%),
   Homemaker's/Madame Au Foyer,
   Quest, City Woman.
   Harlequin Enterprises (58%) paperbacks, learning materials
   Southstar Publishers Ltd. (50%)
   Metrospan Printing & Publishing Ltd.
   Nielsen-Ferns International Ltd. film production

Other interests:
   Infomart, jointly owned with Southam Inc.
   Western Broadcasting Co. (about 33%).
   Harlequin Enterprises Ltd., Toronto. *58% owned by Torstar Corp.*, Toronto. Publisher of paperback novels. Subsidiaries produce educational programs, distribute teaching aids and library books.
Subsidiaries:
   Mills & Boon Ltd. (Britain)
   Mills & Boon Pty Ltd. (Aust.)
   Harlequin Enterprises S.A. (Switzerland)
   Harlequin Enterprises B.V. (Netherlands)
   Harlequin Enterprises GmbH (West Germany)
   Harlequin S.A. France
   Scholar's Choice Ltd.
   Harlequin Books Inc. (U.S.) includes Ideals Publishing Corp. Milwaukee, Wisc., Laufer Co. Calif. (79%, balance under option)
Associates:
   Cora Verlag, West Germany (50%)
   Editors Arlequim SA, Brazil (60%)

Financial Post 22 Sept 79

Wallace Clement's book *The Canadian corporate élite* was reviewed in the *Globe and Mail* when the book first appeared. However, it turned out that the section that dealt with ownership of the media was edited out of the original review . . . This is the section that was left out. It is also of interest that no apology was made for such a glaring omission.

A missing section on the elite

Edward Broadbent's discussion of Wallace Clement's book, The New Corporate Elite (Canadian Elite Stronger Than Ever, April 9), was published without one critical section. Mr. Broadbent called the book an outstanding successor to John Porter's Vertical Mosaic, demonstrating as it does increasing elitism and the fact that Canadians have little opportunity to break into any area of business or to move into the top levels of the power hierarchy; that the best way of perceiving power here is to recognize there is only one crucial elite. Mr. Broadbent went on to say:

Clement persuasively shatters the pluralist argument by combining the arguments made by Macpherson, Maneheim, Marx and Mills about the importance of ideology as an instrument for molding "free" opinion among the majority with his own documentation of the significant overlap between the economic and media elites in Canada. In the process he demonstrates how this core elite is able to run the country in its own interest and simultaneously convince everyone else it's also good for them.

Almost one-half of the members of Canada's economic elite are also members of the media elite, i.e., that small number of people who own and control most of our newspapers, periodicals and radio and television outlets. However, even those members of the media elite who are not members of our economic elite, i.e. in one of the 113 dominant corporations, share similar characteristics with those who are.

In brief, we have one upper class in Canada which dominates our economic and ideological life; this is the corporate elite.

In economic life this elite controls our lives, making decisions whose purpose is to maximize their profits and extend their power, whether or not these objectives are in the short- or long-range interests of Canadians. The vast majority of Canadians, including our Members of Parliament, have no say in these decisions.

In terms of its control of the media the corporate elite present in editorial, news and advertising content not as many views of life to Canadians as they like to contend but simply one basic view with two aspects: (a) that

a life of perpetual and increasing consumption is the best one and (b) that our form of liberal-democracy in which autocratic corporations have almost all the power and elected politicians have almost none is the best kind of democracy.

To believe that a life of equality in which esthetic, community, and fraternal values can flourish can be realized without the disappearance of our elite and the structure which makes it possible is an illusion. This is the point and the documented strength of Clement's book.

With those facts now clear and in the open in a way they were not to Sir John A. Macdonald or even perhaps to Mackenzie King Canadian politicians have only two choices. Either they must start to defend openly the existing inequalities and justify our capitalist liberal-democracy on grounds other than the shattered "equality of opportunity" myth or they can do the hard and uncertain work necessary to help bring about the very different kind of society in which a sense of equality and community can prevail. There is now no honest middle ground.

A cattle farmer and former RAF pilot, Prime Minister Ian
Smith of Rhodesia entered politics in 1948 "with no sense of
destiny." Today, reports **Christopher Munnion,** the future
of his country depends on his ability to lead it down the
perilous road toward majority rule

Last of the Few

HIS DAYS MAY BE NUMBERED,
but Ian Douglas Smith, a small-
town politician who as prime
minister of the unrecognized, war-
torn republic of Rhodesia, has out-
maneuvred many of the world's diplomatic heavyweights, is one of the
longest surviving leaders in Africa.
On a volatile continent this is no
mean achievement. It becomes even
more remarkable when viewed
against the background of Rhodesia's
13 years of isolation from the international community.

From the time that he led Britain's
last remaining African colony into its
unilateral declaration of independence in November 1965, Smith has
been portrayed in many different
ways. To successive British governments he has been the parochial but
devious white reactionary. To the
United Nations and the Third World
he is the arch white racist, symbol of
colonial oppression, exploitation and
hated imperialism. To most of the nationalists among Rhodesia's 6.5 million Africans he is the shrewd leader
of the white settlers, a man who cannot be trusted to relinquish power
readily. To his political opponents in
Rhodesia he is the ruthless and vin-
dictive figure who rarely forgets a
slight and is always ready to repay
in kind. To most of Rhodesia's
250,000-strong white community,
however, he is still "good old Smithy,"
the homespun man of destiny who
championed the cause of "Christian
civilized standards" against overwhelming odds.

All of these images contain an element of his true character, but history will no doubt judge Ian Smith on
what happens to landlocked but
bountiful Rhodesia within the next
few months. If he can successfully su-
pervise a transition to black rule under the moderate, internally based
African leaders with whom he is now
sharing power, Smith may well be
able to fulfil his professed ambition
and retire to his cattle ranch. If he
fails, Rhodesia is likely to be ravaged
by a civil war between rival black nationalist factions, a development that
could send Smith and most other Rhodesian whites into a headlong flight
for safety.

THE SEEDS OF CONFLICT WERE
sown in Rhodesia long before the
pioneer column first hoisted the
Union Jack in Salisbury in 1890.
Some 50 years earlier the western re-

gion of the country had been occupied
by the Matabele people, an offshoot of
the warrior Zulu tribe of South Africa
that had migrated north. In 1890,
when the white settlers arrived, the
Matabele were still in the process of
subjugating the more quiescent
Shona-speaking tribes which had in-
habited the territory for centuries.
Antipathy between the two major tribal groupings—the Shona outnumber the Matabeles 4 to 1—has
prevailed to the present day.

Joshua Nkomo is the undisputed
leader of the Matabele. His support is
largely in the west of Rhodesia, and
his guerrilla army, the Zimbabwe
Peoples Revolutionary Army (ZPRA),
is recruited almost exclusively from
Matabeleland. Conversely, Nkomo's
partner in the fragile patriotic front,
Robert Mugabe, is Shona-speaking,
as is the bulk of his fighting force, the
Zimbabwe African National Liberation Army (ZANLA). The patriotic
front is a flimsy diplomatic marriage
of convenience. The two black leaders
have totally opposite ideological
views, and several attempts to merge
their armies have resulted in
bloodshed.

This background of tribal warfare
has complicated the Rhodesian im-
broglio from the start. Many have argued that white rule in Rhodesia has
survived for so long because of inter-
tribal conflict. Smith's detractors
have often accused him of exploiting
it for his own political ends. In any
case, whites have frequently justified
their hegemony in Rhodesia by claiming that their presence has prevented
open tribal warfare.

The early white settlers were a
motley group. Largely of British and
South African stock, many were originally lured by the never-to-be-real-
ized hopes of rich gold seams, others
by the prospect of an abundance of
land, the fertile acres that later
transformed Rhodesia into one of
Africa's most important agricultural
procedures.

Ian Smith's father, Jock Smith, migrated from Scotland to Rhodesia in
1898 and established himself as a
prosperous butcher in the small mining and farming community of Selukwe in the Rhodesian midlands. By
the time Ian Smith was born on April
8, 1919, his father was one of the best
known and highly respected men in
the area. Young Ian Smith excelled at
sport, particularly rugby, athletics
and rowing. At Rhodes University in

South Africa he distinguished himself more on the playing fields than in
his studies. "I was brought up in
an atmosphere of cattle, race-horses
and sport," he recalls. "Both my parents embedded in me the necessity
for strong, moral character and
principle.".

With many other young Rhodesians, Smith interrupted his university studies to volunteer for the British air force shortly after the
outbreak of war. He trained in Rhodesia as a fighter pilot before being posted to the Middle East. His war record
is a strange mixture of heroics and
uncharacteristic recklessness that
nearly cost him his life on more than
one occasion.

Early one morning at an airfield
near Alexandria in Egypt, Smith in
his own words, "made a bit of a mess
of things." His Hurricane lifted briefly from the runway then dipped
sharply, the undercarriage caught a
sandbagged emplacement and the
aircraft smashed into the ground. His
face and jaw smashed into the instrument panel. One eye hung out of its
socket. For a few days his life was in
danger, but his fitness helped him to
make a rapid recovery. "You don't
think they could account for a Douglas Smith as easily as all that?" he
asked his family in a letter a few
weeks later. Skin grafting concealed
the worst of his scars, but to this day
his face has the slightly odd cast
that cartoonists have seized upon
unmercifully.

Within a few months he was back
with his squadron, flying a Spitfire
from a base in Corsica, strafing German supply lines in Italy. Again he
made a mistake. He was unable to resist a second strafing run against a
train in the Po Valley, and his aircraft caught a burst of ack-ack fire.
He baled out behind enemy lines.

Dodging German patrols, Smith
befriended an Italian family and for
five months operated with the parti-
sans, ambushing and capturing German supply trucks before making his
way back across the Alps to Allied
lines. The rest of the war was relatively uneventful, and in 1946 he returned to Rhodesia, scarred, undecor-
ated, and still only a flight lieutenant.

He returned to university to complete his Bachelor of Commerce degree in order to become a successful
cattle rancher in his beloved Rhodesian midlands. This he achieved within a few years, assisted by his bride,

Janet, a widow whom he married in
1948. A determined, shrewd woman,
she still has a profound influence on
Smith and his decisions. The Smiths
have three children—Jean and Robert by Janet's first marriage, and
Alec, who is an active campaigner for
the Moral Re-Armament movement
in Rhodesia.

IAN SMITH WAS PERSUADED,
somewhat reluctantly, to enter
politics shortly after his marriage
and just as he was establishing his
first farm. A group of local worthies
used his father's influence to persuade Smith to stand for the southern
Rhodesian Parliament. He agreed,
but without any sense of destiny. "All
my life I was one of those people who
was prepared to stand up and say my
piece in order to protect the rights of
people. It so happened that that led to
politics. I was never a rebel for the
sake of being a rebel, but I was never
able to tolerate any injustice or
unfairness."

For many years Smith was a stolid
but undistinguished backbencher for
the now defunct Liberal Party. When
the Federation of Rhodesia and Nyasaland began to crumble in 1960,
however, Smith emerged as a politician of stature. The British government had promised that Rhodesia
would gain its full independence no
later than the other federation partners, Northern Rhodesia (now Zambia) and Nyasaland (now Malawi).
Smith resigned from Sir Roy We-
lensky's United Federal Party in
1961 and became one of the founder
members of a new political group
which became the Rhodesian Front.
He was returned to Parliament in
1962 and was appointed treasury
minister in the new right-wing government. Two years later the Rhodesian Front ousted its leader, Winston
Field, for being too weak in his dealings with the British government
over the independence issue. Ian
Douglas Smith became prime minister of Rhodesia a few days after his
45th birthday amid heavy betting
that he and his "cowboy cabinet"
would not last six months. A local
newspaper described him as "the momentary man."

But the mood of many whites was
swinging toward independence, and
the one aspect of politics at which Ian
Smith excelled was the interpretation and articulation of the settler
mood. The image he projects, espe-

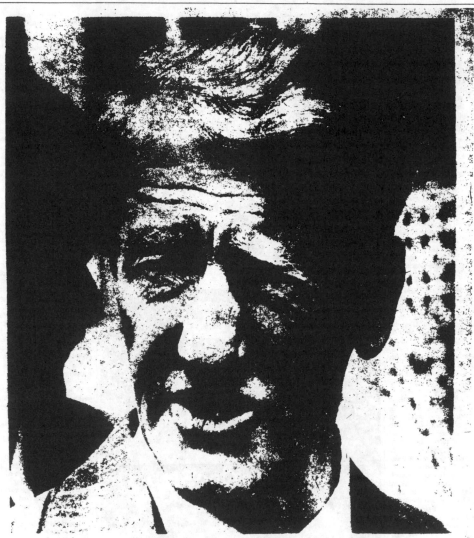

(SBY2)SALISBURY, Rhodesia, Sept.10--SAYS PEACEFUL SETTLEMENT STILL
POSSIBLE IN RHODESIA--Prime Minister Ian Smith of Rhodesia tells
reporters Sunday, he will announce a "new course" for his nation
in a televised address Sunday night. At the press conference, Smith
stated he still believes a peaceful settlement is possible in Rhodesia even though black guerrillas shot down a civilian airliner
last Sunday and massacred 10 survivors of the crash. (AP Laserphoto)
(See AP AAA Wire Story)(rbl1115str)1978.

GOOD OLD SMITHY: Beloved by Rhodesian whites
for his down-to-earth, farmer-turned-politician image,
Ian Smith is paternalistic rather than racist in his
attitudes toward blacks. He was surprised when laughter
greeted his remark that in Rhodesia "we have the
happiest blacks in Africa." He insists that "decent,
middle-class blacks" have always supported him

cially on public platforms, is precisely that with which most Rhodesian whites identified and came to worship. The first Rhodesian prime minister to have been born in the country, he revels in imparting a down-to-earth, straight-talking, farmer-turned-politician image, making a virtue out of his very ordinariness.

Smith found himself dealing with the then British prime minister, Harold Wilson, over the independence issue. It was loathing at first sight for both men, one volatile and devious, the other cool and cunning. Negotiations collapsed, and on November 11, 1966, Smith announced to Rhodesia and the world. that his government had decided to declare independence from Britain. Many believed at the time that Smith had gone along with the decision reluctantly. Wilson was convinced Smith was being manipulated by fanatic right-wingers in his cabinet. In fact Smith has always ruled his cabinet with iron discipline. The two cabinet hardliners suspected by Wilson of influencing Smith, —William Harper and Lord Graham —were dismissed after attempting to challenge the Rhodesian leader in 1968.

SUCCESSIVE BRITISH GOVERN-ments sought to negotiate a Rhodesian settlement. They always found Smith willing to talk but never prepared to concede on what he regarded as crucial issues. A decade after mandatory United Nations sanctions had been imposed on recalcitrant Rhodesia, for example, Smith was still boasting to his white audiences that there would be no black rule in his lifetime— "never in a thousand years," he said on one occasion.

Sanctions, which Harold Wilson had insisted would topple Smith in "weeks rather than months," had failed. The trade barriers leaked like sieves. Gasoline flowed in, and Rhodesia's minerals and agricultural products flowed out. Local industries sprang up overnight to produce passable imitations of myriad commodities that had formerly been imported. Rhodesia reported record economic growth rates year after year. Militant black nationalists despatched guerrillas, armed and trained in the Communist bloc, into the Rhodesian countryside; they were speedily routed by the small but highly efficient Rhodesian security forces. At one point the Rhodesian Front even began to impose more rigid discriminatory legislation on the black population. Jubilant backbenchers were heard at cocktail parties boasting, "We have won."

The turning point came with the collapse of Portugal's African empire in 1974. Mozambique and then Angola came under Marxist rule, and new geopolitical alliances were forged across southern Africa. The republic of South Africa essayed a win-friends-and-influence-people policy and used its considerable clout in Salisbury to persuade Smith to release the black

political leaders Nkomo, Mugabe and Reverend Ndabaningi Sithole. Further attempts to negotiate with the nationalists were abortive, and the war took an ominous new turn. Black schoolchildren fled into neighboring states to return a few months later wielding Kalashnikov rifles and rocket-launchers.

The United States, aroused by the Cuban role in the Angolan civil war, began taking events in Africa seriously. Henry Kissinger, then secretary of state, was soon winging his way to southern Africa. Smith was

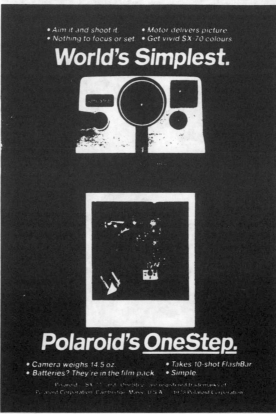

- Aim it and shoot it.
- Nothing to focus or set.
- Motor delivers picture.
- Get vivid SX-70 colours.

World's Simplest.

Polaroid's OneStep.

- Camera weighs 14.5 oz.
- Batteries? They're in the film pack.
- Takes 10-shot FlashBar.
- Simple.

Polaroid, SX-70 and OneStep are registered trademarks of Polaroid Corporation. Cambridge, Mass. U.S.A. 1978 Polaroid Corporation.

impressed by Kissinger's blunt, blackmailing style of diplomacy. Kissinger had covered all the angles, even persuading Pretoria to back his plans for Rhodesia, and Smith returned to Salisbury to tell startled whites that he had accepted the principle of a speedy transfer of power to the black majority.

On March 3 this year Smith signed an agreement with three black leaders: Bishop Abel Muzorewa, a diminutive Methodist with a large black following; the Reverend Sithole, once convicted of plotting to as-

sassinate Smith; and Chief Jeremiah Chirau, an arch-conservative tribal leader. The "internal settlement," as it is called, provided for one-man-one-vote elections and a handover to black rule on December 31. In return the whites were guaranteed a large voting block in Parliament and a substantial say in the running of the country.

So far the internal agreement has faltered badly, and few believe the original timetable can be met. Muzorewa and Sithole have failed to achieve any significant ceasefire ar-

rangement with the 10,000 guerrillas inside the country, discrimination remains in the statute books, and the transitional government is beset by suspicion and bickering. Smith remains committed to the agreement, although he has been conducting secret talks with Nkomo in the hope of persuading the externally based nationalist leaders to participate in a settlement.

Smith's political options are narrowing. If the white confidence he represents is to be retained to help build a new Zimbabwe—the nationalist

name for the country—the war must end soon and sanctions must be lifted.

SMITH HAS SUCCESSFULLY PRO-jected himself as a stolid, phlegmatic figure, unflappable in times of crisis and self-controlled in the midst of emotion. As Janet Smith told a local biographer recently, "he is a very quiet man. We have been married for nearly 30 years and I have never heard him raise his voice, despite the fact that he has been in politics all these years." Rarely has Smith been seen to lose his temper in public, and when he does it is usually a reaction to someone impugning his personal integrity or that of his family. For years, Rhodesia's gossip-prone white community has been alive with rumors that Smith owns a farm in South Africa, to which he would, in the local slang, "take the gap" if the going in Rhodesia became really rough. An angry Smith felt obliged to go on television to deny that he or his family owned any property or assets outside Rhodesia. Outside politics Smith's main interest is his cattle ranch, and he is able to bore the uninitiated for hours at the drop of a new-born calf. He drinks the occasional glass of beer and smokes the odd cigarette "to support Rhodesian industry." He has distinctly suburban tastes in food and entertainment and is delighted when someone breaks the sanctions barrier by giving him some Bovril, the British-made beef extract. He likes "straight-forward, old-fashioned" music, and once admitted he enjoyed "singing along" with the "black and white minstrel show" on local television.

He has retained some of the black staff on his farm for more than 30 years, loyalty he has repaid by elevating two of them to manage his cattle and crops respectively. He seemed genuinely surprised when laughter greeted his remark that in Rhodesia "we have the happiest Africans in Africa," but it was only after he had been obliged to accept the principle of majority rule that for the first time ever he addressed an all-black political meeting. Although his reception was less than lukewarm, Smith insists that he has had a large measure of support from "decent, middle-class Africans."

Robert Mugabe, the most militant of Rhodesia's black leaders, has declared that Smith will have to stand trial and face a firing squad for "war crimes." Ndabaningi Sithole, on the other hand, argues forcefully that he should not only be allowed to stay in Zimbabwe but should also be encouraged to continue in politics, although Smith himself has said he will retire once a black government has taken over. He confidently talks about withdrawing to his 4500-acre farm and 6000-acre cattle ranch near Selukwe. If Zimbabwe allows him to do that after transition to black rule, Smith will have pulled off one of the most remarkable feats in Africa's turbulent political history. ■

Notes

Chapter I: What gave you that idea?

1. Lewis Tressler (1961) *Mastering effective English*, Vancouver: Copp Clark, p. 461, citing James Bryce's essay, "Citizenship".

2. J.A.C. Brown (1977) *Techniques of persuasion*, Harmondworth: Penguin, p. 24-25.

3. Rudolf Flesch (1960), *How to write, speak and think more effectively*, New York: Signet, p. 289.

4. T. Schwartz in "TV: a surrogate world", producer Joyce Nelson, CBC *Ideas* four-part radio documentary.

5. N. Johnson (1970) *How to talk back to your TV set*, N.Y.: Little and Brown, p. 13.

6. N. Johnson (1970), p.13.

7. By the age of twelve, a child has seen 12,000 hours of television. CBC *Anybody Home*, 17 May 80.

8. Information Canada May 1972.

9. *In search/En quete*, Department of Communications, Government of Canada, Winter 1978, p.10.

10. Ontario Royal Commission on violence in the communication industry (1976) Vol. 5, p. 23.

11. T. Schwartz (1973), *The responsive chord*, N.Y.: Anchor Doubleday.

12. N. Johnson (1970), p. 27.

13. R.K. Goldsten (1977) *The show and tell machine: how television works and works you over*, N.Y.: Dial Press, p. x.

14. *New York Guardian* 23 March 77, p. 4.

15. Personal conversation, January 1980.

16. Johnson (1970), p. 28.

17. Goldsten (1977), p. x.

18. Interviewed on *As it happens* CBC Radio 18 May 78.
    In Brazil, an extremely popular band names itself after *Saturday Night Fever* film star John Travolta

—"Travoltinhos", a diminutive form of Travolta, "the little Travoltas" . . . Regular TV fare in the military dictatorship of Chile is the situation comedy *Happy Days* — "Dias Felices".

19. Ontario Royal Commission (1976), Vol. 5, p. 23.

20. *Marketing*, 15 August 77, p. 12.

Chapter II: Getting the message

1. *International Herald Tribune* 5 July 1977.

2. U.S. Air Force Colonel in Phnom Penh, Kampuchea, during the Vietnam war, quoted in *Life* magazine, December 1979.

3. Design or assembly errors were responsible for one plane crash in May 1979 killing 274 people and several other crashes, including a 1974 Paris crash which claimed 346 lives.

4. Similarly the photo widely circulated which shows smiling people in front of homes with a large banner, "WE SURVIVED!". In the *Ecologist* No. 3 May/Jn 1979.

5. Robert Cirino (1971) *Don't blame the people*, N.Y.: Random House, p. 213.

6. Quoted in Darrel Huff (1954) *How to lie with statistics*, N.Y.: W.W. Norton & Co. Recommended reading.
    Regarding media coverage of a pre-election opinion poll, the *Vancouver Sun* noted that ". . . A Gallup poll released seemed to show the Liberals at 48 per cent, the Tories at 28 and the NDP at 23. CTV, in a poll released the same day, seemed to show Liberals 43, Tories 33 and NDP 22. In fact, both polls had distributed the undecided vote . . . The real result for Gallup was Liberal 43, Tory 25, NDP 20 and undecided 11. For CTV, it was Liberal 26, Tory 20, NDP 13 and undecided 40." *Vancouver Sun* 18 February 1980. Quoted in Tony Wilden (1980) *The*

imaginary Canadian, Vancouver: Pulp Press, p. 19.

7. Letter to the editor, *Maclean's* 19 Dec 79.

8. Richard Nixon, later to become President of the United States and as President, deeply implicated in the dirty tricks and illegalities of the "Watergate Scandal". Quoted in the *New Internationalist* No. 73, March 1979, p. 5.

9. *Watson Report* CBC TV 17 Nov. 1980.

10. CBC *Ideas*, 23 May 1978.

11. CBC *Sunday morning* 4 Sept 77.

12. Radio CJCH 31 Aug 77.
    The break-down in logic is not always so harmless, however. In a very professionally produced magazine whose title nonetheless belies its simplistic and erroneous ideas, Philippines President Ferdinand Marcos rationalised his 1972 declaration of martial law, which resulted in brutally repressive measures against tens of thousands Filippinos: "In the words of Mr Marcos himself, 'Martial law was proclaimed to protect our democratic way of life'." *Plain Truth*, May 81, p. 23. (Regular armed forces increased from 60,000 in 1972 to 260,000 in 1980; there are plans for a 900,000-strong "citizens' army".)
    There are countless ways of devising loaded questions which will elicit the desired response. A January 1978 plebicite in Chile received 75% approval. Designed to test the support of the régime which came to power in a 1973 military coup, it read as follows: "In the face of international aggression unleashed against the government of our homeland, I support President Pinochet in his defence of the republic to conduct, in a sovereign way, the process of institutionalisation of the country." Cited in J. D. Cozcan (1979) *Latin America*, Washington: Stryker Post Publications, Inc.
    The former dictator of Nicaragua, Anastasio Somosa Garcia, had this thought on how to conduct the affairs of his country: "I'll give this country peace, if I have to shoot every other man in Nicaragua to get it." *Time* 8 Oct 56.

13. CBC radio news 25 Jl 80. Ironically, as the Canadian journalists were garbling the story with such confusing terminology, their Bolivian counterparts in newspapers, radio and television were prime targets during the horrific state of terror that the military created. Amnesty International reported that one prominent public personality was apparently shown on TV to "prove" that he was still alive, then shot immediately after the broadcast was over. The president of the Journalist's Union of Bolivia, the chief editor of one of Bolivia's prominent weeklies and at least 12 other journalists, writers and radio technicians were rounded up in priority, along with human rights organizations, lawyers, and former ministers of the government. Amnesty Group 15 newsletter Aug 80 (summary of an Urgent Action Appeal).

14. CBC Newfoundland 17 Mar 76.

Of course you'll find it isn't nearly so bad once you've been seasonally adjusted.

15. Hon. P. E. Trudeau, 1 Jl 78, and on other occasions.

16. In a number of Latin American countries, both left-wing and right-wing parties have the word "revolutionary" in their names. For example, the party in power in Mexico since the 1910 revolution is called the P.R.I., Partido Revolucionario Institucional, or "*Institutional* Revolutionary Party"!

17. Knowlton Nash, CBC TV News 19 May 80.

18. *Life* magazine Dec 79.

19. See Rudolph Flesch (1960) *How to write speak and think more effectively* N.Y.: Signet.

20. Sources: **a.** CBC *Sunday magazine* 11 Sept 77; **b.** *Chronicle-Herald* 20 May 78; **c.** *Globe & Mail* 11 Sept 78.

21. *New York Times* 28 Jan 74.

22. *Chronicle-Herald* 7 Jl 79.

23. To John Silber in *Time* magazine, quoted in H. Newcomb, ed. (1979), *TV: the critical view* N.Y.: Oxford University Press, p. 283.

24. *Business Week* 3 May 76.

25. U.S. Vice-President Spiro T. Agnew, in the aftermath of the Kent and Jackson State Universities killings of students by National Guards, quoted in James Aronson (1971) *Packaging the news*, N.Y.: International Publishers, p. 82. Agnew was forced to resign as Vice-President after it was discovered that he had received bribes in an extensive kick-back scheme. As late as 1981 he had still not paid back any of the bribes or interest gained on them, amounting to $250,000.

26. Vice-President Spiro T. Agnew, 1968, quoted in the *New Internationalist* Mar 79, p. 5.

27. *Chronicle-Herald* 8 Jl 78 p. 5.

28. To the Houston Press Club, reported in the *Globe and Mail* 10 May 77.

29. Quoted in W. A. Swanberg (1973) *Luce and his empire* N.Y.: Dell, p. 1.

30. *Globe and Mail* 19 Jl 78.

31. Advertising executive quoted in Ted Wood (1976) "Why do so many ads drive you crazy", *Financial Post* magazine Oct 76, p. 29.

32. *Fortune* magazine 31 Dec 79 p. 31.

33.. In Ted Wood (1976) *Financial Post* Oct 76, p. 43.

34. A 1977 survey found that at one point, 82% of commercials on TV had a fitness-related message. "Sponsoring fitness was, like sponsoring motherhood — we couldn't lose," commented Toronto Dominion Bank's spokesman, John Boles in the *Financial Times* 17 Oct 77, p. 46.

35. *Marketing* 24 Apr 78.

36. *Western Speech* Spring 1962, p. 83-91.

37. Quoted in *The politics of food* (1978) diary, N.Y.: Pluto Press.

38. Quoted in J.A.C. Brown (1977) *Techniques of persuasion*, Harmondsworth: Penguin, p. 180.

39. *Maclean's* magazine 19 Dec 79.

40. CBS Vice-President Edward Klauber to newscaster H. V. Kaltenborn, Radio Daily, Sept 1943, quoted in Eric Barnouw, *The golden web*, Oxford University Press, p. 136.

41. Warner Troyer, *No safe place*, quoted in *Canadian Dimension* Vol. 13, p. 12.

42. The doctor had been in favour of nuclear power until after the accident, when the dramatic increase in numbers of patients suffering from symptoms of anxiety or radiation exposure was ignored by officials. Systematic tests were not done on people close to the site. CBC *Sunday Morning* 27 Jl 80.

43. *Chronicle-Herald* 27 May 80. Thanks to Barbara Rumscheidt for bringing this to my attention.
    A remarkable case of selective omission in newsreporting on Cuba goes a long way to explain the intense and irrational fear and hostility with which most Americans view this Caribbean country. American TV personality Barbara Walters travelled to Cuba to interview Fidel Castro, and later made a television special on the visit. While she said to him that "We don't teach our children to hate the Cubans," this assertion could hardly be confirmed by the way in which the interview was edited. Another American journalist who was present, Saul Landau, reproduced the entire interview, putting in bold face the sections which were selected for broadcast. See "From the cutting room floor: the complete text of Barbara Walters' interview with Fidel Castro," *Seven Days* Dec 77.
    Further irony can be found in the fact that the *full* interview, unseen on television in "free" America, was broadcast widely in Cuba.

44. Edward Epstein (1973) *News from nowhere* N.Y.: Random House, quoted in J. Mander (1978) *Four arguments for the elimination of television*, N.Y.: Morrow Quill Paperbacks, p. 319-20.

45. Ibid., p. 320.

46. R. Cirino (1971), p. 117. To get any coverage at all in the Halifax *Chronicle-Herald*, a member of the human rights group Amnesty International was told by the editor that it would be best to get "a shocker" of a story or not bother trying to get anything in the paper at all. Reported at a meeting 11 Jan 80.

47. *San Francisco Examiner* 22 Sept 1959.

48. U.S. Government Hoover Commission Report (1954), quoted in John Stockwell (1978) *In search of enemies*, N.Y.: W.W. Norton & Co. p. 252.

49. *Advertising Age* 23 Jan 78 p. 5.

50. Quoted in Richard Schickel (1968) *The Disney version: the life, times, art and commerce of Walt Disney*, p. 298.
    Disney's Educational Media Company has given a still more explicit educational role to the cartoon characters. Cartoon filmstrips "introduce students, grade 4 through 6, to the private enterprise system".

If you tell a lie . . .

THE MOMENT OF MADNESS

NEW YORK POST FINAL

ASTOUNDING CLAIM OF THE GUNMAN WHO SHOT POPE:

'I'm with the PLO'

. . . tell a big one

New York Post front-page coverage of Pope John Paul II's assailant, May 14, 1981. The U.S. press downplayed Mehmet Ali Agca's proven fascist connections, and at times even tried to connect him with left organisations, though there was no basis to do so. (He was convicted of murder in the machine-gun killing of a liberal Turkish newspaper editor, had been implicated in at least three other murders, and belonged to Turkey's fascist Nationalist Action Party, known by its Turkish initials MHP.)

Source: N.Y. Guardian 27 May 81

The filmstrips and teaching kit features titles such as "Huey, Dewie and Louie Learn to Expand Their Business," and "Huey, Dewie and Louie Learn About Selling Stock in Their Company". Quoted in *Dollars and Sense* Sept 79, p. 11.

51. D. Kunzle, in the introduction to the English edition of Dorfman and Mattelart (1975) *How to read Donald Duck*, N.Y.: International General, p. 19.

52. R. Cirino (1971) p. 187.

53. Annenberg School of Communication, University of Pennsylvania, cited in *New Internationalist* March 79, p. 10-11, and *Journal of Communications* No. 9, Vol. 28, No. 3 (1978).

54. R. Cirino (1971), p. 182.

55. *Time* 31 Oct 77, p. 63.

56. *Canadian Advertising Rates and Data.*

57. CBC *Sunday Morning* 30 Dec 79.

58. N. Johnson (1970) *How to talk back to your TV set* N.Y.: Little and Brown, p. 25.

59. T. Schwartz in "TV: a surrogate world", Programme No. 4 CBC *Ideas*, producer Joyce Nelson.

60. Ibid.

61. The effect of cable television on communities in the Annapolis Valley has been examined by Prof. D. Grady at Acadia University, Wolfville, N.S.

62. *Financial Post* magazine Oct 76.

63. John Berger (1976) *Ways of seeing*, London: BBC and Penguin, p. 149.

64. Leonard Brockingham to a Canadian Parliamentary Committee in 1939, quoted in S. Crean (1976) *Who's afraid of Canadian culture?* Don Mills: General Publishing.

65. Ad agency advertisement in *Time* magazine, cited in Cirino (1971), p. 299.

66. CBS *Annual Report* 1970, p. 4.

67. N. Trouse, *Your career in advertising*, undated printed pamphlet.

68. J. K. Galbraith in *The new industrial state*.

69. Felix Greene (1971) *The enemy: what every American should know about imperialism*, N.Y.: Vintage, p. 35.

Chapter III: This message was brought to you by . . .

1. D. Schroeder (1978) "Third World gets poor coverage in Canada's press" *CUSO Forum* Special issue. The bulk of international news comes through CP's access to worldwide networks — AP, Reuters and AFP. "These agencies funnel some 250,000 words a day into CP's New York office, where a staff of nine editors select and condense to produce perhaps 60,000 words for transmission to the Canadian circuit." (Sen. I:230).

2. Joseph Scanlon (1974) "Canada sees the world through U.S. eyes: a case study in cultural domination" *Canadian Forum* Sept 1974 p. 35.

3. *Financial Post* 22 Sept 79, p. S2. The Sterling Newspaper chain sold its 20% interest to the Toronto *Sun*.

4. Bob Carr (1979) "All roads lead to Dallas" *Content* Nov 79, p. 13.

5. *Content*, Nov 79, p. 13.

6. Monty Dargan (1977), "Business/PR Newswire: an inside track", *Canadian Journal of Communications* Vol 4 No 2 (1977), p. 9-17.

7. J. Scanlon (1974), p. 36.

8. Quoted in Canadian International Development Agency, *Development Directions* Oct 78, p. 14.

"All power to the board of directors!"

9. D. Schroeder (1978), *CUSO Forum* p. 4.

10. *Content* Feb 1980, p. 2.

11. "Two papers die as Thomson, Southam tighten belts", *Globe and Mail* 28 Aug 80, p. 1.

12. In a ten-year study period (1967-77), the Maritime provinces showed the most dramatic increase in receiving U.S. broadcasting. From none in PEI or Nova Scotia, it rose to 31% of the population and 64% of the population respectively. In New Brunswick 56% of the population could receive at least one U.S. station. CRTC (1979) *Special Report on Canada*, Vol. I, p. 31.

13. John Warnock (1970), "All the news it pays to print," in Ian Lumsden, (1970) ed., *Close the 49th parallel*, Toronto: University of Toronto Press, p. 120.

14. Royal Commission on Corporate Concentration (1976) *Technical Report #17*, p. 51.

15. *Financial Post* 1 May 76, p. S. 18. The extent of overlap of media ownership of the huge complexes is difficult to determine.

16. CBC *Sunday Morning* 30 Dec 79.

17. Royal Commission on Corporate Concentration (1976), *Technical Report #31*, p. xix.

18. Statistics Canada (1979) Corporations and Labour Returns Act (CALURA) *Intercorporate ownership*.

19. Wallace Clement (1975) *The Canadian corporate élite*, Toronto: McClelland and Stewart p. 278-88.

20. *Canada Year Book* 1972, p. 64.

21. W. Clement (1975), p. 325.

22. W. Clement (1975), p. 341.

23. John Saul and Rick Salutin originally noted the appropriateness of this example in *This Magazine* Dec 1978.

24. Russell Hunt and Robert Campbell (1973) *K. C. Irving: the art of the industrialist*, Toronto: McClelland and Stewart, p. 156. Emphasis ours.

25. Russell Hunt and Robert Campbell (1973), p. 160.

26. Senate of Canada, *Debates*, 11 Mar 71.

27. *Time* magazine 18 Apr 69, p. 65. See also R. Cirino (1971) *Don't blame the people*, N.Y. Random House.

28. N. Chomsky and E. Herman (1979) *The Washington connection and Third World Fascism*, Boston: South End Press, p. xvi-xvii.

29. W. Clement (1975), p. 296. On the effects mass media images can have on Canadian perceptions of poverty in Canada, see Ian Adams (1971) *The real poverty report*, Edmonton: Hurtig.

30. Chapter 1 of *Corporate Canada*, Ed. Rae Murphy and Mark Starowicz (1972) Toronto: James Lewis & Samuel, cited in James Lorimer (1972) *A citizen's guide to city politics*, Toronto: James Lewis & Samuel.

31. From a *Maclean's* promotional pamphlet, italics in original, cited in John Sullivan (1977) "A year of the new *Maclean's*: import substitution in the ideology market", *This Magazine* Vol 11 No 1, Jan-Feb 77, p. 8. Recommended reading.

32. *Toronto Star* 6 Mar 79, and B. Zwicker (1980) "Reflections on the take-over of FP", *Content* Feb 1980.

In an astonishingly clear case in South Korea, the difference between the power of censors and the power of advertisers was shown to be one of degree, not kind. In November 1974, the country's most distinguished paper had refused to bend to the Korean Central Intelligence Agency's (KCIA) censorship directives banning the reporting of university demonstrations and actions of Christian churches critical of the government. However, when the paper won the first round and KCIA agents were withdrawn from the paper's offices, a more devious tactic was then used:

'Beginning in mid-December, major commercial advertisers abruptly cancelled their scheduled ads —first one, then another the next day, then a few more, then a host of cancellation notices flooded in . . . By mid-January just about all large firms and countless small ones had withdrawn, reducing advertising revenue by about 60 per cent.

J.J. ...but, my dear boy, don't you realise that we are all eating the same cake...

...it's just my unenviable job to cut it up into slices, and share it out...

...you may think it unfair that big slices are swallowed up by interest repayments...

'Shamefaced and often-frightened clients told a soon-familiar story. Company officials had been summoned by the Korean Central Intelligence Agency (KCIA) and ordered to stop their business with *Dong-A Ilbo*, the paper at once. Many were required to sign written statements that they would not advertise in the forbidden media. 'The advertising director of a large textile chain is reported to have been severely beaten and the company president verbally reprimanded when their ads did not stop quickly enough. The same treatment was meted out to a cosmetics company ad director and his president. This firm's staff was then used to notify other companies . . . .'
— Reported in *Washington Post*, 20 Jan 75. For a description of the church's ensuing involvement in this remarkable story, see George E. Ogle (1977) *Liberty to the captives: the struggle against oppression in South Korea*, Atlanta: John Knox Press, p. 99-100.

33. J. Scanlon (1974), p. 36.

34. Mediocrity in the newsmedia threatens to overtake completely book publishing in Canada as well, if it has not already done so. The biggest three bookstore chains in Canada control 60% of sales. The chains' motivation for profit and large-volume sales has a definite influence on publishers, and eventually on the writers themselves. Quality of writing takes a back seat to "marketability", according to some of Canada's foremost writers who were interviewed on CBC-TV news 10 Apr 81.

35. K. Keller (1978) University of California thesis discussed in *Working papers for a new society*, Vol VII, No 2, Jl/Aug 79, p. 32.

36. K. Keller (1978).

37. Quoted in *Time* 15 Aug 77, p. 47.

38. Institut Canadien d'Education des Adultes (ICEA) (1979), *Les actualités télévisées: le monde recrée au service du pouvoir*, Montreal: ICEA.

39. Robert Shayon, in *Saturday Review* 25 Sept 71, p. 18.

40. Gerry Goodis, president of a prominent Canadian advertising agency, before the Senate Committee on Mass Media (1970), *Proceedings* 21:10.

41. *Globe and Mail* 3 Feb 77, p. 5. It was later established that indeed the author of the Southam story was employed in the marketing department of Southam Press Ltd and not by Southam News Services.

42. Royal Commission on Corporate Concentration (1977) *The newspaper and freedom of information, Study #23*, p. 1. Emphasis ours.

43. R. Cirino (1971), p. 199-200.

44. See Chapter IV, especially p. 148, 171.

45. Quoted in James Aronson (1971) *Packaging the news*, NY: International, p. 13.

46. William Paley, Chairman of the Board of CBS, to journalist Fred Friendly, quoted in Robert Cirino, (1971) *Don't blame the people*, p. 61-62.

47. Interviewed on CBC *Sunday Morning* 17 Aug 80.

48. C. Hamelink (1977) ed. *The corporate village*, Rome: IDOC International, p. 186.

49. CBC *Sunday Morning* 6 Jan 79.

50. CBC *Sunday Morning* 21 Jl 80. The Secretary-General of Amnesty International noted that the Shah's Iran had "the highest rate of death penalties in the world, no valid system of civilian courts and a history of torture which is beyond belief. No country in the world has a worse record in human rights than Iran." Quoted in *Matchbox*, Fall 1976. Estimates of political prisoners ran from 25,000 to 100,000.
   The shah in fact came from a common Iranian family, and was himself brought to power by a brutal, CIA-sponsored coup d'état in 1953.

51. Peter Watkins, "Media repression: a personal statement," Stockholm, 4 January 1980, in *Cineaste* magazine. The accident referred to is the Three Mile Island nuclear accident in Harrisburg, Pennsylvania.

52. "The Canadian film audience pays over 200 million dollars annually to Famous Players and Odeon, both foreign-owned conglomerates (Famous is 51% owned by Gulf and Western, which also owns Paramount Pictures; Odeon is now owned by Rank, a British conglomerate concentrating on U.S. film production. Rank was originally 51% owned by Famous Players' Nathanson.) None of this money is taxed to leave any percentage in Canada to build the Canadian film industry; and there is no stipulation that requires Canadian films to be seen in Canadian theatres." Ardele Lister (1977), "Hewing the wood and drawing the water: women and film in colonized Canada," *Heresies* Vol. 1 No. 2 May 77 p. 103-5.

53. CBC Sunday Morning 12 February 80.

54. ICEA (1979), Les actualités télévisées: le monde recrée au service du pouvoir.

55. *Maclean's* 18 Sept 78, p. 29.

56. *Saturday Night* Dec 80, p. 17.

57. Howley Black, "Censorship Canada", *Saturday Night* Dec 80, p. 9.

58. The largest broadcasting conglomerate in the world is said to be the U.S. Armed Forces Radio and Television Network. See Graham Hancock (1977) "A bread and butter issue" *New Internationalist* May 77, p. 12-13; and Zbigniew Brzezinski, *Between two ages*, quoted in *Le Monde diplomatique* Oct 79, p. 8.

59. "When big business buys the press" *Manchester Guardian* 12 Dec 76.

60. Conference Board in Canada (1976) *Across the board* XIII, p. 2.

61. *Globe and Mail* 21 Jan 80.

62. A. Mattelart (1976) "Multinationales et systemes de communications" Paris: IDOC 20019, p. 191 and 195, cited in Cees Hamelink, ed (1977) *The corporate village*, Rome: IDOC.

63. Disclosed by Standard Oil's Vice-President in a telephone interview, CBC News 23 Dec 79. For Standard Oil of California's agribusiness see the publications of the Institute for Food and Development Policy, California, U.S.A.

64. Walter Powell (1979) "The blockbuster decade: the media as big business", *Working papers for a new society* Jl/Aug 79, p. 30.

65. *The Canadian Student* Sept 1977, p. 12.

66. Alan Wells (1972) *Picture-tube imperialism*, N.Y.: Orbis, p. 117.

67. These two networks do not include the regular broadcasting on other stations by Oral Roberts, Billy Graham, Rex Humbard and others, who each oversee multi-million dollar TV and radio operations. *Press-On* Winter 1980.

68. Peter Schenckel (1977), "Power structure of the communications media" in Cees Hamelink, ed. (1977).

69. Jack Cahill (1980) "Dateline Saigon: dying days of an endangered species" *Canadian Weekend* 9 Feb 80, p. 2.

70. D. Schroeder (1980), *Survey of international news coverage by the Canadian media*, Ottawa: International Development Research Centre (IRDC), March 1980.

71. *Globe and Mail* 2 Dec 78 p. B1.

72. Russel Hunt and Robert Campbell (1973), p. 180.

73. "Time: bigger and richer," *New York Times* 23 Jn 78, p. D1. Time Inc. likes to describe its empire as having "four legs to a stool" — magazines, books, forest products and video communications.

74. Cees Hamelink (1977) ed., p. 96.

75. Jacques Maisonrouge, quoted in R. C. Barnet and R. E. Mueller (1974) *Global Reach*, N.Y.: Simon and Schuster, p. 14-15.

76. Michael Horowitz, quoted in Joyce Nelson (1979) 'The global pillage' *This Magazine* May/Jn 79, p. 35.

77. "Startalk", Mayflower supplement to *Chronicle-Herald* 7 Dec 79.

78. R. Barnet and R. Mueller (1974), p. 144.

79. Prof. de Sola Pool, before congressional committee into "Mass Communications and Foreign Policy", House of Representatives 4 May 67, p.63-64, quoted in H. Schiller (1969) *Mass communications and the American empire*, N.Y.: A. M. Kelly, p. 106.

80. Len Moore (1979), "Sales prove TV's effectiveness" *Marketing* 26 Nov 79.

81. Quoted in R. Barnet and R. Mueller (1974), p. 14.

82. At the 1975 Annual meeting of Philips Corporation, H. A. C. van Reimsdijk, President, quoted in Cees Hamelink (1977) *The corporate village*, p. 164.

83. Canadian International Development Agency, *Development Directions*, Oct 78, p. 7ff.

84. Full-page advertisement, *Financial Post*, 22 Sept 79, Emphasis ours.

85. George Seldes (1958) *The great quotations*, Lyle Stuart, p. 222

Chapter IV: Propaganda, bias and point of view

1. Quoted in the Robert Cirino (1971) *Don't Blame the People*, NY: Random House, p. 134.

2. When there is also disagreement amongst experts on a question, one must usually examine the basis on which assertions are made. For example, in the nuclear safety debate, the pro- and anti-nuclear groups and scientists disagree, *in the final analysis,* over whether there can be such a thing as an "acceptable level of risk" with this form of energy.

3. *Amnesty International in Quotes* (1976) London: Amnesty International

4. See in particular the same issue of *Weekend* magazine, reproduced in the Appendices to this book, p. 6 columns 2 and 3 of the article.

5. For the history and activities of the Selous Scouts, see the publications of the Interntional Defence and Aid Fund for Southern Africa, and *Southern Africa* magazine.

6. *Rhodesia Herald* 11 June 77, quoted in the Catholic Institute for International Relations (1977) *Rhodesia's propaganda war*, London: CIIR, p. 1

7. This figure was widely reported at the time. See the Catholic Commission for Justice and Peace *Newsletter* for Dec 78, for example.

8. *Christian Science Monitor* 11 Jl 78.

9. *Globe and Mail* 23 Oct 78 p. 10.

10. Lest we leave the incorrect impression that *Weekend* magazine was singularly irresponsible in its editorial policies while other media were more fair in their coverage, we should note another, more infamous case of Canadian media treatment of Southern Africa news. In 1978 it was discovered that the Canadian Space Research Corporation was illegally shipping arms to South Africa. Even though an entire CBC *Fifth Estate* programme documented the company's activities, Canadian papers said little and the Toronto *Globe and Mail* said nothing.
"On November 8, the morning after the show went on the air in Canada, its front page included items on the death of Gene Tunney, the safety of municipal bridges, and the water level of Lake Ontario ('average for this time of year'); Space Research merited not a word, even on an inside page . . . Its decision to neglect Space Research, together with the lack of interest shown by Canada's four major syndicated political columnists, helped ensure that the allegations dropped out of public notice almost as soon as they were raised."
— Mark Abley, *Canadian Forum* Apr 79, p. 9.

11. Journalist Robert Lasch, quoted in *Responsibility and mass communication*, Rivers and Schremm, 1969.

12. According to the Columbia University study, the American press consistently repeated the distortion which characterised the broad opostition to the ruling junta as the "extreme left". Scarcely mentioned was the name of this broad opposition, the Democratic Revolutionary Front (FDR) — representing all major peasant organisations, student organisations, trade unions and other popular organisations. Reported in *Latin America Weekly Report* 20 Feb 81 p. 15.

Chapter V: "Underdevelopment": case studies

For the Brazil section of this chapter, I was able to consult files which Kate McLaren and David Currie drew up for the project we were working on together. For the Atlantic Canada section, I had similar access to project files drawn up by Sharon Foley/Reilly.

The only way to create more jobs is to fire a few people!

1. Brazil-Canada Chamber of Commerce (1978) *Background on Brazil,* Toronto, p. 6-7.

2. Report to the Sub-committee on Multinational Corporations of the Committee on Foreign Relations, United States Senate (August 1975), Washington, U.S.: p. 101, quoted in R. Newfarmer and W. F. Mueller, Multinational corporations in Brazil and Mexico: structural sources of economic and non-economic power.

3. Violet Winspear (1977) *The girl at Goldenhawk,* Toronto: Harlequin, p. 25-26 (the dots are in the original).

4. Mary Novik (1978) "A Harlequin serenade", *Books in Canada*, Nov 78, p. 4. It is a well-written, amusing and informative article. Novik quotes Harlequin's message to potential outlets: "Love makes the rack go 'round and the cash registers ring."
Twenty-six out of every 100 paperbacks sold in Canada and 14 out of every 100 sold in the U.S. are Harlequins.
Harlequin is an investor's dream as well. Profit levels have been extremely high, which leads to expansion into other fields of educational materials and movie star magazines. Harlequin Enterprises is 58% owned by Torstar Corporation, the publishers of the *Toronto Star*, and 8 fully-owned weeklies and other publications. Torstar Corporation also owns 40% of Southstar Publishers, which published *The Canadian,* "Canada's largest-circulation magazine", inserted in 21 newspapers in Canada and delivered to thousands of households in many other communities.
See also D. Pullan, "Harlequin: a corporate romance" *Quill and Quire* 45 Nov 9/79

5. In 1973 it was US $142,038 million, Brazil Light Ltd (Canada). Brazilian Government Trade Bureau (1973), *Guide to investing in Brazil.* On 30 April, 1979, the largest transaction in the history of the American Stock Exchange took place, when the ownership of Brascan changed hands. See Peter Newman's "Rolling for billions," in *Maclean's* magazine 9 Jl 79.

6. Though most people would readily recognise that afternoon soap operas are fictional, there are dozens of anecdotes about soap show actors being accosted in New York department stores by hostile viewers. On the effects of television on viewer perception, see Chapter I of this book, and more particularly J. Mander (1978) *Four arguments for*

the elimination of television, N.Y.: Morrow Quill Paperbacks; and the University of Pennsylvania *Journal of Communications*, No. 9, Vol 28, No 3 (78).

7. The ship from the popular television series *Love Boat* figures in actual ads for a line of cruising ships. Travel magazines now deftly apprise the prospective traveller of potential risks or unpleasantness in a country (police or death squads in Turkey or Guatemala; pickpockets in the Caribbean; beggars in India …), all the while steering the reader's attention *away* from the social problems, and *towards* a particularly attractive monument or cosy inn.

   In this way, whole cultures and peoples can be objectified ("reified"), their customs appearing quaint or foolish. In the able hands of *National Geographic* photographers and authors, the life of the inshore fisherman in the Atlantic appears as much an anomaly as does the life of a tribe in the Amazon. Cod-jigging or step-dancing contain no less or no more meaning than does hunting with a blow-pipe and poisoned arrows. While the photographs may render colours and textures with astounding precision, they reduce their subjects to *things*, objects. This view of a world filled with objects (mountains, sunken treasure, people …) allows one, in the long run, to view others as categorically "different" from oneself. It allows the traveller to look at immense poverty and suffering and yet not *"see"* it. It allows the traveller to view a people's efforts to overthrow repressive systems as vague "problems", to be avoided at all costs (or entered into as the ultimate "adventure"). This view builds the illusion that humans are passive *objects* in society and in life, rather than active, responsible and conscious subjects.

   See the works of John Berger; and Terry Dennet/Jo Spense (1979) *Photography/politics: one*, London: Photography Workshop, 152 Upper Street, London N. 1.

8. Brazil also creates dreams for its own population — in the form of mass spectator sports, and the *Carnaval* celebrations of Mardi Gras. The 1977 film *Dona Flor and her two husbands* is a sexual fantasy featuring a beautiful Brazilian soap-opera star. The film takes place during the famous *Carnaval* festivities in Brazil. It has become the most popular movie of all time in that country, where it has been shown to audiences of over 200 million, the majority of whom live in abject poverty and suffer from the effects of malnutrition and starvation. Dona Flor is a gourmet cook …

   Official and corporate backing of spectator sports is common in Brazil. Two journalists report how "the government promotes little 'messages', which are set to music, placarded along with commercial advertising, distributed as bumper stickers. 'Say No To Inflation' was arranged as a samba …. Sports heroes — Pele in football, Emerson Fittipaldi in racing — are boosted by covert government policies, and sports are deliberately used as a means of encouraging diversionary chauvinist feeling. … When the Brazilian football team returned from their World Cup victory in 1970, President Medici greeted them with the phrase 'Niguem segura este pais', *No one can stop this country."* — Fred Halliday and Maxine Molyneux, "Brazil: the underside of the miracle," *Ramparts* Apr 74, p. 17.

   On film, see also Ian Bruce, "Cinema censorship", *Index on censorship* Special Issue on Brazil, Jl-Aug 79; and *Latin American Perspectives* Special Issue on Culture in the Age of Mass Media, Vol V No 1, Winter 1978.

9. "Bond moves to Brazil for a $15-million caper," *Globe and Mail* 21 Jl 78, p. 12.

10. Advertisement in *TV Guide* 6 Dec 78.

11. *Index on Censorship* Jl-Aug 79, p. 24. The U.S. Declaration of Independence was also a forbidden text in Brazil.

12. Joan R. Dassin, "Press censorship — how and why," *Index on Censorship* Jl-Aug 79, p. 17.

13. Roger Revelle (1974) "Food and population," *Scientific American*, Vol. 231, No. 3, Sept 74, p. 167.

14. Georg Borgstrom (1973) *The food and people dilemma*, Duxbury Press, p. 66.

15. Thomas Fenton, *Coffee, the rules of the game and you*, (pamphlet), p. 8. The Christophers, 12 E. 48th St., N.Y. 10017.

16. *New Internationalist*, No. 82, Dec 79, p. 11.

17. Richard Barnet and Ronald Mueller (1974) "A reporter at large: the multinational corporations," *The New Yorker* 2 Dec 74, p. 114.

18. *Ibid.*; see also by the same authors (1974) *Global reach*, N.Y.: Simon and Schuster.

19. *Ibid.* Subsistence farming is actively discouraged by World Bank policies. The Bank's designs to create dependency in underdeveloped countries are clear in a World Bank country report on Papua New Guinea (PNG): "A characteristic of PNG's subsistence agriculture is its relative richness: over much of the country nature's bounty produces enough to eat with relatively little expenditure of effort. The root crops that dominate subsistence farming are 'plant and wait' crops, requiring little disciplined cultivation … Until enough subsistence farmers have their traditional life styles changed by the growth of new consumption wants, this labour constraint may make it difficult to introduce new crops." Cited in Cheryl Payer (1980) "The World Bank and the small farmer," *Monthly Review* Vol. 32 No. 6 (Nov 80), p. 33-34.

20. Penny Lernoux (1977) "Brazil: the church of tomorrow", Latinamerica Press, 5 May 77. See also by the same author (1980) *The cry of the people*, N.Y.: Doubleday.

21. GATT-Fly (1978) *By bread alone?* (broadsheet), p. 2. GATT-Fly, 11 Madison Avenue, Toronto, Ontario. Lest these startling figures from Brazil leave the impression that the problem called "underdevelopment" only occurs "over there", we should remember that Canada lost 50% of its farmers from 1941 to 1976, and continues to lose them. Food security is daily growing more fragile, as Canada continues to grow more dependent on food imports (though remaining a net exporter of food because of grain).

22. Barnet and Mueller (1974) *Global reach*, p. 178.

23. *Ibid.*, p. 179. This food is not necessary for the average North American, whose protein intake is higher than the recommended levels; it in fact contributes to a number of health problems, according to a number of leading nutritionists. See M. Boas and S. Chain (1976) *Big Mac: the unauthorised story of McDonald's*, N.Y.: Mentor, for an entertaining insight into the lucrative fast-food business. The authors cite

"Thinking Aloud Prohibited"

an instance of *Time* magazine's distorted reporting of an address given to the American Public Health Association by the chief of nutrition at New York's Mount Sinai School of Medicine (p. 73). Dr. George Christakis had warned that the fast-food diet of increasing numbers of Americans would have serious consequences for the long-term health of the nation. A future generation of debilitated Americans — "the McDonald's generation" — suffering from heart disease and other ailments would result if trends continued. *Time*, however, quoted Dr Christakis as being "nonfanatical about McDonald's. As a weekend treat, it is clean and fast."

24. K. McLaren, "Hold the gravy! The plight of the potato farmers" *This Magazine* (May 77), p. 7. Statistics are from the New Brunswick Department of Agriculture and Rural Development. In the same period, farm operating expenses and depreciation charges rose by an average of 5.6% each year.

Chapter VI:

Do not adjust . . .

1. The "everything's relative" point of view characterised a confusing New Year's commentary on Iran by journalist Joe Schlesinger. The taking of 50 American hostages was described as "the ultimate in terrorism." The fact that under the former dictator's rule, an estimated 25,000 to 100,000 prisoners suffered summary arrest, torture or death, somehow did not measure up to his definition of the ultimate terrorist act. The commentary also noted that "One man's terrorism is another man's just cause." CBC-TV "Oh what a feeling — the Seventies" 31 Dec 79. On Iran, see N. Chomsky and E. Herman (1979) *The Washington connection and Third World Fascism*, Montreal: Black Rose.

2. H. K. Smith, *Columbia Journalism Review* Fall 1965, p. 13.

Appendix

1. John Porteous (1975) "The brothers Irving" in *Impetus* 22 Nov 75. Entire books have been written in an attempt to establish the worth of this very secretive company. Some indication of its size can be had from the fact that in late 1979 it was revealed that one of the Irving companies, Irving Oil, had neglected to declare part of its earnings — over $500,000,000 in export sales — an amount greater than some countries' annual budgets!

2. *Arcadian Recorder*, 26 June 80, p. 11.

3. *Financial Post* 22 Sept 79, p. S.16. Though the financial newspaper listed the ownership, it was still listed at the regulatory body, the CRTC, as having as its major shareholders LFD Investments Ltd (controlled by the late Lawrence F. Daley, a Halifax lawyer), Premium Holdings Ltd., Newtown Holdings Ltd., and West Gore Investments Co. Ltd.

List of tables

Index